# THE OTHER FIFTY PERCENT

# THE OTHER FIFTY PERCENT

## Multicultural Perspectives on Gender Relations

Edited by

## Mari Womack and Judith Marti

WAVELAND
PRESS, INC.
Prospect Heights, Illinois

For information about this book, write or call:
Waveland Press, Inc.
P.O. Box 400
Prospect Heights, Illinois 60070
(847) 634-0081

Cover illustration by Peter Coes
© Peter Coes 1993

# Contents

# Preface

*The Other Fifty Percent* was conceived at the American Anthropological Association meetings in New Orleans. On the way to dinner in the French Quarter one evening, Mari Womack and Judith Marti compared notes on the sessions and agreed that many of the most interesting and challenging papers had dealt with the role of women in society. At the same time, both confessed to frustration with materials currently available for teaching. Our course was clear: It was time to compile our own text, drawing on the exciting new research now being reported.

We decided to call our book *The Other Fifty-One Percent*, based on the widely held assumption that females outnumber males in the world's population, since women globally have a longer average life-span than men. We were forced to rename the book to *The Other Fifty Percent* when a survey of population figures provided by the United Nations proved our original assumption to be in error. In fact, men make up 50.3 percent of the world's population and women total 49.7 percent, in spite of the fact that the average lifespan for males is 61.8 years compared to 65.9 years for females.[1]

Sex ratios differ by geographic area, favoring women in areas classified by the United Nations as "more developed," while men outnumber women in areas classified as "less developed." According to U.N. criteria, "more developed" areas include North America, Japan, all of Europe, Australia, New Zealand and what was formerly the Soviet Union. "Less developed" regions are Africa, all of Latin America, all of Asia except Japan, and Melanesia, Micronesia, and Polynesia (1991:86).

This doesn't tell the whole story, however, since women outnumber men in all parts of Africa except North Africa and sex ratios are about even in Latin America. In Southern Asia (which includes India), men outnumber women by about 107 to 100; in Eastern Asia (which includes China), men outnumber women by about 105 men to every 100 women. In Southeast Asia, the sex ratio is about even, and Japan conforms to the European and North

American pattern of about 51 percent females. Men outnumber women in most Muslim countries and this, combined with the male-biased population ratios of China and India—which together make up nearly 38 percent of the world's population—offset the female-biased sex ratios of all the rest of the world.

It is beyond the scope of this preface to fully analyze this distribution, but some explanations for male-biased sex ratios have been offered in the literature. Among them are selective childrearing practices—including early weaning for female infants and favoring male children in providing food and medical care—as well as the widespread practice of infanticide.[2]

Although women make up nearly 50 percent of the world's population, the editors believe it appropriate to refer to them as "other," based on the "otherness" of women both in society and in anthropological research. The conceptual basis of "otherness" is treated in a classic writing by Simone de Beauvoir, reprinted in the first section of this volume.

We are also making available articles by Margaret Mead and Hortense Powdermaker, pioneers who, for different reasons, laid the groundwork for present studies of gender. The selection by Margaret Mead illustrates the context of anthropological field work early in this century. Hortense Powdermaker directly addresses the importance of gender in conducting research, and she appears to have anticipated many of the issues being debated today. Other than these three classic writings, the articles in this book were selected according to the following criteria:

1. Case studies were given priority. Our experience in selecting articles for this book suggests that ethnography continues to be a mainstay of anthropology precisely because it elucidates theory while providing information about specific societies.

2. Each article was required to be on the cutting edge of research and most are less than five years old.

3. Articles were evaluated for their contribution to the current debate on the role of women in society.

4. The editors aimed for as much global balance as possible. Though this proved to be an impossible task, we believe the best possible relationship between geography and significant research has been achieved.

5. Topics were chosen to represent a range of important conceptual categories in anthropology. Many of the current

books on gender focus either on the political economy or on religious ideology. It has been our experience, both in teaching and in compiling articles for this book, that it is impossible to understand gender roles without considering *all* aspects of the social context.

The editors began with no specific political or ideological agenda — simply the desire to present exciting new research on gender in an accessible format. However, we discovered that data presented in virtually all articles in this book add up to the same inevitable conclusions — the traditional failure of anthropology to take account of the contributions of women worldwide has resulted in serious misinterpretations of society as a whole. In addition, it is possible to identify two key variables that contribute to the status of women: (1) access to control over economic resources and (2) the ability to form alliances, which may be based on kinship, economic exchange, or residential patterns. Finally, it has become clear that the traditional anthropological emphasis on analysis of social structure has led us to overlook the real "power" of women to negotiate through informal networks.

There are many people who greatly facilitated completion of this manuscript. Paul Bohannan early recognized the merit of the concept and introduced the editors to a publisher who recognized the need for such a work. Tom Curtin at Waveland Press proved to be a valuable resource who made it possible for the editors to focus on compiling the manuscript. Jan Weissman, photo editor at Waveland, searched far and wide for suitable artwork. Greg Womack served as computer consultant, saving the project at several critical junctures. Joan Barker, Naomi Bishop, and Mike O'Sullivan provided helpful criticisms for the introductions to some of the sections, and Oscar Marti contributed editorial advice. Laura Womack and Alethea Marti unearthed some essential research information, while Alice Chesler Abrams and Jeff and Michelle Womack always seemed to know when to nag and when to be supportive. Edward Marti contributed greatly to the completion of the manuscript by patiently tolerating his mother's extended hours at the computer. Of course, it would have been impossible to complete this project without the cooperation of our authors, who worked quickly under deadline pressure, responded to sometimes frantic telephone calls and, in some cases, saved us from embarrassing oversights. We are grateful to all these people and to the women and men whose stories are recounted in this book. If reading this volume proves as satisfying as compiling it, the editors have been well served.

*Mari Womack and Judith Marti*

# PART I

## On
## the Nature
## of Things

Biological Influences on Gender
*Jean Stockard* and *Miriam M. Johnson*

Separate People
Speaking of Creek Men and Women
*Amelia Rector Bell*

Oedipus in the New Guinea Highlands?
*L. L. Langness*

Woman as Other
*Simone De Beauvoir*

Two Balinese women enhance their appearance
with culturally approved adornments.
*Henri Cartier-Bresson/Magnum Photos, Inc.*
▶

# Suggested Readings

**Simone De Beauvoir. 1989.** *The Second Sex.* **H. M. Parshley, trans. and ed. New York: Vintage Books.**
De Beauvoir's English language publisher Alfred Knopf said of her that she "certainly suffers from verbal diarrhea—I have seldom read a book that seems to run in such concentric circles." Indeed, reading *The Second Sex* is not a project to be undertaken lightly, but De Beauvoir identifies many of the issues that continue to preoccupy students of gender. And, in spite of her verbosity, De Beauvoir's provocative style makes this work an engaging read.

**Gilbert Herdt. 1986.** *The Sambia: Ritual and Gender in New Guinea.* **New York: Holt, Rinehart and Winston.**
In this thorough study of male initiation rites among the Sambia, Herdt enters the debate over the importance of socialization in defining male social identity. The author argues in favor of the idea that harsh initiation rites for adolescent boys are aimed at stripping away any residue of femininity the boys may have absorbed as the result of early socialization by their mothers. This is an important theoretical work that also provides powerful descriptions of the rituals and a discussion of their importance in the context of male ideology.

**Sarah Blaffer Hrdy. 1981.** *The Woman That Never Evolved.* **Cambridge: Harvard University Press.**
Hrdy re-examines the evidence on human evolution, especially as reflected in the biology and behavior of nonhuman primates, and establishes a basis for challenging male-centered explanations of human sexuality. In her highly readable analysis of female and male sexual behavior, Hrdy attempts to explain such primate attributes as male and female dominance hierarchies and continuous sexual receptivity of human females.

**Margaret Mead. 1928.** *Coming of Age in Samoa.* **New York: Dell.**
Though criticized for its methodology, *Coming of Age in Samoa* stands as an example of Mead's remarkable ability to observe and record human behavior and to explain what it all means for a Western audience. This book is also a classic early study of socialization into gender roles. Mead firmly believed that appropriate female and male behavior is learned—not innate. That view is reflected in her description of the socialization of Samoan girls.

**Kenneth E. Read. 1965.** *The High Valley.* **New York: Charles Scribner's Sons.**
This compelling account of Read's fieldwork experiences among the Gahuku of New Guinea was not intended strictly as an exploration of gender. However, the author's descriptions of interactions between women and men in a society organized around the supposed complementarity of females and males inevitably stimulate a new consideration of what the social ordering of gender really means.

# Introduction

## *Mari Womack*

In the musical comedy classic *My Fair Lady*, the protagonist Henry Higgins laments: "Why can't a woman be more like a man?"[1] His despair reflects the idea that women are innately so different from men, it is impossible to understand them. Ironically, almost everything that Higgins finds inexplicable—and eventually appealing—in womanhood, in the figure of Eliza Doolittle, are cultural conventions. Eliza's mannerisms, her way of speaking, and her style of dress are shaped by culture.

Women are not born wearing high heels and perfume. The mincing gait so closely identified with the feminine in our culture is produced by footwear and is as culturally formed as the traditional Chinese lotus-shaped feet, the result of binding a girl's feet tightly during the formative years of childhood. It is striking that two such disparate cultures should independently define women as frail and enhance that presumed fragility by, in effect, hobbling them to prevent them from moving about freely.

Why is the presumed weakness of women so desirable that such a quantity of social energy is invested in producing and promoting it? It has been suggested that the presumed weakness of women enhances the prestige of high-status males, who thereby demonstrate their ability to provide for a woman who need not make an economic contribution. Female frailty is not valued when women must contribute to subsistence, as suggested by the former slave Sojourner Truth, in her 1851 speech to a women's civil rights convention:

> That man over there says that women need to be helped into carriages, and lifted over ditches, and to have the best place everywhere. Nobody helps me into carriages, or over mud-puddles, or gives me any best place! And ain't I a woman? Look at me! Look at my arm! I have ploughed and planted, and

gathered into barns, and no man could head me — and ain't I a woman? I could work as much and eat as much as a man — when I could get it — and bear the lash as well! And ain't I a woman? I have borne thirteen children, and seen them most all sold off into slavery, and when I cried out with my mother's grief, none but Jesus heard me! And ain't I a woman?

The concept of what is desirable in a woman depends very much on economics and other social factors. Another irony in the story of Henry Higgins is that the woman he comes to love is his own invention. The Eliza Doolittle he eventually decides to marry is not the unlettered flower vendor he adopts as raw material, but the elegant woman he has trained to behave as a member of his own social class. Not only do we love our cultural inventions, but we insist on believing they are a product of nature or, alternatively, that they are divinely ordained. A wise old woman once pointed out to me, "God hasn't done anything that human beings haven't improved on." She noted that we decorate our bodies and cut down trees to construct our dwellings. Even the plants and animals we know best are carefully engineered through genetic selection. "Why then," she asked, "do we give God credit for what we have done ourselves?"

Perhaps it is because we prefer to have God's — or nature's — stamp of approval on our culturally generated products. From the articles in this book, it becomes apparent that perceptions of gender — attributed to biological, "natural" or divinely ordained differences — pervade all aspects of cultural expression. The social organization of production, allocation of power, rules governing marriage and family relationships, and our perceptions of the natural and supernatural orders all reflect cultural concepts of gender.

Wherever we look, we see "female" and "male." Boats, tropical storms and nations all have symbolic gender. Although the attributes of "femaleness" and "maleness" vary from one society to another, the "gendering" of the universe appears to be universal. According to Western tradition, the sun is masculine and the moon is feminine and this association is explained as "natural" since the cycles of the moon are conceptually linked to the female menstrual cycle. The Japanese do not draw this comparison, however. In Japanese cosmology, the sun is female, the goddess Amaterasu, progenitor of the imperial dynasty. The moon, on the other hand, is Amaterasu's comparatively insignificant brother. The difference is that the Western typology of sun and moon emphasizes the superior position of males; Japanese symbolism provides an explanation for the divine origins of the emperor. In this way, symbolic representations of gender can reinforce social priorities.

The sexual and social dynamics of "female" and "male" are the most powerful of our symbols and perhaps the most troubling of our experiences. Together, women and men have the power to create life and, the ethnographic evidence would suggest, the power to complicate life so much, both often question whether it is all worth it. The frustration of Henry Higgins is echoed in the musings of men of the New Guinea Highlands and of Andalusian Spain alike. And their question is asked in inverted form by women, who wonder, "Why is it men never seem to grow up?"

The biological evidence contradicts the occasionally expressed opinion that males and females are actually of different species. In fact, the two sexes are more similar biologically than the experience of either would suggest. Sexual dimorphism (differences in bodily forms) in human beings is relatively minor when compared to some other primate species, such as orangutans and gorillas. At 150 pounds, the adult male orangutan is twice the size of the adult female.

Although human males are slightly larger, stronger, and exhibit more body hair than females, most attributes that markedly distinguish human males from females are culturally imposed in the form of hair styles and mode of dress. As physical anthropologist Naomi Bishop points out, however, clothing can also obscure sex differences (personal communication 1992). A slender, long-haired young man wearing tight-fitting jeans may be mistaken for a female from the rear. No gorilla would make such an error with reference to a member of his own species. The gorilla has the advantage in that he views members of his species naked, without cultural adornments that might confuse the issue.

The first article in this part "Biological Influences on Gender," by Jean Stockard and Miriam M. Johnson, describes the biological processes that produce females and males, and discusses possible hormonal bases for such behavioral expressions as aggression. Stockard and Johnson note that mood changes in women appear to be linked with hormonal fluctuations associated with the menstrual cycle and that higher levels of testosterone in males may be associated with their greater tendency to display aggression. Testosterone is a form of androgen, which is viewed as the "male" hormone; estrogen and progesterone are considered to be "female" hormones. However, all three hormones are produced by both males and females.

Some anecdotal evidence for the effects of hormones on emotions may be provided by the experiences of a man and woman who underwent sex change operations.[2] The male who became a woman describes estrogen treatments as "like taking a giant tranquilizer." The female who became a man reports feeling "energized" as the result of taking androgen. Such comments are not conclusive, however, since these experiences may be due to the placebo effect, in which individuals respond to medical intervention even when there appears to be no biological basis for the change.

In any case, Stockard and Johnson point out that behavior of both males and females is ordered and evaluated in light of cultural norms, adding, "to say that women should not hold responsible positions because their monthly changes in hormonal secretions affect their moods is akin to saying that men should not hold responsible positions because of their biologically based aggressiveness!" Biological differences alone do not explain why in many societies men are culturally defined and encouraged to be "aggressive" and females are culturally defined and encouraged to be "nurturant."

Biology also does not explain why females are often described as "passive" in spite of behavioral evidence to the contrary. In his article in this part, "Oedipus in the New Guinea Highlands?" L. L. Langness notes that both women and men among the Bena Bena are encouraged to be aggressive. Aggressive acts by females are apparently widespread in spite of the tendency of anthropologists to underreport them. H. B. Kimberley Cook has documented examples of women of Margarita Island off the coast of Venezuela using physical force to control the behavior of men. In one case, a woman intervened to remove a drunken man when the efforts of males proved fruitless:

> Finally a woman in her mid-fifties stood up, walked over to the drunken man, grabbed him firmly under the arm, walked him up town and deposited him on the other side of the street. When she returned the group continued their visit peacefully and uninterrupted (1991:3).

Women are not *passive*, though they may be less physically *aggressive* than males. Culturally produced descriptions of females as passive reflect the patterning of opposition, which is a way of ordering the complex and often bewildering possibilities of social interaction. Mary Douglas notes that people find ambiguity and contradiction—which characterize the disorder of human experience—as inherently threatening. Disorder, she writes, "symbolizes both danger and power" (1966:94). To cope with the "danger" of chaotic experience and to harness its "power" for socially appropriate purposes, it is customary to contain and control disorder through the use of symbols. As noted above, "woman" and "man" are among the most powerful symbols available to human experience.

Claude Levi-Strauss (1963) argues that conceptual categories are typically ordered in the form of binary oppositions, or ideological pairs viewed as being opposed to each other. For example, "male" is viewed as being in opposition to "female"; "aggressive" is opposed to "passive"; "sun" is opposed to "moon"; and so on.[3] Many attributes presumed to be inherent in males and females can best be understood as arising from the opposition of conceptual categories, rather than as being grounded in observations about the actual behavior of men and women. For example, the ancient Chinese concept of the creative forces of *Yin* and *Yang* reflects the ordering of binary opposites. *Yin* is earth, negative, passive, dark, feminine, and destructive; *Yang* is heaven, positive, active, light, masculine, and constructive.

Obviously, not all or even most Chinese females behave in negative, passive, dark and destructive ways, and display a natural affinity for the earth. By the same token, not all Chinese men are positive, active, light and constructive, nor do they have a tendency to seek heaven. These are conceptual categories, not meticulously recorded descriptions of actual personalities or behavior.

This example illustrates why males in our own culture continue to be regarded as "aggressive" and "rational" and women as "passive" and "emotional," even when the behavior and personality traits of most men and women do not bear this out. The persuasive power of our culturally derived assumptions is greater than the evidence of our daily experience. When men frustrate our aims with emotional displays or women insist on being fiercely practical when poetic awe appears to be called for, we rarely respond by rejecting our cultural categories. Instead, we bemoan the perversity of these particular men and women. In acting out and reflecting upon our lives, we tend to focus on the seeming contradictions of our own particular male-female dyad, failing to take note of the cultural context which defines gender roles as being in opposition.

Biological aspects of femaleness and maleness are *sex* differences; the social and cultural ordering of the categories is *gender*. Gender relations are ordered not only conceptually, but in terms of socially defined behavioral roles. "Female" and "male" are in fact social categories that imply organization of production and reproduction, power and compliance. The second article in this part "Separate People: Speaking of Creek Men and Women," by Amelia Rector Bell, demonstrates the pervasiveness of gender ordering on all levels — cosmological, reproductive, economic, ritualistic and linguistic.

Another important aspect of gender relations is that, not only are they ordered socially and conceptually, but values are assigned differently to the two domains. Anthropologists have been hard-pressed to explain why, seemingly universally, male roles and attributes are more valued than female, even where the contribution of women is more important to the survival of the group. For example, in forager[4] societies, hunting is allocated to men, and women provide for the family's daily subsistence needs by gathering.[5] In most cases, gathering is a more consistent and reliable source of food than hunting. Yet, hunting is valued more highly than gathering.

In fact, one generalization that appears to hold true cross-culturally is that women are responsible for those tasks essential to survival: making sure the family is fed on a daily basis; protecting it from the elements through care of the household; and producing and caring for children, without whom no group could survive past the present generation. Men, on the other hand, are allocated the "glamorous" tasks that enrich the cultural life of the group: hunting, making war, maintaining ritual relations with supernatural entities, storytelling, and conducting the affairs of government. Yet, the duties of men are defined as "important" and the affairs of women are defined as "trivial," beneath the notice of men.

A cartoon in the *New Yorker* some years ago illustrates the same principle operating in the division of labor of an American middle-class couple. The couple is asked, "Who wears the pants?" The wife responds: "Oh, my husband, of course. He decides all the big issues, like what to do about the Russians and the Space Program. I decide all the little issues, like where to go on vacation and which house to buy." (Cited in Gilmore 1990:967)

Women's work is *valuable* but men's work is *valued*, and it is difficult to determine precisely why this is so, or why it is such a pervasive feature of human social organization. Sherry B. Ortner asserts that "everywhere, in every known culture, women are considered in some degree inferior to men" (1974:69). She suggests that what she calls the "subordination of women" has three aspects: (1) ideologies that explicitly accord women and their roles less value than men and their roles, (2) symbolic devices that define women as polluting or defiling, and (3) "social-structural arrangements" that exclude women from participating in realms in which "the highest powers of the society are felt to reside" (1974:69).

Nancy Chodorow provides a clue to the devaluing of femaleness in her discussion of the different processes involved in socialization of girls and boys. She contends that female and male personality differences develop out of the process of separation and individuation involved in maturation. She notes that both girls and boys spend the early years of their lives in close association with their mothers. For a girl, this identification continues throughout her life, since her social role as an adult is consonant with her experience of her mother, who provides a model for appropriate behavior.

On the other hand, a boy must disengage himself from identification with his mother to pattern himself after a largely absent "invisible father." Chodorow writes: "A boy, in his attempt to gain an elusive masculine identification, often comes to define this masculinity largely in negative terms, as that which is not feminine or involved with women" (1974:50). Because the boy's sense of self is dependent on rejection of his mother and the feminine within himself, he denigrates and devalues "whatever he considers to be feminine in the outside world" (1974:50).

In a number of societies, a young man's relationship with his mother is severed at puberty through strict taboos defining women as "polluting" or "dangerous." The youth may be subjected to harsh rituals initiating him into male society, including ritual seclusion, beatings, circumcision and subincision, which involves slitting the underside of the penis. Some of these are discussed in L. L. Langness' article "Oedipus in the New Guinea Highlands?" in this part. It has been argued that the purpose of male puberty rites — such as ritualized homosexuality — is to eliminate all traces of the boy's identification with his mother and the female realm in general.[6] On a social level, the female role emerges from and is continuous with the dynamics of the domestic unit. The male role, on the other hand, is socially constructed and discontinuous with the primary unit of socialization.

According to Chodorow, differences in female-male socialization experiences are reflected in their adult personalities. She notes that males establish rigidly defined ego boundaries, whereas females see their ego boundaries as being more flexible, allowing them to care for and assume responsibility for others. Chodorow writes:

> Most generally, I would suggest that a quality of embeddedness in social interaction and personal relationships characterizes women's life relative to men's. From childhood, daughters are likely to participate in an intergenerational world with their mother, and often with their aunts and grandmother, whereas boys are on their own or participate in a single-generational world of age mates (1974:57).

The interconnectedness of women can be politically advantageous, as indicated in David D. Gilmore's article "Men and Women in Southern Spain: 'Domestic Power' Revisited," in Part Four of this volume. Gilmore argues that women are able to exert control over domestic decision-making through mother-daughter alliances. Men, who must rely on support from often competitive age-mates, seldom prevail against this powerful dyad.

However, Chodorow notes the identification of a daughter with her mother can be maladaptive if the young woman fails to differentiate herself clearly from the rest of the world. This results in feelings of guilt and responsibility for situations beyond her control: "This loss of self in overwhelming responsibility for and connection to others is described particularly acutely by women writers. . . ." (Chodorow 1974:59) Chodorow refers especially to, among others, Virginia Woolf, author of *A Room of One's Own*, and Simone de Beauvoir, whose essay "Woman as Other" is the final selection in Part One of this volume.

Chodorow's model provides a new perspective on the debate over Freud's concept of the Oedipal complex, as represented here by L. L. Langness' "Oedipus in the New Guinea Highlands?" the third article in this part. Freud asserted that male children universally must contend with sexual longings for their mothers, which result in feelings of jealousy toward their fathers. The boy wants to kill his father, but feels guilty for these impulses and fears his father's greater power. From this ambivalence develops "castration anxiety," which stems from the boy's unconscious fear that his father will castrate him as punishment for sexual longings for the mother.

Langness rejects both Freud's view that the Oedipal complex is a universal feature of male development and the contention of Chodorow and others that a father's relationship with his children is necessarily marked by distance. On the contrary, Langness notes that, in New Guinea, Bena Bena fathers are involved in ongoing interaction with children of both sexes. He adds that Bena Bena mothers are not charged with the continuous or exclusive care of their children, so it is difficult to see how intense mother-child bonds of the Western type could develop. Langness concludes that Western models of socialization are not applicable universally and that some explanation other than the Oedipal complex must be found to account for harsh male initiation rites at puberty and ritual segregation of men and women.

In my study of male professional athletes in the United States, I note that males are ritually—and therefore most rigorously— segregated from females when activities such as warfare and sports require them to form a cohesive fighting unit. Professional athletes—like New Guinea warriors—practice celibacy before clashing with the opposing group. In explaining the (often self-imposed) rule of celibacy among athletes, I write:

> . . . before a game an athlete must turn his attention from the concerns and social relationships of everyday life and prepare himself to assume the responsibilities of sports. The social relationships which ordinarily occupy his thoughts (such as his wife and children) must be put aside so that he can become a fully participating member of the team. . . . The athletes are not just trying to husband their strength by avoiding sex the night before a game, [they] are subtly putting aside one set of social commitments preparatory to assuming new ones (1982:238).

Women (and sex) are "dangerous" because they threaten the male social "order," which is organized around the necessity of fending off an opponent—an army in warfare or a team in sports. This is not to suggest that *society* is organized around the activities of men, as some earlier theorists seem to imply (See Washburn and Lancaster 1968 and Tiger 1970). In fact, some authors assert that society is more likely organized around the domestic activities of production and reproduction, in which women play a central role (Slocum 1975). However, social *values* often favor the more colorful and dramatic roles of men—including warfare, hunting and public debate—over the more utilitarian roles of women.

In her article "Contested Order: Gender and Society in the Southern New Guinea Highlands," in Part Four of this volume, Rena Lederman suggests that an expressed emphasis on male values is often misconstrued by Western theorists as devaluing women. In fact, she argues, it is a rhetorical device that emphasizes the importance of *collective* male action, defending it against the often more compelling inclinations of *individual* men, who might otherwise prefer the company of women to such group male activities as making war.

The author of the final selection of this part, Simone de Beauvoir, is a product of Western society, and her essay "Woman as Other" reflects contradictions specifically generated by European definitions of gender. De Beauvoir, born in Paris in 1908, poses searching questions about the opposing, though asymmetrical, relationship between men and women: "In actuality the relation of the two sexes is not quite like that of two electrical poles, for man represents both the positive and the neutral, . . . whereas woman represents only the negative. . . ." Ironically, this view is reflected in traditional anthropological studies, discussed in Part Two of this volume, which appear to be based on the assumption that, except for activities specifically designated as female, society is presumed to be male. It may be easier to understand this conundrum if we reflect on the contention that male identity is socially constructed — i.e., explicitly affirmed — while female indentity is never in question. In the articulation of social concepts, then, female is defined as "not-male."

At issue is why women seem to accept and internalize — and pass on to their daughters — the secondary designation of "not-male." De Beauvoir concludes by asserting that one reason woman complies with her social role of "other" is that she is "often very well pleased" with it. However, this is challenged in part by the ethnographic evidence. In his book *The High Valley*, Kenneth Read notes that, given the opportunity through ritual role reversal, women quite often express their repressed anger at occupying a secondary place in society. He describes his own reactions to the unexpectedly strong ritual resistance of teenaged girls in a New Guinea village when Tarova, one of their age mates, is given in marriage to a man of another village:

> Like the contagion spread by panic, the violence of the emotions in the struggling throng swept over me, drawing me to the point where my own fear was indistinguishable from the distraught expressions of the girls whose circle of linked bodies rocked and staggered under the buffeting of the men. It was quite unthinkable that they could win. Not only were they badly outmatched, but also no one in the crowd intended a conscious repudiation of the impersonal order that shaped their lives. The

girls' challenge was not deliberate, not undertaken from any
rational objective that they hoped to gain (1965:259).

Read keenly feels his own powerlessness in the face of inexorable
social forces that will ultimately deliver the female child into the
hands of strangers:

> . . . for a brief moment I hoped for the impossible, and when
> the end came as Helekohe [one of Tarova's townsmen], breaking
> through the circle, grabbed Tarova by the arm and dragged her
> to the base of the wooden staff, I felt so helpless, so emptied by
> distress that my eyes filled with unashamed tears (1965:259).

Read's reaction is not solely due to the fact that, as an outsider
and an anthropologist trained in another culture, he did not share
the values of a society that would forcibly remove a girl from her
own village. Tarova's kinsman Hasu appears to experience the same
feelings of powerlessness:

> Several feet away Hasu was crying silently, completely unaware
> of anyone but Tarova as his eyes enfolded her with a glance in
> which I read my own deep wish to reassure her. Watching him
> I felt that with everyone present he wanted her to understand
> his helplessness to change the course of events and also to give
> her the comfort and protection whose need showed so clearly
> on her face (1965:259-260).

The people of Tarova's village did not tear her away from her age
mates because they were cruel or unfeeling, but because their social
obligations compelled them to do so. We often make the error of
imputing *private* motivations for behavior that derives from our
*public* role. De Beauvoir was a European woman writing for a
European audience and she did not consider that what pleases a
women — and a man — is in large part defined by cultural values that
become internalized as a result of socialization. The roles of both
women and men are part of a network of social obligations that bind
them to culturally defined patterns of interaction.

It is now possible to respond to the rhetorical question posed by
the fictional Henry Higgins at the beginning of this essay: Why can't
a woman be more like a man? On a biological level, women differ
from men as a result of complementary reproductive roles. Even
more importantly, however, a woman cannot be more like a man
because cultural constructs and social roles, impressed upon her
through intensive socialization, constrain her from being more like
a man — just as the same constellation of cultural and social factors
prevent a man from being more like a woman.

# 1

# Biological Influences on Gender

## Jean Stockard and Miriam M. Johnson

**P**opularized theories claim that one biological factor or another determines other psychological and social phenomena. Usually, these analyses try to justify male dominance and the traditional gender division of labor on the basis of some male capacity or female incapacity. This misuse of biology has understandably led many feminists to be extremely leery of any biological perspectives on gender differences. Actually, biological data need not, and in fact do not, imply that women are inferior to men nor that societal systems of male dominance or female mothering are inevitable.

There are obviously biological differences between females and males. There also probably are some psychological gender differences that have a biological base. However, because many studies of these differences have been based on a masculine paradigm, it is important to try to analyze these differences without a masculine bias. At the same time, we must avoid a possible feminist bias, a tendency to distort findings or overlook contradictory evidence because we want to believe certain "congenial truths" (Mackie 1977).

Few people now would argue for the exclusive importance of either nature or nurture in explaining sex gender differences. Biology by no means fully determines what happens to individuals or to social groups. Although physiological variables may prompt individuals to move in certain directions, the social situation,

Adapted from: Jean Stockard/Miriam M. Johnson, *Sex and Gender in Society* (Second Edition), © 1992, pp. 113-133. Reprinted by permission of Prentice Hall, Englewood Cliffs, New Jersey.

including economic and cultural factors, or individual desires, may overrule or drastically alter these biological predilections.

## The Development of Sex Differences in Utero

Biological gender is first determined when the male's sperm unites with the female's egg to form the zygote. Both the sperm and the egg cell have 23 chromosomes. These chromosomes are then paired in the fertilized egg, yielding 23 pairs of 46 individual chromosomes. One of the pairs of chromosomes determines genetic sex. The egg contributes an X sex chromosome; the sperm contributes either an X or a Y chromosome. If the embryo has two X sex chromosomes, it is a genetic female; if it has an X and a Y chromosome, it is a genetic male. Because the female always contributes an X chromosome, it is the male's sperm that determines a child's sex. Scientists estimate that almost 140 XY conceptions occur for every 100 XX conceptions. However, more XY conceptions fail to develop and so, at birth, the ratio of males to females is about 105 to 100 (Money and Tucker 1975:41-42).

For the first six weeks after conception, embryos with either an XX or an XY sex chromosome structure appear the same, although they can be differentiated microscopically. All embryos have "growth buds" that can develop into male or female organs. Differentiation takes place in stages, starting first with the gonads or sex glands (the ovaries and testes), moving then to the internal reproductive structures, and finally to the external genitalia.

If the embryo has XY sex chromosomes, at about the sixth week after conception the bud of the gonads begins to develop into testicles, the male gonads. If the embryo has XX chromosomes, nothing will happen for about six more weeks, when the buds begin to differentiate into ovaries. These will contain many egg cells for reproduction in later life.

The testicles then begin to produce sex hormones: progesterone, androgen, and estrogen. Although we normally think of estrogen as the female hormone and androgen as the male hormone because of the relative proportion of the hormone each sex group produces, it is important to remember that both males and females have all three hormones in their bodies. The proportion of hormones varies both between men and women and between individuals within each sex group and over the life cycle. Testicles produce more androgen than estrogen, and ovaries produce more estrogen than androgen.

At around the third to fourth month after conception, hormones produced by the testicles cause the *wolffian* structures, which are present in all fetuses, to develop as *seminal vesicles*, the *prostate*, and the *vasa*. These are the internal male genitalia. During this time of prenatal life, the testicles also produce a substance that inhibits or stops the *mullerian* structures, also present in all fetuses, from developing into female organs. If testicles have not developed and none of these hormones has been produced, female internal genitalia develop. No hormones appear to be needed to prompt the *mullerian* structures to develop into the *uterus*, *fallopian tubes*, and upper *vagina*, the internal female genitalia (Money and Tucker 1975:46-47). It is possible, however, that hormones from the placenta and the mother, as well as even the ovaries, may influence the development of female genitalia (Fausto-Sterling 1985:81; Otten 1985:160).

Although the male and female internal genitalia develop from different structures, both present in all fetuses, the external genitalia develop from the same preliminary structure. Again, the hormonal mix determines how the preliminary genital tubercle becomes a penis and a scrotum to hold the testicles when they descend. If hormones generally secreted by the testicles are not present, the tubercle stays small to become the clitoris, and the two folds of skin, instead of joining to form the scrotum, stay separate to become the labia minora and head of the clitoris, separating the vagina from the urethra, which connects to the bladder.

One of the most important differences between males and females is the cyclic nature of female hormonal activity. In all female mammals, hormone production follows a regular cycle. Estrogen production is higher from the menstrual period to the time of highest fertility, and progesterone levels are higher after that. These cycles are controlled by the pituitary gland. Males do not have such specific or regular patterns of hormonal activity. Scientists have concluded from experiments on animals that prenatal secretion of androgen by the testicles influences how the pituitary gland will behave later. If androgen is lacking in prenatal life, the female pattern of cyclical secretion develops in later years. Other aspects of the brain are also affected by the prenatal hormone mix including, perhaps, some aspects of personality and behavior.

## The Nature of Physical Differences

Physiological differences between the sex groups continue to appear and develop after birth. Some of these differences, primarily involving traits such as skin sensitivity and strength, first appear at birth. Others become important only at puberty, when sex differences in hormonal levels again occur. Below, we discuss differences in size and strength, susceptibility to illness and disease, and perception.

**Size and Strength.**  At birth, boy babies tend to be slightly longer and weigh slightly more than girl babies. Females' lungs and hearts are proportionally smaller than those of males, and females have a lower percentage of their body weight in muscle, but a higher percentage in fat. Despite these size differences, females mature more rapidly than males. This difference first appears seven weeks after conception. By the time of birth, the female is four weeks ahead of the male baby. Females learn to walk and talk and are toilet trained more quickly than males. They also reach puberty and full physiological maturity earlier.

At birth, male metabolism is faster than female, although the difference may not be statistically significant. From the age of two months, males consume more calories than females. Adult males also have a lower resting heart rate, higher blood pressure, greater oxygen-carrying capacity, and more efficient recovery from muscular activity. These physiological characteristics are one basis of male superiority in strength. Females may certainly develop their strength and endurance through exercise programs. In recent years, as more funds have been devoted to training women athletes, they have rapidly improved their athletic performance (Dyer 1985, 1986). However, it is not yet known whether they will match men athletically in all endeavors.

**Illness and Disease.**  A well-known sex difference that appears even prenatally is the male's greater susceptibility to illness and death. As we noted in the previous section, many more male than female fetuses are conceived, but the sex ratio is almost equal at birth. After birth, males also tend to be more susceptible to both disease and death. In this country, one-third more males than females die before their first birthday. Even as life expectancy in a society lengthens, the benefits accrue faster for women than for men, although this may result from the decline of female deaths associated with pregnancy and birth (Barfield 1976:67; Stillion 1985).

Males are susceptible to physical difficulties that pass females by. Such well-known problems as color blindness, hemophilia, and even baldness result from the males' XY chromosome structure. These inherited conditions arise from genetic information on the X chromosome that the child receives from the mother. Girls may also receive this condition-carrying X chromosome. But because the gene related to hemophilia or color blindness is recessive, the corresponding gene on the girls' other X chromosome can prevent the appearance of the condition in the female. The boy has no other X chromosome to block this effect and thus exhibits the defect. The girl remains a carrier and can pass the characteristic on to her offspring.

The incidence of other disorders may be influenced by our culture. Both males and females have physiological reactions to stress. But in our culture men more often develop peptic ulcers and skin disorders, and women exhibit headaches, migraines, backaches, and insomnia. Sex differences also appear in the incidence of many other diseases and conditions, although the reasons underlying all of these differences are not yet clear. For instance, women develop diabetes, phlebitis, and diseases of the thyroid gland more often than men, whereas men more often develop most forms of cancer and cardiovascular and immunodeficiency diseases (Otten 1985:204-206). In middle age, women more often develop nonfatal chronic diseases, and men more often develop fatal diseases (Verbrugge 1989:345). Differences also occur in the incidence of mental illness. Women more often suffer from depression; men more often suffer from substance abuse and personality disorders that include problems with aggression and impulse control.

Finally, some sex differences in physical vulnerability may come from environmental and activity differences. A higher proportion of male deaths than female deaths results from accidents and injuries. Males also smoke cigarettes more and die from lung cancer more than females. However, as women become more involved in dangerous activities and as they increase their smoking, their death rate in these areas also rises (Travis 1988). Although it is popularly assumed that the stresses men face in the occupational world contribute to the higher number of heart attacks, there is now some evidence that women's hormonal secretions somehow protect them from heart disease. When these secretions diminish at menopause,

women's susceptibility to heart disease rises. Females' lower death
rate may also be promoted by their tendency to seek medical help
more quickly than men (Verbrugge 1976; Hibbard and Pope 1983,
1986).

## Physiology and Psychological Gender Differences

Some differences we think of as "psychological" may have a
physiological basis, including gender differences in nurturance,
aggression and mood change.

*Nurturance.* We use the term *nurturance* to describe the "giving
of aid and comfort to others" (Maccoby and Jacklin 1974:214-215).
Nurturant behavior often involves responding to bids for help and
comfort from others who are younger, weaker, or for some other
reason, such as illness or old age, in a dependent position. Nurturant
care of the young is essential for the survival of the human species,
for human young depend totally on others for their care for a
number of years.

Sex differences in the propensity to nurture appear in studies of
adolescent animals and in studies of humans. Field studies show
that young male langurs and baboons mainly play with other males
and that young females spend a great deal of time with adult females
and help take care of infants (Jay 1963; DeVore 1963; Fedigan
1982). Similar results have also been observed with human children
in a wide cross-section of cultures (Whiting and Whiting 1975;
Whiting and Edwards 1988). Similarly, experimenters who gave
young monkeys to preadolescent pairs of male and female monkeys
found that the preadolescent females were four times as likely as
the males to act maternally toward young monkeys. The males were
ten times as likely as the females to exhibit hostile behaviors
(Chamove et al 1967). Both males and females exhibit nurturant
behaviors; females simply seem to show a greater interest in
learning to do so.

Although biological factors influence nurturance, other factors
also play an important part. Some authors emphasize the importance of physical contact in the postpartum period in cementing
maternal-child ties (e.g., Fabes and Filsinger 1988). Similarly,
however, greater contact between fathers and children appears to
increase fathers' nurturance (e.g., LaRossa and LaRossa 1989).
Attachment and nurturant behaviors appear to develop as parent

and child interact and communicate with each other. Although the prenatal hormone doses males receive may hinder their interest in nurturing young children, they by no means eliminate their capacity for nurturing, as shown by experiences of fathers of newborns. Even among young boys, those with younger siblings at home show more nurturance in doll play than other boys. Girls show nurturance whether or not they have younger siblings (Ehrhardt and Baker 1974:38).

**Aggression.** Males exhibit more aggressive behavior than females in all known societies. Male nonhuman primates also exhibit more aggression than their female counterparts. Certainly, aspects of these differences are socially learned. Most important, the patterns of aggressive behavior that individuals exhibit depend on the social and cultural context. For instance, young boys may wrestle and fight during school recess, but they know that such behavior is not permitted in the classroom. Brawls and fights may occur regularly in some areas of town, but almost never in others.

*Prenatal influences.* As with nurturance, prenatal hormone doses are believed to have an organizing function on aggressive behavior. Evidence from research with animals indicates that males receiving lower than normal prenatal doses of androgens tend to exhibit less aggressive behavior in later life, whereas females who receive higher than normal prenatal doses of androgens exhibit more fighting in adulthood (Edwards 1969; Tieger 1980).

Although one may generalize from such animal studies to humans only with caution, studies with humans do suggest some connection between prenatal hormone doses and later aggression. Some studies indicate that boys and girls who received unusually high doses of androgen were more likely to have a higher level of energy and prefer boys' toys and activities, involving a high degree of rough, outdoor play (Ehrhardt 1973, 1985; Ehrhardt and Baker 1974).

The increased activity of the children with excessive hormonal doses may not be the same as aggression, which is usually defined as actions with intent to hurt another. It may be that in acting out a female gender identity, these girls learn to pattern their activity in nonaggressive ways. This finding suggests that because the feminine role does not include aggressiveness, hormones cannot produce it. The hormones do influence the young women, but the influence is expressed in ways compatible with a feminine identity.

*Postnatal influences.* For both animals and humans, hormonal levels can fluctuate markedly as a result of changes in the social environment. Studies on humans that try to link the level of testosterone within individuals' bloodstream with their level of aggressive or criminal behavior have yielded conflicting results. The relationship may be stronger with certain types of aggressive behaviors and with younger men, but more evidence is needed. Testosterone levels do appear to be associated with positions of dominance. Evidence from studies of nonhuman primates indicates that the more dominant animals have higher androgen levels than the less dominant animals (Moyer 1987), and some have suggested that this model might apply to human groups as well (e.g., Mazur 1985).

Under certain conditions, females are aggressive. Maternal aggression is found in many different species. This behavior, whether involving attacks toward strangers or just general irritability, is usually directly related to pregnancy, parturition, and lactation. Among the primates, this aggression appears to be elicited largely by the distress of the young and is shown by others as well as the mother. Males in a primate troop and other females besides the mother may display strong defensive reactions for the young.

In some cases animal mothers kill their young. However, this probably arises from a different endocrine basis than maternal aggression, including an abnormally high level of androgen (Moyer 1976:182)

**Moods.** Almost 60 percent of all women report that they experience discomfort or changes with their monthly menstrual period (Ramey 1976:139; Ericksen 1984:178). Some of the shifts in mood that women experience may result from negative attitudes toward the bodily functions, but some may result from the influence of different hormonal levels within the body. All living creatures experience cyclic changes. Sleep, pain tolerance, and cell division all appear to vary in regular cycles. Yet, among humans, women's mood changes during the monthly menstrual cycle have received the most research and popular attention. Women secrete hormones in a fixed pattern, corresponding with the menstrual cycle. During the first half of the menstrual cycle, after menstruation, the secretion of estrogen rises. Midway through the cycle, ovulation occurs, as an egg is released from a follicle in one ovary. Estrogen secretion then drops, but begins to rise again about the twentieth day of the cycle and finally drops quickly just before menstruation. Progesterone, also called the pregnancy hormone, increases after ovulation and peaks around the twentieth day of the cycle. Its function is to prepare the body for pregnancy in case sperm fertilizes the egg. Just before menstruation the level of progesterone production falls markedly. There is some evidence that testosterone, a type of androgen, is secreted more heavily just before menstruation and also at ovulation (Bardwick 1974:29; Money and Ehrhardt 1972:222; Barfield 1976:70-71).

Hormones travel through the bloodstream and thus can potentially affect all parts of the body. Although some women have much wider mood changes than others, a good deal of evidence indicates that hostility, anxiety, and depression appear more during the premenstrual stage than in other parts of the cycle. Self-esteem and self-confidence seem to be highest in midcycle at ovulation (Hoyenga and Hoyenga 1979:145-153). Yet, as research in this area accumulates, it has become clear that no simple generalizations can be made about the incidence, symptoms, or source of "premenstrual syndrome" or "PMS." Only a relatively small percentage of women experience the extremely debilitating symptoms associated with a clinical definition of this syndrome. Moreover, cultural beliefs about menstruation and women's cycles are extremely widespread, and hormonal secretions are influenced by environmental variables such as stress. Thus, complete understanding of premenstrual syndrome must consider its multiple dimensions and the interaction of hormonal, cultural, and social influences.

Some evidence suggests that men as well as women experience cycles of hormonal secretions and mood. Several studies have documented relatively regular fluctuations of emotions or moods of both sex groups over a variety of time periods (E.g., Englander-Golden, et al 1986). Other studies have noted fluctuations in the testosterone levels of males, with over half experiencing repeating cycles (e.g., Doering, et al 1975). Even though men may have cyclical changes in mood and other bodily functions, it is not known if individual fluctuations in hormones are related to these changes. Relatively little research has examined this issue, and almost no work has compared women's mood fluctuations with men's.

Whatever may eventually be found with regard to hormonal and mood fluctuations in men, we can say now that the attention given to these matters in women has often been used to disparage them. Both women and men have fluctuations in mood from one time to another. Yet, to say that women should not hold responsible positions because their monthly changes in hormonal secretions affect their moods is akin to saying that men should not hold responsible positions because of their biologically based aggressiveness!

## Avoiding a Masculine Bias

In general, sex differences in physical characteristics appear at birth or develop at puberty. Males are larger and stronger, and they have well-developed visual-spatial ability more often than females. Females mature more quickly, are less susceptible to disease, live longer, and may be more sensitive to taste, smell and touch than males are. Although women have a regular pattern of hormone secretion after puberty, no regular pattern has yet been found for men.

Although these physical differences generally appear cross-culturally, the meaning given to them varies from one society to another. For example, in this society, we have tended to stress women's relative lack of strength and men are expected to be the burden carriers. In other societies, relative strength is apparently unimportant and women carry the heavy loads. Biological differences are also used to justify differential evaluation of the sex groups, but here again the connection is by no means obvious. If one focuses on endurance and freedom from physical defect, one could argue for the natural superiority of women. If one focuses on size and strength, men might be called naturally superior.

Biological influences appear to affect psychological traits by increasing the likelihood that certain behaviors such as aggression or nurturance will appear. It is probably easier to prompt women to nurture and men to be aggressive because of prenatal hormonal influences and hormonal changes later in life. Yet, under certain circumstances, both women and men can nurture and both women and men can be aggressive. Hormones are neither necessary nor sufficient for these behaviors. Thus, that nurturance and aggression are influenced by biology does not mean that the social assignment of mothering to women and warfare to men is inevitable.

Although both men and women are subject to changes in mood, women's moods are somewhat more predictable than men's because they are more clearly influenced by cyclic hormonal changes. It is a masculine bias to assume that these cyclic changes are in themselves bad.

Some writers contend that male dominance itself can be explained by biology. Yet the activities and roles toward which females are biologically prompted are more important to the long-term survival of the group than those of males. For example, the affectional bonds between mother and young and between female members of primate groups promote group cohesion and survival much more than dominance and aggression. Although biology can help explain the social role divisions between women and men, it cannot explain why men's activities are valued more highly than women's. In order to explain this, one must look for theories that take into account the unique capacity of humans to imagine, to interpret, and to create meaning from their physical and social world.

# 2

# Separate People
## Speaking of Creek
## Men and Women[7]

### *Amelia Rector Bell*

Corn-Mother is the paradigmatic Creek mother, who feeds her children from corn that grows on her legs and is scraped off daily. She contains the germ of life within her. In the myths, male children, when old enough to see her secretly scraping corn from her legs, are horrified and kill her. They flee their home and live as warriors hunting in the forest. By the death of Corn-Mother, women and male children are separated, boys become warriors, and corn grows henceforth apart from the body of the mother. This creation myth articulates the basis for separation of female and male realms in terms of economic and reproductive roles and clan affiliations, as well as the expression of these complementary relationships in language.

In Creek thought, a female, watery cosmological domain generates all life. From this watery fundament, the sun, called "grandfather," emerges cleansed and purified to define each day. A symbol of male definitional power, the sun passes through and separates from the water in rays of light each morning. This mythical metaphor encapsulates the Creek ideology of the separation of gender: human social ordering requires light and heat obtained by and through the male capacity to differentiate from the mother.

The sun separates from the original watery domain each day. The myth of Corn-Mother describes this transition: boys must leave the maternal domain or become polluted by it, as eating corn from the

Adapted from *American Anthropologist* 92:2, June 1990, by permission of the American Anthropological Association. Not for sale or further reproduction.

legs of Corn-Mother portrays. Males separate from their mothers by killing her and then killing animals in the forest. Through such acts they arrest the uncontrolled life in the universe and, as the myth shows, corn grows separate from the body of Corn-Mother. Thus corn, the staple Creek food, grows because uncontrolled female generativity is defined and controlled by male action.

## Ritual and the Social Order

Creek Indians once lived in *i:tálwa* "tribal town[s]" along river valleys of what is now Alabama and Georgia. In the 1930s most Creeks were moved into Indian Territory on the midwestern plains of what is now Oklahoma. Today, thirty to forty thousand Creeks reside in small communities scattered over eleven counties which subdivide the Creek Nation, now a regional administrative unit. Creeks still live in settlements grouped according to *i:tálwa* affiliation, although homes are more dispersed than in the past.

Creek are matrilineal, which means a woman is a member of her mother's clan and *i:tálwa*, an association of several linked clan segments. A woman maintains primary affiliation to her natal *i:tálwa* all her life. A Creek man is a member of his mother's clan and *i:tálwa* until he marries, when he changes his primary *i:tálwa* affiliation to that of his wife.

The marriage creates a political alliance between the *i:tálwa* of the wife and that of the husband, and this alliance is emphasized in summer rituals, or stomp dances, held at ceremonial grounds. Each *i:tálwa* usually conducts four major stomp dances from March to November, including a midsummer *póskita* (green corn ceremony). Only *i:tálwa* joined by marriage alliances may participate in these ritual dances. Members are encouraged to attend their own stomp dances and participate in dances of their allies.

During stomp dances, men sing loudly in response to the verses of a leader, while women shake turtleshell rattles strapped to their legs. Women do not sing. Dancers form a spiral line of alternating men and women who stomp briskly around a central fire. Participants in the dance seek to become "one body" — a harmonious and well-choreographed group uniting men and women, hosts and allies.

## Women and Corn

A Creek woman is fundamentally a "food maker"—a cook. Women are expected to be good cooks as part of their nature. A woman who cannot cook is thought to have bad "medicine" within her, "blown" into her through the agency of a jealous rival. A poor cook must go to a medicine maker to have the intrusive agent expelled, which restores her natural ability to cook.

Women cook a symbolically important food called *sófki:*, a watery corn gruel made of water, crushed flint corn, and wood ashes. Cooked at a simmer for several hours until the proper thickness is reached, *sófki:* resembles thickened milk with bits of corn floating within it. Eaten hot or cold, *sófki:* is best when it has been allowed to sour for about three days. At this stage, it has a sharp, bitter taste and exudes a strong vinegary, beerlike odor. If allowed to sour much longer, it will begin to putrefy, and is so used to make cornbread. Creek believe a meal is not complete if *sófki:* is not served.

*Sófki:* preparation is undertaken entirely by women. Men take no part in making *sófki:* except to provide wood for the cookstove or cooking fire, which both boils the *sófki:* and provides ashes to mix with corn. A woman prepares *sófki:* for her children and husband as well for as any visitors. *Sófki* preparation marks a woman as the head of her own household; before marriage, girls and boys eat their mother's *sófki:*. Girls begin making their own *sófki:* at the age of courtship, apparently without explicit instruction. When a woman agrees to prepare *sófki* for a man, it marks the beginning of a relationship that may become a marriage. After marriage a woman cooks *sófki:* for her husband and children. If a woman ceases to cook *sófki:* for her husband, this is a sign the marriage is about to end.

Conceptually, *sófki:* is related to the procreative power of women, as reflected in attitudes and practices associated with menstruation. Many contemporary Creeks, particularly the more traditional stomp dancers, require separation of men from women during menses. When a woman is menstruating, her husband and older male children stay in the backyard brush arbor, a rough structure constructed of logs and roofed with oak leaves. In cold weather men and menstruating women usually sleep in different bedrooms. Some women own a special set of dishes and cups to be used during menstruation. Most use plastic tableware and paper plates and cups, which are thrown away after meals. During menses, women can cook for men but cannot eat food served from communal bowls or platters. Benches and other common seats are avoided. A menstruating woman cannot eat at the same table with men. During stomp dances, she is prohibited from entering the *paskó:fa*, the area for dance. It is believed that women who violate these regulations cause sickness for themselves and others.

The strong smell of *sófki:* contrasts with the strong smell of menstruation: *fámpiwákkin* or "stink lying down." Menstruation, "lying down," is not shaped by men. Both smells indicate the presence of a woman. Men say if they smell *sófki:*, they know a good (controlled) woman is around. When they smell menstrual "stink," which they believe can be perceived from a great distance, they know a dangerous (uncontrolled) woman is nearby. *Sófki:* shows that interaction between men and women is controlled. The male element, heat and ashes from firewood, is provided by men who cut down trees and deliver wood to their wives.

## Warriors, Wood, and Fire

The unmarked category of Creek life is female. Men are "made" through ritual processes that separate them physically and existentially from their mothers. A Creek baby is considered to be female and part of its mother, suckling the *sófki:*-like milk from her body, as did the sons of Corn-Mother. In the Creek idiom, babies have no bones. Creek babies of either gender are female and ideologically lack the "phallus." That is, they are female until transformed into men.

The Creek view of the importance of the phallus in defining social position is similar to the Western concept, noted by many anthropologists, that male ultimately defines female. However, Western concepts also assume that women's "lack of the phallus" implies lack of agentivity and a voice in the body politic. Among the Creek, women are not viewed as lacking agentivity. Rather, they provide the generative force that must ultimately be defined and ordered by men.

When children are born, both boys and girls are given names from their mother's clan. During the *i:tálwa*'s green corn ceremony (*póskita*, "to fast, separate"), pubescent boys (but not their sisters) receive a war name from their father's clan. These names are given after a successful foray into the forest. Historically, these forays were for warfare or hunting, primary expressions of male power; boys returned with enemy scalps or deer. Today, smaller animals such as squirrels are more typical trophies. Males who never attain these benchmarks of manhood are ridiculed and called *isti: tóko:* "not a person" or simply "old woman." The transformation of males into men and warriors is marked by bestowal of wooden ballsticks, instruments of aggression used in warlike games, and other implements of warfare, such as shotguns.

Woodcutting and the production of fire is an especially important activity of Creek men in sustaining their households and communal rituals, since both require large fires giving much heat and light. For Creeks, the sun and ritual fire inside the ceremonial dance ground are believed to be the same. Both are distinctively male in their function to define and light the otherwise undifferentiated (female) darkness. Men deliver firewood to their wives to be used for daily cooking and weekly summer stomp dances.

Today, logging firewood recapitulates hunting and warfare. To fell a tree is to kill its intrinsic vitality by converting its female aspect — its capacity for growth — to male-defined form as a firelog. It can then be used by the domestic household or *i:tálwa* for heat and light. Through killing and thus arresting female-like uncontrolled generativity, men change trees into firewood that can be appropriated for domestic use. By bringing wood from the (external) forest into the (internal) domestic realm, men provide the heat that will catalyze the intrinsic female capacity for nourishment — change corn into *sófki:*. Men provide the means — the heat — to integrate male and female. The implications for the Corn-Mother's death at the hands of her sons can thus be understood. Males separate that which is male from the primordial (mother) female through killing, which allows the reuniting of male and female in marriage and the birth of children.

## Marriage and Children

Marriage is tentative until the birth of a child. Pregnancy both proclaims and proves that a marriage has taken place, since the woman's productive, generative potential has been directed into reproduction of Creek (human) form. When menstruation ceases in pregnancy, her endogenous capacity for unformed growth and life is controlled by the definitional power of her husband. The productive capacity of a woman is thereby demonstrated to have been shaped and defined by a man.

Pregnancy is also political. When a man leaves his natal *i:tálwa* to join the *i:tálwa* of his wife he secures an alliance between *i:tálwa*. The *i:tálwa* of the husband's mother and father are thereby linked to the *i:tálwa* of the wife's mother and father by the birth of a child. Because pregnancy indicates male control of female generativity, a Creek baby brings *i:tálwa* into controllable and visible political domains. Through this gendered process, political alliances are constituted, as demonstrated at summer stomp dances when participants dance together to create "one body"—a new "child" symbolic of the manifest alliance.

## Speaking Creek

Creek gender is represented through ideologies of language which categorize speech as *female gossip*, *male oratory* and *baby talk*.

**Women and Gossip.** For Creeks, women's speech can be dangerous; it is typified in gossip "flowing like a summer flood." Women are said to be able to "bring down an *i:tálwa* quicker than a tornado," by causing its members to argue with each other and break up the "one body." Gossip generates conflicts that men must settle through combat. Such conflict is especially evident in dramatic confrontations where men battle and drive off (symbolically kill) Creek *sti:kinni*, feared "witches." A *sti:kinni* is an owl in whose body a malicious Creek hides to fly around a home and "shoot bad medicine into the family." If the attacked home is not defended, family members will sicken and die. A man must drive away a *sti:kinni* to save his family; in such confrontations he demonstrates his capacity as a warrior.

Women also bring problematic situations into public knowledge through gossip. An example follows:

> A young Creek man was arrested for drunk driving. His mother identified the person who caused his misfortune to be a man of the opposing *ankipáya*[8] *i:tálwa* alliance who was jealous of her son's new car. One night, after days of ceaseless gossip between the mother, sisters, aunts, and their women friends, a *sti:kinni* appeared. The son's father shot the *sti:kinni* which was identified as the man jealous of the son's car.

A potent aspect of women's gossip is that it brings about a context where men must battle—kill and arrest "growth." Menstruation and gossip are equivalent signifiers of women's endogenous capacity to "flow." This "flow" challenges men to "kill" and thereby shape (define) situations into appropriate Creek social form.

**Men and Oratory.** Women do not speak in most public and ritual contexts, especially at stomp grounds. While dancing, they are verbally silent. Women freely assent to withhold their speech in these public contexts as a sign they are not dangerous. Such female "flows" as speech or menstruation would signify their uncontrolled (and thus conflict-producing) generativity — totally inappropriate at these peacemaking alliance dances.

In contrast to women's gossip, orations, public speeches, and stomp dance songs are delivered only by men. Men's speech can order, control, and, in its most public context, define social form. Men's speech is typified in oratory that begins and ends all ritual stomp dances. A male *tolóswa* ("tongue"), an official of the *i:tálwa*, starts the ceremony by delivering, in a formulaic litany, an opening oration in which the "rules and regulations" of the particular stomp ground are stated. These "rules" are to be followed by everyone present, an act that acknowledges the host's control of activities. Assent is dramatized as the dancers synchronize their movements and stamp in single file around the fire. At dawn their "body" — the alliance — is ratified in the first rays of the sun, when the closing oration is delivered. This signatory oration states that the stomp dancers were successful in following the host's rules and regulations.

**Baby Talk.** For Creeks, language originates in a baby without form or shape. It flows in babbles. "Language" in this state is female. When a child is born it "knows" everything; it is still connected to the female "watery fundament" in which universal knowledge exists. However, when the child begins to speak, primordial (female) knowledge is forgotten and the founding connection with the mother is severed. When a child speaks, it is defined as a visible social being, under control of male social ordering.

Until the child talks, it is carried almost exclusively by mothers, grandmothers, and sisters. It "has no bones." When it begins to speak coherently, it demonstrates its control by the male defining order and is almost immediately encouraged to walk by itself — it now has "bones." Older siblings are scolded for carrying a "speaking child." The act of speaking Creek forces an initial separation between child and mother because it "gives the child bones." For Creek, bones are equivalent to wood and other hardened implements identified with males. The correlation of the "phallus" and bones is evident in Creek perception: a child's lack of bones expresses this differentiation from the male signifier (the phallus) and its identification with its mother. When speech begins, the male signifier is shown to have defined the previous female-like babbles as being Creek in form.

When the child learns to speak Creek correctly—separating, defining, and acknowledging the order of language—the child enters into the "rules and regulations" of the Creek sociocultural and linguistic order. By speaking Creek, the child's female-like subjectivity is thus changed by a male-defined sociosymbolic order. To speak Creek is to assent to the control and hegemony of male order.

## Summary

The Creek case presents a view of subjectivity, gender, and language in which the male shapes and defines innate female generativity. For Creeks, female generativity and unboundedness, made explicit in menstruation, provide the basic growth principle that is life's force and vitality. Men's ability to define and shape social form is demonstrated through identification with fire, sun's light, logs, bones, and instruments for combat. The politics of gendered subjectivity ramify throughout Creek social action and speech.

Creek subjectivity constitutes men and women through the "phallus"—the male ability to define social form. However, the Creek woman's empowerment (and disempowerment) does not come simply from her ideological lack of the phallus. It is inherent to her intrinsic ability to menstruate and *force* separation of men from women. Thus, she forces men to be made from her own body (politic). Creek females are not inert, as "lack of the phallus" often implies; they provide the basic principle of vitality to which males respond. Creeks maintain that men and women are separate people. What they mean is that men and women are *separated* people. This is because the basic Creek problem of social relations is to separate men from women in order to constitute a reproductive world that can continue to be Creek.

# 3

# Oedipus in the New Guinea Highlands?

## *L. L. Langness*

The male Oedipus complex, according to Freud . . . , is a
*triangular* constellation involving a boy, his father, and his
mother, in which the boy's *sexual desire* for the mother, whose
love he wishes to monopolize, *leads* to hostility toward his father
(and his siblings), whom he views as a rival for the mother's love.
As a result of his wish to possess the exclusive love of the mother,
the boy moreover develops the wish to kill the father and to
replace him in his relationship with the mother. (In the mind
of a little boy, of course, "to kill" means to eliminate, to banish,
to be rid of.) (Spiro 1982:4)

**T**he gist of the argument centering on the Oedipal
complex is that boys spend the first few years of life in
intimate (or "exclusive") association with their mothers
(which includes sleeping with them) and fathers are
typically absent and/or aloof. Therefore the boys are in danger of
being "feminized" and must undergo a "radical resocialization"
at adolescence if they are to become fully "masculinized." In the
case of the Sambia and some other New Guinea groups this involves
male homosexuality, although very similar rites can and do exist
without this particular element. Among the Sambia, for example,
men provide adolescent males with semen believed necessary for
their growth into manhood through homosexual rites performed
during initiation ceremonies. Ritualized homosexual activity begins
when the child is about seven and continues until he is about

Adapted from *Ethos* 18:4, December 1990, by permission of the American
Anthropological Association. Not for sale or further reproduction.

seventeen (Herdt 1981). The purpose of these rites, it is argued, is to accomplish resocialization, turn the boys into warriors, and to "contain" the Oedipal wishes of the boys, while at the same time gratifying the "complementary Oedipal complex of the men" (Spiro 1982:170).

As the kinds of ethnographic details about marriage and child rearing necessary to demonstrate the accuracy of this view are largely absent for the New Guinea Highlands, it is difficult to determine precisely what occurs during the child-rearing process. Thus, these claims are little more than assumptions based on ethnographic glosses that need more careful scrutiny than they have received to date. Let us begin with the notion of intimate or exclusive mother-son ties.

Clans in the New Guinea Highlands were relatively small autonomous groups seldom exceeding 250 persons. In the Bena Bena[9] area, at least, clan members rarely traveled far from their own territory. There was strong solidarity and everyone was well-known to everyone else. The birth of a child was known about and shared by all. All females in the clan old enough to be the child's mother were called by that term and all other females were termed sisters. The terms implied nurturance, and in fact virtually all clanswomen were nurturant toward the infant even though, naturally, the actual mother of the child was dominant in this respect.

Infants were nursed when they cried and could be nursed by females other than their mother. Lactating women sometimes suckled piglets as well. Infants could sometimes also be seen sucking on the dry breasts of grandmothers. Whether being suckled or not, infants and toddlers were commonly passed from person to person and received affection from all. They were generally weaned by the time they were approximately three. This same general pattern of child rearing occurs among the Fore (Sorenson 1976) and was so strong among the nearby Tairora that Watson was led to describe it in terms of "collective nurturance" (1983:265), in which the "nurturing collectivity is a generationally defined group of parents" (1983:271). He also describes this in terms of "the community-as-parent" (1983:273).

While infants were still nursing they accompanied their mothers, usually sleeping in a net bag suspended from the mother's forehead and hung on a nearby tree while the mother was working. As the women typically worked in groups there was usually more than one child to be cared for and there was also typically an older clan sister or a premenstrual bride in attendance for this purpose. When male infants became toddlers and nursed less frequently, they did not always accompany their mothers.

Boys and girls played together as toddlers, but this changed quickly and by four or five they began to play almost exclusively with children of their own sex. Female children continued to accompany their mothers and were schooled in women's work and duties. Although male toddlers were usually supervised by an older female sibling, supervision even at this young age tended to be minimal and the boys ran and played pretty much as they chose. If they climbed too high or otherwise got into danger they would usually be rescued, but not until the situation was extremely dangerous by western European standards. It was not at all unusual to see even very small toddlers playing with sharp bush knives with no intervention on the part of caretakers.

While it was true that infants and toddlers slept with their mothers in the mother's house while adult males slept separately in a communal men's house, how exclusive an arrangement this was is open to question. As there was no such thing as an only child (except, of course, firstborns) there were always siblings who shared the mother's bed (a raised platform that occupied roughly half of the small circular women's house). As children nursed less frequently or were weaned they tended to sleep together in the women's houses with their chums.

A number of Bena Bena customs tended to promote multiple parenting and caretaking. For example, all little girls were "marked" by a clansman other than their father who became responsible for their initiation and subsequently received their brideprice. "Men," the Bena Bena said, "cannot take pay for their own semen." These relationships usually involved affection between the "adopting" family and the child. Similarly, the adoption of boys was relatively common in Bena Bena as well as elsewhere in the Eastern Highlands. But the boys did not usually leave the clan, they simply changed the place where they typically slept and ate and thus in effect maintained multiple parents.

Likewise, it was common for a man, if he took a particular fancy to a child, to create a special relationship with him (or her, occasionally) by giving the child his name. There was a special term for this, *apatnigasi*, and it resulted in bonds of genuine and lasting affection. As it was necessary to have daughters in order to provide wives for sons,[10] it was my impression that these customs allowed people to balance their families in such a way as to ensure these results. One consequence of this was the multiplication of personal ties between families and subclans and the further dilution of exclusive parental bonds. It was also not unusual for even small children to choose to spend the night or even a few days with their father's brother or some other clansman.

Bena Bena children, from the time they were infants, received a great deal of affection from clan mothers and sisters (and others, as we shall see below). While it is true to say they slept and spent time with their mothers, their child-rearing experiences when compared with western European standards were quite different. Even as toddlers and youngsters they had a great deal of independence and played primarily in like-sexed groups. Although the mother-son bond was intimate, intimacy is a relative concept, and among the Bena Bena the relationship would not be well described as exclusive. Indeed, women who had several children, who worked long hard hours daily, who ended their day coming in from their gardens with heavy loads of sweet potatoes and also carrying firewood, and then had to call and feed their pigs as well as cook the evening meal, would seem to have had little time to invest in giving exclusive attention to or infantilizing their sons. Furthermore, as women were well aware that their sons had to grow up to be warriors and, indeed, took pride in the ritual advancement of their sons, they had little incentive to do such things.

It is claimed by Herdt and Stoller and apparently accepted by many that while in the (exclusive?) hands of women the little boys are "feminized." This is a poor choice of terms as the connotation in English is hard to overcome even when reminded that it is meant to apply to the feminine nature of New Guinea women. This would seem to imply, among other things, that the boys were taught feminine tasks. This was certainly not true in the Bena Bena case. They did not help women with their gardening, they were not taught women's gardening magic, they did not learn to make net bags or string, they rarely if ever baby-sat, they were taught nothing about childbirth or child care, nor, in fact, did they have or perform duties of any kind. As soon as they were physically able they basically just ran wild, getting into mischief, willfully doing whatever they pleased, and were rarely if ever punished. Mothers would sometimes yell and threaten their children, but such threats fell upon deaf ears and usually failed to materialize. This was not unique to the Bena Bena. It was true of the Ndumba and probably many other Highlanders as well: "The life of a Ndumba boy (*nraammwa*) is one of play and indulgence, with virtually no explicit discipline and no responsibilities (in contrast to a Ndumba girl, whose child-care and gardening tasks begin early in life)" (Hays 1987:188; also see Sorenson 1976). Men also virtually never punished their children, as it was believed that until they were at least seven or so they were incapable of either understanding or reasoning.

As women were aggressive in their dealings with other women, and also toward their husbands when angry, as they subscribed to the same values of "strength" and "hardness" as did men, and as they encouraged this in their children, it is difficult to see how they could be said to have been feminizing their sons. Some idea of the basic "flavor" of Bena Bena child rearing can be seen in the following excerpt from my fieldnotes:

> B and his wife, I, were sitting by the fire in front of I's house this evening. B gave a stick to F, his three-year-old son, with instructions to "stick it up Y's vagina," Y being his six-year-old daughter. F proceeded to try to do just that, chasing Y around the yard poking at her with the stick. Y started to cry. Both B and his wife laughed and apparently thought this to be very funny.

Women of the clan argued openly at times, and fights between co-wives[11] were by no means uncommon. These sometimes involved serious physical violence and even an occasional death as the women attacked each other with rough planks that were used to fasten their doorways, tore at each other's clothing and hair, and wrestled each other to the ground. As role models they were hardly what western Europeans would regard as feminine. Men, in fact, valued these qualities in women, and would often comment admiringly that "so and so is a strong woman." When women fought, men seldom intervened unless it continued for too long. A better idea of how far a "strong" woman could go can be seen in this somewhat unusual case from Auyana:

> At the opposite extreme was Pu'a, a quiet, tongue-tied, shy young man in his middle twenties in 1962. Pu'a had somehow been matched with a flirtatious, loud-mouthed, assertive woman. As their house was close to mine, I heard many arguments between them and the tongue lashings she gave him. The ultimate degradation arose when he decided to donate a pig[12] which she did not want killed. Knowing she would attack him in order to prevent him from killing it, he told some men in his pooling unit that he wanted to donate the pig and for them to kill it. They cheerfully did so the morning of the pooling.

> Pu'a's wife did not interfere and did nothing except avoid him until he came home that evening after the distribution had been completed. As he entered the house, she screamed at him for having killed the pig and hurled vicious insults. He only shouted back at her occasionally. By this time, we all were intently listening in order not to miss any part of the show. Suddenly there was a howl and Pu'a staggered out of the door with his wife flailing at him with a firebrand. Just as he got outside, she smashed him on top of the head, knocking him to his knees. She took one brief look at him, whirled around, and stalked back into the house. He knelt a few seconds, appearing dazed and then got up and staggered back into the house. Nothing further was heard (Robbins 1982:87).

When a woman refused to accept an arranged marriage and ran away to a different place, most probably to a former lover, her father, guardian, and brothers would find her and bring her back, sometimes rather brutally. But if she was persistent and kept running away, there was no recourse for them but to give in to her wishes and return the brideprice. They would say of her, with begrudging admiration, "She is strong. We can't make her stay."

While it was the case that uninitiated Bena Bena boys were regarded as polluting because of their contacts with women, this was apparently a much milder version of that belief than that found among either Sambia (Herdt 1981) or Hua (Meigs 1984). Similarly, while it was also the case that, at least in infancy, they might be said to have inhabited primarily a "woman's world," to say that they were regarded as feminine because of this would be to truly stretch the point.

Aside from the case of hermaphrodites (which I never encountered or even heard of in the Bena Bena) there was no doubt about an infant's sex. Boys possessed a penis and little girls did not. As in Auyana: "The criterion of sex was binary, agreed upon at birth, and was nonnegotiable. Strong women might act like men and weak men might act like women but for a person to become the opposite sex was only a fantasy" (Robbins 1982:163). That boys were male was known to everyone, as they went naked until approximately age seven and little girls, who wore a small string apron virtually from birth, did not. This identification was made even more apparent by the fact that people commented about the little boys' penes, frequently pulled on or fondled them, and thus constantly called special attention to them. Men, it was true, quite commonly threatened to cut them off, but as this was so common and so obviously said in jest it seems not to have bothered the boys very much. On one occasion I witnessed, for example, an adult clansman told a boy of about four that he would cut off his penis. The boy looked at him for a couple of seconds and then calmly replied, "you have a big nose." On one occasion I saw a woman playfully threaten her son (of about six) that she would bite his penis off. There was a great deal of fondling of the boys' penes by males. Women fondled infants but not older boys. Individuals of both sexes would pick up infants and mouth their genitals and kiss them all over.

There was an enormous amount of physical contact between clanpersons of all kinds (except husbands and wives). While this did have a sensual quality to it, it is important to remember that it occurred in a culture where the traditional greeting meant, "I eat your genitals," and one in which every part of a person was believed to be an important element in their being—hair, urine, feces, fingernails, pus, phlegm, and certainly their skin. In addition to the verbal greeting, men (and women, too) would embrace each other, touch each other's genitals, and rub their hands all over the other person's body often for several minutes at a time. There was an enormous amount of physical contact between almost everyone but husbands and wives. To interpret all this fondling as simply "sexual" must be carefully considered.

Male toddlers were given miniature bamboo bows and arrows by their fathers and encouraged to practice. Girls were not supposed to touch bows and arrows. Boys were present when pigs were being butchered and, indeed, were often underfoot and roughly shoved aside. Girls were much less present at such male tasks and then mainly on the sidelines. Boys, as in the case quoted above, were actively encouraged to dominate girls. Even when young, long before they were to be initiated, they were encouraged by men and their peers not to spend time with their mothers. They were, in fact, treated differently in virtually every way. Thus, granted that being male was not identical with being masculine (or perhaps more appropriately, "manly") as Herdt and Stoller argue, there could be no doubt in anyone's mind that Bena Bena boys were male and not female and there must have been at least some significance in a boy's early recognition of this simple and basic fact.

Thus, masculine (male) gender identification began very early and was continuous; it did not just take place during male initiation rites, as Herdt and Stoller seem to imply for the Sambia. Why, in this situation, given her low status and relative powerlessness, would a male child identify or overidentify with his mother? Further, what can it mean to claim that male children inhabited a "female world" (Read 1982; Herdt 1981) when, although in primary association with females during infancy, those creatures were not in important respects "feminine," did not instruct them in female ways, and, indeed, encouraged them to acquire the presumably "male values" of strength and aggressiveness?

And what of absent or aloof fathers? It is not my experience that Bena Bena fathers were absent either physically or psychologically, although it is certainly true that they slept in the men's houses and, in important respects, avoided contact with females. Typically a man visited his wife and children at his wife's house for a late afternoon meal. If he had more than one wife, as approximately 25 percent of the Bena Bena males where I worked did, he took turns visiting them. One of the first signs of marital strife or pending divorce was a man's failure to do this. He accepted sweet potatoes cooked by his wife for himself and his children and usually ate his meal in their company. He carried away cooked sweet potatoes for his breakfast and/or lunch the next day. The children did likewise.

Far from being aloof, Bena Bena fathers were affectionate and even demonstrative with their children of both sexes, holding them, cuddling them, giving them little gifts of pork, and so on. A man could not see his infant child for the first month (again, a very moderate version of a widespread Highlands avoidance pattern) and, while it was true that there was a taboo against a man carrying his firstborn child, men had more than one child and they also had adopted children and others to carry if they wished. Similarly, as among Hua, these taboos appeared to be more serious at the verbal level than the behavioral:

> A man may not carry his firstborn baby (male or female) on his shoulders lest he be prematurely "put or pressed down." Nevertheless the Hua are warm, loving and gentle with their children: resentment of the firstborn is expressed verbally and symbolically, never to my knowledge physically (Meigs 1984:104).

Men would sometimes take their sons with them while they were making or repairing garden fences, building houses, digging garden ditches, or engaging in other domestic activities. They were proud of their children and did not hide their feelings about them, especially when they were "strong" and handsome (when they had clear, lighter skins, aquiline noses, and were tall and physically adept). Because the gardens of the Bena Bena immediately surrounded the villages rather than being more distant, the adult males were usually working nearby, where they could be seen by everyone, including children. Similarly, because hunting was virtually absent among the grassland-dwelling Bena Bena, men were rarely away from their own villages and even then only for days rather than weeks as in the case of the Baruya or Sambia (Godelier 1986:14; Herdt 1981:138).

Public events at which fathers presided were frequent and witnessed by everyone, including children. Cooking with earth ovens, for example, a common event in Bena Bena life, was always done by men and witnessed by everyone. Men were an everyday presence in village life, just as were women. Thus, while they may have been absent from the mother's house during the night, they were not often absent from the village or from the "life space" of their children. Some quotes from my fieldnotes illustrate this:

> March 22, 1961: Even very small children spend quite a lot of time with their fathers. You can often see the men sitting around holding a child. Sometimes when a child is tired he will be held until he falls asleep and then put down somewhere. The children, of course, run to their fathers for protection. When I come around, for example, if they are afraid they will run to their fathers who invariably hold them until they are ready to run off and play again.

> April 21, 1961: Fimaso (about 2) cried today when Bonobo (his father) tried to leave him with his mother. Finally the parents gave in (as usual) and Fimaso ran down the path after Bonobo. . . .

> Children are spoiled very badly by the men — less so, but also, by the women. But in any case they are rarely disciplined, seldom punished, and usually get their way. They do little work to speak of but do sometimes carry firewood, food, or *pit pit* (cane). Also an older boy will sometimes sleep in the gardens to chase pigs away.

> April 26, 1961: The men treat all the boys more or less like their own sons. Today, for example, Abio was walking with his son Finamuna (about 4). Amuloya, Sepik's boy (about 5) came up and began talking to Abio and held his hand. Later, in Sapuro village, Abio called out to Finamuna to go with him to his coffee. Finamuna was playing and did not heed so he and Amuloya walked off hand in hand. . . .

Today Tubutaboe gave some pig fat to Mate (about 3), a girl whom he has "marked." Cilarki tried to give her a piece also but she just made a face at him and refused it. Tubutaboe then took it from Cilarki and held it out to her and she accepted it. A man who has marked a girl like this seems to go out of his way to be nice to her. . . .

Even small children of 3 or 4 wander about by themselves, gathering passion fruit, playing and so on. No one seems to worry about them. Often I will see Yosimi or Gooyi (both about 3 or 4) or other children about that size playing either in the village or in a garden with no older person in sight. This is by no means uncommon.

May 13, 1961: The boys seem to resent it if a boy walks around with his mother rather than his age mates. Today Bianiso (about 7) remarked about one boy that he didn't pal around with them but went all the time with his mother. All of the boys expressed their disapproval of his behavior.

July 20, 1961: The people, men especially, are much more tolerant of children than we (Europeans) are. A man will put up with any kind of climbing, pulling, pestering, etc., on the part of his children. When not moving about working or otherwise busy a man is almost constantly holding, petting, or talking to a child. Most frequently this is a boy but often girls as well.

August 21, 1961: Bonanihi's wife was holding Wapio, Ietopesso's infant son. She remarked to a woman near her about the baby's genitals and then she took her hand and pretended to carry them to her mouth and eat them. She would touch them with her fingers and then put her fingers to her mouth as if kissing them. Later, Sepik's first wife was holding Wapio, kissing him on the stomach and holding him up and tickling his feet with her mouth, etc. Naguropave (a teenager) later came and took him from Ietopesso, also fondling him for a time.

November 15, 1961: Men as well as women are extremely playful and affectionate with babies. This morning Sepik (an adult male) was holding Wapio (his adopted brother's infant son), flicking out his tongue at him and even in his mouth, talking "baby talk" to him and so on. Wapio loved it. Kikipe (an older adult male of the subclan) held him also and made much of him. When Wapio looked as if he might cry Kikipe kidded him and sort of "loved" him out of it. . . . Wareka is taking care of his baby today, holding it and fondling it. . . . The men make it a point to give food to the boys (and girls) when they are around. For example, while sitting there today waiting for the stones to heat, Afooya came with Finamuna (about 4) and his other little grandson (about the same age). Bonobo (an adult male) immediately broke off part of his tapioc and gave it to Finamuna. Klehopave (also an adult male) gave a piece of sweet potato to the other child and the two children were then encouraged by all the men present to eat it.

March 31, 1962: Kaesso (an adult male) today, as Kano (about 3) passed by him, reached out and played with his penis. He then took the boy in his arms and fondled him. Later I saw Gugupa (an adult male) kissing a small boy.

There is a great deal of affection between adults and children — and this has little to do with the family or subclan. Any adult is apt to love and fondle any child almost at random. Today, for example, I saw Kaesso (an adult male) fondling Kano (not of the same subclan), Gugupa (an adult male) kissing him, Bonanihi (an older adult male) fondling Mate (a girl of 3), Mumugefa (an older adult male) fondling her and Bubisso (a boy of about 5). Adults are very fond of children and very permissive and loving. Even so, today when all the men were gathered and three small boys were with them, when a small girl (about 8) came too close and peered over the fence Katopi (an adult male) got up with a switch and chased her away.

Prior to pacification, of course, fathers could not have had as much time as they did when my observations were made. But I do not believe the basic pattern was different. They were not *always* at war. When groups were strong and dominant, as was the group of Bena Bena I worked with, there were substantial periods of time when life was relatively easy, gardens flourished, the pig herds could be increased to make possible the periodic exchanges (and initiations), and *people could enjoy their children*. I certainly do not believe that prior to pacification Bena Bena men were indifferent to their children, absent and aloof, and only learned to be affectionate and caring during the postcontact period. The Bena Bena may be different than other Highlanders in this respect, but to simply dismiss fathers and husbands as aloof or physically and psychologically absent is just not satisfactory. Fathers and husbands are far more absent from the ethnographic literature (indeed, they are amazingly absent from it) than they probably were from their families. The Bena Bena case is somewhat like that of the Siane described by Salisbury:

> After a relatively short period when young children are looked after exclusively by their mother, and when they visit their

father for fondling and affection, the training of children is
undertaken by males and females generally, rather than by the
elementary families. As soon as boys are old enough to talk and
to understand, they are toilet trained by their fathers and by
older boys: after their ceremonial weaning between the ages of
3 and 6, their principal companions are other boys (1962:18).

The Bena Bena share most of the beliefs about women and men
that are reported from all over New Guinea. They engaged in most
of the same rituals. Bena Bena male initiations involved ear and
nose piercing, bloodletting from tongue, nose, and urethra, cane
swallowing, and vomiting. They also involved the use of semen,
although there was no homosexuality. Women were believed to be
polluting, primarily because of menstruation. They were said to be,
and appeared to agree that they were, weak and inferior to men in
every way. Men (and even boys) were actively discouraged from
spending time with them. There were no overt displays of affection
between husbands and wives (although there was a great deal of
this between clan brothers and sisters). Sexual intercourse was
engaged in privately and to produce offspring and, supposedly, not
otherwise. After intercourse, aboriginally, men were expected to
cleanse themselves by swallowing canes and nose-bleeding
themselves before returning to the men's house. I have been told
that most men did so. If a man did not perform these actions he
was criticized by other men, as he was polluting to them.

There were many taboos having to do with male/female
relationships. Women could not touch men's hair, could not be
above them in any way, could not cast their shadows on them, had
to retire to their menstrual huts during their menses, could not
garden or cook food for anyone at such times, and so on. Men
worked together in groups, as did women, although sometimes a
man and a woman would work together temporarily in an
established garden. There were clearly male and female tasks.
Women grew sweet potatoes and most introduced vegetables; men
grew yams, bananas, and taro. Men fenced garden plots and dug
drainage ditches after women had broken the ground with shovels.
Men staked the labor-intensive wing bean gardens; women
possessed the magic to make the beans grow. Women manufactured string, net bags, and arm bands; men made bows and
arrows and male decorations for the various events they were in
charge of organizing. Girls almost exclusively fetched water in the
long bamboo tubes they used for that purpose, although if no girl
was present men and boys would do so. It was not that women were

domestic and men were not, but rather that men were engaged in both domestic and public endeavors and women much less so in the latter.

Most Bena Bena beliefs about men and women, as well as the day-to-day behavior that reflects them, were not, indeed, could not have been entirely secret. Children growing up heard women being disparaged daily, they witnessed the care with which men approached females, they saw that men were in charge of public events and almost everything else, that they ordered women about and in general dominated them. Although their parents did not actually reside together, husbands and wives had their own space in the women's houses where they kept their sparse belongings. Children were aware of this from an early age. Thus, although nuclear families could be recognized, they existed in a special cultural context. When fathers interacted with their children they were almost totally nurturant. When they were absent they were known to be residing in the mysterious and prestigious men's house with other men and engaging in men's activities, which were thought by everyone to be superior in every way. Thus, given the men's house, strong proscriptions relating to relations between husbands and wives, the absence of overt expressions of affection between husbands and wives, the beliefs about female pollution and the status of women in general, and given the privacy (and presumed infrequency) of the parental sex act, it is difficult for me to believe that fathers could be perceived to be rivals for mothers' attention, particularly sexual attention. It is difficult to see why a child would envy his mother's status, and in this context it is equally difficult to understand why a child's love of his mother would result in his hating his father. The entire ethos of the culture worked against such an outcome.

There is a question here, of course, as to precisely what the mother's role might have been in bringing about Oedipal conflict. It has been suggested by Whiting and others (Whiting, Kluckhohn, and Anthony 1958) that because of the long postpartum sex taboo women might well have been seeking sexual gratification from their sons. The question of New Guinea Highlanders' heterosexual relationships is far too complex and paradoxical to deal with here. It could be argued on the one hand that women, like men, must have greatly feared sex, but on the other that they, like Tairora men, "regard[ed] sexual intercourse as one of the most urgent and unremitting pleasures of life" (Watson 1983:101). It was not my impression that Bena Bena women were particularly seductive toward their sons (or, indeed, that they would have reason to be), but this will have to be dealt with elsewhere.

It could also be argued, of course, as Spiro suggests, that fathers are dealing with their own Oedipal problems during the violent initiations. However, it is clear from the literature as well as from my own fieldwork that the initiates' fathers were not responsible for inflicting any of the brutality or pain (Godelier 1986; Robbins 1982:95). And among the Sambia, as well as the Bena Bena, they apparently took pains to control what happened to their sons: "a man would be foolish to risk cruel ritual treatment toward his son in initiation at an alien dance ground where he lacked the presence of reliable supporters" (Herdt 1981:32). Similarly, among the Ndumba it is the fathers and their clansmen who attempt to hinder the initiation procession (Hays 1987:195).

Without father-son rivalry, no Oedipal complex could develop, whatever the pre-Oedipal situation might have been. Thus, while Oedipal conflict *can be* postulated as an intervening variable in the ongoing drama of the Bena Bena, to use that concept in spite of what appears to be evidence to the contrary violates the law of parsimony. While it may have been possible for some particular Bena Bena individual or family to experience Oedipal conflict, this cannot have been typical of the culture. Thus, the existence and persistence of male initiation rites among the Bena Bena must, and I believe can be, explained without recourse to Oedipal considerations.

# 4

# Woman as Other

## Simone De Beauvoir

**W**hat is a woman?

To state the question is, to me, to suggest, at once, a preliminary answer. The fact that I ask it is in itself significant. A man would never get the notion of writing a book on the peculiar situation of the human male. But if I wish to define myself, I must first of all say: "I am a woman"; on this truth must be based all further discussion. A man never begins by presenting himself as an individual of a certain sex; it goes without saying that he is a man. The terms *masculine* and *feminine* are used symmetrically only as a matter of form, as on legal papers. In actuality the relation of the two sexes is not quite like that of two electrical poles, for man represents both the positive and the neutral, as is indicated by the common use of *man* to designate human beings in general; whereas woman represents only the negative, defined by limiting criteria, without reciprocity. In the midst of an abstract discussion it is vexing to hear a man say: "You think thus and so because you are a woman"; but I know that my only defense is to reply: "I think thus and so because it is true," thereby removing my subjective self from the argument. It would be out of the question to reply: "And you think the contrary because you are a man," for it is understood that the fact of being a man is no peculiarity. A man is in the right in being a man; it is the woman who is in the wrong. It amounts to this: just as for the ancients there was an absolute vertical with reference to which the oblique was defined, so there is an absolute human type, the masculine. Woman has ovaries, a uterus; these peculiarities

From Simone De Beauvoir, *The Second Sex*, trans. and ed. H. M. Parshley. New York: Alfred A. Knopf, 1952.

imprison her in her subjectivity, circumscribe her within the limits of her own nature. It is often said that she thinks with her glands. Man superbly ignores the fact that his anatomy also includes glands, such as the testicles, and that they secrete hormones. He thinks of his body as a direct and normal connection with the world, which he believes he apprehends objectively, whereas he regards the body of woman as a hindrance, a prison, weighed down by everything peculiar to it. "The female is a female by virtue of a certain lack of qualities," said Aristotle; "we should regard the female nature as afflicted with a natural defectiveness." And St. Thomas for his part pronounced woman to be an "imperfect man," an "incidental" being. This is symbolized in Genesis where Eve is depicted as made from what Bossuet called "a supernumerary bone" of Adam.

Thus humanity is male and man defines woman not in herself but as relative to him; she is not regarded as an autonomous being. Michelet writes: "Woman, the relative being. . . ." And Benda is most positive in his *Rapport d'Uriel*: "The body of man makes sense in itself quite apart from that of woman, whereas the latter seems wanting in significance by itself. . . . Man can think of himself without woman. She cannot think of herself without man." And she is simply what man decrees; thus she is called "the sex," by which is meant that she appears essentially to the male as a sexual being. For him she is sex—absolute sex, no less. She is defined and differentiated with reference to man and not he with reference to her; she is the incidental, the inessential as opposed to the essential. He is the Subject, she is the Absolute—she is the Other.

The category of the *Other* is as primordial as consciousness itself. In the most primitive societies, in the most ancient mythologies, one finds the expression of a duality—that of the Self and the Other. This duality was not originally attached to the division of the sexes; it was not dependent upon any empirical facts. It is revealed in such works as that of Granet on Chinese thought and those of Dumezil on the East Indies and Rome. The feminine element was at first no more involved in such pairs as Varuna-Mitra, Uranus-Zeus, Sun-Moon, and Day-Night than it was in the contrasts between Good and Evil, lucky and unlucky auspices, right and left, God and Lucifer. Otherness is a fundamental category of human thought.

Thus it is that no group ever sets itself up as the One without at once setting up the Other over against itself. If three travelers chance to occupy the same compartment, that is enough to make vaguely hostile "others" out of all the rest of the passengers on the

train. In small-town eyes all persons not belonging to the village
are "strangers" and suspect; to the native of a country all who
inhabit other countries are "foreigners"; Jews are "different" for
the anti-Semite, Negroes are "inferior" for American racists,
aborigines are "natives" for colonists, proletarians are the "lower
class" for the privileged.

Levi-Strauss, at the end of a profound work on the various forms
of primitive societies, reaches the following conclusion: "Passage
from the state of Nature to the state of Culture is marked by man's
ability to view biological relations as a series of contrasts; duality,
alternation, opposition, and symmetry, whether under definite or
vague forms, constitute not so much phenomena to be explained
as fundamental and immediately given data of social reality."[13]
These phenomena would be incomprehensible if in fact human
society were simply a *Mitsein* or fellowship based on solidarity and
friendliness. Things become clear, on the contrary, if, following
Hegel, we find in consciousness itself a fundamental hostility toward
every other consciousness; the subject can be posed only in being
opposed—he sets himself up as the essential, as opposed to the
other, the inessential, the object.

But the other consciousness, the other ego, sets up a reciprocal
claim. The native traveling abroad is shocked to find himself in turn
regarded as a "stranger" by the natives of neighboring countries.
As a matter of fact, wars, festivals, trading, treaties, and contests
among tribes, nations, and classes tend to deprive the concept *Other*
of its absolute sense and to make manifest its relativity; willy-nilly,
individuals and groups are forced to realize the reciprocity of their
relations. How is it, then, that this reciprocity has not been
recognized between the sexes, that one of the contrasting terms is
set up as the sole essential, denying any relativity in regard to its
correlative and defining the latter as pure otherness? Why is it that
women do not dispute male sovereignty? No subject will readily
volunteer to become the object, the inessential; it is not the Other
who, in defining himself as the Other, establishes the One. The
Other is posed as such by the One in defining himself as the One.
But if the Other is not to regain the status of being the One, he must
be submissive enough to accept this alien point of view. Whence
comes this submission in the case of woman?

There are, to be sure, other cases in which a certain category has
been able to dominate another completely for a time. Very often
this privilege depends upon inequality of numbers—the majority
imposes its rule upon the minority or persecutes it. But women are

not a minority, like the American Negroes or the Jews; there are as many women as men on earth. Again, the two groups concerned have often been originally independent; they may have been formerly unaware of each other's existence, or perhaps they recognized each other's autonomy. But a historical event has resulted in the subjugation of the weaker by the stronger. The scattering of the Jews, the introduction of slavery into America, the conquests of imperialism are examples in point. In these cases the oppressed retained at least the memory of former days; they possessed in common a past, a tradition, sometimes a religion or a culture.

The parallel drawn by Bebel between women and the proletariat is valid in that neither ever formed a minority or a separate collective unit of mankind. And instead of a single historical event it is in both cases a historical development that explains their status as a class and accounts for the membership of *particular individuals* in that class. But proletarians have not always existed, whereas there have always been women. They are women in virtue of their anatomy and physiology. Throughout history they have always been subordinated to men, and hence their dependency is not the result of a historical event or a social change — it was not something that *occurred*. The reason why otherness in this case seems to be an absolute is in part that it lacks the contingent or incidental nature of historical facts. A condition brought about at a certain time can be abolished at some other time, as the Negroes of Haiti and other have proved; but it might seem that a natural condition is beyond the possibility of change. In truth, however, the nature of things is no more immutably given, once for all, than is historical reality. If woman seems to be the inessential which never becomes the essential, it is because she herself fails to bring about this change. Proletarians say "We"; Negroes also. Regarding themselves as subjects, they transform the bourgeois, the whites, into "others." But women do not say "We," except at some congress of feminists for formal demonstration; men say "women," and women use the same word in referring to themselves. They do not authentically assume a subjective attitude. The proletarians have accomplished the revolution in Russia, the Negroes in Haiti, the Indo-Chinese are battling for it in Indo-China; but the women's effort has never been anything more than a symbolic agitation. They have gained only what men have been willing to grant; they have taken nothing, they have only received.

The reason for this is that women lack concrete means for

organizing themselves into a unit which can stand face to face with the correlative unit. They have no past, no history, no religion of their own; and they have no such solidarity of work and interest as that of the proletariat. They are not even promiscuously herded together in the way that creates community feeling among the American Negroes, the ghetto Jews, the workers of Saint-Denis, or the factory hands of Renault. They live dispersed among the males, attached through residence, housework, economic condition, and social standing to certain men — fathers or husbands — more firmly than they are to other women. If they belong to the bourgeoisie, they feel solidarity with men of that class, not with proletarian women; if they are white, their allegiance is to white men, not to Negro women. The proletariat can propose to massacre the ruling class, and a sufficiently fanatical Jew or Negro might dream of getting sole possession of the atomic bomb and making humanity wholly Jewish or black; but women cannot even dream of exterminating the males. The bond that unites her to her oppressors is not comparable to any other. The division of the sexes is a biological fact, not an event in human history. Male and female stand opposed within a primordial *Mitsein*, and woman has not broken it. The couple is a fundamental unity with its two halves riveted together, and the cleavage of society along the lines of sex is impossible. Here is to be found the basic trait of woman: she is the Other in a totality of which the two components are necessary to one another.

One could suppose that this reciprocity might have facilitated the liberation of woman. When Hercules sat at the feet of Omphale and helped with her spinning, his desire for her held him captive; but why did she fail to gain a lasting power? To revenge herself on Jason, Medea killed their children; and this grim legend would seem to suggest that she might have obtained a formidable influence over him through his love for his offspring. In *Lysistrata* Aristophanes gaily depicts a band of women who joined forces to gain social ends through the sexual needs of their men; but this is only a play. In the legend of the Sabine women, the latter soon abandoned their plan of remaining sterile to punish their ravishers. In truth woman has not been socially emancipated through man's need — sexual desire and the desire for offspring — which makes the male dependent for satisfaction upon the female.

Master and slave, also, are united by a reciprocal need, in this case economic, which does not liberate the slave. In the relation of master to slave the master does not make a point of the need that he has for the other; he has in his grasp the power of satisfying this need through his own action; whereas the slave, in his dependent condition, his hope and fear, is quite conscious of the need he has for his master. Even if the need is at bottom equally urgent for both, it always works in favor of the oppressor and against the oppressed. That is why the liberation of the working class, for example, has been slow.

Now, woman has always been man's dependent, if not his slave; the two sexes have never shared the world in equality. And even today woman is heavily handicapped, though her situation is beginning to change. Almost nowhere is her legal status the same as a man's, and frequently it is much to her disadvantage. Even when her rights are legally recognized in the abstract, long-standing custom prevents their full expression in the mores. In the economic sphere men and women can almost be said to make up two castes; other things being equal, the former hold the better jobs, get higher wages, and have more opportunity for success than their new competitors. In industry and politics men have a great many more positions and they monopolize the most important posts. In addition to all this, they enjoy a traditional prestige that the education of children tends in every way to support, for the present enshrines the past—and in the past all history has been made by men. At the present time, when women are beginning to take part in the affairs of the world, it is still a world that belongs to men—they have no doubt of it at all and women have scarcely any. To decline to be the Other, to refuse to be a party to the deal—this would be for women to renounce all the advantages conferred upon them by their alliance with the superior caste. Man-the-sovereign will provide woman-the-liege with material protection and will undertake the moral justification of her existence; thus she can evade at once both economic risk and the metaphysical risk of a liberty in which ends and aims must be contrived without assistance. Indeed, along with the ethical urge of each individual to affirm his subjective existence, there is also the temptation to forgo liberty and become a thing. This is an inauspicious road, for he who takes it—passive, lost, ruined—becomes henceforth the creature of another's will, frustrated in his transcendence and deprived of every value. But it is an easy road; on it one avoids the strain involved in undertaking an authentic existence. When man makes of woman the *Other*, he may, then, expect her to manifest deep-seated tendencies toward complicity. Thus, woman may fail to lay claim to the status of subject because she lacks definite resources, because she feels the necessary bond that ties her to man regardless of reciprocity, and because she is often very well pleased with her role as the *Other*.

# PART II

## Why Not Ask the Women?

# Samoa
## The Adolescent Girl
*Margaret Mead*

# A Woman Alone in the Field
*Hortense Powdermaker*

# Access to Women's Knowledge
## The Azande Experience
*Stephen David Siemens*

# Adventures in the Field and in the Locker Room
*Mari Womack* and *Joan C. Barker*

Margaret Mead (center) poses with two women of Samoa, where she conducted her early fieldwork. *Photo courtesy of the Institute for Intercultural Studies, Inc., New York/Library of Congress.*

▶

# Suggested Readings

**Martha C. Ward. 1989. *Nest in the Wind: Adventures in Anthropology on a Tropical Island*. Prospect Heights, IL: Waveland Press.**
Martha C. Ward's account of her fieldwork on a Pacific island is so entertaining, it is easy to overlook the fact that she has provided insight into under-reported aspects of doing anthropological research—including the perils of being the female half of a husband-wife team and the methodological implications of becoming pregnant. As *Nest in the Wind* illustrates, the perspective of the "other 50 percent" is essential for understanding both halves of the gender equation.

**Elenore Smith Bowen. 1954/reissued 1993. *Return to Laughter: An Anthropological Novel*. Prospect Heights, IL: Waveland Press.**
Writing under a pseudonym, the eminent anthropologist Laura Bohannan describes her fieldwork experiences in Africa, including her negotiations with powerful male village leaders and her friendship with a woman who dies in childbirth. Bohannan uses the novel form to recount her responses to the sometimes harsh conditions of the field. Margaret Mead calls *Return to Laughter* "the first introspective account ever published of what it's like to be a fieldworker among a primitive people." The Waveland edition includes a new retrospective introduction by the author which puts the story into context and includes personal reactions, reflections and interpretations, not only of that time, but of the years since its original publication.

**Ute Gacs, Aisha Khan, Jerrie McIntyre and Ruth Weinberg, eds. 1989. *Women Anthropologists: Selected Biographies*. Urbana: University of Illinois Press.**
As this volume suggests, a list of noted women anthropologists reads like a "Who's Who" in the history of the field. Some, like Margaret Mead, Ruth Benedict, Ruth Bunzel and Elsie Clews Parsons, helped to shape American anthropology. Others, like Hilda Kuper and Hortense Powdermaker, were trained in the British tradition. Although it omits important physical anthropologists like Jane Goodall and Dian Fossey, this book provides an important indicator of the contribution of women anthropologists.

**Margaret Mead. 1972. *Blackberry Winter: My Earlier Years*. New York: William Morrow.**
In this work, Mead turns an analytical eye onto her own life and career as an anthropologist. She describes her relationship with significant women in her life, including her mother, grandmother, daughter, and granddaughter, as well as her friendship with the famous anthropologist Ruth Benedict. Mead also describes what it was like to be the student of Franz Boas, considered the father of American anthropology.

**Marjorie Shostak. 1983. *Nisa: The Life and Words of a !Kung Woman*. New York: Vintage.**
This ethnography is innovative both because it provides a woman's view of !Kung society and because Shostak allows Nisa to tell her story in her own words. Nisa describes her marriage and her introduction to motherhood and shamanic healing, and she discusses frankly and openly the practice of infanticide, which requires a woman to kill her own infant when there are no resources to care for it.

# Introduction

*Mari Womack*

Sigmund Freud, who spent much of his career analyzing the female psyche, eventually confessed that he was at an impasse. "The great question," he mused, "which I have not been able to answer, despite my thirty years of research into the feminine soul, is 'What does a woman want?'"[1]

The irony is that, in spite of thirty years of access to the carefully guarded secrets of Victorian women, he never bothered to ask the women what *they* wanted. Instead, bolstered by the authority of his physician's role and insulated from their feminine concerns, he told them what he thought they wanted—or ought to want. It is staggering to think that all those hours of heartfelt confessions, brought forth in tears and pain, have never really been heard—not even by Freud.

It is even more staggering to realize that, more than a hundred years after the emergence of the discipline, anthropology is just beginning to discover what women want, and do, and think about. Anthropologists, like Freud, didn't think to ask. Furthermore, with rare exceptions, they didn't think it was important to ask. Anthropologists diligently reported on political systems, kinship systems, economic systems and religious systems—based on data collected almost entirely from men and describing almost exclusively the activities of men. In her article "Woman the Gatherer: Male Bias in Anthropology," Sally Slocum writes:

> Anthropology, as an academic discipline, has been developed primarily by white Western males, during a specific period of history. . . . Given the cultural and ethnic background of the majority of anthropologists, it is not surprising that the discipline has been biased (1975: 37).

Slocum asserts that such concepts as "man the hunter" promote the assumption that society is itself male and that only the activities of males are important. She notes that "hunting . . . is pictured as a male activity to the exclusion of females. This activity, on which we are told depends the psychology, biology, and customs of our species, is strictly male. A theory that leaves out half the human species is unbalanced" (1975:39).

There is some evidence that even such generally accepted anthropological "truths" as the idea that men hunt and women gather are flawed due to male bias. Anthropologists have long noted that women in many societies "gather" fish and small game animals along with plant foods. However, anthropologists have reserved the concept "hunting" for such male-dominated activities as killing a large animal with a bow and arrow or spear. Hunting is restricted to men, according to this view, because pregnancy and caring for infants prevents women from chasing after game animals.

This view of hunting may be flawed, however. In her article "Daughters of the Forest," reprinted in Part Four of this volume, Agnes Estioko-Griffin observes that Agta women of the Philippines hunt wild pigs and deer using bow and arrow and knives. Further, these women express great enthusiasm for the chase and the kill, even when they engage in these energetic activities while caring for small children.

Women have been overlooked in anthropology, both as subjects of study and as researchers. Catherine Lutz argues that the contributions of women anthropologists are consistently devalued by their colleagues. Based on her survey of anthropological publications from 1977 to 1986, Lutz observes that women wrote thirty percent of articles appearing in four prominent journals— *American Anthropologist, American Ethnologist, Ethos* and *Human Organization*—and a similar proportion of the books. However, women authors were cited significantly less often than male authors, indicating a gender disparity in citation, an important measure of the impact of a publication on the field. Female authors were cited more often by other women than by males. One reason for this, Lutz notes, is that studies based on women tend to be described as relevant primarily to the field of gender, whereas studies based on men are considered to be more general studies of society as a whole:

> . . . the view of male as a universal person and female as marked,
> gendered, partial person is replicated in academic work by the
> failure of those who focus on aspects of men's lives (on hunting,

religion, politics, warfare, or colonial culture, for instance) to consider the work of feminism relevant to their own (Lutz 1990:621-622).

The historical male bias in anthropology is evident in spite of the fact that women have made significant contributions to the field. In fact, the anthropologists best-known outside the discipline are all women: Ruth Benedict, Margaret Mead and Jane Goodall. Ruth Benedict was author of the widely read book *Patterns of Culture*, in which she argued that "culture is personality writ large." Margaret Mead pioneered in a number of anthropological techniques, paving the way for psychological anthropology and visual anthropology. Through her popular writings, Mead also introduced anthropological concepts to the general public. Jane Goodall, a physical anthropologist, conducted a landmark study of chimpanzees that set the standard for similar research on other nonhuman primates.

Two important women anthropologists, Margaret Mead and Hortense Powdermaker, describe their field experiences in the first two articles of this part. Mead was trained in the 1920s by Franz Boas, often called the father of American anthropology. In her autobiography *Blackberry Winter*, Margaret Mead notes that Boas' attitude toward his students, who called him "Papa Franz," was both protective and somewhat controlling. It was Boas who insisted that Mead study adolescent girls to test whether the troubles of teenagers were the result of cultural practices or were biologically based. Mead would have preferred to study culture change, a subject still of great interest to anthropologists, and one that would have been a landmark topic at that time.

Boas was strongly opposed to Mead's plan to conduct research in Polynesia, on the grounds that it was too dangerous. This does not appear to have been necessarily a sexist view on Boas' part, however. Mead says he recited to her "a litany of young men who had died or been killed while they were working outside the United States" (Mead 1972:141). Although Boas tried to persuade her to study American Indians instead, Mead proved to be as adamant as her mentor:

> I was determined to go to Polynesia, but I was willing to compromise and study the adolescent girl. . . . So I did what I had learned to do when I had to work things out with my father. I knew that there was one thing that mattered more to Boas than the direction taken by anthropological research. This was that

he should behave like a liberal, democratic, modern man, not
like a Prussian autocrat. It was enough to accuse him obliquely
of exercising inappropriate authority to have him draw
back. . . . Unable to bear the implied accusation that he was
bullying me, Boas gave in. But he refused to let me go to the
remote Tuamotu Islands; I must choose an island to which a
ship came regularly — at least every three weeks. This was a
restriction I could accept (Mead 1972:142).

It was as a result of her compromise with Boas that Mead
conducted her study of adolescent girls in Samoa, research that
formed the basis for perhaps her most famous work, *Coming of Age
in Samoa*. In the first article of this part "Samoa: The Adolescent
Girl," Margaret Mead recounts her introduction to field work,
providing insight into the personalities and philosophical context
of an era that shaped American anthropology. In addition, this
selection describes important but often overlooked aspects of
anthropological field work: finding a place to stay, learning the
language, meeting the people, coping with discomfort, dealing with
missionaries and other gatekeepers, and making the difficult
transition from the classroom to the field. Mead does not specifically
link her adjustment to the field to being female. Instead, she appears
to take the limitations and opportunities gender presents for
granted.

On the other hand, the second selection, "A Woman Alone in the
Field" by Hortense Powdermaker, focuses on the ability of a woman
anthropologist to move between female and male realms in doing
field work. Powdermaker was a dedicated and imaginative
researcher who conducted studies in a Melanesian village on an
island off the coast of New Guinea, in a black community in
Mississippi, among filmmakers in Hollywood, and in a mining town
in Zambia.

Powdermaker's most widely read publication is her classic work
on anthropological method, *Stranger and Friend: The Way of an
Anthropologist*, from which the selection "A Woman Alone in the
Field" is taken. In it, the anthropologist describes her experiences
in Lesu, the Melanesian village. She identifies key aspects of field
work, such as the importance of formal and informal contexts in
shaping the types of data anthropologists collect. As Powdermaker
notes, the gender of the researcher — and of the people involved in
an activity — may determine which type of access an anthropologist
can gain. This aspect of field work is also identified as significant
in two other articles in this part: "Access to Women's Knowledge:

The Azande Experience," by Stephen David Siemens, and "Adventures in the Field and in the Locker Room," by Mari Womack and Joan C. Barker.

Powdermaker was one of three students — including E. E. Evans-Pritchard and Raymond Firth — to study with Bronislaw Malinowski at the London School of Economics in the 1920s, in what has been called "the Golden Age" (Powdermaker 1966:33). Powdermaker's illustrious classmate Evans-Pritchard figures prominently in the third article of this part: "Access to Women's Knowledge: The Azande Experience" by Stephen David Siemens. Siemens compares his experiences studying the Azande of the southern Sudan with that of Evans-Pritchard, who wrote a classic study of their religious practices, *Witchcraft, Oracles and Magic among the Azande*. Siemens, whose wife accompanied him to the field, gained access to events — including rituals of birth and death — that were not accessible to the noted British anthropologist.

The gender of the anthropologist as a factor in methodology is also the topic of the final article in this part, "Adventures in the Field and in the Locker Room," by Mari Womack and Joan C. Barker. In this case, two women analyze the difficulties and research opportunities arising from their studies of male-dominant groups with a strong machismo ethic. Womack observed and interviewed professional athletes; Barker conducted research among Los Angeles police officers. The experiences of Womack and Barker shed new light on such concepts as the marginal role of the anthropologist. The two researchers argue that empathy as a factor in conducting interviews is often overlooked in discussions of methodology and, since women are often viewed as being more understanding and less critical than men, the empathy factor may favor the female anthropologist. Like Powdermaker before them, Womack and Barker conclude that being a woman researcher may be an advantage under certain conditions.

Of the articles in this part, Siemens' discussion of his experiences among the Azande illustrates the importance of studying women as a key to understanding human beings in general. In the 1970's, when feminist anthropologists called for an end to the male bias in research, no one could have anticipated how a systematic attempt to include women in anthropological research design would alter our view of society as a whole. One result, transcending gender, is a shift from the traditional anthropological focus on structure, as reported by male informants, to a greater emphasis on social interaction, which can only be understood through long-term observations of how people actually live. One revelation is that the constellation of *patriarchy, patrilineality* and *patrilocality* is not prima facie evidence of male dominance in all realms of society. *Patriarchy* is the term for male control of political power; *patrilineality* is the practice of tracing descent through the male line; *patrilocality* refers to residence with the husband's family after marriage. The concepts describe formal structures of social interaction.

The distinction between *social structure* and *social dynamics* can have profound implications for understanding the delicate balance of power within a society, as indicated by Margery Wolf's (1972) study of family relations in Taiwan. The rural Taiwanese follow traditional Chinese marriage customs, in which a woman severs formal ties with her natal family upon marriage and goes to live with her husband's family, where she is an outsider. This is considered the classic pattern of female subjugation, since the young woman has no allies in her new home and is subject to the control of her husband and mother-in-law. However, Wolf points out that a woman can protect herself from harsh treatment by allying herself with the women's community in her husband's village and by using the threat of gossip, which will result in loss of face for her husband and his family. She also notes that the uterine family, which centers on a woman's bond with her sons, allows women to control significant aspects of domestic life in a society that is structurally patriarchal, patrilineal and patrilocal.

Women's control of "domestic power" is also the subject of David D. Gilmore's analysis of two rural communities in Southern Spain, in Part Four of this volume. Even though males are expected to "rule," and being unable to rule is linguistically equivalent to being castrated, men must defer to women in many important matters due to female control over the domestic realm. This control extends to such issues as where to live, how to spend domestic funds, and when to have children.

Wolf's and Gilmore's conclusions that female sources of power are grounded in informal networks are paralleled by Rena Lederman observations, as reported in her article "Contested Order: Gender and Society in the Southern New Guinea Highlands, reprinted in Part Four. Lederman notes that the traditional anthropological emphasis on formal institutions and "social structure" obscures the importance of such informal interactions as women's economic exchange, even though these may contribute significantly to the overall economy and to gender relations.

Studies such as these are revolutionizing anthropological theory by providing support for the idea that relationships are negotiated in an ongoing social context rather than determined by formal conceptual categories. In focusing on formal structure, male accounts present an *idealized* view of social interaction. The delay in arriving at a dynamic view of social life has been in part due to limited access to women's activities and by an anthropological bias that largely dismissed them as unimportant.

Roger Keesing notes that his access to life histories of Kwaio women of Solomon Islands was restricted by attempts of Kwaio men to control codification of women's rules and roles and to determine who would be allowed to describe them to the anthropologist. It was only after Keesing was able to convey to women his interest in hearing their view of "reality" that they freely revealed "women's knowledge" which, he discovered, accords women a central place in social life:

> A woman, standing in the center of the clearing, the heart of a tiny Kwaio social universe, standing astride the generations, with the powers of life and death in her and her daughters' hands, creates and perpetuates order, maintains the boundaries the unseen spirits police. Feeding and teaching, canonically social and cultural acts, are key symbols of a woman's life. The cycles that connect mothers and daughters in these constructions women place on their lives and culture are as central as the cycles that connect men to their ancestors through patrifilial links, in male accounts (1985:34).

Studies that overlook informal uses of power and influence, and accept without question male definitions of their own activities as central to social life, provide an incomplete picture of social dynamics. It is tempting to speculate that, had Freud attempted to answer his question "What do women want?" by asking his women patients and listening to their answers, he might also have learned more about people in general.

# 5

# Samoa
## The Adolescent Girl

### *Margaret Mead*

**W**hen I sailed for Samoa, I realized only very vaguely what a commitment to field work and writing about field work meant. My decision to become an anthropologist was based in part on my belief that a scientist, even one who had no great and special gift as a great artist must have, could make a useful contribution to knowledge. I had responded also to the sense of urgency that had been conveyed to me by Professor Boas and Ruth Benedict. Even in remote parts of the world ways of life about which nothing was known were vanishing before the onslaught of modern civilization. The work of recording these unknown ways of life had to be done now—*now*—or they would be lost forever. Other things could wait, but not this most urgent task. All this came to a head at the Toronto meetings in 1924, where I was the youngest participant and everyone else had talked about "my people" and I had no people to talk about. From that time on I was determined to go to the field, not at some leisurely chosen later date, but immediately—as soon as I had completed the necessary preliminary steps.

But I really did not know much about field work. The course on methods that Professor Boas taught was not about field work. It was about theory—how material could be organized to support or to call in question some theoretical point. Ruth Benedict had spent a summer working with a group of quite acculturated Indians in California, where she had taken her mother along for a vacation, and she had worked in Zūni. I had read Ruth's descriptions of the landscape, of how the Zūni looked, of the fierceness of the bedbugs

From: Margaret Mead, *Blackberry Winter: My Earlier Years*. New York: William Morrow, 1972.

and the difficulties of managing food, but I knew little about how she went about her work. Professor Boas always spoke of the Kwakiutl as "my dear friends," but this was not followed by anything that helped me to know what it was like to live among them.

When I agreed to study the adolescent girl and Professor Boas consented to my doing this field work in Samoa, I had a half hour's instruction in which Professor Boas told me that I must be willing to seem to waste time just sitting about and listening, but that I must not waste time doing ethnography, that is, studying the culture as a whole. Fortunately, many people—missionaries, jurists, government officials, and old-fashioned ethnographers—had been to Samoa, and so the temptation to "waste time" on ethnography would be less. During the summer he also wrote me a letter in which he once more cautioned me to be careful of my health and discussed the problem he had set me:

> I am sure you have thought over the question very carefully, but there are one or two points which I have in mind and to which I would like to call your attention, even if you have thought of them before.
>
> One question that interests me very much is how the young girls react to the restraints of custom. We find very often among ourselves during the period of adolescence a strong rebellious spirit that may be expressed in sullenness or in sudden outbursts. In other individuals there is a weak submission which is accompanied, however, by a suppressed rebellion that may make itself felt in peculiar ways, perhaps in a desire for solitude which is really an expression of desire for freedom, or otherwise in forced participation in social affairs in order to drown the mental troubles. I am not at all clear in my mind in how far similar conditions may occur in primitive society and in how far the desire for independence may be simply due to our modern conditions and to a more strongly developed individualism.
>
> Another point in which I am interested is the excessive bashfulness of girls in primitive society. I do not know whether you will find it there. It is characteristic of Indian girls of most tribes, and often not only in their relations to outsiders, but frequently within the narrow circle of the family. They are often afraid to talk and are very retiring before older people.
>
> Another interesting problem is that of crushes among girls. For the older ones you might give special attention to the occurrence

of romantic love, which is not by any means absent as far as I have been able to observe, and which, of course, appears most strongly where the parents or society impose marriages which the girls may not want. . . .

. . . Stick to individual and pattern, problems like Ruth Bunzel on art in Pueblos and Haeberlin on Northwest Coast. I believe you have read Malinowski's paper in *Psyche* on the behavior of individuals in the family in New Guinea. I think he is too much influenced by Freudianis, but the problem he had in mind is one of those which I have in mind.

For the rest, there was G. Stanley Hall, who had written a huge book on adolescence in which, equating stages of growth with stages of culture, he had discussed his belief that each growing child recapitulated the history of the human race. There were also the assumptions set forth in textbooks, mainly derived from German theory, about puberty as a period of storm and stress. At that time puberty and adolescence were firmly equated in everyone's thinking. Only much later, students of child development began to say that there was perhaps a "first adolescence" around the age of six and a second crisis at puberty and that adolescence could be prolonged into the twenties and might in some sense reappear in adults in their forties.

My training in psychology had given me ideas about the use of samples, tests, and systematic inventories of behavior. I had also some very slight experience of social case work. My aunt Fanny was working at the Juvenile Protective Association at Hull House, in Chicago, and one summer I had sat on the floor and read their records. This had given me an idea of what the social context of individual behavior was—how one had to look at the household and place the household in the setting of the community.

I knew that I would have to learn the language. But I did not know anyone who was colloquially proficient in the language of the people they studied except missionaries, or the children of missionaries, turned ethnologists. I had read only one essay by Malinowski and did not know how he had used the Trobriand language. I myself had never learned a foreign language; I had only "studied" Latin and French and German in high school. Our training in linguistics had consisted of short demonstrations of extremely exotic languages in the course of which we were confronted, without previous preparation, with phrases like these:

"Adē'," nē'x•lata NEmō'guis lāxîs   ts'ā'yē          Lō'La'watsa;
"Friend, he said NEmō'guis to his younger brother Lō'La'watsa;

"gōa'LEla sEns  hēquä'lē          yā'wix•'idag•a  x•ins  qa
do not let us    go on in this way  let us act         us     to

yā'yats'ē        sEns  xunō'kuēx."
go on the sea    our    son this."

In a way this was an excellent method of teaching. It prepared
us—as our classes on forms of kinship and religious belief also
did—to expect almost anything, however strange, unaccountable,
and bizarre it might seem to us. This is, of course, the first lesson
the field anthropologist must learn; that he may well meet up with
new, unheard-of, unthought-of ways of organizing human behavior.

The expectation that we may at any time be confronted by some
as yet unrecorded mode of behavior is the basis on which
anthropologists often clash with psychologists, whose theories have
developed out of their efforts to be "scientific" and out of their
skepticism about philosophical constructs. It is also the basis of our
clash with economists, political scientists, and sociologists, to the
extent that they use the model of our own social arrangements in
their studies of other societies.

The tough treatment given us by Professor Boas shook us up,
prepared us for the unexpected, and be it said, the extremely
difficult. But we did not learn how to organize work on a strange
new language to the point at which a grammar could be worked
out on the basis of which we could learn to speak the language.
Sapir remarked parenthetically on the immorality of learning
foreign languages; one was never really honest, he said, except in
one's mother tongue.

There was, in fact, no *how* in our education. What we learned
was *what* to look for. Years later, Camilla Wedgwood, on her first
trip to Manam Island, reflected on this point when she wrote in her
first letter back: "How anyone knows who is anybody's mother's
brother, only God and Malinowski know." Lowie, too, illustrated
the startling differences between his field methods and mine when
he inquired, "How does anyone know who is whose mother's
brother unless somebody tells you?"

Our training equipped us with a sense of respect for the people
we would study. They were full human beings with a way of life
that could be compared with our own and with the culture of any

other people. No one spoke of the Kwakiutl or the Zūni—or any other people—as savages or barbarians. They were, it was true, primitive; that is, their culture had developed without script and was maintained without the use of script. That was all the term "primitive" meant to us. We were carefully taught that there was no regular progression from simple "primitive" languages to complex "civilized" languages; that, in fact, many primitive languages were far more complex than some written ones. We were taught also that whereas some art styles had been elaborated from simple designs, other art styles were reduced to simpler forms from originally more elaborate ones.

We had, of course, had lectures on evolution. We knew that it had taken millions of years for the first human-like creatures to develop language, to make tools, to work out forms of social organization that could be taught to the next generation, for all these things, once acquired, had to be taught and learned. But we went to the field not to look for earlier forms of human life, but for forms that were different from those known to us—different because particular groups of primitive people had lived in isolation from the mainstreams of great civilizations. We did not make the mistake of thinking, as Freud, for example, was misled into thinking, that the primitive peoples living on remote atolls, in desert places, in the depths of jungles, or in the Arctic north were equivalent to our ancestors. True, we might learn from them how long it took to chop down a tree with a stone axe or even how much of the food supply women may have contributed in societies based on male hunting. But these isolated peoples were not in the line of our ancestors. Obviously our ancestors had been located at various crossroads where peoples met and exchanged ideas and traded goods. They had crossed mountains, they had sailed the seas and returned. They had borrowed and copied. They had stimulated and had been stimulated by the discoveries and inventions of other peoples to an extent that was not possible among peoples who lived in much greater isolation.

We knew that in our field work we could expect to find differences—differences far greater than those we would expect to find among the related cultures of the Western world or in the lives of people at different periods in our own history. The record of what we found out about the way of life of each primitive people we studied was to be our principal contribution to the accumulating store of exact knowledge about the world.

As far as anthropology was concerned, this was my intellectual equipment. I had, of course, acquired some knowledge of the techniques in use for categorizing, for example, the uses a people made of their natural resources or the forms of social organizations they had developed. And I had some practice in analyzing the observations that had been made by other fieldworkers.

But nobody really asked what were the young fieldworker's skills and aptitudes — whether he had, for instance, the ability to observe and record accurately or the intellectual discipline to keep at the job, day after day, when there was no one to supervise, no one to compare notes with, to confess delinquencies to, or even to boast to on an especially successful day. Sapir's letters to Ruth Benedict and Malinowski's private diary are filled with self-flagellating confessions of idleness written at a time when, as we also know, they were doing prodigious work. No one considered whether we could stand loneliness. No one inquired how we would get along with the colonial or military or Indian Service officials through whom we would have to work; and no one offered us any advice.

The style, set early in the century, of giving a student a good theoretical orientation and then sending him off to live among a primitive people with the expectation that he would work everything out for himself survives to this day. In 1933, when I gave a girl student who was setting out for Africa some basic instructions on how to cope with the drinking habits of British officials, anthropologists in London sneered. And in 1952, when I arranged for Theodore Schwartz to spend a year learning the new technologies — running a generator, making tape recordings, and working with cameras — that we intended to use in the field, his professors at the University of Pennsylvania thought this was ridiculous. Men who are now professors teach their students as their professors taught them, and if young fieldworkers do not give up in despair, go mad, ruin their health, or die, they do, after a fashion, become anthropologists.

But it is a wasteful system, a system I have no time for. I try to work against it by giving my students a chance to work over my own field preparations and notes, by encouraging them to work at photography, and by creating field situations for my class, in which they have to work out a real problem and face up to the difficulties of an actual situation in which there are unknown elements. For only in this way can they find out what kind of recording they do well — or very badly — or how they react when they discover they have missed a clue or have forgotten to take the lens cap off the camera for a critical picture.

But I am also constantly defeated. A year's training in how to protect every object so that it will withstand humidity or being dropped in the river or the sea does not keep a young fieldworker from turning up with a unique copy of a manuscript wrapped in brown paper, or with her passport and money in a flimsy handbag, or without an airtight container for a valuable and essential camera. Yet students in other disciplines do learn; chemists learn laboratory procedure and psychologists learn to use a stopwatch and to write protocols.

The fact that anthropologists insist on learning everything over again for themselves, often including all the theory they have been taught, is, I think, an occupational disease that may well be inseparable from field work itself. For field work is a very difficult thing to do: To do it well, one has to sweep one's mind clear of every presupposition, even those about other cultures in the same part of the world in which one is working. Ideally, even the appearance of a house should come to one as a new, fresh impression. In a sense it should come to one as a surprise that there are houses and that they are square or round or oval, that they do or do not have walls, that they let in the sun or keep out the wind or rain, that people do or do not cook or eat in a dwelling house. In the field one can take nothing for granted. For as soon as one does, one cannot see what is before one's eyes as fresh and distinctive, and when one treats what is new merely as a variant of something already known, this may lead one far astray. Seeing a house as bigger or smaller, grander or meaner, more or less watertight than some other kind of house one already knows about cuts one off from discovering what this house is in the minds of those who live in it. Later, when one has come to know the new culture, everything has to be reassimilated into what is already known about other peoples living in that area, into our knowledge about primitive peoples, and into our knowledge about all human beings, *so far*. But the point of going to the field at all is to extend further what is already known, and so there is little value merely in identifying new versions of the familiar when we might, instead, find something wholly new. But to clear one's mind of presuppositions is a very hard thing to do and, without years of practice, all but impossible when one is working in one's own culture or in another that is very close to it.

Before one's first field trip one doesn't know all this. All one knows is that there is a tremendous job ahead—that it will be a struggle to learn the language well enough to hear and speak it, to find out who everyone is, to understand a myriad of acts, words, glances, and silences as they are integrated into a pattern one has no way of working out as yet, and, finally, to "get" the structure of the whole culture.

Before I started out for Samoa I was warned that the terms in which others had written about the culture were anything but fresh and uncontaminated. The recorded grammar was contaminated by the ideas of Indo-European grammar and the descriptions of local chiefs by European notions about rank and status. I knew I would have to thread my way through this maze of partial understandings and partial distortions. In addition, I had been given the task of studying a new problem, one on which no work had been done and for which I had no guidelines.

But in essence this is true of every worthwhile field trip. Today students sometimes are sent into the field to work on a small problem that does not involve much more than making the observations necessary to fill out a prearranged questionnaire or giving a few specific tests. Where the questions are unsuitable or the tests are wholly uncongenial to the unwilling subjects, these may not be the easiest things to do. But if the culture has already been properly studied, this kind of work may do as little harm as it does good. But it is not the same thing as being charged with getting the whole configuration of the culture down correctly.

But at the same time one has always to remember that the pattern one discerns is only one of many that might be worked out through different approaches to the same human situation. The grammar you work out is not *the* grammar but *a* grammar of the language. But it may be the only grammar anyone will ever make, it is crucial that you listen and record as minutely and as carefully as you can and, as far as possible, without reference to the grammar you are tentatively putting into shape.

All this is important, but it gives no sense of what the day-to-day tasks will be. For there is no way of knowing in advance what the people will be like or even what they will look like. There may be photographs of them, but by the time one arrives they may look different. The summer I worked among the Omaha Indians, the girls were getting their first permanent waves—something I could not have foreseen. One doesn't know what the particular officials, the planters, the police, the missionaries, or the traders will be like. One doesn't know where one will live or what there will be to eat or whether it will turn out to be a good thing to have rubber boots, mosquito boots, sandals that keep one's feet cool, or woolen socks to absorb the sweat. So there is a great tendency—and when fieldworkers were poor there was a greater tendency — to take along as little as possible and to make very few plans.

When I set out for Samoa I had half a dozen cotton dresses (including two very pretty ones) for I had been told that silk rotted in the tropics. But when I arrived, I found that the Navy wives dressed in silk. I had a small strongbox in which to keep my money and papers, a small Kodak, and a portable typewriter. Although I had been married for two years,[2] I had never stayed alone in a hotel and I had made only short journeys by train as far as the Middle West. Living in cities and small towns and in the Pennsylvania countryside, I had known a good many different kinds of Americans, but I had no idea of the kind of men who enlisted in the United States Navy in peacetime, nor did I know anything about the etiquette of naval life on an outstation. I had never been to sea.

At a party in Berkeley, where I stopped briefly on my way out, Professor Kroeber came and sat next to me on the floor and asked in a firmly sympathetic voice, "Have you got a good lamp?" I did not have any lamp at all. I had six large fat notebooks, some typing and carbon paper, and a flashlight. But no lamp.

When I arrived in Honolulu I was met by May Dillingham Freer, a Wellesley friend of my mother's. She and her husband and daughter were living in their house up in the mountains, where it was cooler, but she said I could live in Arcadia, their beautiful big house in the town. The fact that my mother had known May Dillingham and her sister-in-law Constance Freer at Wellesley made all the difference in my comings and goings in Honolulu for many years. May Dillingham was the daughter of one of the original missionary families, and her husband Walter Freer had been governor of the Hawaiian Islands. She herself was strangely out of place in her great, extensive, wealthy family; she was full of delicate sentimentalities and was childlike in her approach to life. But she was able to command any resources she needed and her influence, which extended even to Samoa, smoothed my path in a hundred ways. Under her guidance everything was arranged. The Bishop Museum made me an honorary member of the staff; Montague Cook, a member of another old Honolulu family, drove me to the Museum every day; and E. Craighill Handy gave up a week of his vacation to give me daily lessons in Marquesan, a language related to Samoan. A friend of "Mother May" — as I immediately named her — gave me a hundred little squares of torn old muslin "to wipe the children's noses," and she herself gave me a silk boudoir pillow in response to one of the few bits of practical advice I was given, in this case by a biologist who said, "Always take a little pillow and you can lie on anything." Someone else took me to visit two part-Samoan children in school; this meant that their family would be on hand to help me in Samoa.

It was all extremely pleasant. Basking in the Freer and Dillingham prestige, I could not have had a more felicitous beginning to my field trip. But this I only vaguely realized, for I did not know how to sort out the effects of influence and the courtesies that were entirely routine. But many a young fieldworker has known heartbreak in those first weeks. He has been made to feel so miserable, so unwelcomed, and so maligned—perhaps in terms of another anthropologist who got everyone's back up—that his whole field trip has been ruined before he has really got under way. These are the incalculable risks from which one can only try to protect one's students. But the factor of accident is great. Mrs. Freer might have been away from Honolulu when I arrived. Just that.

After two weeks I left, weighed down with flower leis, which in those days we threw from the ship's deck into the sea. Nowadays the Samoans give shell leis, because the admission of flowers and fruits into other ports is forbidden, and they bring a plastic bag in which to carry the leis home. But in those other days the ship's wake was bright with floating flowers.

And so I arrived in Samoa. Remembering Stevenson's rhapsodies, I was up at dawn to see with my own eyes how this, my first South Sea island, swam up over the horizon and came into view.

In Pago Pago there was no one to meet me. I had a letter of introduction from the Surgeon General of the Navy, who had been a fellow student of Luther's father at medical school. But that day everyone was too busy to pay attention to me. I found a room at the ramshackle hotel and hurried back to the square to watch the dances that had been arranged for the visitors from the ship. Everywhere there were black umbrellas. Most of the Samoans wore cotton clothes—the men were dressed in standard style and the women in heavy, unbecoming overblouses. Only the dancers wore Samoan dress. The chaplain, thinking I was a tourist with whom he could take liberties, turned over my Phi Beta Kappa key to look for my name. I said, "It isn't mine." And this confused things for many months afterwards.

Then came the period that young fieldworkers find so trying, even today, no matter how hard we try to prepare them for it. I was in Samoa. I had a room in the hotel—the hotel that had been the scene of Somerset Maugham's story and play, *Rain*, which I had seen performed in New York. I had letters of introduction. But I still had to establish some kind of base for my work. I called on the governor, an elderly and disgruntled man who had failed to attain the rank of admiral. When he told me that he had not learned the language and that I would not learn it either, I incautiously said that it was harder to learn languages after one was twenty-seven. That did not help.

Without the letter from the Surgeon General I do not know whether I would have been able to work as I wished. But that letter opened the doors of the Medical Department. The chief nurse, Miss Hodgeson, assigned a young Samoan nurse, G. F. Pepe, who had been in the United States and spoke excellent English, to work with me an hour a day.

I then had to design a way of working the rest of the time. I was very conscious of being on my own and yet of being responsible to the Fellowship Committee whose members had objected to giving me three months' stipend in advance. As there was no other way of measuring how hard I was working, I decided that I must at least work for eight hours a day. For one hour I was tutored by Pepe. The other seven I spent memorizing vocabulary and so, by accident, hit on the best way to learn a language, which is to learn as much of it as fast as possible so that each piece of learning reinforces each other piece.

I sat in the old hotel and ate the dreadful meals prepared by Fa'alavelave—whose name meant Misfortune—which were supposed to accustom me to Samoan food. Occasionally I was asked up to the hospital or to the home of one of the medical staff. The National Research Council had insisted on mailing my checks to me, and the next boat overcarried the mail. This meant that for six weeks I had no money and could not plan to leave until I had paid my hotel bill. Every day I walked about the port town, and tried out Samoan phrases on the children, but it was not an atmosphere in which I could do field work.

Finally the boat arrived again. And now, with the help of the mother of the half-Samoan children I had met in Honolulu, I was able to move to a village. She arranged for me to spend ten days in Vaitogi and to live in the household of a chief who enjoyed entertaining visitors. It was there I had all my essential training in how to manage Samoan etiquette. His daughter Fa'amotu was my constant companion. We slept together on a pile of mats at the end of the sleeping house. We were given privacy from the rest of the family by a tapa curtain, but of course the house was open to the eyes of the whole village. When I bathed I had to learn to wear a sarong-like garment which I could slip off under the village shower as I slipped a dry one on in full view of the staring crowds of children and passing adults.

I learned to eat and to enjoy Samoan food and to feel unabashed when, as a guest, I was served first and the whole family sat about sedately waiting for me to finish so that they, in turn, could eat. I learned the complex courtesy phrases and how to pass kava — something I never did as it is only appropriate for an unmarried woman to do so. However, in Vaitogi I did not tell them that I was married; I knew too little about what the consequences might be in the roles that would be assigned to me. Day after day I grew easier in the language, sat more correctly, and suffered less pain in my legs. In the evenings there was dancing and I had my first dancing lessons.

It was a beautiful village with its swept plaza and tall, round, thatched guesthouses against the pillars of which the chiefs sat on formal occasions. I learned to recognize the leaves and plants used for weaving mats and making tapa. I learned how to relate to other people in terms of their rank and how to reply in terms of the rank they accorded me.

There was only one difficult moment when a visiting talking-chief from British Samoa started a conversation based on his experience with the freer sex world in the port in Apia. Still struggling with the new language, I explained that marriage would not be fitting owing to our respective ranks. He accepted the phrasing, but added regretfully, "White women have such nice fat legs."

At the end of the ten days, which were as delightful and satisfying as the previous six weeks had been laborious and frustrating, I returned to Pago Pago to prepare to go to the island of Tau in the Manu'a group. Everyone agreed that the Manu'an islands were much more old-fashioned and were, therefore, much better for my purposes. There was a medical post on Tau, and Ruth Holt, the wife of Chief Pharmacist's Mate Edward R. Holt, who was in charge of the post, was in Pago Pago having a baby. The chief medical officer arranged that I would live on the post, and I crossed over with Mrs. Holt and the new baby on a minesweeper that had temporarily replaced the station ship. In the dangerous landing through the reef a whaleboat carrying schoolchildren upset, and Mr. Holt was relieved to get his new baby, named Moana, safely ashore.

My living quarters were set up on the back veranda of the dispensary. A lattice separated my bed from the dispensary porch and I looked out across a small yard into the village. There was a Samoan-type house in front of the dispensary where I was to work with my adolescents. A Samoan pastor in the next village presented me with a girl who was to be my constant companion, as it would have been unsuitable for me ever to be alone. I set about working out living arrangements with the Holts, who also had a little boy, Arthur, who was not quite two years old and spoke both Samoan and English.

I soon found that having my base in the dispensary household was very useful, for had I lived in a Samoan household I could have had nothing to do with children. I was too important for that. People knew that when the fleet came into Pago Pago I had dined on the admiral's flagship; that had established my rank. Reciprocally, I insisted that the Samoans call Mrs. Holt *faletua*, so that there would be no questions about where and with whom I ate.

Living in the dispensary, I could do things that otherwise would have been wholly inappropriate. The adolescent girls, and later the smaller girls whom I found I had also to study, came and filled my screen-room day after day and night after night. Later I borrowed a schoolhouse to give "examinations," and under that heading I was able to give a few simple tests and interview each girl alone. Away from the dispensary I could wander freely about the village or go on fishing trips or stop at a house where a woman was weaving. Gradually I built up a census of the whole village and worked out the background of each of the girls I was studying. Incidentally, of course, I learned a great deal of ethnology, but I never had any political participation in village life.

My field work was terribly complicated by a severe hurricane that knocked the front veranda off the dispensary, knocked down the house I was to have had as a workroom, and destroyed every house in the village and ruined the crops. Village ceremonies were almost completely halted while the village was being rebuilt and, after I had painfully learned to eat Samoan food, everyone had to live on rice and salmon sent over by the Red Cross. The Navy chaplain who was sent over to supervise the food distribution added to the crowding of our small house. In addition, his presence was deeply resented by Mr. Holt, who was only a chief pharmacist's mate because he had refused to go to college; now he smarted under every display of rank.

In all those months I had almost nothing to read, but it did not matter very much because I worked as many hours a day as I could stay awake. My only relief was writing letters. My accounts of life in family bulletins were fairly evenly balanced between pain and pleasure, but in my letters to friends I laid such heavy stress on points of difficulty that Ruth concluded I was having a hard and disappointing time. The truth was that I had no idea whether I was using the right methods. What were the right methods? There were no precedents to fall back on. I wrote to Professor Boas just before I left Pago Pago, outlining my plans. His reassuring answer arrived after I had finished my work on Tau and was ready to leave!

Still, it is letters that bring back to life that distant scene, and in one I wrote:

> The pleasantest time of day here is at sunset. Then accompanied by some fifteen girls and little children I walk through the village to the end of Siufaga, where we stand on an iron bound point and watch the waves splash us in the face, while the sun goes down, over the sea and at the same time behind the coconut covered hills. Most of the adult population is going into the sea to bathe, clad in lavalavas with buckets for water borne along on shoulder poles. All the heads of families are seated in the *faletele* (village guesthouse) making kava [an intoxicating beverage made from the root of a pepper plant]. At one point a group of women are filling a small canoe with a solution of native starch (arrowroot). And perhaps, just as we reach the store, the curfew-angelus will stop us, a wooden bell will clang mellowly through the village: The children must all scurry to cover, if we're near the store, it's the store steps, and sit tight until the bell sounds again. Prayer is over. Sometimes we are all back safely in my room when the bell sounds, and then the Lord's Prayer must be said in English, while flowers are all taken out of their hair and the siva [dance] song stopped in the middle. But once the bell sounds again, solemnity, never of a very reliable depth, is sloughed off, the flowers replaced in the girls' hair, the siva song replaces the hymn, and they begin to dance, by no means in a puritan fashion. Their supper comes about eight and sometimes I have a breathing spell, but usually the supper hours don't jibe well enough for that. They dance for me a great deal; they love it and it is an excellent index to temperament, as the dance is so individualistic, and the audience thinks it is its business to keep up incessant comment. Between dances they look at my pictures. I am going to have to put Dr. Boas much higher on the wall, his picture fascinates them. . . .

The times I remember with most pleasure are the expeditions we made to other villages, to the other Manu'an islands, and to the other village on Tau, Fitiuta, where I lived like a visiting young village princess. I could summon informants to teach me anything I wanted to know; as a return courtesy, I danced every night. Those expeditions came at the end of my field work, after I felt I had completed my project and so could "waste time" on ethnology by bringing up to date all the detail on ways in which Manu'a differed from the other islands.

On all my later field trips when I was working on cultures about which nothing was known, I had the more satisfactory task of learning the culture first and only afterward working on a special problem. In Samoa this was not necessary, and this is one reason why I was able to carry out my work on the life of the adolescent girl in nine months.

By studying the pre-adolescent girls also I invented a cross-sectional method that can be used when one cannot stay many years in the field but wants to give a dynamic picture of how human beings develop. In Samoa I went back only one step. Later I went back to small children and then to infancy, realizing that I needed to include all the stages of growth. But in Samoa I was still under the influence of the psychology I had been taught, and I used case histories and tests that I invented, such as a picture-naming test, using pictures someone had sent me from a magazine story about Flaherty's *Moana of the South Seas*, and a color-naming test, for which I painted the hundred little squares.

When I wrote *Coming of Age in Samoa* I carefully disguised all the names, sometimes using double disguises so that the actual individuals could never be identified. In the introductions I wrote to new editions I did not include the girls I had studied among the readers for whom I was writing; it seemed extremely unlikely that any of them would ever learn to read English. Today, however, the children and grandchildren of girls like the ones I knew in Tau are attending American colleges—for nowadays half the Samoan population lives in the United States—and as their classmates read about the Samoans of fifty years ago, they wonder how what I have said applies to them.

# 6

# A Woman Alone in the Field

## Hortense Powdermaker

In casual daily life [in Lesu] I was much more with the women than with the men; the sexes were quite separate in their social and economic life. I often sat with the women of my hamlet and of neighboring ones, watching them scrape the taro, the staple of their diet, and prepare it for baking between hot stones. Notes on the different ways of preparing taro became so voluminous that I sometimes thought of writing a Melanesian cook book. I was apparently compulsive about writing everything down, but I justified the fullness of the cooking notes by saying that they illustrated Melanesian ingenuity and diversity with limited resources. More important than the cooking notes were my observations on the relationships of the women with their daughters and with each other; listening to the good-humored gossip provided many clues for further questions and added subtlety to my understanding.

Pulong, whom I saw daily, was in the middle stage of her pregnancy, and I could observe her customs such as not eating a certain fish believed to "fight" an embryo in the stomach. Full details about pregnancy customs and taboos came later and gradually. When I first asked Pulong if there was any way of preventing pregnancy, she said she did not understand and looked vague. It seemed evident that she did not want to talk about the subject. Somewhat later, she and my adopted "mother" and a clan "sister" brought me leaves that they said would produce an abortion if chewed in the early stages of pregnancy. I put them carefully in a botanical press for identification when I returned home.

Reprinted from: Hortense Powdermaker, *Stranger and Friend: The Way of an Anthropologist*. New York: W. W. Norton, 1966.

It was taken for granted that I should go to all the women's feasts in or near Lesu. The morning of a feast was usually spent in preparing the food, then came the dances, distribution of food, and speeches. At one such feast in a nearby village to celebrate the birth of a baby, the hundred or so women were in a particularly gay mood, which I enjoyed. One woman, a born jester, who was not dancing because her relationship to the newborn baby precluded it, grabbed the drum and began doing amusing antics. It was like an impromptu skit and all the onlookers laughed loudly. Encouraged, she continued. Then came the distribution of bundles of baked taro, most of it to be carried home, and the women's speeches praising the ability of their respective husbands as providers of food. However, one complained that her husband was lazy and did not bring her fish often enough. In the late afternoon, my Lesu friends and I trudged home. A basket of food and sometimes a baby was on each woman's back (except mine), and although we were all tired after a long day, a pleasant, relaxed feeling pervaded the small group.

As I ate my dinner that night and thought about the day's events, I felt happy to be working in a functioning traditional culture rather than one in which the anthropologist has to get most of his data about tribal life from the reminiscences of the elders. Sometimes I asked for details of a ritual in advance of its performance; when it took place, some differences usually showed up, even though the customary pattern was followed. After one rather important ceremony, I made this point to an informant who had given me particularly full details in advance. He looked at me as if I was either stupid or naive (or both), and asked if I didn't know that nothing ever took place *exactly* as it was supposed to. Nor can generalizations by Melanesians, or anyone else, include all the specific details of actual happenings.

Although it would not have been appropriate for me to be with the men in their casual social life as I was with the women, it was understood that I must observe and learn about men's economic and ritual life, which was apart from the women's. I worked on my veranda with individual men as informants and as teachers of the native language. I did not go to men's feasts and other rites unless I was invited, but I was invited to everything. When the men were having a feast, usually in the cemetery, two elders called for me and escorted me there. I sat on one side, apart from the men, and munched on a banana as I recorded what was said or done. Later I would go over the notes with one or two of the men who had been present. One morning, although I arose very early — before dawn — to go to a men's feast in a neighboring village, I was still eating my breakfast when the Lesu men were ready to leave. Without saying anything to me, they detailed one man to wait. The sun was just rising when he and I started our walk to Ambwa, about three miles away.

I had to go to all feasts for the same reason that my presence was required at every mortuary rite [because the people involved would be offended and think that I did not regard the rite as important]. But no law of diminishing returns operated for the feasts, since the events they celebrated were so varied: birth, bestowal of name on a newborn baby, appearance of his first tooth, early betrothal, first menstruation, initiation of boys, marriage, completion of any work, death, and practically every other event — small or big — in life. Through these feasts I gained not only a knowledge of the normal round of life, but I saw also the economic system functioning. It was evident from the speeches and from my informants that the exchange of bundles of baked food was by no means casual, but followed a rather rigid system of reciprocal gifts. I heard praise for those who were generous and gossip about those who were slow to make gifts in return for those taken. As I typed my notes and mulled over them, I thought that perhaps I would organize all my data around feasts. An article on them, rather than a book, did eventually emerge after I left the field. There, I found it difficult to think in terms of articles, because I was always trying to relate one aspect of the culture to everything else.

I was more selective in going to other activities. I could not afford the time to go regularly with the women to their gardens. They left in the early morning and did not return until midafternoon. But I did go often enough to observe the various stages of their work. Fortunately, there was no feeling that my presence was necessary at all gardening activities. It was the same situation with the men's fishing. I waded into the shallow water by the beach and watched the different forms of fishing: with spears, nets, traps, and hooks. But I was content with seeing each kind of operation once or twice and discussing details of it afterwards with informants. Later, I wrote down the magical spells connected with gardening and with fishing.

I was lucky that during my stay the initiation rites for eight boys from Lesu and from two neighboring villages took place. (They did not occur every year, but only when the number of boys reaching puberty was sufficient to justify the elaborate rites.) Less than a month after I settled in Lesu, the women began practicing a dance each evening. An elderly man was teaching them, but it was taboo for other men to see the rehearsals, although they would see the dance at the ritual.

Finally, one evening, I gathered my courage and began dancing. My place in the circle was between Pulong and an important old woman in her clan. The old women danced with more vivacity than the young ones; the gayest woman of the village was a grandmother. Good-natured laughter greeted my mistakes, which were carefully corrected. The steps were not difficult and I soon caught on to them. No longer were the evenings monotonous. Every night, as the moon became fuller, I danced. But, somehow, I did not think ahead to the night of the big rites.

Finally it came. That morning, Pulong and several other women came over and presented me with a shell arm band and a *kepkep*, a tortoise-shell breast ornament, and asked that I wear their favorite dress—a pink and white striped cotton. I gulped, and said I was not going to dance; I would just observe. But why, they asked in astonishment, had I been practicing every night? I could not explain that I had started because I was bored and that now I felt too self-conscious to participate in rites which I knew would be attended by thousands of natives from all over the island and nearby islands. Soon I saw that I had to dance. A refusal now would be a rejection.

All day there was an increasing "before the ball" excitement. Hair was colored with bright dyes and bodies of men were ornamented. The tinsel trimming which I had brought with me was in demand by the women dancers, who wound it around their hair. At sunset my dancing companions assembled at my house and we walked together to the far end of the village. Like the other women, I had a yellow flower behind my ear; the *kepkep* strung on a piece of vine hung from my neck; shell bracelets were on my left arm just above the elbow. I wore the pink and white striped dress. I was excited and nervous.

When we arrived, about two thousand Melanesians from all over New Ireland and neighboring islands were sitting around the fires. We took our places and watched the dances, which went on continuously all night long in an open clearing before an intently absorbed audience. Most of the men's dances were dramatic, often acting out a story such as the killing of a crocodile. Masks were elaborate; dancing was strenuous and the drums beat vigorously. The women wore no masks and their dances, which alternated with the men's, were far less elaborate and formed abstract patterns of lines, squares, and circles. Young men held burning torches near the dancers, so that all could see them.

I was unable to pay much attention. Consumed with self-consciousness, I imagined my family and friends sitting in the background and muttering in disapproving tone, "Hortense, dancing with the savages!" How could I get up before all these people of the Stone Age and dance with them? I prayed for an earthquake—the island was volcanic. But the earth was still, and all too soon it was our turn to dance. I wondered if I would not collapse on my way to the open clearing which served as the stage. But there I was in my proper place in the circle; the drums began; I danced. Something happened. I forgot myself and was one with the dancers. Under the full moon and for the brief time of the dance, I ceased to be an anthropologist from a modern society. I danced. When it was over I realized that, for this short period, I had been emotionally part of the rite. Then out came my notebook.

In the early morning the boys were circumcised inside the enclosure. I was invited to watch the operation, but decided not to. Nor had I gone into the enclosure during the preceding few weeks when the boys were confined there. The normal social separation between the men and women was intensified during the initiation of the boys. The mothers (real and classificatory) openly expressed their sorrow at losing their sons who would now join the adult men. The women wept (not ritual wailing) when the boys went into the enclosure for the operation, and began a dance which expressed their feelings. Men ran out from the enclosure and engaged in a spirited fight with the women. They threw stones and coconut shells at each other and exchanged jeering talk. Since I had been identified with the women, even to the extent of dancing with them, it seemed unwise in the hostile atmosphere between the sexes to swerve suddenly from the women's group to the men's. Or, perhaps, I was unable to switch my identifications so quickly.

Later in the morning the piles of food (contributed by the clans of boys who had been circumcised) were given to the dancers. A particularly large pile was put in front of me and a speech was made praising my dancing and expressing appreciation. From then on the quality of my relationships with the women was different. I had their confidence as I had not had it before. They came of their own accord to visit me and talked intimately about their lives. I secured eight quite long detailed life histories. My relationships with the men were also subtly strengthened. The formal escort to their feasts continued as before, but there was a greater sense of ease between us and they gave me freely any data I asked for. I was glad for many reasons that I had not given in to my self-consciousness. Thinking about it, I was amused to realize that all the things white people had tried to make me fear—snakes, sharks, crocodiles, rape—had not caused me anxiety. Nor had the expedition taken any particular courage. As one of my friends remarked, I had the courage of a fool who did not know what she was getting into. But to dance with the women at the initiation rites—that had taken courage.

A woman alone in the field has certain advantages. Social separation between the sexes is strict in all tribal societies. Male anthropologists say it is difficult for them to be alone with native women because the men (and the women, too) suspect their intentions. When traders and other white men have had contact with native peoples, they frequently have had sexual relations with the women, with or without their consent. No precedent existed, at least in Melanesia when I was there, for a white woman to live alone in a native village. We could establish our own patterns, and obviously these large strong Melanesians could not be afraid of me. (The gun which Radcliffe-Brown had insisted I take with me for protection remained hidden in the bottom of a trunk.) My relations with the women were more chummy than with the men, and data from the former were more intimate. But the men completely understood that I had to find out as much as possible about all sides of life and, very definitely, did not want the masculine side omitted. It was the men, not I, who suggested escorting me to all their feasts. My impression is that field work may be a bit easier for a woman anthropologist alone than for a man alone.

Being alone for a male or female anthropologist gives a greater intensity to the whole field experience than living with company, and frequently provides more intimate data because the field worker is thrown upon the natives for companionship. On the other hand, it has the disadvantage of loneliness, and, perhaps, getting "fed-up" more often. A mate and children reduce the loneliness, and they may be of help in securing data from their own sex and age groups. Children are often an entering wedge into the study of family life. A team of colleagues, particularly from different disciplines, makes possible a many-sided approach to complex problems and offers the stimulation of exchange of ideas while in the field. A disadvantage of the family and team is that they may make relationships with natives more difficult. One member may be quickly accepted and the other disliked. It is usually easier for people to relate to one stranger than to several. The initial pattern in participant observation was the lone anthropologist. Today the family and team are becoming more common.

# 7

# Access to Women's Knowledge
## The Azande Experience

*Stephen David Siemens*

Does one get the native view about life (and about women) from men or can one get to know the women as well and see things from their viewpoint? Much depends on the people one is studying and the status of women among them. . . . The Zande[3] [women] were almost an inferior caste, and unless elderly matrons, shy and tongue-tied. . . . (Evans-Pritchard 1973:7)

When I was in Zandeland I felt on the whole on the side of men rather than of the women. . . ." (Evans-Pritchard 1974:10)

For E. E. Evans-Pritchard, the "woman's viewpoint" was peripheral to what he considered the more important task of getting the "native view about life," which was virtually synonymous with the man's view. When I conducted my own research among the Azande more than fifty years after Evans-Pritchard, the "woman's view" moved to center stage.[4]

I conducted field work in Southern Sudan, very near its border with Zaire (the Nile/Congo divide). My field site was about five miles from Evans-Pritchard's field site, in a community as similar to his as can be expected given the difference in time. Evans-Pritchard was there twenty months during the period 1927 to 1930. I was at my field site nineteen months from 1984 to 1985. I met many people who were children of the people in his books.

My experience supports the view that the assumptions of the fieldworker and the people of the community are more important than the fieldworker's gender in gaining access to women's (and men's) knowledge (Gregory 1984). Although Evans-Pritchard and I were both male, we obtained our knowledge of Zande culture from Azande of different sexes. Evans-Pritchard spoke mainly to men and found no reason to spend time with women.

Women initially viewed me as unapproachable and unconcerned with them. However, once they realized that I was interested, they were eager to share their knowledge with me. Nevertheless, since their viewpoint was not represented in Evans-Pritchard's writings, it was new to me and it took me some time to realize women were engaged in cultural processes of great interest to me.

Zande men and women have authority over different aspects of social life. Men are concerned with political offices, litigation and oracular procedures. Women are concerned with birth, bringing children into society, and mourning. From Zande women, I learned to be interested in "rites of passage" for babies and for bereaved mourners. In fact, these became the focus of my research (Siemens 1990). Evans-Pritchard's account only vaguely alludes to such knowledge. He learned to be concerned with witchcraft, oracles and magic from the Zande men: "I had no interest in witchcraft when I went to Zandeland, but the Azande had: so I had to let myself be guided by them" (Evans-Pritchard 1973:2). Because he did not interact with women, Evans-Pritchard did not know there was anything to be learned from them: "[Women] played no part in public life. . . . [h]ence we shall not find women taking a prominent part in magical and oracular processes" (Evans-Pritchard 1937:16).

My experience in the field gave me some insight into the way Evans-Pritchard was perceived and his consequent lack of access to women's knowledge. Evans-Pritchard and I were defined similarly by our Zande hosts, but I gradually contested the definition whereas Evans-Pritchard accepted it.

As a white male educated outsider, I was given the treatment accorded to high status males. Indeed, even before I met anyone in the Zande community, I was defined by the summoning beat of the drum: àbàrémù, àbàrémù ("government men").[5] This was my introduction to the community. The drum summoned people (mostly men) to the chief's court.[6]

Through an interpreter, I informed the assembled court that the government had not sent me; rather, I had come to do something like Evans-Pritchard had done. Everyone cheered enthusiastically, much to my bewilderment. I later found out that Evans-Pritchard was legendary for giving huge feasts. The fathers of some of those present on my arrival had been employed in Evans-Pritchard's extensive cultivations. I had unintentionally introduced myself as a rich, important man. People exalted my status by addressing me as "elder" (bakumba), even though I did not fit the usual criteria: I was too young and I didn't have children.

It is clear that Evans-Pritchard was also put into an exalted status, as evidenced both from his writings and by Azande comments to me: "Azande treated me as a superior; Nuer as an equal" (Evans-Pritchard 1940:14-15). Titako-Paulino,[7] one of my interpreters, told me that Evans-Pritchard was considered to be like a subchief. This is consistent with the jealousy directed at Evans-Pritchard by neighboring subchiefs. He documented much political intrigue among the sons of chiefs (cf. 1971a:130-157), and himself became a target of their hostile magic. Their malicious "medicine" was discovered in his homestead by his workers:

> They said that the purpose of the medicines was to destroy the popularity of the settlement where I lived by killing some people and making the rest afraid to stay there, or to make them merely discontented with their present residence. It so happened that after I had come to live in the settlement its population had more than doubled and the nobles of the locality were annoyed because each person who came to live in my settlement was a loss from one of their settlements. . . . My oracle declared that sons of [the chief] in our neighborhood were responsible for the medicines. . . . [The chief] sent for his sons and severely admonished them. . . ." (Evans-Pritchard 1937:402-404)

An important aspect of Zande social interactions is that high-status individuals are usually isolated from low-status individuals. At many events, the "elders" in attendance form an exclusive group. My own experience of being isolated sheds some light on what was probably Evans-Pritchard's experience of the Azande.

All large feasts are commemorative feasts, honoring someone who has died. At the first such all-night feast I attended, my hosts honored me as befits a chief. My wife and I, with my interpreter, were generously given a separate hut in which to sit and a separate pot of beer to drink. Our host instructed my interpreter to chase away anyone who might try to come in. After hours of isolation, I finally risked offending my host by leaving my designated place to try to gain a broader perspective on what was taking place.

At commemorative feasts later in my field work, I was expected to stay with the men of my assigned clan or of the royal clan. Among the men, there is almost no discussion of the ritual taking place. Elsewhere, women relatives of the dead person conduct a ritual that ends the mourning of the feast's host and other bereaved people. I had to refuse the company of men and go watch the women to learn the ritual and symbolism of mourning.

It seems likely that Evans-Pritchard accepted his male role on such occasions and discussed matters of politics and the history of the royal clan. When I excused myself to observe the women, I was surely viewed as odd and probably insulting to reject the company of men in favor of women. Near the end of my stay one of the men told me that I was not an "elder." Perhaps I had disappointed him.

My access to women's knowledge was partly deliberate and partly serendipitous. My assumptions about what was important were clearly different from the assumptions of my chief, Gbamuti-Charles, and my subchief, Pangūra-Simon. Early in my field work, I explained my plan to make a census survey of my neighborhood. I planned to survey all households who shared my headman but, since I could not cover all the households under my subchief, I planned to do a random sample. The chief recommended that I survey only the households of important people. He could see no reason for me to waste my time with households of unimportant people. I showed deference to my subchief by surveying his household first, but I caused resentment by skipping some important households in my efforts to obtain a random sample. I caused some consternation, too, by interviewing small homesteads headed by poor women. Some households even gained an exaggerated sense of importance because their homesteads were selected in the random drawing that determined my sample.

Ultimately, I owe my introduction into the community of women to my wife, Wendy Rader. This probably took longer than it might have because she did not behave like a Zande woman. She sat with me and the men at most social gatherings and, in general, she avoided classification as a Zande woman. She did not treat me like her husband: she did not cook for me, cultivate for me or wait on me. I did not seem to treat her as my wife: I involved her in decisions about money. Since she did many of the same things I did, including perform some census interviews without me, no one believed we were married (although they did refer to her as my "wife"). The consensus was that we had signed up for the same course and were sent out together so we wouldn't be lonely. The fact that I had not paid bridewealth for Wendy clinched it for the Azande.

Wendy had become especially involved with health concerns, and this brought us a lot of attention. Bundu-Nelson and a few other prominent members of the community requested that Wendy conduct a health class. They were especially worried about low fertility, a problem for the Azande, unlike for many African peoples (cf. Farrell 1954). Zande men asked, "Why is it that you pay the bridewealth for a young woman and then she comes to live in your homestead for a couple years and does not have a baby?"

As a result of the health class, a desperate husband Kpakasiro-Petero came to Wendy asking for pills to make his wife give birth quickly, since she had started labor. Despite Wendy's protestations that she did not have any such pills, Kpakasiro-Petero insisted, so she gave him some Vitamin C pills. He gratefully hurried home and gave them to his wife, who immediately gave birth. Kpakasiro-Petero subsequently appeared at our homestead asking for a loan to buy soap for the midwife, Natika-Mary, and a cloth for the baby. When we loaned him the money, he invited Wendy to the small feast called "bringing the baby out of the house."

"Bringing the baby out of the house" is a complex "rite of passage" that immediately caught my interest. A mother and baby are secluded in a hut immediately after birth to avoid seeing anyone who had sex the previous night. Were this to happen, the mother and baby would get sick and perhaps die. (Post-childbirth infections are considered normal.) The danger passes when the baby's umbilical cord falls off. Then the midwife ritually "brings the baby out of the house" for the first time. The ritual includes holding the baby in the smoke of magical wood to strengthen the child and remove its smell. The baby is also introduced to its cohort by having a child jump over it. The baby is introduced to the homestead courtyard by being placed on the dirt momentarily. After these acts have been performed, sexually active relatives can see the baby without danger. I now see this ritual as endowing the baby with certain crucial aspects of personhood.

I began to pay closer attention to news of births because I knew they would be followed by "bringing the baby out of the house." After attending one ritual, I interviewed the midwife in charge and found there is another ritual, "decorating the baby," that happens months later. This ritual is also performed by the midwife.

Suddenly, I found myself with lots of questions only midwives and other women could answer. Males knew little of the things that interested me. As I sought out midwives to ask questions, they responded to my interest. These were usually older women, such as Natika-Mary and Narugiyo-Rebeka, who were quite sure of themselves and who helped me a lot by volunteering information even if my questions missed the important points. No doubt, Natika-Mary and Narugiyo-Rebeka exemplify the "elderly matrons" to whom Evans-Pritchard referred and in whom he expressed so little interest.

Soon a midwife told me that "decorating a baby" is like "removing mourning taboos." This connection between baby "rites of passage" and mourning required me to take a closer look at mourning. Until then I had mostly concerned myself with the dead person rather than the mourning survivors. Consequently, I had concentrated on the funerals and had missed many important transitions of the mourners.

It turned out that women are in charge of mourning rituals as well as baby rituals. I had not been aware of these activities because they do not concern the men unless the men are mourners. Mourning rituals are often private. Even when a mourning ritual is a public event, much of it takes place away from the public space where men sit and converse. For example, when a widow "puts on mourning taboos" the clan "sister" of the dead husband pretends to feed the widow "medicine" in the sleeping hut she and her dead husband used. Meanwhile, the older men sit under the granary and veranda, away from the activity. Similarly, at large all-night feasts to "remove mourning taboos" the men sit in arranged places or go to the dancing area. Meanwhile elsewhere, mourners are bathing and dressing in "red" clothes under the direction of the dead person's clan "sister."

Men generally find mourning distasteful because a mourner avoids the signs of high rank: sitting on a chair, putting oil on the skin and wearing colorful clothes. Women are more willing to take on the signs of low status, perhaps because they generally have lower status than men, and mourning is a way for women to gain recognition. Even though mourning is a period of low status, holding a commemorative feast raises the prestige of the host. By entering mourning women have a way of increasing their prestige.

Mourning is obligatory for bereaved spouses and very close relatives, but is voluntary for most other relatives. Both Gero's (1968) account and Evans-Pritchard's account (as reported in Seligman and Seligman 1932)[8] are based on the assumption that there is a single commemorative feast for a dead person, but I found there can be any number of such commemorative feasts. Evans-Pritchard assumes that the male household head who hosted the funeral also hosts the commemorative feast. I found that the funeral host ("the owner of death") does have a responsibility to provide for building a stone mound over the grave and for holding a feast, but many other relatives may also hold their own commemorative feasts of varying sizes.

The number and importance of these additional commemorative feasts has probably increased over the last fifty years. In Evans-Pritchard's time, heads of large households had considerably greater control over the labor of young men and women. At the time of my field work, there were ways for young men to raise money without relying on their fathers and uncles. Similarly, women could raise money by brewing beer and liquor and selling it. These economic factors reduced the control that a head of household could exert and the amount of labor and wealth he could marshall for a commemorative feast. Alternate sources of money also opened the possibility of small households increasing their prestige by hosting a feast.

Evans-Pritchard promised to write about these important rituals (a part of "family life" which includes "religion," as he put it), but continued to postpone it to the end of his life. Could it be that he was frustrated by his own sense of lacking important information in this area? Evans-Pritchard certainly recognized the importance of the rituals of the commemorative feast:

> Above all it is necessary to know on what occasions dances are held and if they form a part of some ceremonial complex, and what role, if any do the dancers take in the performance of the rites. It is quite possible that Zande beer dances are held on a variety of occasions, but amongst the Azande of the bush I have only come across their performance in connexion with the cycle of mourning and mortuary feasts. . . . We must therefore not think of the dance as a play activity but as forming an important social undertaking associated with religious ritual. . . . This crowd gives a background against which the rites are performed. . . . their presence gives support to the more serious events of the occasion. The crowd gives social recognition to the carrying out of a sacred duty towards the dead. . . . (Evans-Pritchard 1928:460-461)

Yet, Evans-Pritchard tells us little about "the more serious events of the occasion." Perhaps he is referring to the placing of the last stone on the grave mound, which usually happens in the daytime before the dance. Even so, he never mentions crucial ritual actions that occur simultaneously with the dance. Possibly, the omission is because "removing mourning taboos" is controlled by women.[9]

Evans-Pritchard also neglected the "rites of passage" for babies. Although he mentions the ritual of "bringing the baby out of the house," many essentials are omitted. Most importantly, the ritual of "decorating the baby," which completes the ritual sequence, is entirely unreported. The baby's initial seclusion in a hut is not mentioned, nor is the danger from sexually active people. The period of homestead confinement is not mentioned, either. These aspects of the "rites of passage" are probably not innovations, since some elements are found in Lagae's account (1926:170-172), which predates Evans-Pritchard's field work.

The knowledge of how to "bring out babies" and "decorate babies" is held and developed by midwives and the women who help them. High status males know little of such things. Evans-Pritchard found the cultural knowledge of women to be of little concern. His male hosts considered women's concerns beneath them and certainly unworthy of the attention of their "superior" guest. Thus, the Zande "rites of passage" were not understood and barely documented by Evans-Pritchard, even though they were a prominent concern of Zande women. The Zande women knew how to act in front of "superiors" and did not call attention to themselves. Consequently, Evans-Pritchard was free to concentrate on the history of the rulers (1971a) and the magic by which they carried out intrigue (1937).

By contrast, I was concerned to get a view of Zande society at all levels, especially the lower levels missing in Evans-Pritchard's account. This put me in a position to show interest when opportunity arose and enabled me to learn how Azande mourn their dead and introduce their babies into society. These concerns are "matters of life and death that are ultimately in women's hands" (Keesing 1985:29). The importance of these practices is demonstrated by their persistence despite opposition by church and government.[10] Rituals and practices pertaining to mourning and to new babies — which are under the authority of women — are a necessary part of being Azande and need to be brought into ethnological view.

# 8

# Adventures in the Field and in the Locker Room

*Mari Womack and Joan C. Barker*

**W**hen Mari Womack decided to study rituals of professional team sport athletes, virtually all of whom are male, she was advised by several anthropologists to work with a male co-researcher. It was feared she would not have access to such key sites as the locker room and that male athletes would be reluctant to discuss their magic with a woman. There were also suggestions that, as a female and an outsider, she might be labeled a "jinx" if the teams went into a slump while she was studying them.

Joan Barker found herself in a similarly equivocal position when she studied officers in the Los Angeles Police Department. Her research began at a time when the organization had recently implemented affirmative action policies which, in some cases, created tensions between men and women on the force. As women studying male-dominant groups, the two researchers discovered that being an obvious outsider conferred some unanticipated advantages and that the experience shed new light on the traditional relationship of anthropologists to the people they study.

## Gender, Participant Observation and the Insider Perspective

The gender of the anthropologist has been identified as an important issue in conducting field work. Most of the discussion has centered on the implications of men studying women or, even more problematic, men studying men and allowing that to stand for society as a whole. E. E. Evans-Pritchard pondered whether it were possible to gain access to the women's viewpoint, or whether one could get the "native view about life" from men alone (1973:7). In her now-classic article "Woman The Gatherer: Male Bias in Anthropology," Sally Slocum answers this question with a resounding "NO!": "The perspective of women is, in many ways, . . . foreign to an anthropology that has been developed and pursued primarily by males. There is a strong male bias in the questions asked, and the interpretations given" (1975:37).

On the other hand, James R. Gregory (1984) notes that the emphasis on gender as a factor in limiting access to certain kinds of information obscures the fact that, by the nature of field work, anthropologists are subject to being misled by the people they study:

> . . . the myth of the male ethnographer and the woman's world is a false statement in the sense that it implies that such problems with distortions, omissions, and half-truths are unique and that there are no comparable problems for male ethnographers in working with male informants. In my experience, nothing could be farther from the truth. . . . (1984:321)

Gregory suggests that gender is one of a number of factors that may affect the anthropologist's ability to gain information. The process of collecting data can be influenced by such conditions as the nature of the information being sought (whether it is sensitive or dangerous), the group's previous experience with outsiders, and whether the information is provided privately or in the presence of others. This view is consistent with the experiences of Womack and Barker.

Participant-observation is a preferred methodology for the field but, as Gregory points out, the ability of anthropologists to "participate" in any society has probably been exaggerated. The researcher is prevented—due to barriers of sex, age or differential status—from having access to many customs and practices of a culture. Suspension of norms is typically allowed only when the anthropologist is considered a nonperson or outsider. In one case, a Japanese woman anthropologist was barred from observing certain Shinto ceremonies, whereas an American woman anthropologist was permitted to observe them (Lisa Cerroni-Long, personal communication, 1989). As an insider, the Japanese anthropologist was bound by rules that define women as ritually polluting. The American woman—an outsider and non-person—

was not. The same logic favored a male anthropologist who, during his study in New Guinea, observed some female rituals normally forbidden to males (Philip Newman, personal communication). Hortense Powdermaker (1966) notes that she was invited to attend men's feasts on the island of Lesu and even to observe closely guarded male circumcision rituals.

Suspension of rules for outsiders often favors the female researcher in an all-male group. In studying police, Barker discovered that being female relieved her of the necessity of being an "O.K." male, a category with standards almost impossible for a non-police officer to meet. She did not have to be athletic, a skilled fisherman or have mastery over large and powerful motorcycles. She did not have to have "command presence," or have an acceptable profession, such as police officer, firefighter or professional athlete. She could eschew risk taking, but could participate in these activities as an onlooker. This is acceptable behavior for a woman, but not for a man.

Barker also learned that being female was a partial solution to overcoming "clannishness" among police officers because it allowed her to interact with them in a relaxed, off-duty setting. Her research began when she was challenged by a police officer, one of her students, to apply the concept of cultural relativism to a study of "cops." She was invited to socialize with off-duty officers at a "cop bar." She later discovered that her entry into the group was greatly facilitated by the fact that her initial contact was a highly respected officer who, in effect, vouched for her good behavior and signalled to other officers that she was trustworthy.

Barker and Womack were obvious outsiders, since there was no likelihood that either would become a member of the group. Womack was barred from becoming a professional athlete by her gender and lack of adequate playing skills. Barker had not undergone the rigorous training and graduation ceremony of the police academy.

Womack began her study as the inadvertent result of becoming friends with a professional hockey player, who introduced her to teammates and their wives. It was in this casual context that she became aware of the importance of sporting rituals. Thus, both researchers experienced a transition from informal participant-observation to formal interviews, and both found the quality and kinds of information gathered differed when the context of information gathering shifted from "conversation" to "interview."

Both Womack and Barker were assisted in their research by the fact that their field site, Los Angeles, is a media center. Athletes and police officers are accustomed to being the focus of the media spotlight. Though both groups express a great deal of hostility toward journalists, they do not question cultural norms that accord strangers with note pads and tape recorders the right to ask intrusive questions.

However, the transition from "conversation" to "interview" was more acute for Barker, who discovered that police reacted warily to being "interviewed." Many officers avoided scheduled interviews altogether, and many of those who were interviewed initially tended to give idealized and very brief responses, with little of the elaboration open-ended interviews are designed to encourage. Police are adept at giving minimal information, especially in situations that resemble questioning by news media.

Athletes, on the other hand, are usually relaxed during interviews. However, they are more likely to try to "shape" an interview by listening for the question behind the question and by framing their answers so they sound good on the air or in print. In informal conversations, athletes are more reflective and less concerned with controlling the outcome of the exchange.

Because of their different research settings and research questions, the two anthropologists took opposite approaches in asking questions. In fact, this is probably a key difference between Womack's research context and that of Barker. Barker conducted her study in informal settings and downplayed any associations with media; Womack emphasized her journalistic connections. Barker was most effective by "being the person who wasn't there." Because her interactions with police officers took place in recreational contexts where women are accepted, Barker could, in effect, disappear into the woodwork. Womack couldn't disappear. She was treading the hollowed ground of baseball dugouts and team locker rooms, where few women had gone before. Therefore, Womack underscored her visibility. She gained access to high-level athletes through her credentials as a professional journalist, access that would be difficult to achieve in any other way. Her press pass allowed her to interact with athletes before and after games and during practice.

Womack relied on visual cues to enhance or downplay her association with sportswriters as the research required. For example, she displayed a note pad or tape recorder to signal her purpose for being there. Athletes are accustomed to being followed around by reporters bearing tape recorders, note books, and television cameras and lights. They are suspicious and disdainful of strangers without these paraphernalia who hang around locker rooms and playing fields. Females are usually assumed to be "groupies"; males are part of the despised social category known as "jocksniffers." Reporters are also viewed as "jocksniffers," but athletes acknowledge that journalists are required to hang around because of their jobs, which is a more acceptable motivation than simple curiosity.

To avoid undesirable aspects of being associated with journalists, Womack distanced herself from them by always dressing in skirts and dresses, since almost all sports writers at the time she began her research were male. At the same time, she dressed discreetly in a business-like "uniform" to distinguish herself from "groupies," women who gain access to the group through sexual favors. Womack also distanced herself behaviorally from sportswriters by avoiding the kind of "good old boy" display that sports writers often affect. She refrained from giving the athletes pointers on their games, as sports writers sometimes do, and generally avoided conveying a sense of superior knowledge about sports. Although males commonly use this means to get to know each other and establish patterns of dominance and deference, it infuriates professional athletes when they are subjected to it by outsiders. In fact, being a woman was an advantage in this respect, because athletes presumed her innocent of any knowledge of sports and, therefore, found her non-threatening. This became apparent one day in the Dodger dugout when Womack was chatting casually with a high-ranking member of the team. A male visitor began to instruct her on the finer points of baseball, while affecting an easy familiarity with the team. The athlete looked at him disdainfully and scornfully made his exit. This incident, and others like it, definitively resolved for Womack the issue of whether she was correct in choosing not to work with a male co-researcher.

## Male Solidarity

Both police officers and professional athletes adhere to an ethic of "esprit de corps," in which they strongly ally themselves with their fellows. A number of athletic customs and rituals emphasize the solidarity of the group and link the identity of the individual player to his position on the team. For example, a hockey player new to a team is subjected to a ritual shaving by his teammates.

This forcible removal of head and body hair is usually administered when the new team member demonstrates a disregard for his teammates by inconveniencing them in some way. Professional football teams serve communal meals on the day of a game, and some hold vesper services as well.

The custom in baseball of shaking hands after hitting a home run reminds the triumphant athlete that he is still a member of the team. During the course of Womack's field work, Reggie Jackson created a scandal by refusing to shake hands with his teammates on the New York Yankees. When a member of another baseball team was asked about the incident, he replied: "That would never happen on our team. We're all one team, you know. (Getting a home run) is part of a team effort. I don't know what Reggie had in mind — maybe there's something there I don't know about — but it's like taking it all for yourself."

This sports figure is expressing the pull of two loyalties created by the emphasis on solidarity among athletes. He is reluctant to criticize a fellow insider in baseball to an outsider, but it was evident in the context of the interview that he strongly disapproved of Jackson's behavior because it emphasized the individual over the team.

Team (and police) solidarity is generated and maintained by excluding outsiders, especially those who might threaten the integrity of the group. As Mary Douglas (1966) has noted, it is ambiguity and mixing of cultural categories that is particularly threatening. Thus, *male* outsiders are more "dangerous" than *female* outsiders, who are members of a "safer" conceptual category because they can never become insiders.

During Womack's field work, a court decision was handed down that forced teams to admit women to their locker rooms. The announcement came on a day she made a scheduled visit to the Los Angeles Dodgers, resulting in the only overt display of hostility Womack experienced while studying the team. A member of the coaching staff approached her in the dugout and said, "Why don't you go on into the locker room?" Womack correctly interpreted this as a challenge and replied, "I think I'll pass on it today." Rebuffed in his attempt to attack her directly, the team member launched into a tirade against women reporters in general, concluding his speech with the assertion: "Women who want to go into the locker room aren't women at all. The players have nothing but contempt for them."

Although this team member was the only one who verbalized his anger, his attitude was no doubt generally shared, as evidenced by Womack's later experiences on entering the locker room. On one occasion, she was taking a picture of a fully clothed athlete when his unclad teammate deliberately stepped into the frame, affording the anthropologist a photograph of a full frontal male nude. Admitting women to the locker room was perceived as a challenge to the solidarity of the group because it permitted "outsiders" to invade the male team realm. Women, who were "safe" in a clearly delineated external role, became "dangerous" when they were allowed to get too close. In another context, male "wanna-bes" or "jocksniffers" are dangerous because their attempts to get close to the athletes are experienced as threatening the solidarity of the in-group.

Police display a similar reaction to outsiders who fail to observe the proper distance. Many people seeking to ingratiate themselves with police officers drop names of other officers and try to impress them with "inside" knowledge. This has the opposite effect, since police view such attempts as inappropriate familiarity.

No outsider will ever be perceived as an insider by police or by professional athletes. However, an outsider who occupies a clearly defined, delimited, and non-threatening role — and who conveys an understanding of that role — will be accepted and even welcomed. As noted later in this paper, Womack and Barker discovered that both athletes and police were eager to tell their stories after they learned to trust the researcher. For both, earning trust included passing a few well-chosen tests.

## Passing the Test

Womack and Barker were forced to establish early in their research that they were not "groupies," part of the experience of professional athletes and police officers alike, and both researchers were subjected to various types of tests in the field. Early in her research, Barker discovered that police officers would deliberately try to shock her by describing a grisly event on the job or by making a provocative political statement. At these times, their emphasis was different from when they discussed such subjects among themselves. Barker learned to distinguish whether they were exchanging information among themselves and allowing her to overhear, or whether they were directly addressing her and, in many cases, trying to assess her reaction.

In one sense, police officers were trying to determine whether she was "for" or "against" them. This went beyond a simple insider-outsider distinction, and was an attempt to find out more general kinds of information about her. They wanted to know whether she was a "pushover for the image" or, conversely, whether she would be hypercritical of them. In the first instance, they would disdain her for being gullible; in the second, they would be offended by her close-mindedness. They were asking the tacit question: Are you interested in me because of what you think I am or because of who I really am?

In another sense, Barker was being subjected to a test of character. Officers value the ability to be noncommittal until, as they put it, they "know all the knowns" — that is, until all the facts are in. Yet street officers must often respond instantly to situations in which they do not "know all the knowns," and they must draw conclusions based on fragmentary information. These conflicting abilities are essential in the performance of their jobs, and the ability to sort out complex social situations is required of fellow officers and valued in people generally.

Also as a result of their jobs, police officers automatically try to find out "where you're coming from." They are trained interviewers and know many tricks of the trade designed to gain information from others while revealing little about themselves. Barker found herself subject to many of the techniques officers rely on to elicit information from suspects and victims. She would be conversationally "set up" by officers introducing a subject about which they knew she had information and then waiting to see her response. This was a test of her discretion and trustworthiness. On some occasions, Barker found herself the object of an adapted version of "good cop, bad cop."

Like police officers, professional athletes are accustomed to being courted or vilified because of their image, and they are scornful of those who are blinded by the uniform. Womack was often offered a chew of tobacco by baseball players intent on putting her on the spot. Just as with police officers, the real test was how she felt about them. If she had reacted with disgust, she would have been scorned as one who wanted the glory of being associated with them but was unwilling to accept them as they are. Had she accepted, she would have earned the contempt athletes reserve for women who try to be men or for outsiders who try to be insiders. Passing the test required an understanding of how to maintain the proper distance while demonstrating the ability to take the heat. In other words, the athletes wanted to know whether Womack possessed the appropriate qualities of innate character and social sensitivity. Once she demonstrated her ability to reject the tobacco but not the man, the discussion proceeded comfortably and cordially.

There was one particularly severe test that Womack failed honorably, however. While interviewing a hockey player on the sidelines during practice, other players carefully aimed hockey pucks so they would sail within ten feet of her and the athlete. This is no gentle threat, since hard-hit hockey pucks have been timed at ninety miles an hour, and can cause serious injury. After enduring this aggressive display for several minutes, the researcher confessed, "This is making me a little nervous."

The hockey player replied, "It's making me pretty nervous, too."

Come to think of it, Womack may have passed that test.

## Machismo and the "Empathy" Factor

Both researchers discovered unexpected advantages to being a woman studying a male-dominant group, and some of these are due to the values of machismo culture. Women are non-threatening, whereas men are competitors. Women are viewed as sympathetic listeners, especially when the discussion involves a revelation of self. Womack found that athletes were often eager to talk to her about rituals, a subject so personal one team member said it was "like asking them what brand of shorts they wore." In general, talking about magic is viewed as dangerous, both because athletes fear being considered "superstitious" and because, as baseball player Ron Cey put it, "If I told you my rituals, they wouldn't work."

Whereas talking with another male can be an encounter fraught with danger, talking with a woman can be an opportunity for display. Barker discovered that police officers were flattered by the attention and pleased that an outsider was interested in them as individuals, as well as the work they did. She also feels she may have been aided by the fact that they viewed her project as being of little consequence and, therefore, non-threatening.

The empathy factor—and face-to-face interaction—played an important part in getting athletes to talk about their rituals, yielding information that is virtually impossible to get any other way. After presenting some of her data at a conference, Womack was approached by a researcher conducting a study on athletes, who asked, "How did you get all this information? I tried to get a group

of athletes to answer a questionnaire and got all negative results.''
Athletes are experts at refusing to answer a question they don't like,
or seeming to answer a question without actually doing so, and at
misleading an interviewer they don't particularly like.

In some ways, Womack's and Barker's equivocal role as women
in male-dominant groups provided a service to the subjects, in that
they were able to talk about their lives in a way that was customarily
denied them. Barker notes that police could reveal vulnerability
with her, and describe their emotional reactions to some of their
experiences. They were especially disturbed by brutality to children
and frustrated by their sense of being unable to intervene effectively.
However, in spite of their strong reaction to scenes of children who
were killed, beaten or sexually abused, police were limited in their
ability to distance themselves from it. Unlike the public, police must
focus on the experience in filling out their reports, but report writing
emphasizes detachment rather than emotion. Police are subject to
extended contact with events that provoke strong emotion, but are
generally deprived of an outlet for expressing it. Barker's research
drew this description of his work from one officer:

> I can take anything the job throws at me except the kids. First
> fatal [case involving a death] I drew was my third day on and
> there were two children and their mom. She lost control and
> T-boned a telephone pole. The infant in the child seat, the three-
> year-old and the mom. We were the first on the scene and the
> three-year-old kept asking for her mother, and you could see the
> mother was dead. The baby was gone, and this little girl was
> so broken up, and all you could do was talk to her — you couldn't
> pick her up, or hold her, because of the injuries. I kept talking
> to her, but she never even made it out of the wreck. Welcome
> to the wonderful world of public service. That almost ended my
> career. I thought I could never go through that again. On every
> call I just pray there are no kids, no children.

As another officer put it, "Police must be pretty well balanced
to take the 'stuff' over and over again." Most male police attempt
to protect their wives from such experiences, so they don't talk
about them at home. Police may talk about such events with their
partners, who have gone through the experience with them, but
in this case a fellow officer is too intimately involved to provide a
useful sounding board, and there may be some reluctance to let
down all professional barriers. Even if the partner is a woman, she
is not viewed as quite so understanding as a woman who has not
been through the rigorous police training and toughening

experiences of the street. A policewoman is one of them and, therefore, "tough." She is also subject to the same professional constraints that prevent officers from venting their feelings as openly as they did with Barker. It may well be that to do so would add to their sense of frustration and powerlessness since, in their view, they are admitting to being unable to "take it."

Barker occupied the appropriate position to bridge the empathy gap: she knew the job and was also a woman. The researcher provided an opportunity to reprocess the experiences, this time including the outrage, pain and frustration. Barker was more knowledgeable about the job of policing than officers' wives, who are removed and "protected," but at the same time she was enough removed from the experience to provide scope for reflection. Barker provided the perfect sounding board because she was softer than a policewoman and more knowledgeable than a wife.

Womack found much the same to be true of professional athletes. She was softer than reporters or athletes and more knowledgeable than fans. On a number of occasions she was told, "I'm glad you're doing this. People need to know what it's really like to be an athlete." Although they are the focus of much attention and are grilled for information about everything from their attitudes to their weight, athletes as human beings attract little interest. They are in the unique position that everyone wants to know them, but no one cares who they are. Womack asked them to reflect upon their experiences.

Like police, athletes are subject to intense stress and lack of understanding from outsiders. Both need a well-considered approach to life to survive in a highly stressful social environment and perform consistently beyond the capacity of most humans. The careers of many physically gifted athletes are cut short by the inability to handle stress. Most athletes have thought carefully about who they are and what their performance means, but no one wants to hear about it. Athletes are presumed to be unintellectual, so no one is interested in their opinions. When a sympathetic listener sits down and asks, "What do you think about . . . ?" and is willing to listen to the answer, they are only too happy to talk. This is especially true if the listener is a woman and, therefore, assumed to be sympathetic. Womack observed men settling in for a chat with athletes and noted that, often, the exchange held an edge of tension related to competition. The male outsider appeared eager to demonstrate his knowledge of the game, and the athlete appeared eager to avoid being put on the spot.

The willingness to listen is a key factor in Womack's and Barker's research experiences and is probably a crucial aspect of anthropological research in general, transcending gender. The importance of empathy in anthropological methodology is often overlooked. Books on field work may devote a great deal of space to discussing how to ask questions, but virtually none considers the perhaps more important aspect of conducting interviews — how to listen. This is an issue that transcends differences of gender and distinctions of insider and outsider and goes to the heart of anthropological research. It is not enough to ask the good question. Whether female or male, the anthropologist who wants to understand the insider perspective must turn off the internal dialogue, settle back, and really *listen* to the answer.

## The Feminine Factor

Males who are part of a machismo culture often seem to view it as incumbent upon them to please a woman by giving her what she wants or what they *think* she wants. Therefore, they feel an obligation to answer questions posed by a woman in a one-on-one context, even if they view the question as intrusive. This circumstance favors the female researcher, but the advantage is lost if the interview takes place in the presence of other males. For example, in her job as a sports reporter, Womack was conducting an interview in the locker room of a professional boxer immediately after he had lost a fight. "What are your plans now?" she asked. The boxer's manager flew at her in a rage, saying, "How can you be so insensitive? This man has just lost a fight. How can you ask a question like that?" Just then a male reporter entered the locker room and, not hearing the previous exchange, asked the same question, "What next?" Without a moment's hesitation, the manager answered the question.

This episode illustrates one disadvantage of being a female researcher in an all-male group — becoming a scapegoat. As an onlooker with distinctive characteristics, a woman is likely to be singled out for blame in times of trouble. Just as women have the power to sink ships, they are also capable of sinking a baseball team. In this respect, the outsider status of female is more risky than the traditional outsider role of the anthropologist, since women are viewed as polluting by many groups, including professional sports teams. Elsewhere, Womack (1982) has noted that women are barred from group interactions organized around male solidarity because female-male pair bonding threatens the male-male group bond. Similarly, Rena Lederman (1989) notes that male rhetoric that purports to devalue women is actually aimed at shaming men into fulfilling their assigned responsibilities in the all-male group.

It is impossible to assess whether a male researcher could have acquired the kinds of information about athletes and police officers available to two female researchers. Certainly, none has so far done so. However, this may be because male researchers have not posed the same questions, rather than that they would not have received the same kinds of answers. On the basis of their experiences, however, both Womack and Barker concluded that being a woman researcher working with a male-dominated group offered certain key advantages:

1. As women, they were able to transcend traditional male rivalries.

2. They were able to negotiate their equivocal status to gain access to information not otherwise available.

3. They were perceived as empathic listeners.

Gender as a factor in field research shares some advantages associated with the traditional outsider role of the anthropologist. However the female researcher/male-dominant group dynamic is further influenced by concepts of femaleness and maleness. Thus, negotiating the relationship of insider and outsider is necessarily more complex.

# PART III

## Love, Marriage, and Power

## Status, Property, and the Value on Virginity
*Alice Schlegel*

## Symbol and Meaning in Nayar Marriage Ritual
*Melinda A. Moore*

## Why Women Take Men to Magistrate's Court
*Mindie Lazarus-Black*

## In-Law Relationships in the American Kinship System
### The Impact of Divorce and Remarriage
*Colleen Leahy Johnson*

The economic and social importance of marriage is indicated by the lavishly decorated chariot transporting the bride and groom to their new status as a married couple. *The Bettmann Archive.*

▶

# Suggested Readings

**Margaret Atwood. 1986. *The Handmaid's Tale*. Boston: Houghton Mifflin.**
In her best-selling science-fiction novel, Atwood correctly identifies childbearing as central to human social organization and explores the role of sexuality in the status of both men and women. At a time in United States history when reproductive rights are being hotly debated in the press, in the parlor, in the pulpit, in the Congress, and in the doctor's office, this book stands as a powerful reminder that the production and care of children are everybody's business.

**Akemi Kikumura. 1981. *Through Harsh Winters: The Life of a Japanese Immigrant Woman*. Novato, California: Chandler and Sharp.**
On January 15, 1923, nineteen-year-old Michiko Tanaka left Hiroshima, Japan, with her husband to begin a new life in the United States. On May 15, 1980, Tanaka became a United States citizen. In the intervening years, she gave birth to thirteen children, worked to support them in the fields of California, and spent World War II in an intern camp in Arkansas. She never returned to Japan. In this biography of her mother's life, Kikumura describes a woman of courage and strength, who bears little resemblance to the frail creature depicted in Western stereotypes of Japanese women.

**Amy Tan. 1989. *The Joy Luck Club*. New York: G. P. Putnam's Sons.**
In her novel focusing on four Chinese immigrant women and their American-born daughters, Tan explores the mother-daughter relationship from the perspective of two generations. Although the stories reflect the experiences of Chinese-Americans, the conflicts and confluences Tan describes transcend ethnicity and contribute to the understanding of the often-frustrating and always-complex mother-daughter relationship.

**Alice Walker. 1982. *The Color Purple*. New York: Pocket Books.**
Relationships between poor, black men and women of the American South are explored in this novel that resulted in a controversial film of the same name. Walker provides a sensitive look at the lives of women as reflected in their relationships with their men, children, and God. The story is woven in a series of letters written to God by Celie, a child-woman who grows in self-esteem and autonomy through her friendship with an unlikely female mentor.

**Margery Wolf. 1972. *Women and the Family in Rural Taiwan*. Stanford: Stanford University Press.**
Wolf's study of women's ability to exercise power in the domestic realm challenged anthropological assumptions about the absolute dominance of men in traditional Chinese society. It forced anthropologists to re-examine the role of social structure in defining gender roles and led to a new approach emphasizing the informal negotiation of power.

# Introduction

*Mari Womack*


It was a story right out of a fairy tale, and the American public eagerly followed press reports on the marriage of Prince Charles of England to Lady Diana Spencer. He was the man who would someday be king; she was the living image of the beautiful young princess. He was the sophisticated man of the world; she was a shy, gentle, young school girl. It was a match made in heaven. Or was it?

Ironically, this most romantic of love stories was constructed, not in the glimmering castle of a fairy tale paradise, but in the more substantial halls of political necessity. The marriage was not the response of two lovers to an irresistible attraction; it was arranged to ensure the succession to the throne of England. Diana's role was not to be the object of Charles' romantic desire, but to be the future queen of England and the mother of future kings. When the troubled marriage later became the subject of headlines, a disappointed public believed the fairy tale had ended. In fact, the marriage was never a love match, but a political alliance.

The story of Charles and Diana illustrates the importance of a distinction that is often lost sight of: the sometimes competing relationship between private inclination and public convention. Regardless of the individual desires of the participants, all marriages are political. It is through marriage that social relationships are ordered and realigned. Perhaps more importantly, it is through marriage and its legitimizing of sexuality that society is perpetuated through the birth of children. Without children, the most powerful lineages would fall and, without successors, the most distinguished of royal families must surrender the reins of power.

In fact, it could be argued that all of social life — the duality centering on maleness and femaleness — is ordered around the compelling necessity to produce the next generation. This powerful aspect of sexuality is obscured when we approach it from the Western bias that presumes male and female roles to be developed

**117**

around the sexual desires of the male, or the romantic feelings men and women have for each other. Quite often, in fact, individual pleasures are subverted by the necessity of conforming to social convention. In *The High Valley*, Kenneth E. Read describes the dilemma of a new husband who eventually succumbs to social pressures coercing him to beat his young wife. Because he didn't want to beat her at all, but does so only after enduring the repeated exhortations of his male elders, he finally reacts by beating her severely.

Marriage is political because it is a public social statement about the relationship of husband to wife, wife to husband, parent to child — and of the reproductive unit to the larger social context. Marriage legitimizes sexuality and provides a kin group with descendants. It establishes an economic partnership that is legally binding. It links together two kin groups — that of husband and wife — in an alliance in which both have an economic, political, and biological stake. The bringing together of two kin groups is usually marked by a transfer of property that serves to reinforce the marriage bond. The various forms of marriage exchange are described by Alice Schlegel in the first article of this part, "Status, Property, and the Value on Virginity." The American custom in which the bride's parents pay the wedding expenses is a form of *dowry*, which is the property that a woman brings to the marriage.

It is through marriage that kinship is ordered and redefined. Relatives by descent or "blood" are *consanguineal* kin; relatives by marriage are *affines*. Marriage links together in an affinal relationship two descent groups, which are organized around a network of consanguineal kin. The system for organizing descent groups varies from one society to the next, with a primary distinction between *unilineal* and *bilateral* forms of descent.

In a society with a *unilineal* kinship system, descent is reckoned either through females, as in *matrilineal* descent, or through males, as in *patrilineal* descent. If you were born into a matrilineal system, you would be considered a member of your mother's kin group and would have an altogether different relationship with your father's kin group. The term *matrilineal*, which refers to a system of reckoning descent, is often confused with *matriarchy*, a political system in which positions of power are reserved for women. Anthropologists have yet to discover a *matriarchal* society, though they have described a number of *matrilineal* societies.

In recent decades, as anthropologists have delved more deeply into the dynamics of kinship, they have discovered that societies can also be *matrifocal*, either in terms of their kinship system or in the organization of gender relations. Matrifocal kinship systems are those in which "the role of the mother is structurally, culturally, and affectively central" (Tanner 1974:131). Even patrilineal societies can be matrifocal in some respects, as in the example provided by David D. Gilmore in Part Four of this volume, "Men and Women in Southern Spain: 'Domestic Power' Revisited." Gilmore argues that women control both finances and gender relations within the domestic unit.

As Gilmore indicates, matrifocality may be the result of residence patterns after marriage. Residence with or near the wife's family is a *matrilocal* pattern; residence near the husband's family is *patrilocal*. When a couple establishes a new home independent of both families, the residence pattern is *neolocal*. In Gilmore's example, women consolidate their power by insisting on residing near their mothers.

The American residence pattern is *neolocal* and the system of descent is *bilateral*, which means that descent is reckoned through both male and female sides of the family. On the level of interpersonal relations, this means that you are considered to be equally related to your father's siblings and your mother's siblings. In American terminology, an uncle is an uncle whether he is related to you through your mother or your father.

Although the kinship system is structurally bilateral, Americans display certain biases for one side of the family or the other. As Colleen Leahy Johnson notes in the last article of this part, "In-law Relationships in the American Kinship System: The Impact of Divorce and Remarriage," there is a matrilateral bias in awarding custody of children after divorce. Americans also express a patrilateral bias in such customs as providing a child with a surname. Although no law exists to regulate the practice, a child is usually given its father's surname. This custom emphasizes the kin relationship—with all its rights and obligations—between a child and its father. For example, the father is legally bound to provide economic support for the child and, in return, may expect certain behaviors indicating obedience and respect. Identifying the child by its father's surname emphasizes the role of the child in continuing the father's descent group. This is sometimes referred to colloquially as "keeping the name alive."

The father-child relationship is established legally through the marriage of the father to the child's mother at the time of its birth. The marriage is in and of itself sufficient to establish the paternity of the child and to set up a reciprocal system of rights and obligations, including the child's right to use its father's name. This legal and social relationship is the basis for the concept of "legitimacy." When the parents are not married, other means are required to socially mark the father-child relationship.

Depending upon economic and political organization, the form of marriage varies from one society to another. In all cases, however, marriage establishes the social paternity of a woman's children. In other words, it legitimizes them. *Monogamy* is a marriage between one man and one woman. *Polygamy* is a system of multiple marriage that has two forms: *polygyny* and *polyandry*. Polygyny refers to the marriage of one man to more than one woman; polyandry is the marriage of one woman to more than one man.

One result of polygyny is that it reinforces the power of older males over younger ones. For example, in Papua New Guinea, males cannot gain status in society without a wife. Because of the practice of polygyny, however, older men with access to political and economic resources are better able to accumulate the *bridewealth* necessary to acquire a wife. A young man must have sponsorship of an older male to get the *bridewealth* to marry a first wife, or he must render *brideservice* in the form of labor for his future wife's family. Women care for yams and pigs, both a source of food and important ceremonial objects that ultimately can be exchanged for additional wives. As a man gains wives, he gains economic power and political influence through the establishment of kin networks. Women seek co-wives to ease the burden of caring for gardens and pigs, and because they can thereby gain allies to offset the power of the husband. Polygyny may also allow women to exert control over other women, through the greater status of the senior co-wife.

Where it occurs—primarily in Nepal, Tibet and Sri Lanka—polyandry appears to be related to the need to conserve land. For example, in mountainous Nepal, land is scarce and owned by patrilineages. Brothers marry a single wife, who produces the next generation of brothers. Tibetans living in northern Nepal say polyandry guards against dividing the land to support the different wives. If each had a wife, the Tibetans say, the wives would quarrel over which of their children should have more, and eventually this would force division of the land (Goldstein 1987).

These different forms of kinship and marriage—shaped in an economic and political context—are associated with differences in values assigned to the role of women in general and to specific attributes, such as virginity. In her article "Status, Property, and the Value on Virginity," Alice Schlegel notes that a virgin bride is not equally prized in all societies. She suggests that carefully guarding sexual access to an unmarried girl is a barrier to *hypergamy*, the practice of marrying one of a higher social class. Schlegel observes that a lower-status male can gain access to the resources of a higher-status kin group by seducing and impregnating a daughter of the family.

There may be other factors that make virginity desirable, such as ensuring biological succession in a patrilineal kin group. Though the visibility of pregnancy makes motherhood readily apparent, establishing biological fatherhood is more elusive. The case of the royal family of England is instructive in this regard. The emphasis on Diana's virginity at her marriage increased the likelihood that at least her first child — who, if male, would be the future king of England — would be fathered by Charles. By the time Charles' younger brother Andrew married Sarah Ferguson, Diana had already produced an heir, removing Andrew from direct succession to the throne. Therefore there was little interest in the state of Sarah Ferguson's hymen.

The second article of this part "Symbol and Meaning in Nayar Marriage Ritual," by Melinda A. Moore, illustrates the importance of a woman's fertility and sexuality in contributing to the prosperity and prestige of her kin group. Nayar are matrilineal and matrilocal, which means that a woman's children will be members of her own kin group and she and her children will continue to reside in the household of her family. Nayar make no effort to identify the biological father of her children, and the woman may take a number of sexual partners after she has undergone rituals that validate her status as an adult and potentially fertile woman. Yet, even though Nayar women do not need the economic support of males outside their kin group, they must still rely on a "husband" to "legitimize" or provide a social father for their children. Nayar make every effort to ensure that the woman's marriage alliances and sexual partners reflect creditably on the social standing of the lineage.

The third article of this part "Why Women take Men to Magistrate's Court," by Mindie Lazarus-Black, illustrates what happens when kin networks are replaced by state institutions in negotiating parental rights and obligations. Lazarus-Black notes that unmarried women of Antigua use child support laws to ensure that their children's fathers observe appropriate standards of responsibility and "respect" even when their relationships are not "legitimized" by a marriage contract.

In the last article of this part "In-law Relationships in the American Kinship System: The Impact of Divorce and Remarriage," Colleen Leahy Johnson examines the process of reordering kinship rights and obligations when the marriage contract is dissolved. In American families, where the emphasis is on the nuclear family, descent is still a major factor in the renegotiation of kinship relations. Johnson notes that grandmothers use a variety of strategies to retain access to their grandchildren in the aftermath of their children's divorces.

Americans place a great emphasis on the romantic aspects of marriage, while tending to ignore the position of the marrying couple within the larger network of kinship obligations. However, when the kin network is realigned—through marriage, the birth of a child, or divorce—the real significance of the descent group becomes apparent. When the fairy tale unravels, the network of social rights and obligations must be reordered.

# 9

# Status, Property, and the Value on Virginity

## Alice Schlegel

One way to assess a woman's autonomy is to ask whether she controls her own sexuality. Thus, the prohibition on premarital sex for females is often considered a measure of men's control over women's lives. There are certain difficulties with this assumption, however. First, the way a people feels about premarital sex is not necessarily consonant with its attitude toward extramarital sex, as many people allow premarital freedom but condemn adultery, while others, such as the South African Lovedu (Sacks 1979), insist on premarital virginity but turn a blind eye to discreet extramarital affairs.

Second, this assumption fails to recognize that in most societies, the value placed on virginity applies to adolescent girls, not to adult women. With few exceptions worldwide, girls are still physically adolescent when they marry, generally within three or four years after puberty. More important, young people are generally not social adults until they marry, so that the premarital female is socially an adolescent girl. Some societies, such as our own and that of 17th-century England (Stone 1977), for example, are exceptions to this, having a stage that I call "youth" intervening between adolescence and full adulthood. However, in most parts of the world the bride is a teenage girl who in most aspects of her life is still very much under the authority of her parents.[1]

If virginity is not, then, a very good measure of female subordination, we must look for other aspects of girls' and young women's lives that are associated with the proscription of premarital sex. One common notion is that virginity is valued when men have

Adapted from *American Ethnologist* 18:4, November 1991, by permission of the American Anthropological Association. Not for sale or further reproduction.

to "pay" for wives by transferring goods in the form of bridewealth to the women's families. This notion is based on the assumption that there is some innate preference for virgins which can be activated when men have the upper hand, so to speak, because they are paying for the bride. It must be noted, of course, that there is no universal preference for virgin brides. Such an assumption projects onto other cultures the attitudes that have developed historically in our own. Moreover, the belief that when men give bridewealth they pay for virgin brides is shaken when we read in Goody (1973:25) that dowry-giving societies, in which the bride's family pays, are generally intolerant of premarital sex for girls. Here the family pays to give, not to receive, a virgin bride.

There is a connection between marriage transactions—the movement of goods or services at the time of a marriage—and the value on virginity, but it is not obvious what that connection is. In this paper, I argue that the virginity of daughters protects the interests of brides' families when they use marital alliances to maintain or enhance their social status. To illuminate this issue, it is necessary to understand the varying effects that marriage transactions have on the transmission or retention of property and on the social debts thus incurred.

## Marriage Transactions[2]

The form of marriage transaction that has received the most attention in the anthropological literature is *bridewealth*, goods given by the groom, usually with the assistance of his kin, to the family of the bride. Bridewealth generally does not remain with the family that receives it: it or its equivalent is used to obtain wives for brothers of the bride or an additional wife for her father. Thus, goods and women circulate and countercirculate. In the large majority of bridewealth-giving societies, which are patrilocal, households end up with as many women as they have produced, by replacing daughters with daughters-in-law and sisters with wives.

*Women exchange* is also a form of replacement, the exchange being direct rather than mediated by a transfer of property. Women exchange and bridewealth are most frequently found where women have economic value through their large contribution to subsistence (cf. Schlegel and Barry 1986). In each case the result is a kind of social homeostasis, both among the families through which women and goods circulate and within the household that sooner or later gains a woman to replace each one it has lost.

*Brideservice* is often considered to be analogous to bridewealth, with payment in labor rather than goods. They differ significantly, however, in that the benefit of brideservice goes directly to the bride's household and is not circulated as are bridewealth goods. Thus, families with many daughters receive much free labor, while families with few get little.

While *gift exchange*, in which relatively equal amounts are exchanged between the families of the bride and groom, can occur at all levels of social complexity, it is often found in societies with important status differences in rank or wealth; it occurs most often in Asia, native North America, and the Pacific. Since residence is predominantly patrilocal in gift-exchanging societies, the bride-receiving household is socially, although not economically, in debt to the bride-giving one. The exchange of equivalent goods is a way of ensuring that the intermarrying families are of the same social status, as indicated by the wealth that they own or can call up from among their kin and dependents.

Status is a major consideration in *dowry*-giving societies. The bride's dowry is sometimes matched against the groom's settlement, thus ensuring equivalence, a usual practice among European land-owning peasants or elites. Dowry can also be used to "buy" a high-status son-in-law, a common practice in South Asia and one also known in Europe. Dowry or a bride's anticipated inheritance can be used to attract a poor but presentable groom, a client son-in-law whose allegiance will be primarily to the house into which he has married and on which he is dependent. This strategy seems to have been practiced by mercantile families in Europe and Latin America. Dowry was associated historically with the property-owning classes of the Old High Culture areas such as the Mediterranean (ancient Mesopotamia, Greece, and Rome) and Asia (India, China, and Japan), and was the common form throughout Europe until recently.

The final form of marriage transaction to be examined here is *indirect dowry*, which contains some features of both bridewealth, in that goods are given by the groom's family, and dowry, in that the goods end up with the new conjugal couple. Sometimes the groom's kin give goods directly to the bride, but more often they give goods to her father, who then gives goods to the new couple. The latter form has frequently been confused with bridewealth, as in the Islamic *mahr*. Indirect dowry tends to be found both on the fringes of and within the Old High Culture areas, such as Egypt, where it has been introduced along with conversion to Islam, replacing the simple dowry of earlier times. In its classic form, indirect dowry appears to be a way of establishing the property rights of the conjugal couples that make up larger households, in anticipation of eventual fission. In addition, it allows for status negotiation without either family being put in the other's economic or social debt.

There are variations within these major types, and there are additional features (such as the European dower[3]) that are secondary and limited in distribution. In complex societies, the form of transaction may vary according to region or class. In prerevolutionary China, for example, the landed or mercantile elite gave dowry while the landless peasantry gave indirect dowry. In modern China, marriage transactions have disappeared from urban areas, whereas bridewealth has replaced indirect dowry among peasants (Fang 1990).

## Why Value Virginity?

Since the burden of controlling a girl's sexuality through socialization or surveillance falls upon her family, it is instructive to consider what benefits are to be derived from preserving the virginity of daughters and sisters. Goody (1976) sees restrictiveness as a way of avoiding inappropriate marriages: by controlling a girl's sexuality, her family can better control her marriage choice, for the loss of virginity may "diminish a girl's honour and reduce her marriage chances" (Goody 1976:14). However, this presupposes that preserving virginity has some inherent value, whereas that value is precisely what needs to be explained.

I argue that virginity is valued in those societies in which young men may seek to better their chances in life by allying themselves through marriage to a wealthy or powerful family. In preserving a daughter's virginity, a family is protecting her from seduction, impregnation, and paternity claims on her child. This is most critical when certain kinds of property transactions are involved. In societies in which dowry is given (or daughters inherit), it would be attractive to seduce a dowered daughter (or heiress), demanding her as wife along with her property. Her parents would be reluctant to refuse, since the well-being of their grandchildren would depend upon their inheritance from both of their parents, and another man would be unlikely to marry the mother if it meant that he had not only to support her children but also to make them his heirs. (The widow with children would be a different matter, since these children would have received property through their father and would make no claims on their stepfather beyond support, for which their labor would provide compensation.)

To illustrate that upward mobility through marriage with a dowered daughter or heiress is known in dowry-giving societies, let us consider a common theme of European fairy tales. A poor but honest young man goes through trials to win the hand of the princess, who inherits her father's kingdom. Or, he wins her heart, and through the good offices of a fairy godmother or other spirit helper, they evade her wrathful father and are eventually reconciled with him. This more or less legitimate means to upward mobility is not so different from the illegitimate one, by which he wins the girl through seduction.

This line of reasoning was familiar to the seventeenth- and eighteenth-century English, as Trumbach tells it:

> Stealing a son . . . was not the great crime. It was, rather, the theft of a daughter that was the real nightmare. For a woman's property became her husband's and she took his social standing. . . . To steal an heiress was therefore the quickest way to make a man's fortune — this was the common doctrine of the stage before 1710 — and it had a special appeal to younger sons (1978:101-102).

As the following table shows, the value on virginity is statistically associated with the type of economic exchange linked to the marriage transaction.

All of the dowry-giving societies in the sample value virginity except the Haitians. Nevertheless, as Herskovits, writing about Haiti, points out: "Even though pre-marital relations are commonplace, . . . the pregnancy of an unmarried girl is regarded as both reprehensible and unfortunate, and she is severely beaten for it by her family " (1971:111). Their fear of her seduction is well founded, for if they disapprove of a suitor and reject him, the young man "uses all persuasion to give her a child and, this achieved, abandons her to show his contempt for the family that has formally refused to accept him as a son-in-law" (Herskovits 1971:110). To avoid childbearing, women and girls resort to magical means of contraception and the more effective abortion.

The majority of societies that exchange gifts and give indirect

## Correlations of value on virginity
## with type of marriage transaction[1]

**Marriage transaction**

| Virginity valued | None | Bride-wealth[2] | Bride-service | Gift exchange | Dowry and indirect dowry | Total |
|---|---|---|---|---|---|---|
| Yes | 3 | 16 | 6 | 9 | 18 | 52 |
| No | 26 | 27 | 10 | 3 | 7 | 73 |

N = 125; Chi-square = 27.13; p <.0001

[1] Information on attitudes toward premarital sex for females comes primarily from the code "Attitude Toward Premarital Sex (Female)" in Broude and Greene (1980), which is based on the Standard Sample of 186 preindustrial societies. I have altered the code established by Broude and Greene for four societies based on the ethnographic literature. The second source is a body of data collected by Herbert Barry and me on adolescent socialization in Standard Sample societies not coded by Broude and Greene.
[2] Includes token bridewealth.

dowry also expect brides to be virgins. This is particularly true in the case of gift exchange, in which a bride's family gives quantities of property along with her, receiving a more or less equivalent amount from the family of the groom. As noted earlier, gift exchange is a way of ensuring that the two families are of equal wealth or of equal social power. Impregnating a girl would give a boy and his family a claim on that girl and an alliance with her family, even though they would have to come up with something themselves for the exchange (not necessarily equivalent to what a more appropriate suitor would give; see the case of the Omaha, discussed below). As in dowry-giving societies, an emphasis on virginity discourages a man who is tempted to jump the status barrier by claiming fatherhood of a woman's child. The sample does, however, include three exceptions to the general requirement of virginity in gift-exchanging societies, and it is instructive to examine these deviant cases.

Malinowski (1932) has discussed at some length the sexual freedom of girls in the Trobriand Islands in Melanesia. However, we must recall that the Trobriand Islanders do not, at least ideologically, associate sexual intercourse with pregnancy. Weiner (1976:122) relates two cases in which pregnancy was attributed to magic, and her informants maintained that women could conceive without male assistance. No boy, then, can make a claim on a girl simply because he has been sleeping with her and she has become pregnant. Fatherhood can only be attained after marriage, when it is socially defined.

Among the Omaha Indians of the Great Plains, virginity was not considered important for most girls (as coded in Broude and Greene [1980]), but according to Fletcher and LaFlesche (1911), virgins were held in greater esteem than those who had lost their virginity. It was a special privilege to marry a girl who had been tattooed with the "mark of honor," which was given to a virgin of a prominent family on the occasion of her father's or another close relative's initiation into one of the ceremonial societies. Only the marriages in prominent families involved significant gift exchange. In ordinary marriages, the young husband was expected to work a year or two for his father-in-law, making brideservice a more common feature than gift exchange. Thus, it was in the important marriages, accompanied by the exchange of goods of much value, that the bride was expected to be a virgin. Omaha elite families faced the danger that a daughter might be seduced by a youth who would persuade her to elope. As long as his family recognized the marriage and brought some gifts to the bride's father, the marriage was legitimate in the eyes of the community. Maintaining the virginity of high-status girls protected their families from unwanted alliances.

In the Polynesian islands of Samoa, similarly, girls from untitled families had sexual freedom (as coded in Broude and Greene [1980]) but the daughters of titled chiefs did not. Samoa had an ambilineal descent system, in that children could be affiliated either to the mother's or the father's group. If the mother's rank was higher than the father's, the children's status would be elevated above their father's. High-status families would wish to guard their daughters against potential social climbers, who might be tempted to improve their children's position in life by seducing and marrying socially superior girls. It appears that only the arranged marriages, generally of high-status people, involved much gift exchange. Most marriages were of the "elopement" type and were much less expensive than the arranged ones (Shore 1981). Thus, as in the case of the Omaha, intracultural comparison demonstrates a correlation between the type of marriage transaction and the value on virginity.

It is clear that when no property accompanies the marriage, virginity is of little interest. If the groom gives goods or labor, the picture is mixed, but fewer societies are restrictive than permissive. In societies in which the bride's side gives considerable property, as with gift exchange, dowry, and, in many cases, indirect dowry, virginity is most likely to be valued. Thus, there is an association between the giving of property, particularly from the bride's side, and control of the girl's sexuality. I have interpreted this as a means by which the families of girls prevent their being seduced by ineligible boys, resulting in alliances that could be an embarrassment. This is particularly the case when status negotiation is a prominent feature of marital alliances, in those societies in which families use the marriages of their daughters to maintain or enhance their social position. Such considerations are likely to be found only in rank or class societies.

## Virginity and Fatherhood

The question of the value on virginity revolves around two issues: whether premarital sexual intercourse leads to pregnancy, and whether biological fatherhood alone gives a man a claim on a child and its mother. There should be less concern over virginity when sexual intercourse is not likely to lead to pregnancy than when it is. Safe, socially condoned abortion is a reliable way of preventing unwanted births, and virginity is not such an issue if abortion is freely available, as it has been in Southeast Asia since at least the sixteenth century. Even there, however, the elite have secluded their daughters, possibly in imitation of the Hindu, Buddhist, or Moslem aristocrats whom they have emulated in other ways (cf. Reid 1988:163).

Although abortive techniques are widely known and practiced, even where proscribed (Devereux 1976), there is little evidence to indicate the extent to which illicit abortions are available to unmarried girls. Desperate girls, with the help of their mothers, surely must resort to them, as anecdotal information indicates; but whether or not they are successful, and whether or not the girls can keep them secret, are open to question. Illicit abortion is a last-ditch measure for preventing unwanted births and must take a distant second place to the maintenance of virginity.

Impregnating a girl does not automatically give a boy or man a claim to her child or to her. In the Trobriand Islands, as we have seen, biological fatherhood alone is simply not recognized. In other places, it may be recognized without giving the impregnator a paternity claim. Such a claim may have to be paid for either directly or indirectly through bridewealth and marriage to the mother; if it is not, the child is absorbed into the mother's kin group. This practice appears to be more common in Africa than in other regions, although the question requires a study in its own right. I suggest that the acceptance of illegitimate children is greater when children are a distinct economic asset. They are likely to be so in underpopulated areas, such as are found throughout much of Africa (Kopytoff 1987). In such places, the availability of labor rather than of land is the major constraint on the economic success and expansion of the productive unit, the family and the kin group, and illegitimate origins do not detract from the potential labor value of a child. A similar explanation may hold for some European peasantries.

Where land is in short supply in preindustrial societies and family resources consist of private property, heirship is a central concern. A bastard is less likely to be welcomed, since it is totally dependent on the mother's family and does not draw in resources from the father. Bastards may be better received when the father is of much higher status than the mother — when he is, for example, a king or the noble impregnator of a peasant girl. In such cases, so long as paternity is acknowledged, the child provides a left-handed link to wealth and power, one that otherwise would be beyond the reach of the mother's family.

If children are not an unqualified asset to the mother's family, the rules of social life are likely to include the prescription that fathers take responsibility for their children, thus bringing biological and social fatherhood closer together. The responsibility for one's child can be restated as the right to that child, and biological fatherhood becomes a claim on social fatherhood. When the status of the mother is equal to or lower than that of the impregnator, it is to her advantage to use the rule of responsibility to press for marriage or at least support, so long as the impregnator is willing (or is unable to escape). Turning this on its head, when the mother is of greater wealth or higher status, particularly when her status or property will be inherited by her child, it is to the advantage of the impregnator to use the rule of responsibility to press *his* claim on the child and its mother. It is in precisely such situations, I propose, that virginity is valued, as it is the surest way of preventing such claims.

This is not to deny that virginity may acquire secondary meanings. In its extreme form, a value on virginity can lead to a value on chastity so great that widows are discouraged from remarriage. Such was the case in India for the higher castes (Ullrich 1977), throughout prerevolutionary China (Chiao 1971), and in early Christian Europe (Verdon 1988). In such places celibacy comes to be seen as a spiritually higher state than married sexuality. In this form, the ideal of virginity has been incorporated into some religions and has been diffused along with conversion.

While the eighteenth-century English, living at a time of expanding wealth and social mobility, were aware of the social advantage of seducing an heiress and spoke freely about it, it is improbable that most peoples would give this as the reason for keeping their daughters virginal. In Eurasia, at any rate, one is much more likely to get explanations involving purity and the shame that follows its loss. We weave significance around the hard facts of existence, and virginity, a practical concern, can be a sign of spiritual purity when the invasion of the body implies the invasion of the spirit or when the seduction of female kin comes to symbolize the violability of the lineage.

The idealization of virginity is most common in Eurasia, and it is found in some other areas, such as Polynesia or native North America, where certain categories of girls are expected to be virginal. It is noteworthy that belief in the purity or spiritual power of virginity, chastity, and celibacy developed in those regions where dowry or gift-exchange was the established form or the form practiced by the elite and aspired to by those who would imitate them. Ideology does not arise *de novo* but is grounded in existential concerns and issues. I suggest that the ideology of virginity has its source in pragmatic concerns about status maintenance and improvement.

As a practical matter, ensuring that daughters and sisters remain virginal puts a heavy burden of surveillance on parents and brothers. The effort required is worthwhile when the stakes are high, as when considerable property and status are involved, or the secondary meanings of virginity are such that the purity of the girl and thus the honor of her family are at issue. In many parts of the Mediterranean world, control over female sexuality is a lived metaphor for control over social relations. The transgressing girl is defying her male kin and giving away what only they have the right to bestow (cf. Schneider 1971).

Elsewhere, particularly among poorer people in societies that value virginity, the daughter's choice of husband is of minor consequence. Thus, there is no point in restricting her. Even when virginity is generally accorded a high value, it may be an ideal to which only a minority aspire. Recognizing this makes it easier to reconcile the seeming contradiction between the high value placed on virginity and the high rate of bastardy at various times and places throughout European history.

## Implications of the Proposition

Regarding a value on virginity as a way of forestalling male social climbing through seduction causes us to take a fresh look at the interest, in some places, in seducing virgins and the self-congratulation or acclaim by peers that accompanies the successful boy or man in this pursuit. It has nothing to do with sexual pleasure, for the experienced girl or woman is a more satisfying sexual partner than the virgin. What, then, is the point?

First, of course, is the thrill of the forbidden. However, seducing a virgin can be as much of a coup in sexually permissive societies like Samoa as it is in the restrictive ones. In a discussion of adolescent sexuality in the Trobriand Islands, Weiner (1988:71) has pointed out that attracting lovers is not a frivolous pastime but rather "the first step toward entering the adult world of strategies, where the line between influencing others while not allowing others to gain control of oneself must be carefully learned." If the game of seduction is serious business, then how much more is this true when seduction can lead to status improvement. We can understand the Cinderella story and its variants as a tale of upward mobility for women through sexual attraction—but what about upwardly mobile men?

Winning the heart of a high-status woman as a path to a better life may be a male fantasy in all societies that are divided by rank or class, or at least those in which men will not be killed or severely punished for the attempt. Boys and youths have nothing to lose and much to gain if they can make a paternity claim on the child of a high-status girl. In such a setting, where only a few can succeed, all boys will be tempted to refine their skills with virgins of their own rank while hoping for their big chance with a *taupou* (the Samoan "village princess") or her equivalent.

It is well recognized that women use their sexual attractiveness to try to improve their position through a socially advantageous marriage or liaison, when such possibilities are open to them. (The seclusion of girls not only protects daughters against seduction but also protects sons against inconvenient romantic attachments, thus reinforcing parental control over the marriages of children of both sexes.) It should not surprise us that men and boys do the same if the opportunity arises. When sexual success can be translated into social success, it is predictable that men and boys will make themselves attractive to women and that sexual exploits will become a major topic of discussion, teasing, and boasting. In such cases, male competitiveness is channeled into overt sexual competition. The man who seduces a dowered virgin has his fortune made.

## Conclusion

The trend in the modern world follows the pattern established for the preindustrial societies in the sample. With readily available contraception and abortion, extramarital sexual relations do not have to result in pregnancy or illegitimate birth. Even if a paternity claim is pressed, there is no obligation in our individual-centered society to honor it, as economic opportunities for women as well as welfare payments by the state make it possible to support a child without a husband.

Equally important, the dowry has lapsed in most European and European-derived cultures. Parental investment in daughters is increasingly in the form of education, not dowry. Furthermore, the daughter's choice of a husband does not have the significance for the family today that it did in earlier times. For most people in the industrial world, there is little in the way of a family estate to preserve. Even among the rich, a rebellious daughter and her husband can be cut out of the will, since in modern societies the disposal of assets is up to the individual with legal ownership of them. Thus, a daughter's choice of a husband is not critical to the well-being of the family and the maintenance of its assets.

Most commentators on the "sexual revolution" point to the availability of new contraception and abortion technology as the deciding factor in the changing of our sexual habits. But contraception and abortion have a long history in civilization; techniques to reduce fertility have been known and used in Europe and elsewhere for centuries, albeit clandestinely. Technology alone, without significant changes in social relations, is not enough to alter such deep-seated cultural values as the value on virginity. As marriage transactions disappear and social status is gained more through achievement than through the family into which one is born or marries, parental control over marriage declines and disappears. The choice of a son-in-law is no longer a central concern, and the virginity of daughters loses its salience.

# 10

# Symbol and Meaning in Nayar Marriage Ritual

*Melinda A. Moore*

Few societies have succeeded in capturing the anthropological imagination as much as the Nayar caste of Kerala in southwestern India. Not only did the Nayar practice an extreme form of matrilineality, but their marriage practices have challenged anthropological definitions of marriage (Gough 1959). Nayar marriage involved two ceremonies (the *talikettukalyanam* and *sambandham* rite), rather than one. Both, often involving different men, legitimize a woman's children.

In its older form, the Nayar marriage system is no longer practiced. This study relies on ethnographic interviews conducted in central Kerala during 1978–1980, and during 1975 in southern Kerala. It also makes use of written sources, including indigenous fiction, memoirs, folklore, family histories, and court records, as well as accounts of ethnographers and explorers. It is recognized that the rituals varied a great deal, especially along the lines of region, wealth, status, subcaste and (in alliances involving non-Nayars) caste.

Nayar were organized into property-holding groups, segments of a matrilineage composed of a group of brothers and sisters, together with the children of the sisters and their daughters' children. This group lived in one house and was under the legal guardianship of the oldest male (*karanavan*) of the group. Both the property-holding group and the lineage were called *taravad*. Nayars were members of the warrior or *Kshatriya* caste, the second highest caste of Indian society. Nayar men trained as professional soldiers, often serving in the armies of chieftains of the Brahmin or priestly caste.

Adapted from *American Ethnologist* 15:2, May 1988, by permission of the American Anthropological Association. Not for sale or further reproduction.

# The *Talikettukalyanam* or *Tali*-tying Rite

The *talikettukalyanam or tali*-tying ceremony was performed before a girl had begun menstruation. The ceremony lasted four days and included all prepubertal girls of the *taravad* between the ages of seven and twelve. On the first day, the girls sat on white sheets on the *tara*, a floor area around the central courtyard of the house. Each girl was paired with a selected young unmarried man of appropriate caste and lineage. At an auspicious time decided by astrologers, the groom tied the gold ornament or *tali* around the neck of the girl. The couples continued to sit on the *tara* all day.

During the night, the boys and girls were separated, but they stayed in one house. Each morning they returned to the *tara*, sat all day, and were separated at night. On the fourth day, the couples, who had not bathed for four days, led a procession of guests to a water tank for a ritual bath. Ideally, they returned to the house riding on elephants. After they returned, there was a ceremony in which the senior member of the girl's family cut a cloth into two pieces, then gave one piece to the boy and one to the girl. This severed their relationship.

The ritual acts comprising the *talikettukalyanam* center around three main symbolic themes. The first of these is female fertility and auspicious marriedness exemplified by the concept of *mangalyam*, for which the *tali* (a gold neck ornament) itself stands. The second is the connection of the girl and her *taravad* with the goddess Bhagavati. The third is the prestige, and place in society, of her *taravad*.

### The Tali, *Female Auspiciousness, and the Married State.*
The *tali* itself is regarded by Nayar as a sign of the state of auspicious marriedness called *mangalyam*. Wearing the *tali* makes a girl a woman. Many objects used in the *tali* rite represent fertility and the related concept of prosperity, but some of these are not unique to this ritual. For example, paddy [grain] and rice placed near a lighted brass lamp symbolize the prosperity of the household, but their significance is not specifically associated with the *tali* rite, since this set of objects is set out at nearly every ritual occasion in the household. On the other hand, coconut flowers are included among these objects only for marriage-like rituals, such as the *tali* rite and the *sambandham* rite, as well as the modern Nayar marriage rite.

The tray of eight auspicious objects called *ashtamangalyam* is especially prominent in the *tali* rite, but it is used in some variants of the *sambandham* rite. Taken as a whole, the *ashtamangalyam* represents fortune and well-being, and is etymologically related to *mangalyam*, the state of auspicious marriedness signified by the *tali*. Taken separately, the items can be divided into the groups of (1) objects used by a married woman for personal adornment (a woman's loin-cloth, a rouge-box, a mirror); (2) items representing household prosperity (rice, paddy, and a lit wick); and (3) items connected with sexuality and fertility (an arrow, the "tool" of the god of love Kamadevan, a coconut flower). The *ashtamangalyam* is also associated with another occasion of "beginning": the New Years Day, which marks the start of the agricultural calendar.

One act particular to the *tali* rite is the girl's worship of the sun. Although the associations of this act are unclear, it may relate to women's role in showing the household lamp to the sun daily at dawn and dusk, an act which is supposed to bring household prosperity. Also unique to the *tali* ceremony is carrying a jasmine branch in procession. In the aristocratic Nayar ceremony described by Anantha Krishna Iyer, this proceeds as follows:

> a cutting of the jasmine placed in a brass vessel is carried by the Elayad or family priest, who, mounted on an elephant with it, and accompanied by a grand procession with the beating of drums, a display of fire-works, and the joyous shouts of men and women, goes to the nearest Bhagavati or other temple, where the plant and the *tali* (marriage badge) placed in a vessel are consecrated by the performance of a *puja*[4] by the temple priest. The party then return home with it (1912, 11:24).

The jasmine branch is carried to the platform where the girl has worshipped the sun, the setting of "some minor ceremonies, consisting of women young and old dancing or playing beneath a bunch made of ears of corn held in their hands over their heads" (Panikkar 1900:137-138). Such sheaves of paddy are powerful symbols of household prosperity. Old, dry ones are often kept hanging in the house, left over from the rite that begins the harvest.

Bringing jasmine to a house is an important aspect of marriage ritual for Nambutiris, members of the Brahmin caste to whom some Nayar owed allegiance. Nambutiris maintained a permanent pedestal for jasmine plants (*mullattara*) in the central courtyard of their house, and these provided a focus for certain aspects of the marriage ceremony:

> The bride first makes three clockwise circumambulations
> around the *mullattara*. A *nilavilakku˘* (brass lamp), an
> *ashtamangalyam*, and a *nirapara* (full measure of grain) are
> placed in the *nadumittam* [courtyard] which is decorated with
> flour made from rice paste. After making the circumambula-
> tions, she will take a handful of rice and place it in the
> *mullattara*. The rice used for this must be brought from her old
> house. This ritual action, called *samarppanam*, is symbolic of
> her becoming a member of the new house and bringing
> prosperity; it has the meaning of "you throw your heart on that
> as a kind of dedication."
>
> Following this, the bride places a jasmine branch, brought from
> her own house, into the *mullattara*. This will grow into a new
> plant. Jasmine is always associated with marriage and therefore
> it is particularly fitting that the bride should plant a jasmine in
> her husband's house.

In this Nambutiri rite, as in all the Nayar rites using jasmine,
objects standing for women and their state of married auspiciousness are combined with those standing for a house and its well-
being. Just as rice is connected with household prosperity, the
jasmine is connected with the condition of having a husband alive
(*mangalyam*)—it is used to decorate the hair of Nambutiri women
who are not widows.

The contrast with the Nayar situation is also instructive. Nayars
do not keep such jasmine pedestals in their houses, nor do they
transfer women to different houses at marriage. Nayar women
remain in the household of their *taravad* after marriage, and their
children are raised as members of the matrilineage. A woman visits
her husband's house only after *sambandham* and is greeted by a
ritual different from the Nambutiri one—she sits in or near the
courtyard and is fed sweets by the groom's female relatives. This
act fits with the limited rights a Nayar wife, as opposed to a
Nambutiri one, acquires through marriage. Nayar women do,
however, deck their hair with jasmine, which they associate with
marriage, and are never prevented from doing so by widowhood.
In the Nayar *tali* rite the jasmine, instead of being brought from
a sacred area in the bride's own house, as among the Nambutiris,
is taken to or from some other sacred place along with the *tali* and,
when brought back, both are set alongside the girl during her three-
day vigil in an inner room. Eventually the jasmine is discarded
during her bath. Just as the jasmine is not transferred to the home
of the groom, the girl's sexual and reproductive powers are retained
by her own household.

**Bhagavati and the Tali Rite.** Bhagavati is the member of the Hindu pantheon most associated with the *tali* rite. This association takes several forms. The *tali* may be carried to Bhagavati's temple and set before her, along with the pot of water and jasmine mentioned above or with a piece of red silk cloth, as an informant told me, to "get her blessing." Alternatively, ritual acts may be performed "to bring Bhagavadi to the *taravad* and set up a temple in the house," where she is given offerings and allowed to express her satisfaction through oracles (Gough 1955:49ff.). The girl is continually brought into association with objects representing the goddess, such as the plank of the milk-exuding tree on which she sits during the *tali*-tying. There is also a picture of the goddess on the floor of the marriage shed.

Although by no means the only deity associated with the Nayar *taravad*, Bhagavati was certainly the most common. If only one permanently installed deity was present in the *taravad* house or a temple near it, it was likely to be Bhagavati. Particular manifestations of the goddess were associated with particular *taravads*. Bhagavati was also associated with the Nayars' hereditary occupation of warrior. A representation of the goddess would be installed in the building for martial arts training where Nayar male initiation rites were held. Household prosperity is linked to the presence of the goddess Śri, who is equated with Lakshmi and Bhagavati.

The association of girls with Bhagavati during the *tali* rite links them to household prosperity. In older times it might also have implied connection with the source of their sons' martial ability. Indeed, it is tempting to see the girls as actually embodying Bhagavati, becoming this goddess in the household. There is at least some evidence that the girl was treated as a goddess during the *tali* rite itself. In one version of the rite, the girl is taken on the first day of the rite to a temple and given a ceremonial ablution like that offered to an installed image of a deity. On being taken home, she is seated in an inner room of her house, the *maccu*; a room on the western side which is associated with objects of worship. There she is made to sit in a manner reminiscent of installed deities:

> The girl sits on a piece of pala (*Alstonia scholaris*) wood, which is called a mana. She is elaborately adorned . . . . In her right hand she holds a valkannadi (brass hand mirror, and in her left a charakkal (a highly ornate arrow). In front of the girl are placed, in addition to the five-wicked lamp and nirachaveppu, a metal

dish or talam of parched rice, and the eight lucky things known
as ashtamangalyam. A woman, termed Brahmini or Pushpini,
usually of the Nambissan caste, sits facing her on a three-legged
stool (pidam), and renders appropriate and lengthy songs, at the
close of which she scatters rice over her (Thurston 1909, V:317).

These songs wish the girl longevity ("years as numerous as rice
counted"), children, and possession of a husband, comparing such
a state to the bliss of gods and goddesses paired in mystic union:
"as they [Rama and Sita] lived there happily as husband and wife,
so let these live here long in the enjoyment of happiness" (Report
of the Malabar Marriage Commission 1894:25ff.). We are reminded
of the Nambutiri ceremony, with its worship-like treatment of the
new bride, who will be like a goddess to her husband's house by
bringing it wealth, children, and her husband's longevity. It is
tempting to regard the *tali*-rite as the Nayar equivalent, which
equates the girl's relationship to her natal house to that of the
Nambutiri bride's to her husband's house. That is, she will bring
it prosperity and children, having been put into a state of
marriedness that lasts, as far as her *taravad* is concerned, for the
entirety of her life. The role of the goddess Bhagavati in the *tali*
rite suggests an association of girls with household well-being, a theme
also central to the *tali* itself.

**The Tali Rite and Taravad Prestige.** A third complex of
symbols in the *tali* rite is concerned not so much with women and
their transformation as with *taravads* and their place in society.
The ritual seems to have required all the ostentation a *taravad*
could afford. To celebrate it simply, as when a girl's mother tied
her *tali* before an idol, was to admit poverty, whereas even wealthy
*taravads* could make a simple affair of the sambandham rite. We
should take seriously the statements of those who one hundred
years ago testified before the Malabar Marriage Commission that
the *tali* rite "meant" little more than an occasion for spending
wealth for display to the point of ruin (Report of the Malabar
Marriage Commission 1894:27-30; Thurston 1909, V:326). On the
other hand, very wealthy *taravads* might allow the sambandham
to be hastily arranged and simply celebrated should a fortuitous
match appear.

The special emphasis of the *tali* rite on displaying a *taravad*'s
wealth and prerogatives is paralleled by an emphasis on the
reaffirmation of its social connections. The feasting associated with

it extended to the *taravad*'s whole social universe, including villagers and servant castes. Permission to perform the rite had in many cases to be granted by a hierarchy of overlords, who in some cases had themselves the prerogative of *tali*-tying or even defloration (Gough 1955:51-52). A *taravad*'s relation to its *tali*-tiers was relatively permanent, and when new *tali*-tiers were acquired this was usually accompanied by events of political significance. In this respect it is useful to contrast the term for "affines" by the *tali* rite (*inangar*) with that for "affines" by *sambandham* (*bandhukkal*). While the former were regarded as linked to the *taravad* permanently, having obligations in many contexts, the latter were seen as connected through relationships between particular men and women, and would break off should these do so.

## The *Sambandham* Rite

The *sambandham* rite marks the beginning of a sexual union between a woman and a man, who need not be the *tali*-tier. Like the *tali*-tying rites, the *sambandham* rite has many variants but, in addition, *sambandham* variants are known by a number of names. My informants thought "*sambandham*" itself to be a rather "impolite" term, citing *pudavakoda* and *pudamuri* as examples of "better usage." The latter two words refer to cloth (*puda, pudava*), meaning respectively "cloth-giving" and "cloth-cutting"; *sambandham* literally means "joining together." A major distinction is made between variants that involve gifts of cloth from groom to bride and those that do not.

Unlike the other two rites, those grouped under the heading of *sambandham* necessarily imply sexual intercourse. One is tempted to regard this as a defining feature around which the ritual centers, but *sambandham* prestations can be used to legitimize a woman's child regardless of whether the man who gives them is its genitor or even the woman's lover. The prestations do, however, make heavy reference to eroticism.

Sexuality also plays a role in two key orientations by which the *sambandham* differs from the *tali* rite. The first of these has to do with the point of view of the groom, and the second with a contrast in the way each rite — like the union it establishes — brings prestige to the girl's *taravad*.

Whether a man has tied any girl's *tali* seems to be a matter of indifference as far as his biography is concerned. *Sambandham*, on the other hand, has relevance for men as both a rite of passage and a definer of character. The number of *sambandham* relationships a man establishes provides him with a reputation; an example is the legendary hero Taccoli Otenan, notorious for his sexual as well as military exploits (e.g. Mathew 1979:63-64).

Certain symbolic acts in the *sambandham* rite focus on the groom. He must get an elaborate set of blessings from elders — those of his own *taravad*, father's *taravad*, and other *taravads* related by marriage — to whom he gives betel and from whom he receives cloths for the bride. Puthenkalam (1977:97-98) describes in addition a ritual shaving in front of a *niracca veppu*[ritual display of paddy, rice, and a lighted lamp], after which the groom bathed and "sat in padinyatta (western room) where the assembled elders sprinkled rice and blessed him." One is reminded of a similar treatment of the bride, seated in the same western part of her house, in the *tali* rite. The groom continues his ritually active role at the bride's house as well, where he gives betel and cakes to the members of his party directly after presenting the bride with cloth (Thurston 1909, V:331). These examples show the concern in the *sambandham* rite with the groom's ritual state and social connections, in contrast to the *tali* rite, where the groom merely serves to effect ritual changes in the bride.

The role of the groom also relates to a key difference in the way the *sambandham*, as opposed to the *tali* rite, enhances the prestige of the girl's *taravad*. While the relationship of a *taravad* to its *tali*-tiers was relatively fixed, there was often a fortuitous and fluid quality about its *sambandham* relationships. Stories abound of women who attracted a partner by her beauty, when glimpsed at a temple or bathing tank. Such partners were often of higher rank than any with whom the *taravad* could aspire to establish a connection, even given hypergamy or marrying up. *Sambandham* matches could also break up, not only because of disagreements between partners, but because *karanavans* [*taravad* head] forced them to break up to accommodate a high-ranking man's desire for exclusive possession of a woman.

Where *sambandham* did not result from such fortuitous sexual attraction, great care was taken that the parties be suitably matched. The emphasis in many accounts of the *sambandham* rite on matching horoscopes, and on preliminary visiting between houses, seems to contrast with the emphasis in other accounts on relationships contracted quickly and without much ritual — with a visiting stranger, for example. Yet there is a common theme here:

both views of *sambandham* show its concern with establishing a relationship between a *taravad* and an outsider — a groom and his relatives who were not necessarily connected to it in any previously established way. These became a *taravad's bandhukkal*, connections by *sambandham*, a category in contrast to its *inangar*, with whom it had permanent links and from whom *tali*-tiers were drawn. In accord with this emphasis on the establishment of new connections, the *sambandham* rite has as its dominant theme the notions of (1) hospitality and (2) relations of support and dependency that cut across *taravad* boundaries. While the former is symbolized especially by exchanges of betel and areca nut and light food, on reciprocal visits the latter is symbolized by prestations of items for personal use (for example, oil for the bride's hair) and, above all, by gifts of cloth.

These dual themes are seen in the first ritual acts of the *sambandham*, the preliminary arrangements. The groom's elders (*karanavan* or father) initiate the match (if it is not one the groom himself initiates); they consult the bride's people to ask their consent, both sides consult astrologers and, finally, a party from the groom's house visits the bride's for the purpose of fixing the marriage by a formal statement of intention and date. The party is entertained with betel and sweetmeats. In some variants, the groom's party gives money for the wedding expenses or even cloth at this time; in others he receives either of these. After this may occur the groom's visits to relatives described above, during which he gives betel and receives cloths for the bride.

On the appointed day, the groom goes to the bride's house with an entourage of persons of specified caste and relationship, as many as fifty male elders. Puthenkalam (1977:98) describes an entourage which includes an oil monger who carries the bundle of betel leaves; a Nayar washerman who carries the cloths which the groom will present, and a weaver who carries a lighted lamp. There is also a group of the groom's *inangar*. Women — as well as the groom's father, mother's brother, or brothers — are not included. The party usually stops to rest at a house near the bride's, where it is met by a party from the bride's house and conducted there ceremoniously. The groom is greeted at the gate, as in the *tali* rite, by women carrying lamps and auspicious objects, and by a ceremonial foot-washing. In one account, the groom's party is feasted by the bride's house, and members of the two *taravads* exchange gifts (Panikkar 1900:26-27).

The next act is the presentation of gifts to Brahmins. In some accounts this is done by the bride, in some by the groom, and in some accounts by both. Such gift-giving to persons outside the groom's and bride's *taravads* calls for interpretation. In one sense, it bears comparison to North Indian practice, in which "the gift" is a means of removing sin or inauspiciousness. The *sambandham* rite, as an occasion where a couple are about to unite sexually to produce a child, would seem an appropriate time for removing negativity.

Secondly, a comparison can be made with the *tali* rite. Some variants of the *tali* rite involve gifts by the bride's *taravad* to Brahmins; in many cases the groom was presented with a money gift. Whether or not the latter occurred seems to have depended on caste. If the *tali*-tier and the bride were of the same caste, their horoscopes were compared but no fee was paid; if the groom were higher, he received the fee but no horoscopes were examined.

In any case, the *sambandham* rite differs from the *tali* rite in that both groom and bride, not just the latter, are expected to give gifts. Gifts to Brahmins are only the beginning. The single most characteristic act of the *sambandham* rite is a gift—the presentation of cloth by groom to bride. It alone, with no other ritual acts, is sufficient to constitute the union. Although it was not necessary—unions could be constituted without it—it was nevertheless regarded as "typical" of the *sambandham*.

Cloth-giving is the symbol par excellence of the theme of support/dependency. Informants say that cloth-giving means "the groom will support the bride." The theme is further elaborated by comparison with the other major context where Nayars give cloth in the exact ritual manner of the *sambandham* (folded, on a platter, with certain prescribed gestures): at the harvest festival of Onam. This gift, called *onapudava*, was given by a *karanavan* to the junior members of his *taravad*. In modern households it is given by the father or other eldest male to juniors. Household servants also receive such an Onam cloth. Artisans and tenants do so as well, but are expected to present a counterprestation. In all of these cases, it is a relationship of dependency that is asserted. The analogy between cloth-giving at *sambandham* and Onam is made very apparent in my South Malabar village area, where the term *onapudava* is used for the cloth given at marriage—in both the modern ceremony and the remembered *sambandham*.

This theme of dependency and support is continued in another set of events, unique to *sambandham*, that occur after the cloth has been given: (1) taking the bride to the groom's house and (2) gifts from groom's house to bride's house by which the *sambandham* is maintained.

In every *sambandham*, whether cloth is given or not, the groom's right to enter the bride's house, perhaps on a regular basis, is established. By contrast, establishing the equivalent right for the bride may require the gift of cloth. Quoting Chanthu Menon, Thurston (1909, V:332) notes that, where the *sambandham* relationship is established without cloth-giving, this may take place years later, when children of the couple are grown, so that the husband may take his wife to his house.

Taking the bride to the groom's house was common, even outside North Malabar, where it was customary for her to reside there until divorce or the husband's death. In my village area in South Malabar, Nayar brides would be taken even to the houses of Nambutiri husbands, staying from a few days to several months. Even in the most matrilineal regions, wives of *karanavans* would take up permanent residence in their husband's houses.

Among Nayars, neither bride nor groom was made a permanent member of the other's house; their right to live and take sustenance in it was never permanent. Hence they celebrated nothing equivalent to the Nambutiri marriage ceremony. Yet there was a ritual connection, though of lesser strength, between a Nayar bride and her husband's house. In some cases, she could even be spoken of as a goddess bringing it good or ill fortune. The following description of the ceremony which welcomes a Nayar bride to her husband's house not only contrasts with that of the Nambutiri, but reveals the importance of the prestations that will define and maintain the *sambandham*:

> A few days after the completion of the ceremony, the senior woman of the bridegroom's house sends some cloths including pavu mundu (superior cloths) and thorthu mundu (towels), and some oil to the bride for her use for six months. Every six months she does the same, and, at the Onam, Vishu, and Thiruvatrira festivals, she sends besides a little money, areca nuts, betel and tobacco . . . . Before long, the women of the husband's house express a longing for the girl-wife to be brought to their house, for they have not seen her yet. Again the astrologer is requisitioned, and, on the day he fixes, two or three of the women go to the house of the girl, or, as they call her, Ammayi (uncle's wife). They are well treated, and presently bring away the girl with them. As she is about to enter the gate-house of her husband's taravad, the stile of which she crosses right leg

first, two or three of the women meet her, bearing a burning lamp and a brass plate (thalam), and precede her to the nalukattu of the house. There she is seated on a mat, and a burning lamp, a nazhi (measure) of rice, and some plantains are placed before her. One of the younger women takes up a plantain, and puts a piece of it in the Ammayi's mouth; a little ceremony called madhuram tital, or giving the sweets for eating. She lives in her husband's house for a few days, and is then sent back to her own with presents, bracelets, rings or cloths, which are gifts of the senior women of the house. After this she is at liberty to visit her husband's house on any day, auspicious or inauspicious (Thurston 1909, V:334-51).

The prestations that maintain the *sambandham* — the continued gifts of cloth, towels, oil, money, and betel and arecanut — are here shown to be not a private matter between groom and bride but a concern of the groom's female *taravad*, as shown by its ability to keep its own women as well as the wives of its men supplied with items for comfort and beauty. This association with prestige exists alongside a strong association of such items with sexuality.

The symbolism of the *sambandham* rite is organized around two themes. The first is sexuality — here, a pure eroticism that is not heavily connected with fertility as in the *tali* rite. The second is the creation of an intersection of *taravads* as places and holders of property, as open for hospitality and as extending to a nonmember some of the member's prerogatives of support. In contrast to the *tali* rite, the symbolism of the *sambandham* is of an ongoing process rather than a rite of passage. The actions that constitute it are kept up indefinitely or terminated accordingly as the relationship lasts.

## Symbolism in Nayar Marriage Ritual

Nayar marriage rituals are about female sexuality and fertility, but with significant shifts in emphasis. The themes of female eroticism and beauty, central in the *sambandham*, get eclipsed in the *tali* rite by a complex of symbolism centered around assuring the girl's fertility and associating her with household prosperity. She is ritually made ready not only to bear children who will insure the continuity of her *taravad*, but also, goddess-like, to bring it wealth. While the rite seems to have some connection with the concept of *mangalyam*, it is more in its sense of the woman's general state of married auspiciousness than in its sense of her connection with her husband. Alongside *mangalyam*, the transformation worked by the *tali* rite is characterized by the term for the girl's new status, *amma*. This term not only means "mother" (the girl is a potential mother for children of her *taravad*), but also is the term for a female member of the Nayar caste, and may be attached to the woman's name as a term of address. The status of *amma*, therefore, is triply meaningful. Not only does it imply womanhood and potential motherhood, but it is also a kind of honorific title.

In the Nayar system much more attention was given to the marriage of the female than the male. The elaborate "male initiation rites" that existed in pre-British times among many Nayar subcastes had to do with war rather than marriage. Yet the marriage rituals did not neglect men entirely. Here a sharp distinction between the *sambandham* and the *tali* rites becomes apparent. Only the *sambandham* rite was treated as an expected rite in the life-cycle of men as well as women. In the *tali* rite men participated as representatives of their *taravads*, paid officiants, and such. The *sambandham* not only includes significant ritual pertaining to men — like greeting of their relatives — but creates other significant situations for men as well — such as the ability to bring a bride to one's house.

Parallel to this differential emphasis of the rituals on women and men is the way they vary in asserting the prestige of the bride's and groom's *taravads*. The *tali* rite not only contains a greater amount of ritual relevant to *taravad* prestige, but the ritual it contains is almost solely about the prestige of the bride's *taravad* — whereas the *sambandham* gives equal or greater weight to the ritual assertion of the prestige of the groom's *taravad*. Still, the *tali* stands first both in the richness of its ritual statements about persons (women) and the grandeur of its assertion of *taravad* prestige.

A similar parallel is found in each ritual's treatment of the *taravad*'s social connections. The *tali* rite is especially rich in the number of such connections it celebrates, but there are two other important differences which distinguish the *tali* rite from the *sambandham* rite: (1) the former is concerned with reaffirmation of old relationships rather than creation of new ones and (2) only in the latter is there reaffirmation of social connections by the groom's *taravad* as well as the bride's.

Running through both rituals, and uniting all themes, is the symbolic construction of the *taravad* as house-and-land unit. The transformation of girls into women is symbolized in terms of their symbolic relation to a house. In the *tali* rite they are celebrated as goddess-like bringers of household prosperity and continuity. The opening of the house to outsiders is ritually effected and celebrated in the *sambandham*. The latter may be made reciprocal: in the most complete form of *sambandham* the groom's house, too, is ritually opened to the bride and its resources are extended for her support, symbolized by the same act (cloth-giving) that symbolizes a *taravad*'s support of its own members. Similarly, in the *tali* rite, it is the wealth of the girl's house, its status in a hierarchy of overlordship, and its permanent social connections that are conspicuously displayed; in the *sambandham* the wealth, prerogatives, and prestige of the groom's house must be displayed as well.

# 11

# Why Women Take Men to Magistrate's Court

## Mindie Lazarus-Black

**E**very Thursday afternoon a list of "Order in Bastardy, Maintenance, and Arrears" is posted on the wall of the St. John's magistrate's court in Antigua, West Indies. In a typical week, six to eight new cases are scheduled for hearing, while twenty or thirty others are brought by the collecting officer of the state against men who have neglected to pay child support. There were 1,493 cases of maintenance and arrears in 1984, 1,287 cases in 1985. Given a population of approximately 80,000 in Antigua and Barbuda, such case loads indicate that the court is frequently utilized.

Academic, legal, and popular wisdom holds that these West Indian women are going to magistrate's court for money because the babies' fathers fail to support them or to pay regularly enough. They go to court because they are unemployed or underemployed with too many illegitimate children to raise and too few dollars with which to do so.[5] But when I asked one woman if she went to court for money, her answer surprised me. She looked at me indignantly and said, "I carry my case up there for justice. I complain him for justice."

This article explores ideas about justice which are integral to kinship relations in Antigua and Barbuda. "Carrying a case" to the magistrate's court exemplifies the interaction between state forms and community norms and demonstrates that certain rules and judicial processes of the Antiguan state are now constituent of local family ideology and practice. That is, Antiguan women regularly take cases to court to demand justice in their kinship relations, to

Adapted from: Mindie Lazarus-Black, "Why Women Take Men to Magistrate's Court: Caribbean Kinship Ideology and Law," *Ethnology* 30(1991):119-133.

assert their autonomy and rights, and to resist the pervasive hierarchical structures of gender and class.

## The Legacy of Colonialism

British and European colonists brought to the West Indies cultural traditions in which families were legally constituted and then duly went about relegislating kinship. In the case of Antigua, as early as 1672 and at regular intervals over the next three centuries, legal codes were absolutely critical to creating and maintaining different social ranks in the colony and to regulating families, gender and race. Local legislators wrestled with questions about who might marry whom, which persons constituted "family," and what rights and duties such connections bestowed. The kinship order these lawmakers instituted for Antiguans departed dramatically from the rules that guided kinship in Great Britain. The legacy of colonialism included both detailed kinship laws and an elaborate hierarchy of courts.

Antigua was first colonized in 1632, mainly by English and Irish adventurers, soldiers, farmers, and laborers. Early lawmakers and judges consisted of a very small group of men of property, most of them planters. The switch from tobacco and cotton to sugar began in the 1650s. At that time, the colony was comprised of small farmers and a good number of European indentured servants. A century later, 93.5 percent of the population were slaves and most worked on large sugar plantations (Gaspar 1985:83).

The kinship laws Antiguan planters wrote were directed at controlling marriage and human reproduction, and also at reproducing the hierarchical social and economic structure of capitalism. Codes made it illegal for slaves to marry free persons, prevented indentured servants from marrying without their masters' permission, granted the right to perform marriage ceremonies only to Anglican ministers, and made white men responsible for their white bastard children.

The *Leeward Islands Amelioration Act*, passed in Antigua in 1798, also set up a separate system of marriage for slaves. According to this act, a slave marriage was monogamous but not contractual, since the nuptials bestowed none of the rights and duties implied in marriages of free persons. Nor did a slave marriage convey upon children the status or title of the husband/father. The law did include provision for public declaration of a couple's intention to live together and for monetary awards from their masters.

The colonists also established a hierarchy of courts. By the end of the eighteenth century, there was a Court of Chancery, a Court of Error and Appeal, a Court of King's Bench and Grand Sessions, a Court of Common Pleas, a Court Ordinary, a Court Merchant, and a Court of Admiralty. In addition, complaints between indentured servants and masters, and masters and slaves, were heard by itinerant justices of the peace.

Slavery was abolished in Antigua in 1834. In reality, abolition brought few dramatic changes to the lives of the ex-slaves. Limited availability of free land and the infamous Contract Act, which set new terms between workers and planters, combined to make it difficult to leave the estates. The Contract Act not only made it arduous to find a new employer, it also directed who might legally reside with whom in the estate huts, and commanded labor from each member of a man's family. Other social welfare legislation of this period made the destitute, the infirm, and the elderly the economic responsibility of their kin, not of the government.

Lawmakers passed in 1875 *An Act for the Better Support of Natural Children, and to afford Facilities for obliging the Putative Father to assist in the Maintenance of such Children.* The statute set procedures for obtaining affiliation orders, bestowed power upon magistrates to establish relationships between illegitimate children and their fathers, and designated stipends for men to provide for their offspring. Any woman who delivered a bastard child could apply for a support order. The request had to be made within a year after the baby's birth unless she could prove that previously the man had cared for the child. At the hearing parties could bring witnesses and had the right to counsel.

Weekly support payments were limited to five shillings for the first six weeks and to two shillings and six pence thereafter until the child attained the age of twelve or until the mother married. Stipends were payable directly to the mother and she had to apply for arrears within thirteen weeks or they were forfeited. The magistrate also had discretionary power to order the father to pay the costs of the case, a payment to the midwife, and funeral expenses if necessary. He could appoint a guardian for a child if the mother died, was of unsound mind, or went to prison. A putative father could appeal his case to the High Court, but the magistrate had power to send him to jail and to sell his property for failure to comply with the bastardy order.

With only slight modifications, the bastardy law still functions today. The act exemplifies both the continuous intervention of the state in matters of kinship and the hegemonic character of legalities in local communities. The bastardy law is regularly invoked by contemporary Antiguan women, although not always for reasons envisioned by nineteenth-century and later lawmakers.

## The Economic and Political Context

Antigua's present population is almost entirely African-Caribbean. A few people have British and other European forefathers, others are descendants of Syrian and Lebanese traders who arrived early in the twentieth century, and there are some expatriate Americans and Canadians. English is the standard language, although there is a creole dialect. Most islanders are literate and most consider themselves Christian.

Historic dependence upon sugar exports prevented Antigua from achieving economic self-sufficiency. Agriculture remains in general decline today, despite a variety of efforts to revive it. Manufacturing and industry is developing slowly, but in the last two decades tourism has emerged as the most important economic sector (Henry 1985). Its direct value now accounts for approximately 21 percent of the gross domestic product, and at least 12 percent of the labor force works in tourism (The World Bank 1985:24). Government employs about 30 percent of all working persons (The World Bank 1985:4). Unemployment remained at around 20 percent through the first half of the 1980s (*Statistical Yearbook* 1985).

Antiguan planters controlled local politics until labor unrest heralded a movement for social and economic reform early in this century. Unions were legalized in 1940 and adult suffrage was granted in 1951. Shortly thereafter, election rules were changed to allow greater representation of the working people. In 1979, the islands became an Associated State, gaining control over local affairs but still under British authority with respect to external relations and defense. Independence came in 1981. Antigua and Barbuda is now a parliamentary democracy with a Prime Minister, Senate, and House of Representatives. The government proclaimed a nonaligned foreign policy at independence, but maintains strongest political and economic ties with Britain, Canada, and the United States.

Antigua's two social classes, middle and lower, can be differentiated into smaller strata based upon members' socioeconomic status and ability to wield formal political power. At the top of the present hierarchy is a small local elite which holds elected political authority. In contrast to the days when sugar dominated, this elite is Antiguan-born, black, and increasingly educated in the Caribbean. Within this same stratum are foreign businessmen and expatriates who play important roles in the economy but who are noticeably absent from the official political process. The lifestyle and domestic organization of the elite, however, are virtually indistinguishable from Antigua's middle class. Such similarities help explain why middle-class persons almost always say that Antigua has only two classes. Middle-class women rarely use the magistrate's court to order their kinship relations. Moreover, the ideology of class protects middle-class men from being named publicly as the fathers of illegitimate children.

Quite the opposite is true of the lower class, which uses the courts regularly. In some respects, the lower class is also more heterogeneous than the middle class. Its upper stratum consists of a petite bourgeoisie, "who own small amounts of productive resources and have control over their working conditions in ways that proletarians do not" (Rapp 1982:180). Petite bourgeoisie men are often jacks-of-all-trades. They may own some land, raise a few cattle or goats, and work a job or two for weekly cash. Petite bourgeoisie women run their own small shops or work from their homes as seamstresses or hairdressers. In contrast, members of the working class have little or no property and only their own labor to sell. They include agricultural workers, fishermen, sales persons, domestics, hotel workers, and laborers. They are low-income, hard-working people for whom multiple jobs and job-sharing are common.

In contrast to Antigua, class is not relevant in Barbuda. Antigua's sister island was leased to the Codrington family in 1685 and 1705. The Codringtons used Barbuda as a supply depot and manufacturing center for their estates in Antigua. Until 1898 when the Antiguan legislature assumed financial responsibility for its government, Barbuda was virtually without political representation, welfare or educational services, or legal institutions.

The island has remained sparsely populated. Codrington, the only village, is home to approximately 1,200 people—almost all descendants of Codrington's slaves. Today many Barbudan men fish for their living. Others raise cattle. Both men and women work subsistence gardens and continue to insist upon communal ownership of land outside the village despite opposition from the government in Antigua (Berleant-Schiller 1977). Barbuda has a few shops, a couple of hotels where people find seasonal work, an elementary school, a health clinic, several churches, and a few government buildings. During my field work,[6] a room in the police station served as a temporary courtroom upon the arrival of the magistrate.

## The Courts, the Codes, and the Litigants

The organization of the courts and the legal codes partially determine who comes to the magistrate's court, the types of complaints that are filed, and how any particular case will fare. A four-tiered court system presently serves the islands. The first tier consists of the magistrate's courts. Affiliation and maintenance cases, arrears, disputes between persons over small property claims, personal grievances, traffic matters, and minor assaults are brought to these courts. In addition to the magistrate's court serving the capitol city of St. John's, three "country courts" meet weekly in the villages of Bolans, All Saints, and Parham. By law, the magistrate holds court in Barbuda four times a year for two or three days, depending upon the case load. The Barbuda court draws quite a crowd. Interested bystanders make humorous comments about the litigants and their cases, sometimes to the chagrin of the magistrate.

A case heard in a magistrate's court may be appealed to the second tier in the system, the High Court. The High Court also settles major property and criminal cases, and family matters such as divorce, adoption, and contested wills. The third tier, the Appellate Division of the Supreme Court of the Eastern Caribbean, meets intermittently in the different Leeward Islands. Finally, since Antigua and Barbuda is a member of the Commonwealth, cases decided by the Supreme Court may be appealed, as a last resort, to the Privy Council in England.

Kinship statutes instruct who shall use which of these courts to resolve family disputes. When I conducted field work, statutes distinguished persons on the basis of their marital status (single or married) and their birth status (legitimate or illegitimate). Married persons have the option of applying either to the High Court or the magistrate's court for legal remedy with respect to certain kinship disputes. For example, a married woman may apply to the magistrate for relief if a spouse has committed adultery or aggravated assault upon the applicant, or is guilty of persistent cruelty or desertion, or is a habitual drunkard. The magistrate has authority to order that the complainant no longer be bound to cohabit with the defendant, award legal custody of children to the applicant, and direct the defendant to pay weekly support for the plaintiff and any "children of the family" for whom the man is legally responsible. Only a woman in a legal union can ask for support for herself (*The Revised Laws of Antigua* 1962:417-421). All conflicts between unmarried couples over child care and maintenance must be adjudicated in the magistrate's court.

The persistence of these two alternative legal channels preserves the hierarchical social structure. The system, in place since the nineteenth century, funnels women with illegitimate children through one set of processes and married women through another. The law also differentiates in practice between persons of different social classes, since the two courts are widely acknowledged to have quite different consequences for individuals' family ties and the economy of their households. When I asked whether the magistrate's court might be characterized as a "poor peoples' court," eighteen of twenty-one attorneys concurred.

There are structural, economic, and ideological reasons beyond the factor of legal jurisdiction as to why that characterization holds. First, the magistrate's court is more readily accessible to the lower class. It is cheap to take a case there: the cost of a three-dollar stamp. One need not hire an attorney and, indeed, the majority of litigants with maintenance cases are not represented. Second, in 1987 a magistrate could award a maximum of fifteen Eastern Caribbean dollars per week for child support ($5.67 U.S.) and up to twenty-five E. C. dollars per week ($9.36 U.S.) for support for a married woman. Such small sums are unlikely to draw middle-class women to the court. Moreover, since they are usually married, middle-class women prefer to divide their property and arrange for the welfare of their children at the High Court where judges have much greater discretion in awarding support. In contrast to magistrates, High Court judges investigate the income and property of both parties and the ages and educational needs of the children. Finally, there are ideological reasons why the middle class avoids the magistrate's court. Members of this class, and some lower-class persons as well, consider kinship cases analogous to "hanging one's dirty laundry in public." The court's long association with persons of low status—with rogues and criminals—also dissuades Antiguans concerned about reputation from bringing a case there.

For all of these reasons, the magistrates primarily hear kinship disputes of working-class persons. The large number of family cases is partly due to the frequency with which men who have been adjudged as legal fathers and ordered to pay weekly support fail to make those payments. When a man does not pay for five or six consecutive weeks, the collecting officer requests the magistrate to order the man to give reason why he has neglected to pay. At present, if he chooses not to pay he does not pay until the police track him down. Meanwhile, the number of cases against him continues to multiply on the books.

After cases of unpaid arrears, the most frequently heard family disputes are those in which a woman requests that the man be judged the putative father of her child and an order be made for the child's support. These petitions constituted about 70 percent of all new kinship cases brought before the magistrates each year between 1980 and 1986.

Excluding cases of arrears, almost all of the kinship cases heard by the court are brought by women. Women rely on the courts to establish affiliation and maintenance, to increase support orders, to deny husbands the right to cohabitation, to request maintenance for themselves and their children, to protect the financial interests of a child if a father is about leave the country, and to remove a youth from the home of a negligent parent. Men, on the other hand, file most of the requests for a discharge of a magistrate's order. They have that option as soon as a minor reaches the age of sixteen, if the child comes to reside with them, or if the mother takes the child out of the state.

The plaintiff with a kinship case in the magistrate's court is almost always a lower-class woman, finding herself at odds with a man and her children neglected. The woman may or may not have other children at home to support. In a great many instances, she juggles child care and some form of part-time employment to pay for shelter and food. Usually the union between the man and woman has not been a casual one; most frequently the couple have been seeing each other for over a year and up to several years. Of twenty-two such trials I observed in St. John's, seven involved one child, nine involved two children, four involved three children, and two involved four children. The parties tend to be young, commonly eighteen to thirty-five years of age, but the vast majority were not pregnant teens. Most plaintiffs had never been to court before and most were uncertain about what was expected of them.

The litigants usually did know, however, that a magistrate could award only up to $15 E. C. per week for child support. Indeed, the amount is so low that it can make a difference only to the most indigent. Moreover, if financial considerations were the primary cause for women going to court, we would expect to see a steady rise in the number of cases filed after 1982 when the stipend was raised from $7 to $15 E.C. That was not the case. There was an immediate but temporary rise in the number of requests for affiliation and maintenance in St. John's right after the stipend increased, probably due to the publicity surrounding the change in the law. This may have encouraged some women with easy access to this court to apply for aid for the first time and others to request an increase in the support they already received. Within two years of the passage of the bill, however, the number of new requests had dropped to earlier levels. The court records also show that over the relevant five-year period there were no significant changes in the number of new cases filed in any of the country courts or in Barbuda. Apparently neither urban nor village women were motivated to go to court for purely financial reasons.

## Why Women Use the Magistrate's Court

Case histories, interviews with litigants and lawyers, and observations of trials at the magistrate's courts show that Antiguan women take men to court when those men violate local norms about respect, support, and appropriate relations between the sexes. Women invoke the state in the name of justice, using law and forensic processes to ritually enact the meaning, rights, and responsibilities of kin. Two case histories illustrate this phenomenon.

In 1985, Cicely was 38, unmarried, with four children, each of whom had a different father. Cicely supported herself and the children by cleaning offices two days a week, working in a private home one afternoon, and sometimes selling candy, cigarettes, drinks, and other small items on a street-corner from a tray perched upon a styrofoam cooler. Her regular salary was only $95 E. C. per week (about $35 U. S.) and she frequently needed help from her mother, who worked as a kitchen aid, or from her younger sister, a primary school teacher.

Her situation had improved somewhat a year later. She had a full-time cleaning job for which she earned $108 E. C. per week. She had also obtained some funds from an American organization which assisted poor children. The composition of her household had changed as well. Her oldest daughter had returned to live with her, but a little girl she had been "minding" in 1985 had gone to live with her father's sister. One thing was unchanged: Cicely had virtually no support for her children from their fathers. Yet Cicely took only two of those men to court. The first man was a bartender, the second was a police officer. The other fathers were laborers.

Josephine's story reveals some interesting parallels to Cicely's case. Her father, Tyronne, was a carpenter and electrician. Tyronne had no formal training, but he was a master at fixing and inventing things, and could connect a house to the government electricity without its knowledge. Tyronne ran a small shop and drove a big car. When he died in 1981, Josephine met siblings at his funeral that she had never known.

Josephine's mother, Evelyn, worked as a domestic servant. Evelyn and Tyronne had not stayed together long. When Evelyn married for the second time at the age of 44, she had had eight children by six different men. Only her first husband had consistently supported his two children. The other men, laborers and fishermen, went their separate ways. Only Tyronne, however, was taken to court. By coincidence, two other women also summoned Tyronne to court for maintenance on the same day and all three were awarded the maximum that the law allowed.

The timing of Tyronne's cases may have been coincidental; the fact that he and two of the fathers of Cicely's children were brought to court, was not. The case studies show that women use the courts selectively. The profiles of these men are keys to identifying ideas about family, gender, and status that explain why Antiguan women go to court and why these particular men received summons. Moreover, these notions are intrinsic to family ideology and to the even flow of family life in the community.

In the Antiguan lower class, men and women are held to have distinctly different natures. Although West Indians highly value individual autonomy and economic independence for both men and women, I found that Antiguans repeatedly stressed the biological and social differences between men and women and used those differences to support the premise that there is a proper domain for each sex. Both men and women distinguish between the "inside" world of women and the "outside" world of men, and neither views those two domains as equal in any respect. The creed of gender hierarchy within the family contributes to the subordinate position of women in this society. Nevertheless, as we shall see, a highly developed sense of justice ensures there are limits beyond which a man may not assert the special privileges accorded to his sex.

Antiguan men and women love and need each other—children are one consequence of that fact—but because their natures are so different, men and women parent in different ways. Women nurture children, cook for them, wash them, teach them, and discipline them. Men provide some of this care, but their primary responsibility is to "feed a child," which means that the man maintains a particular kind of relationship with the child and the mother. An alliance exists in the first place because the man and the child share the same blood. Antiguan men are proud of their children and boast about their number. As another indication of their willingness to accept fatherhood, men rarely deny paternity at court, even if there are raging disagreements about how much they can afford in weekly payments.

A child generally uses his or her father's surname in the community and is entitled to that man's attention and "support." Support may take the form of cash, gifts, food, clothing, school supplies, or services provided by either the man or members of his family. For example, a woman generally does not take a man to court if his mother babysits or provides clothing for her grandchild. In contrast to the law, community norms are flexible with respect to the amount and type of support due to an illegitimate child. Support may vary in amount or kind from month to month, but it must be given somewhat regularly to maintain the alliance.

Finally, in addition to support, a man owes the mother of his child "respect." Like the notion of feeding a child, respect embodies a host of expectations. It means that even after their separation the man speaks politely about his child's mother and the people she is close to, that he acknowledges them publicly if the occasion arises, that he acts with discretion, and that he never flaunts a new relationship in her presence.

Breaking the norms which govern the alliances between men, women and children sometimes results in a man being hauled to court. One woman I interviewed, for example, took the father of her child to court only after he had insulted her publicly in the market. Often, however, a norm involving respect is broken in conjunction with another which speaks directly about principles of hierarchy within the lower class. Consider the men whom Cicely and Evelyn brought to court: the bartender, the policeman, and Tyronne, the electrician. These men share a social stature that distinguishes them from the other fathers of Cicely's and Evelyn's illegitimate children. Locally, they are called "big men." A "big man" in Antigua has a respectable job with a steady income. Beyond this, he has won admiration by virtue of his leadership qualities, command of language, intelligence, wit, education, and generosity. He can maintain multiple unions, even when married, keep his women "in order," and father and "feed" many children. Big men uphold certain standards in their family relationships. They provide gifts to their wives and "outside" women and support all of their children in a manner which accords with their standing in the community.

Violating this code of behavior makes a big man an Antiguan woman's choice for a trip to the magistrate's court for a ritual shaming. The courtroom becomes for these men what Garfinkel (1956:89) calls a "degradation ceremony." When a man's name is called in court, his position as a big man is challenged. The trial indicates that he is not generous, not responsible, not a suitable father, and incapable of controlling his women.

By all accounts and my own observations, the shaming of men at the magistrate's court undeniably achieves this aim. Often a woman need only file legal papers and the man changes his ways. Those who come to court are chastised and warned that they may face prison if they fail to pay for their children. Some men refuse to attend, but in that case the suit is heard in their absence and the effect upon their reputation in the community is the same. The shaming ceremony, then, renews and validates legally constituted kinship responsibilities while mitigating the prestige of a big man.

## Inversion of Gender Relations

The court ritual that challenges a man's personal competence and his status among his peers also inverts the usual hierarchical status between men and women. When she brings a man to the magistrate's court, a woman forces a conjuncture of the domestic and the public spheres; the dirty laundry is made public. During the case, she uses law, courts, forensic processes, and legal personnel to manage male behavior and to lay claim to the rights due her and her children. If only for the duration of the ritual, she is a status equal and the public spokesman and representative for her children. Such behavior has its costs. A woman may be chided for going to court; she may be accused of spite. Nonetheless, the achievement of equality, the validation of individual rights, and the recognition of moral duty — central elements of Antiguan family ideology — are proclaimed during the trial. These constitute a vital part of the "justice" for which Antiguan women go to court.

Ironically, the expressed intent of the lawmakers — the regular provision of support for illegitimate children — is not nearly as effective as the threat or the actual performance of the shaming ceremony. Almost every woman I spoke with during my follow-up study complained about not receiving weekly payments. Their complaints were borne out by the collecting officer's records. Most women waited weeks between payments; some waited months. Women who take policemen to court face an added difficulty because officers are reluctant to hand warrants for failure to pay child support to fellow officers.

One last issue with respect to kinship cases at the magistrate's courts needs to be raised. There is a point at which a big man is too big a man to impugn in court, which accounts for the infrequency of inter-class family disputes in the lower courts. For at least three reasons, upper-middle-class status shields a man against the justice that lower-class women seek from the courts. First, charges of corruption against public officials occur frequently enough that the lower class remains cynical about the justice that poor people can expect at court when their opponents are wealthy and powerful people. In their view, pragmatism teaches that there is not much use in suing a middle-class man whose fancy lawyer will break your case or who is himself a friend of a friend of the judge. Second, rich and powerful men are likely to be married to rich and powerful women, who are formidable adversaries in their own right because they wield considerable influence over employment and educational opportunities in the community. Finally, some lower-class women do not take the wealthy fathers of their illegitimate children to court because they cherish the hope that some day these men will "rediscover" their children, come to love them, and provide them with their rightful due. That hope is part of the ideology of Antiguan family life and is crucial to understanding why a woman has a child "for" a man.

Although a maintenance case may appear to be a request for cash, it is in fact a way to substantiate familial alliances and to shame men who purport to be "big men" but who break a "big man's" code of conduct. A woman brings a case to magistrate's court to claim normative rights which regulate family, gender, and hierarchy within the lower class. Women rely on and use a literal translation of Antiguan kinship law to manage male behavior, to voice objections to their own inequality, and they reaffirm the rights of their children. They "carry" their cases for "justice."

# 12

# In-Law Relationships in the American Kinship System
## The Impact of Divorce and Remarriage

*Colleen Leahy Johnson*

The dominant model of American kinship systems used by anthropologists today was developed by David Schneider (1968) over twenty years ago when divorce and remarriage were viewed as exceptions rather than the norm. Now, during an era when the high incidence of divorce and remarriage is publicly acknowledged and "blended families" are common, this model should be reevaluated. The structure and organization of the kinship system changes with divorce and remarriage, as do the meanings individuals assign to kinship relationships.

This paper[7] reports on the impact marital changes are having on American middle-class kinship systems. The analysis illustrates that the American kinship system is mutable and flexible as its members accommodate to the realities of marital change. The findings suggest that this flexibility is delimited, however, because the key issue in family and kinship reorganization following divorce centers on access to the children of divorce. To retain a connection to these children, individuals redefine relationships and initiate strategies by which they navigate through a complex network of relatives by blood, marriage and divorce. The analysis focuses on the grandparents and their roles in these emerging kinship systems, because grandparents are at particular risk of having their access to grandchildren blocked when their children divorce. The means

Adapted from *American Ethnologist* 16:1, February 1989, by permission of the American Anthropological Association. Not for sale or further reproduction.

they use to retain access to their grandchildren are described in order to illustrate how the sense of blood relatedness continues through generations.

## Approaches to Kinship Analysis

Anthropologists have focused on several conceptual principles in approaching the study of kinship. Drawing on the cultural domain, Schneider (1980) considered kinship relations in light of two categories: the *order of nature*, or biological relationships [consanguines], and the *order of law*, or those related by marriage [affines]. Schneider (1965) suggests also that when the cultural material is abstracted out from social actions, these elements form a system of oppositions and contrasts, which may make distinctions between relatives by blood and by marriage.

On the other hand, a structural-functional analysis views individuals as status occupants and role players interacting in a social relationship. Radcliffe-Brown (1950) outlines a process under which in-law relationships may become redefined. When a child is born, the father-in-law of the child's father becomes the grandfather, a brother-in-law becomes one's child's uncle, and so on. Thus, once the marriage has produced issue, in-laws become affinal relatives who are defined not only by the order of law, but also by their recognition of a biological linkage to the child. As my research indicates, with high rates of marital instability, these dual definitions of kin contribute an additional category of relatives, those who are defined on the basis of shared biological relatedness only. After divorce, in-laws are unrelated by nature and by law, but they share a biological linkage to another individual.

A structural-functional approach also is useful in identifying points of tension in the kinship system. For instance, joking and avoidance relationships function to reduce the potential conflict that occurs when two families are joined by marriage (Radcliffe-Brown 1952). Points of tension generally arise in those in-law relationships that pose the greatest conflict in loyalties—for example, that between husband and wife and her mother. The frequency with which the mother-in-law is the brunt of jokes in our society suggests there is a marked underlying tension associated with this kinship role.

Since the points of tension in any kinship system are readjusted following divorce and remarriage, it is useful to examine the system at a more abstract level in order to identify the configuration of relationships in reorganized kinship systems. Using models based upon structural linguistics, Lévi-Strauss (1963) demonstrates how the oppositional nature of kinship systems creates tension in one set of relationships, leading to cleavages and often dissolution. At the same time, coalitions develop in other parts of the system. In societies such as ours, with bilateral descent and neolocal residence, conflicts between in-laws in intact marriages are less likely to occur because of the distance created by neolocal residence. Psychological distance also is likely due to the strongly endorsed norms on independence, the mandate of privacy for the nuclear unit, and the belief that marriage should entail a sharp break between parents and adult children. Nevertheless, our kinship system has a matrilateral emphasis, so subsequent kinship relationships are usually linked and orchestrated by women (Newman 1986; Troll 1971; Yanigasako 1977). Theoretically then, one can predict that women will play a more important role than men in the reorganization processes following divorce. Such a role may be in part by default, for the empirical literature convincingly documents that men's parental and economic responsibilities drop off sharply after divorce (Johnson et al 1988).

Divorce is a greater problem in our culture than is typical in cultures with more explicitly defined rights and obligations, because our households are based upon a marital relationship relatively isolated from kin (Bohannan 1971). Since the nuclear family is thereby structurally and economically isolated, dependent children are in a vulnerable situation. In such cases, grandparents are the logical relatives to provide help, but their status is derived from the parents or their grandchildren (Johnson 1983, 1985). Although custody is usually granted to mothers, the husband has some legal access to his children. His mother, however, has no legal rights over her grandchildren, so her access is informal and mediated through her son or his former wife. If his relationship with his wife is such that he cannot provide his mother with access to the children, then the points of tension between the husband and his wife are likely to be associated with other dyadic relationships—between the husband and his child, his mother and his wife, and his mother and his child. Obviously with some divorces, relationships break down and contacts among in-laws cease. As will be illustrated here, however, evoking the shared biological connection occurs when grandmothers are strongly motivated to retain their relationship with their grandchildren through a former in-law.

## The Social and Cultural Context

This study focuses on white families, the majority of which were selected from public divorce records of middle-class suburbs in the San Francisco Bay Area. The grandmothers were interviewed three times, the first time soon after a child's divorce but less than three years after the separation, a second time an average of fourteen months later, and a third time forty months after the first contact.

These families were experiencing frequent marital changes. By the selection criteria, all grandparents had at least one divorced child, and 30 percent had two or more. Over a quarter of the grandparents had been divorced themselves. Remarriage was also taking place at a fast pace. Almost 40 percent of the divorcing parents had remarried by our third contact and 18 percent had acquired stepchildren. Their former spouses showed a similar pattern: 53 percent were remarried or cohabiting, and 21 percent had stepchildren.

With divorce, most grandparents came expeditiously to the aid of their children and grandchildren (Johnson 1983, 1985, 1988). The greatest source of variation in their contact and services was found to be the ages of grandparents and their grandchildren. Younger grandmothers with younger grandchildren were significantly more active following the separation and divorce. On the whole, grandmothers maintained cordial relationships with their children and grandchildren, most likely because they attempted to avoid being moralistic and judgmental about their children's lives. They also tried to avoid "repeating the parent role" with their grandchildren by concentrating on pleasurable activities.

In addition, maternal and paternal grandmothers differed significantly in their involvement (Johnson 1988). Maternal grandmothers were in more frequent contact with their children and grandchildren, and over time, their contact increased. In contrast, paternal grandmothers had about the same frequency of contact with their children as did maternal grandmothers, but they had less contact with grandchildren immediately after the divorce. This contact became even less frequent over time. Not surprisingly, many more paternal grandmothers reported that a child's divorce had a negative impact on their lives. With this loss of contact also came a loss of aid to grandchildren.

The decline in contact of paternal grandmothers suggests that they may have had some difficulty in maintaining access to grandchildren, possibly because their sons were not able to provide this linkage. As one solution to the problem of access, paternal grandmothers were significantly more likely to stay in contact with their former daughters-in-law than maternal grandmothers with their former sons-in-law. Even by our third contact, almost one-quarter of the paternal grandmothers still had weekly contact with their former daughters-in-law and the majority described that relationship as close and friendly. This frequency contrasts with that of maternal grandmothers, among whom no one at our third contact reported a close relationship with a former son-in-law.

## Meaning of Kinship with Marital Change

While the rules delineating membership in the American kinship system are clear, individuals have considerable latitude in deciding whether some in-laws are related to them. No one questions, for example, their relationships by blood and marriage, but there are no rules indicating that in-laws on the paternal and maternal sides should be related to each other. Consequently, the way individuals define these relationships can be an important determinant of the ensuing relationships. These definitions center on those characteristics that define how ego[8] is related to a relative — in Schneider's (1968) terms, those relationships in nature (by blood) or in law (by marriage). Second, by the rules of our flexible systems, individuals can draw upon voluntary criteria and define these relatives by custom, or on the basis of notions of closeness and distance, norms of friendship, "liking," or norms of responsibility.

***Relatives by Blood.*** Evoking the metaphor of a blood connection was one means grandmothers used to define their former children-in-law, a definition that makes a strong claim of relatedness. Thus, some referred to a daughter-in-law as "my child" but more commonly they defined that individual as "like a child to me." Such a direct biological connection appeared to be a relatively temporary phenomenon. While it was quite common to hear former children-in-law referred to as "like my own son or daughter" at our first contact, only in rare cases did such an equation to a blood tie persist. Over time and as the grandchildren's needs diminished, such definitions were usually modified. If the relationship persisted, a former child-in-law who was previously "like a son to me" became redefined as either "my friend" or "my grandchild's parent."

*Relatives by a Shared Biological Linkage.* More commonly, grandmothers defined the in-law as being related through a shared biological linkage to the children of the dissolved marriage. With this dual measure of relatedness (Radcliffe-Brown 1950), the divorce eliminated only one criterion. A former spouse, no longer a spouse, remains "the parent of my children." A former child-in-law remains "the parent of my grandchildren," even though he or she is no longer the child's spouse. That individual's parents remain "my grandchildren's other grandparents." Such a definition is most commonly found among paternal grandparents who were more likely than maternal grandparents to invoke the shared biological linkage. This adherence to a shared biological tie accounts for the retention of in-law relationships even when divorce, both legally and often emotionally, ends the tie. Common responses were, "How can I divorce the mother of my grandchildren?" or "She may no longer be my son's wife but she'll always be my grandchildren's mother."

In some cases, both sets of grandparents joined together to reaffirm their shared biological linkage to the grandchildren. For example, in one case, maternal and paternal grandparents had their pictures taken together with their grandchildren to symbolize their commonality. Others had jointly intervened to help grandchildren who were in vulnerable situations. Former in-law relationships also were recognized by a common practice of parents-in-law and children-in-law sending each other cards on Mother's Day and Father's Day, a custom occurring even in families where there was considerable conflict after the divorce.

The importance of the shared biological connection was demonstrated also by negative evidence. Grandmothers were less active in maintaining in-law relationships after divorce if there were no children in the marriage. In fact, with remarriages of their children, some made no attempt even to meet their new child-in-law's parents if the marriage was childless. Others were hesitant to include step-grandchildren in their definition of kinship, because "their father is not my son."

*Definitions of Relatives "In-law".* If ego's relatives by marriage are defined as in-laws, this suggests that the relationship dissolves with divorce. Such a situation occurs in three contexts. First, it is far more commonly found among maternal grandmothers who tend to sever their relationship with their former son-in-law. "He is no

longer in my family — he is my former son-in-law."
Correspondingly, a man is likely to refer to his former wife's mother
as "my former mother-in-law." Second, if the marriage has not
produced children, the grandparents more often define a child's
former spouse as, "He is no longer in my family — there is nothing
that keeps us in contact." Third, former in-laws tend to be
eliminated from one's definition if the situation demands a transfer
of loyalties from former in-laws to new in-laws with a child's
remarriage.

For example, if a child and his or her new spouse demanded a
grandmother's undivided loyalties, then mothers tended to follow
their child's wishes and redefine the former child-in-law as no longer
a relative. This rejection of the in-law of divorce occurred often with
resistance and some grandmothers reported feelings of sadness at
the loss of a friend. One maternal grandmother described how hurt
she was when her former son-in-law introduced her to his new wife
as "my former mother-in-law." Another women described the
situation as even more distressing. "It is hard to let go. The young
man almost became like a son to me. It is like death — I don't see
him anymore." There was also some fear in forming close relationships with new intimates of adult children. "I'm not as friendly to
the people my daughter brings around. I don't want to be
disappointed again. We really like her first husband. With the
divorce, it was like losing a friend."

***Relatives by Custom.*** Another definition of in-laws centered on
invoking the norms of friendship. One paternal grandmother
described the situation, "We are close. She is not my daughter-in-
law any more, but she is still my friend." Another said of her son's
former wife, "We've always been friends. The only difference now
is we don't talk about my son." Still another responded, "Just
because two people are relatives means nothing. Why can't you
choose who you're related to? It is far better to choose to be friends
rather than relatives." Other grandmothers defined their relationships by degrees of affection. In comparing her ex-daughters-in-law,
one respondent concluded, "My son Bill's ex-wife is easier to like
than my son Bob's ex-wife."

Subjective norms of distance were used also as rationalizations
for the level of social contact maintained with children and former
in-laws. One use of distance centered on geographic proximity. "We
have always been friendly neighbors. The divorce hasn't changed

that," or "If he still lived nearby, we'd be friends." Subjective conceptions of distance were used to reflect the extent of social and emotional commitment to former in-laws. For example, one grandmother was in more frequent contact with the two former children-in-law who divorced her own children and then married each other. She justified this closeness by saying that her own children "lived too far away." In reality, the geographic distance was about the same, but she had less conflict with these former in-laws than with her own children. At the same time, both her grandchildren resided in the reconstituted family of her former children-in-law, and her friendships with them thereby assured contact with the younger generation.

In sum, numerous techniques are used to define a person as a "relative." These include not only the usual genealogical connections and sociodemographic features, but also norms regarding friendship, social responsibility, and so on. Given the optional character of our kinship system, where norms exist, they are flexible and without formal rights and obligations. Thus individuals use various strategies in organizing in-law relationships.

## Reorganization of In-law Relationships

American families affected by divorce and remarriage differ in resolving the problems that arise concerning in-law relationships. The variability of response depends on the generation level and post-divorce positions in the household, family, and wider kinship structures. For example, divorcing parents do not share households, yet they share parenting activities, at least initially. Children of divorce have potential membership in two families. Also, these families often expand as their parents remarry and bring new partners and their children into the household.

The status of grandparents in our kinship is a derived one: structurally and organizationally their grandchildren's parents provide them with a linkage to their grandchildren. From the point of view of the grandparents, three types of conflicting interests pose tensions as new patterns of solidarity emerge. First, as noted above, noncustodial grandparents have difficulty retaining access to grandchildren. Second, grandparents and other relatives cannot completely sever in-law relationships either emotionally or instrumentally, particularly if there is recognition of a shared biological linkage. Yet they must also transfer their loyalties to new in-laws when their children remarry. Third, for those who remarry, a division of loyalties can arise between step and biological kin.

These events are best illustrated by analyzing the tension that develops over a grandparent's access to grandchildren. Four dyads are likely to be affected: (1) the grandmother and her divorcing child, (2) the grandmother and her grandchild, (3) the grandmother and her former child-in-law, and (4) the divorcing individual and his or her ex-spouse. Even when affectionate ties are maintained among them, in-laws find it difficult to retain equal affiliations and loyalties after divorce between former in-laws and their own children. Because of custody patterns, the data suggest that most children of divorce live with their mother, and their mothers' parents are more actively involved in their lives. As noted, relationships between maternal grandmothers and their former sons-in-law are more likely to dissolve or become distant after divorce, perhaps because they do not generally need him to provide access to their grandchildren.

As indicated also, it is more difficult to dissolve the relationship between paternal grandparents and a former daughter-in-law, because grandparents may need her cooperation in gaining access to their grandchildren. In resolving the grandparents' access to their grandchildren, tensions between relatives of blood and of marriage and divorce are expressed in dual oppositions somewhat similar to those proposed by Lévi-Strauss (1963). The difference here is that the oppositions lie not between generations as Lévi-Strauss suggests, but along the lines of tensions between relatives of blood and those of marriage. The following models suggest how the processes of reorganization operate for the paternal grandmothers as they redefine and reorganize their relationships with children and children-in-law after divorce.

1. **The blood tie is emphasized.** This is the most common pattern. A paternal grandparent's affiliation with a former daughter-in-law diminishes or ceases. The grandparent maintains a strong supportive relationship with her son, who can provide her access to her grandchildren. The custody relationship is usually joint or with liberal visitation, so even if conflict arises, the son has no difficulty in gaining access to his children. When the linkage between generations comes from the son, the grandparent-parent-child bond or the blood tie is strengthened after divorce.

2. **The shared biological link to the grandchildren is elaborated.**  The relationship between a mother and her son may be conflictual, as is his relationship to his ex-wife. Thus the son is unable or unwilling to provide his mother with access to his children. The grandmother then has the option to retain her affiliation with her former daughter-in-law and thus to strengthen her link to her grandchildren. In such cases, the grandmother may be compensating for her son's deficiencies as a parent (Johnson and Barer 1987). She may attribute blame to him for the divorce and transfer her loyalties to his wife. Contact with the grandchildren is thereby maintained through the female-linked in-law tie, and this flexible use of the kinship system encourages the solidarity between women.

Some models do not fit neatly into the dual scheme revealed by the current findings, but take on more complex forms. For example, a son who remarries usually wants his mother to distance herself from his former wife and transfer her loyalties to his new wife. Here, the son's relationship with his mother is associated with her relationship to his new wife and that relationship is also associated with her relationship with his former wife.

The grandmother may retain a friendly relationship with their former daughter-in-law and, through her, gain access to the children of her son's first marriage. This coalition places a strain on her relationship with her son and his new wife. Invariably in such a situation, the latter express anger at what they perceive as his mother's disloyalty. In this context, access to a new grandchild may be erratic.

Alternatively the grandmother may transfer her loyalties to her son and his new wife and distance herself from his first wife. Such a move creates distance from the grandchild of her son's first marriage. Because of the fundamental cleavages the divorce process creates, it is rare for individuals to balance their loyalties and retain stable and close relationships with both sets of in-laws.

## Conclusions

Marital changes can be analyzed as vehicles for broader changes in constructions of the American family and kinship relations. While divorce rearranges family and household units, the decisions of both parents and grandparents are dominated by the overriding desire to stay in contact with biological heirs—what Craig (1979) refers to as "the vertical transmission of substance and symbolic estate." The problem of access to children in divorcing families is the strategic factor influencing the processes of reorganization and the meanings assigned to kin relations. Bonds of affection and friendliness also form among in-laws, and these allegiances can continue after a divorce. In other words, in-laws can be defined as one chooses, by norms of kinship, friendship, amity or enmity.

As Lévi-Strauss has illustrated in another context, one is likely to find a duality of oppositions with positive and negative valences between relatives by blood and those by marriage. A positive relationship between blood relationships is likely to be paired with negative relationships with in-laws. The opposition between parents and grandparents does not stand in isolation, because the structural problem centers on the grandparents' access to their grandchildren. This access is related not only to the grandmother's relationship with her child and former child-in-law but also to her son's relationship to his former wife.

With maternal grandparents, their relationship to their sons-in-law during the post-divorce period is less variable. Women usually have the primary responsibility for children, so maternal grandmothers have little difficulty in retaining their access to grandchildren. Since they do not need their son-in-law for such purposes, he is likely to be described as "my ex-in-law" and thus no longer a relative. After divorce, women are more likely than men to become dependent on their parents. Over time, men become increasingly distant from their child, in the process shedding many parenting responsibilities. They are also more likely to remarry, which further separates divorced fathers from their children. In this common situation, the maternal grandparents fill the void the divorce creates in their grandchildren's family.

# PART IV

*Economics,
Power and
Gender Relations*

## Men and Women in Southern Spain
"Domestic Power" Revisited
*David D. Gilmore*

## Contested Order
Gender and Society in the
Southern New Guinea Highlands
*Rena Lederman*

## Breadwinners and Decision-Makers
Nineteenth-Century Mexican Women Vendors
*Judith E. Marti*

## Daughters of the Forest
*Agnes Estioko-Griffin*

A Guatemalan woman works at her traditional
craft of weaving, an economic activity that may
be threatened by new production techniques.
*Photo courtesy of Tracy Bachrach Ehlers.*

▶

# Suggested Readings

**Aristophanes.** *Lysistrata.* **Garden City, New York: Halcyon House.**
More than 2000 years ago, the Greek dramatist Aristophanes created a play about women's revolution against male authority. Angered by their husbands' continual pursuit of warfare, the women wage a subtler form of battle: they withhold their sexual favors until the men put down their "arms" and open their arms to their wives. Aristophanes suggests the victory of the women is a victory for the men as well.

**Florence E. Babb. 1989.** *Between Field and Cooking Pot: The Political Economy of Marketwomen in Peru.* **Austin: University of Texas Press.**
This book weaves theory with description to introduce us to the daily working lives of women market and street vendors in Huaraz, Peru. Generally depicted as unimportant and even detrimental to Peruvian society, we see how crucial they are to the economy of Peru and the link between producers and consumers. We also discover how women vendors, often illiterate, exhibit a "good deal of business sense" and selling strategies, and have real impact in the male-dominated union.

**Beverly Newbold Chiñas. 1993.** *La Zandunga: Of Fieldwork and Friendship in Southern Mexico.* **Prospect Heights, IL: Waveland Press.**
In this personal narrative, Chiñas recounts the difficulties and rewards of being a "lone foreign woman" doing fieldwork in a small Mexican village. The Isthmus Zapotec women she has come to study, and who become her close friends, wield considerable economic and social power in the culture. They also play a major role as peace keepers, as conflict avoiders and conflict resolvers.

**Ursula K. Le Guin. 1974.** *The Dispossessed.* **New York: Avon Books.**
Who better to construct a fictionalized futuristic society than the daughter of an anthropologist? The winner of a number of science-fiction awards and the daughter of Alfred and Theodora Kroeber, Ursula K. Le Guin contrasts two cultures on two different planets. One, like our own society, is stratified according to social class and gender. The other is egalitarian; women and men live communally and share equally in all tasks. Locked in cosmic orbit, each planet is in fact a mirror image of the other. Le Guin masterfully crafts this tale that exposes the drawbacks and strengths of each type of social system.

**Annette B. Weiner. 1988.** *The Trobrianders of Papua New Guinea.* **Fort Worth: Harcourt Brace Jovanovich College Publishers.**
The banana bundles exchanged by Trobriand women at funeral rites and described by Bronislaw Malinowski as useless are shown by Weiner to be evidence of women's wealth. Her extensive research, done sixty years after Malinowski's classic study, gives women an economic and political importance that was only attributed by Malinowski to men.

**Virginia Woolf. 1929.** *A Room of One's Own.* **New York: Harcourt, Brace, Jovanovich.**
Long before feminist anthropologists identified access to economic resources as a key factor in the autonomy of women, Woolf argued that a woman must have a secure annual income and a place to write in order to make an impact on the literary world. Unlike Simone de Beauvoir, Woolf manages to make her point in succinct and almost lyrical prose.

# Introduction

*Judith Marti*

Who holds the power in the family, in the village, in the community? Men or women? Who makes important economic decisions? Who controls the pocketbook? Power has been identified as economic power and, by extension, it is generally assumed that men hold power because they control the economic system. The articles in this part challenge that view. The authors argue that power and economic decision-making are not a strictly male province and that the demarcation between male and female roles—generally drawn sharply in theory—are blurred in real life. The debate hinges on two conceptual distinctions: the opposition between *domestic* and *public* domains and the *division of labor* along female and male lines.

The distinction between *domestic* and *public* domains has been used to explain differences in activities associated with female and male roles. Women's activities belong to the domestic domain, which includes care of home and children, and the production of basic necessities for family use—for example, making baskets and weaving cloth. According to this view, women stay near home and village, and their social life revolves around close female relatives. Men's activities, on the other hand, belong to the public domain. As wage-earners, men venture outside the home and interact with a wider circle that includes non-family members associated with business or politics (Tierney 1991). Men have access to the world at large, public cafes, distant villages and towns. Women make their way from kitchen to village bakery to general store and back and, when venturing into a public square, skirt its edges, heads down, quickly crossing what is a man's world.

The idea that women and men occupy separate spheres was first formulated in Europe in the early nineteenth century and was used to describe economic life. Until that time, goods had been produced in the home, which served as both a domestic and economic unit occupied by both sexes. Industrialization forced men into factories to manufacture goods outside the home. Men became the bread-winners and carved for themselves the wider public sphere. By default, the domestic sphere became the domain of women (Tierney 1991).

Contemporary research thus inherited the assumption that men, operating in the public sphere, make the important economic and political decisions, and that women's input is secondary, more a matter of *influence* than of *power*. Power is defined as the ability to carry out one's own will despite resistance or opposition (Weber 1947). On the other hand, Louise Lamphere notes:

> A woman exercises influence when she is able to bring about a decision on another's part to act in a certain way, because it is felt to be good for the other person, independent of changes in his or her situation and for positive reasons, not because of sanctions that might be imposed[1] (1974:99-100).

As a consequence of the distinctions between *public* and *private* and between *power* and *influence*, men have been perceived as universally dominant, powerful and assertive; women are seen as subservient, compliant, and acquiescent.

Recently, researchers have begun to question the validity of assumptions that assign women to the domestic domain and men to the public domain, with status and power accruing to the latter. As June Nash points out, "even a single well-recorded case of egalitarian gender relations . . . discredits the thesis of universality of male supremacy" (Nash 1989:230).

Authors in this part refute assumptions of male supremacy in the political and economic arenas, as well as theoretical concepts that have opposed women and men, with women traditionally at the losing end. In his article "Men and Women in Southern Spain: 'Domestic Power' Revisited," David Gilmore undermines the stereotype of women as passive and men as dominant by demonstrating that power is not necessarily linked to the public sphere. Gilmore argues that lower class western Andalusian women have "domestic power [that] is real and unqualified."

The power of women is based in residence patterns. Newlyweds typically follow the bride's choice in living close to her mother, which allows the women, allied with other female kin, to form a base of power. In this community of women, the man is the outsider. In addition, even as men have little power in the domestic sphere, neither do they have it in the public domain. They are equal with their peers and ineffective against the power structure that controls the public realm. In Gilmore's article, the concept of male dominance is revealed to be a "myth."

In "Contested Order: Gender and Society in the Southern New Guinea Highlands," Rena Lederman also challenges the myth of male dominance. The idea that males define power within a group, she argues, results from the Western bias of viewing power and gender relations in terms of public and domestic domains. Ethnographers have assumed that power is derived exclusively from public rituals and ceremonies, such as the clan-sponsored pig festivals given by adult males among the Mendi of Papua New Guinea. The exclusion of women from these clan activities has been seen as evidence of their secondary position in the society.

Lederman argues that the facts show otherwise. Men as well as women are more concerned with their own exchange networks than with clan projects and, in the realm of exchange, men and women are on equal footing. Both build networks of exchange partners and both take total responsibility for their actions. A woman trades in her own name and builds up a network of partners separate from that of her husband. Lederman concludes that it is a mistake to assume that women are restricted to the domestic domain, or that male clan activities are necessarily more important than exchange activities of both men and women.

In her article "Breadwinners and Decision-Makers: Nineteenth-Century Mexican Women Vendors," Judith Marti demonstrates that women, as well as men, can negotiate power in the public domain. Women have often been portrayed as confined to the domestic sphere prior to the industrialization of Mexico at the end of the nineteenth century. However, Marti's study of women market vendors—many widows and heads of households—shows that, though illiterate and uneducated, these women were capable of negotiating power in the public domain, often successfully, as they dealt with the municipal government through petitions and complaints.

The division of power and labor into public and domestic domains has resulted in some misreading of human evolutionary development and mistaken interpretations of present-day hunter-gatherer (forager) societies. Traditionally it has been argued that men hunt and women gather. Foragers live in small bands, subsisting on wild plants and roots gathered by women and wild animals hunted by men. Their societies are egalitarian, without social classes or a ruling elite (Friedl 1978).

It has been generally assumed that, in foraging societies as in more complex societies, the status of women is inferior to that of men. Early studies linked this presumed inequality to the belief that men were responsible for the group's survival. The meat provided by men through hunting was thought to make the most significant contribution to the subsistence of the group, while women's gathering of fruits, nuts, berries and roots was believed to be of secondary importance.

These theories underestimated the contribution of women and the importance of plant food in the diet. In the 1960s, research showed that gathering activities of women often provide most food consumed by hunter-gatherers. For example, the women of one foraging !Kung group in the Kalahari desert contributed as much as 80 percent of the daily diet (Lee 1965, in Draper 1975). "A common sight in the late afternoon is clusters of children standing on the edge of camp, scanning the bush with shaded eyes to see if the returning women are visible. When the slow-moving file of women is finally discerned in the distance, the children leap and exclaim" (Draper 1975:82).

Ernestine Friedl links the status of women in foraging societies to variations in the importance placed on meat in the diet. Since it is men who hunt, the greater the dependence on meat, the more dominant the male and subservient the female. When men return from the hunt, the meat is divided in a public ceremony, with all members of the group participating and eagerly anticipating a share of the game. The largest and best portions of the meat go first to the hunting party, then to their blood relatives, in-laws, and so on, until all members of the band have received a share. Women, on the other hand, share the foods they gather only with members of their own household, creating no obligations and receiving no honors. The source of men's power, Friedl argues, lies in their control of the meat they hunt—a scarce and therefore valuable commodity. Thus it is in societies most dependent on meat that women are subordinate to men. Where gathered foods make up the daily diet, women and men are most likely to hold equal status (Friedl 1978).

A different interpretation of the public ceremony of meat distribution is given by Draper. Meat distribution does not demonstrate the power of men, she argues. Quite the contrary. Society's strict rules governing the distribution of meat show how *little* control men have over the food they contribute, whereas women retain control over what they have gathered, distributing it as they please (Draper 1975).

Still, there is prestige involved in hunting skills and anthropologists have assumed that the opportunity to demonstrate one's prowess is denied women. According to the model of man-the-hunter and woman-the-gatherer, women do not hunt because they are primarily responsible for child care and because they lack the strength to draw a bow or to throw a spear with sufficient force to bring down a large game animal. Women perform tasks compatible with child care, tasks that can be interrupted, that do not require long stays away from home, and that do not place children in danger (Brown 1970). Gathering is such a task. Hunting, on the other hand, takes concentration and quiet and can require days of stalking, at great distance from camp. Nursing an infant and pursuing a game animal were considered to be incompatible tasks. Hunting, it was thought, is best suited to men—a natural division of labor.

Agnes Estioko-Griffin's article, "Daughters of the Forest," questions these assumptions. Among the Agta of the Philippines, both women and men hunt, and women seem to find the pursuit of large game animals compatible with childrearing. Girls as well as boys play with bow and arrows, learning their skills from both mother and father. From the age of about ten, girls go on hunting expeditions with fathers, mothers, grandmothers and other members of the family. Women hunt with nursing infants and, less frequently, while pregnant. When caring for children might slow the chase, women share this responsibility, freeing the swifter among them to pursue the animal to its death.

The idea that hunting and childrearing cannot be combined is based on Western views of mothering, which overlook the fact that, in most societies, women share childrearing tasks and that men may be more involved in child care than has been generally assumed. As noted in L. L. Langness's article in Part One of this volume, women may nurse each others' infants and discipline each others' children—and fathers are often not very far away. The idea that parenting is an exclusively female role and that political and economic activities are exclusively male may well be a distorted interpretation resulting from the Western experience of industrialization, in which the *public* sphere centered on manufacturing and commerce is distinct from the *domestic* realm centered on the family. In nonindustrial societies, public and private may well overlap or even merge.

# 13

# Men and Women in Southern Spain
## "Domestic Power" Revisited[2]

### David D. Gilmore

A nthropologists have begun to challenge standard assumptions about gender in southern Europe. Initiated by feminists compensating for male bias in data collection, recent studies[3] have revitalized Mediterranean ethnography by transcending sexual stereotypes of woman as reticent, passive, and submissive, and man as active, powerful, and assertive. Disavowing the alleged "invisibility" of peasant women and providing new insight into women's daily routines both in and out of doors, these studies take us far beyond the crude sex-based oppositions such as honor/shame, kinship/friendship, and public/private, with their often hidden androcentric biases.

The argument is that if we look at what goes on within and among households rather than public policy-making, women are neither so recessive nor so powerless as male anthropologists and their informants have stated. My topic here is the question of "domestic power" and who has it. Data are taken from two rural communities in western Andalusia (Seville Province). "Fuenmayor" and "El Castillo"[4] are located some ten miles apart on either side of the national highway linking the provincial capitals of Seville and Cordoba. No comparison is intended here; the two examples are treated as a single case study.

Adapted from *American Anthropologist* 92:4, December 1990, by permission of the American Anthropological Association. Not for sale or further reproduction.

## Rural Towns

Fuenmayor is an agricultural town of about 8,000 people in the alluvial Guadalquivir River Basin. Its economy is based on dry cultivation of Mediterranean staple crops such as olives, wheat, and sunflowers. El Castillo is about half the size of its neighbor, with about 4,000 people. The two towns represent matched "twins" sharing similar market adaptations, history, and mutual participation in a generally shared ritual cycle. As in the larger town, the Castilleros are almost all involved in rainfall agriculture. The smaller community has somewhat more land under garden irrigation and so has a slightly higher per capita income.

El Castillo also has a vestigial cottage industry of esparto-grass manufacturing, producing tiny quantities of sandals, mats, and bridles, but this is hardly thriving today with the competition of mass-produced goods. In contrast, Fuenmayor has one of the few liquor mills in the *comarca* (ecological zone), producing small amounts of bottled anisette and cheap brandy. Sometimes this contrasting specialization gives rise to jokes about drunks versus cobblers, but otherwise the two towns enjoy friendly relations and their people mingle freely, intermarrying without comment.

Both towns are class-stratified, with relatively minor differences in wealth being the source of much discussion and concern. The main difference is that El Castillo does not have a significant resident gentry (*señoritos*) because its municipal territory is more subdivided. In addition, El Castillo has no aristocratic absentee landowners as does Fuenmayor, whose municipal territory includes a huge latifundium[5] owned by a Madrid-based duke. So, while the people of Fuenmayor recognize three resident social classes — the gentry, the peasants (*mayetes*), and the landless laborers (*jornaleros*) — the Castilleros proudly say they are more egalitarian, with only peasants and farm workers present. "We are more together," they say, glossing over the fact that there are a few wealthy peasant families who hire labor.

Today, both communities are Left-leaning, with strong Communist and Socialist representation, although in keeping with the generally more sophisticated quality of Fuenmayor's political life, most of the current regional leaders come from Fuenmayor. In most other respects, also, the two towns are similar, especially in their lingering observation of traditional sex and gender distinctions. In what follows I discuss primarily the men and women of the working classes: smallholding peasants and rural proletarians.

The gentry of Fuenmayor and the relatively few rich farmers of El Castillo form an important contrast that I will address later.

The rigid sexual segregation typical of Andalusian agrotowns prevailed in these two towns until the 1970s, which represents our ethnographic present. As throughout the region, men are expected to remain outside the home, either at work, or, when unemployed or after hours, at the neighborhood tavern. Men who linger at home are morally suspect; their manhood is questionable. Community gossip is relentless on this score. Men who avoid the male camaraderie of the bars at night are often likened to "motherhens," and "brooding cows." Very concerned about their manly image, most men avoid spending too much time indoors.

In El Castillo, there is one exception to this. Some men have organized an "eating club," which meets alternately in each club member's home. The man in question prepares a feast with his wife's help and invites all the others to the festivities. This, however, is somewhat of an anomaly, and even the Castilleros say openly that this is daring and "modern."

Men and women in both towns say that men "belong" in the streets, women in the home. A good woman is "mistress of her house": chaste, housebound, secluded, a careful housekeeper and a devoted mother. A good man, conversely, although he is a concerned husband and father and a good provider, is not expected to be deeply involved in domestic activities. As we have seen, any retreat away from the hurly-burly and the often exhausting male rivalries of the extra-domestic world is, for a self-respecting man, a cultural solecism as damaging to reputation as a woman's immodesty. Thus, while women are "forced" to avoid the public places, one may say equally that men are "forced" to give up the tranquility and comfort of the home for the greater part of the day.

Depending upon individual personality, this spatial "gender schema" (Bem 1983) can be said to be equally repressive for both sexes. One is tempted to add that the association of "public" with freedom and power, and of "private" with deprivation and oppression, is an ethnocentric imposition upon a much richer reality.

## Conjugal Decision Making
### Prenuptial Example

In Andalusia, the engagement is usually a long, drawn-out process often involving years. Consequently, such decisions often presage future directions and set the stage for marital relations to come. The following incident involves fiances (*novios*) from El Castillo. It involves the most important decision a couple can make: when to marry.

Eulogio, a man of about 30, and Carmen, 28, had been engaged for four years—a relatively long period, but not unusual by any means. Carmen decided it was time to marry: she had compiled her *ajuar* or trousseau; her parents had finally rebuilt and furnished an upstairs apartment in the parental home for the newlyweds. Besides, she was impatient for the big day. However, Eulogio resisted setting a date, and the wedding was becoming a bone of contention. A trucker with a growing business transporting comestibles to and from Seville, he felt he needed more time to amass capital before marriage. As he put it to friends, a man wants to gain financial independence before, not after, marriage—a common sentiment finding wide approval among his friends and confidants. So a basic disagreement erupted, setting the stage for a battle of wills, directly observed by Eulogio's male friends.

The unfolding of their rather stormy nuptial story is revealing for two reasons: first, because of the personal characteristics of the fiances, and second, because of the fact that within Eulogio's circle of bachelor friends, he was considered an exemplary "strong man," whose relations with his fiancee were watched closely for evidence of the hoped-for male domestic prerogative. That is, Eulogio was considered somewhat of a test case in the sense of masculine "right," a model for other as-yet unmarried men in his circle. Whether or not he would prevail over a woman was therefore regarded among his fellows as an augury. As elsewhere in Spain, El Castillo men pay lip service to an ideology of patriarchal privilege—at least in their bachelor days.

Eulogio was a gregarious man, tall and athletic, a successful risk-taker in business, stentorian in conversation, somewhat boastful, generous, "correct" in his dealings with men. Up to that point, too, he had appeared dominant in courtship (he appeared to be in charge, at least in public). In his teens, he had been a leader of his *pandilla*, or youthful clique, had achieved noncommissioned officer's rank in the army, and was considered to have leadership qualities. Independence and self-assurance were his hallmarks, consciously cultivated and acknowledged among both men and women in El Castillo. Contrariwise, Carmen was a small, demure, physically unimpressive women, who gave no indication, at least among men, of any outstanding qualities of character.

When Eulogio told his friends that his wedding would be postponed for another year because, as he put it, *he dicho* ("I have spoken"), there was general agreement that Carmen would simply have to wait. Yet within a month, Eulogio astonished his friends by sheepishly confiding that the wedding date had been set, that Carmen had gotten her way on an early marriage and that there was "no remedy." What had caused this dramatic turnaround? One day I sat in a bar with a number of mutual friends who were discussing the fiasco.

The men earnestly debated Eulogio's demise. One bachelor, Geraldo, expressed shock over his friend's craven capitulation. How was it possible, he asked, that a big strong man like Eulogio could relent so easily, put up so weak a struggle, and be so dominated by a small and apparently demure woman? "Who rules," Geraldo asked plaintively, "the man or the woman?"

The verb used here is *mandar*, "to command or dictate," a commonly heard term in discussions of politics. This concept of *manda*, or rule, has historically played an important role in masculine self-image in Andalusia, especially among rural farm workers. For these men to maintain their honor they must rule themselves, be their own master; hence they are manly. To be "ruled," by which is meant to be controlled by or dependent upon others, is to be dominated, with almost a ring of emasculation about it. One who is ruled is *manso*, "tame," the same term used in the farm context for a steer, a castrated bull (Marvin 1984:65). The "rule" concept finds symbolic expression in all walks of life, political, sexual, and interpersonal. Hence its use is affectively important in contexts in which male self-image is involved. Geraldo's question therefore had resonance beyond the call to colors in the battle of the sexes. It brought a reflective response from another, older man.

This man, Carlos, himself married, had the advantage of personal experience in such matters and also knew the fiances better than the rest. As such men often do in Andalusian bars, Carlos gave a little speech, beginning with the standard pontifical prelude: "look man, what happens is the following" (*lo que paza e' lo ziguiente*). Listening attentively, the others found his subsequent comments both amusing and profoundly true.

Carlos spoke candidly about the balance of power between the sexes. He allowed that the man rules in Spain, except, he added ironically, "when he doesn't." This latter occurs in most matters that are important to the woman. The reason for this is that the man is preoccupied by other matters and cannot give his full attention to details to which his wife, or fiancee, devotes all her energies. The final say in such matters, according to Carlos, is held not by the man or the woman, but by the support they can muster from interested kin. In this sense, the woman will prevail in domestic matters because she has the unfailing support of her mother, whose role in life is to protect her daughter and to advance her interests, while the man stands alone. The women, then, in tandem, can almost always "wear the man down." Carlos thus introduced two important principles: the inherent power of women in conjugal matters as a result of the divided attention and solitariness of men; and more telling, the considerable role played by the infamous *bête noire* of Andalusian husbands, the mother-in-law (*suegra*), in terrorizing her son-in-law. The invocation of the mother-in-law drew sighs of recognition and self-pity from most men present.

Carlos added that personality is of course very important here. For the man to prevail against wife and *suegra* he must be unusually "strong," meaning stubborn. However, even if he is strong and his wife is "submissive" (*floja*), his *suegra* is always strong, and the alliance of women is too potent to resist without an intolerable exhaustion of male energies. Equally important is the fact that the husband is rarely at home, leaving the field open to usurpation by wife and *suegra*, who are deeply invested in matters of the home. In any case, it is clear that "power" in this case, at least from the male perspective, was wielded by a woman, or perhaps more accurately, women in domestic alliance, since the ability to prevail in an important decision was "unexpected," unequivocal, and independent of "right" as men see it. Although my informants would be surprised to hear the word power used in this seemingly trivial context, they would nevertheless agree that important decisions affecting a man's life are often beyond his control and in the hands of manipulative or scheming women.

As Carlos was finishing his peroration about the power of the *novia* allied with the dreadful mother-in-law, one of the most popular local poets and comedians, a man known to everyone by his nickname "Juanito el Chocho," walked into the bar. Overhearing our conversation, the poet joined in by performing a credible pantomime of his "pugilistic" *suegra*, replete with right hooks and uppercuts. These comical convulsions culminated in a crescendo of obscene gestures indicating "she has me by the ass." Finally, before wandering off to the bar to reward his own performance with a drink, he sang a *copla* from one of his own epics, entitled "La Vida del Hombre" ("Man's Life")—a typical way of concluding such discussions by invoking the summary power of wit. After catching the lyrics, the other men joined in:

| | |
|---|---|
| *Yo pelé con mi novia* | I had a fight with my *novia* |
| *Y mi suegra se enteró.* | And my mother-in-law (to be) found out. |
| *Me pegó con una caña* | She jumped on top of me with a club |
| *Y encima me la cascó!* | And gave me a thorough drubbing! |

Again, the term *encima* has emotional resonance. Literally "above," or "on top of," it is used to express social hierarchy and domination, as in the commonly heard expression *los ricos nos están encima*, "the rich are on top of us." To be "encima" also has obvious sexual connotations.

While these men clearly felt abused by the outcome of Eulogio's premarital squabble, I am unfortunately unable to provide his antagonists' view. For reasons of discretion, I was unable to interview Carmen or her mother alone. Despite recent arguments to the contrary (Gregory 1984), it is still inadvisable for a male fieldworker to approach unchaperoned women in places like Andalusia, because men take umbrage at such things.

Yet I did get some casual female input. The few women I was able to query regarded Carmen's victory as "only natural" because, as they said, technical matters involving marriage are a "woman's business" (*cosa de mujeres*). For a man to interfere in such matters was to them as unseemly as his attempting to dictate a silverware pattern or an upholstery color. So here is an area where male "right" seems to contrast with female "prerogative" or sexual "seemliness," and the former may indeed be contested, since the prerogatives of sex role seem ambiguous.

## Conjugal Decisions

Once a couple marries, the newlyweds are faced with three immediate problems, the solutions of which will have permanent impact upon their future: first, where to set up residence; second, how to administer domestic finances and how to allocate previous savings in order to set up an immediately comfortable home; and, finally, when to have children and how many to have. Naturally there are other questions that arise, depending upon idiosyncrasies, but these three represent the major, initial, seminal or "organic" decisions that all newlyweds must make at the outset of establishing an independent household.

Postmarital residence in Fuenmayor shows a very strong neolocal, but "matrivicinal" (Carrasco 1963) tendency; that is, newlyweds tend to choose a new home that is near that of the wife's family. By "near" is normally meant within five minutes' walking distance. Minuscule degrees of distance are a major issue among engaged couples. I have heard both men and women state seriously that a house two blocks away was *lejos,* or "distant." People describe a house on the other side of town (about ten minutes' walking time) as *muy lejos,* or very far away. In addition, when the newlyweds must remain in one of the parental homes because of financial constraints (neolocality is preferred), there is a marked uxorilocal [residence with the parents of the bride] tendency. In Fuenmayor, 71 percent of households show a matrilateral extension. This same matrilateral tendency is equally well marked in El Castillo, where 79 percent of the extended multigenerational families were living with the wife's parents in the 1970s.

As a result, many Andalusian towns display a female-oriented residence pattern and sororal neighborhoods [neighborhoods in which sisters live close together], as is true of some Greek, Portuguese, and southern Italian peasants (Casselberry and Valavanes 1976; Pina-Cabral 1986:72; Brøgger 1990; Davis 1973:22-25). These data challenge conventional wisdom about patriarchal, patrilocal peasantries. As Davis reports for the town of Pisticci in southern Italy, this residential preference tends to create a permanent female infrastructure, or matri-core; that is, neighborhoods are dominated by women's ties because women remain co-residential more often and longer than men and because they reside in close association with childhood neighbors, kinswomen, and parents after marriage. According to village perceptions of spatial-social distance, it is the husband who is most often the "stranger" in his home or neighborhood, residing "very far" from his parents, who may be located more than two blocks away, and from his agnates.[6] In a statement that may serve for Andalusia, Davis writes: "The neighborhood is a community of women: women bring their husbands to live there; women have their close kin there; daughters will continue to live there when parents are dead" (1973:71-72). As Davis astutely notes, this matri-core is a woman's "chief source of power" (1973:22), since it provides her access to allies and to sources of information and gossip, and establishes a continual basis of kinship support.

Equally true in western Andalusia, this quasi-matrifocality raises two epistemological questions in considering domestic power: first, to what degree is this matrilocal-matrivicinal pattern consonant with the assumed male domestic prerogatives; and second, what is the effect of such a residence pattern on conjugal decision making? Although there is the usual amount of individual variation, certain patterns emerge.

When I first became aware of the matrifocal tendency, I queried men about it, since it seemed at variance with the androcentric emphasis, Most men said that they quietly acquiesced to the wife's request to "live near mamma," for a number of reasons, any one of which may have been paramount in any particular case. As in Seville City (Murphy 1983), some men said they wanted to evade the continuing supervision of their fathers, although this seems less pressing in these rural towns. The most common response was that residence was an issue that meant a great deal to women and less to men, as men are by nature more "independent" of parental ties. The wife, men allow, especially a new bride, needs the support of her mother in establishing a new home; so why break up this proven domestic team?

Basically the men felt that any attempt on their part to "come between" wife and mother-in-law by insisting on virilocal residence [residence with the parents of the groom] would backfire, leading to a passive-aggressive campaign by both to undermine his comfort and his peace of mind for the rest of his life, and that therefore the battle for dominance was just not worth the penalty.

To be sure, part of the answer reflects selfishness rather than mere passivity, since men want their homes to be run well and efficiently. Andalusians believe that since women are in charge of domestic operations they must be allowed full control; otherwise the man's life will suffer from disorganization. As one man put it: wife and mother are a "clique" that works well only when there is physical proximity. In a sense, therefore, the mother-in-law is regarded as a necessary nuisance, a kind of existential penance. The most common response to questions about the uxorial dominance in residence choice was therefore a resigned acceptance of proven practice with the frequently heard conversational suffix: *no hay remedio* (there is no remedy for it). This is a rhetorical device that one encounters in many male pronouncements concerning wives, mothers-in-law, and women's capacity to get their own way in general. Although this may reflect, in part, the usual male indifference to "feminine" preoccupations, it also seems to indicate a degree of moral surrender, as the issues concerned were indeed of great importance to men and were often, as they knew, the sources of dissatisfaction later. In this sense, we may characterize male abstention from such domestic matters as de facto, although ambivalent, recognition of uncontested female authority in domestic decision making.

The most important consequence of the husband's ambiguous acquiescence is that the *suegra* maintains a high profile in the man's life, often intruding into domestic arrangements and sometimes asserting the balance of power in marital quarrels or disagreements. The powerful image of this invasive female scourge is found also among urbanites in western Andalusia, testifying to a regional stereotype deeply rooted in male consciousness (Press 1979). On the surface, the Andalusian's fearful attitude about his mother-in-law seems ubiquitous rather than area-specific, aside from the possibly anomalous intensification of affinal ties as a result of matrivicinal residence. Most bilateral societies, including our own, have their own folklore about the horrors of this stock villain in the domestic comedy. Yet, because of the associated structural preponderance of the domestic matri-core, the Andalusian husband often finds himself outmatched by the weight this fierce harridan throws in supporting her daughter, and his laments often evoke a revealing sense of masculine alienation before a female dyad elevated to domestic sovereignty.

Naturally the *suegra*'s power is enhanced by simple residential propinquity, but even more psychologically salient is the fact that she and her daughter enjoy a moral symbiosis that the husband cannot match. Although he may have many friends, his male friendships are founded as much on competition as cooperation, and he cannot plead for help in domestic skirmishes without endangering his reputation as a "strong man." His own mother of course may intercede, but no man wants to have his mother fight his battles. So for various reasons, he acquiesces, maintaining a respectable facade of indifference before his peers. In addition the husband knows all too well that "trouble" (*jaleo*) with the *suegra* leads to marital discord, unless the wife is "strong" and prefers to mollify her husband while alienating her own mother. However, this is said to be rare.

With their vibrant oral traditions (Brandes 1980), Andalusians are consummate artists of the human condition. Because of the powerful proscription on fighting and violence in their culture, they prefer to express their sorrows and troubles in song and art rather than in outbursts. Accordingly, the alliance of wife and *suegra*, with the latter assuming mythopoetic status as a masculine nemesis, has achieved a kind of apotheosis in verse and poetry. In both Fuenmayor and El Castillo, the men sing *coplas* during Carnival to great acclaim and applause, reflecting common male concerns. What is most interesting about these verses is the formidable physical power ascribed to the *suegra* in metaphors and tropes of specifically virile animal and military imagery, a tradition rendering "marital" as "martial," in which the male appears victimized and indecisive. This may reflect, as Driessen perceptively suggests (1983:126), deep-seated insecurity or cognitive dissonance about the power of women, which the "cover" of male indifference or self-abstention is meant to assuage. During the Fuenmayor Carnival of 1970, one famous poet sang the following *copla*, receiving accolades from the cheering men:

> All mothers-in-law in the world
> Are pretty much the same.
> I fight with mine, too,
> So listen how it goes.
> She kicks me out of her house
> Forty times a day.
> Good, bad, indifferent,
> They all belong in the cavalry.[7]

Another poet describes his *suegra* as a *bicho fiero* ("fierce beast") which he hopes someday to *desbravacer* ("tame" or, more colorfully, "geld") as though she were a wild animal.[8] One man told me that his *suegra* was a "dragon" who expelled him from "her house" (which was his house, as well) whenever he disagreed with her. Other men described their *suegra* as a "brave bull," a "tomcat," an "armor-plated lizard," and other such scaly or vicious animals.

With all their hyperbole, these pseudo-jocular laments are revealing because of the intimations of sex-role reversal and power inversion with their unconscious implications of sublimated male gender-identity insecurities. Also revealing is the sense of powerlessness expressed as an evanescent integration into the domestic setting as a result of the man's tenuous connection to the home, which is, after all, haunted—sometimes owned outright—

by his *suegra*. Even if the man lives neolocally, the *suegra*'s intrusion into his home is so all-encompassing that the man feels menaced in his own house. As we have seen, this domestic weakness is partly attributable to a masculine abdication of domestic responsibilities in exchange for a full larder and efficient housekeeping, but belying the ready acceptance of this domestic "service" is the continual eulogizing over lost powers.

Faced with this powerful matri-core, the working-class husband often finds some of the most basic decisions in his life taken over unilaterally by affines. For example, many men complain plaintively that although they hate to emigrate to work outside of Andalusia, they are literally forced to go when faced with the *fait accompli* of a decision made by wife and *suegra*. One man in El Castillo, a peasant farmer, echoed a commonly heard complaint when he confided that he went to work in Madrid after his wife decided they needed a new refrigerator—a prestige item that many women buy for competitive "show" rather than real need (since women shop daily, the refrigerator often stands empty in the kitchen). Most men are committed to providing as well as possible for their families, but often decisions about consumption needs, and therefore about employment, are made by the joint demands of kinswomen, with the *suegra* again figuring demonically in this process. Another popular carnival *copla* puts it this way:

> Working, working,
> Working night and day,
> Because when I'm unemployed
> And not earning any money,
> No one can control my
> Wife and mother-in-law.[9]

Later in this song the *suegra* and wife are scolded for their voracious appetite for consumer goods, which forces the poor man to emigrate to Germany as "the only way to pay back what I owe in Spain." Again, the point to be made is that a worker or poor peasant, who has very little input into purchasing decisions, senses a helplessness before the power of the matri-core. The wife, in alliance with her mother, may make the most important life decision, and the man may feel a passive victim.

Occasionally, a man may express the opinion that his wife cares more about her mother than her husband, a complaint that may convey a hidden sense of both injustice and affective exclusion. For example, there was one man in Fuenmayor, Adolfo, whose wife kept forgetting his lunch (the main meal of the day). Her excuse was that her mother was old and needed her constant attention. One day I went home with Adolfo directly from the bar where we had been enjoying a pre-prandial beer. He had invited me home for the midday meal, after which I was to interview him. But when we arrived, Adolfo was chagrinned to find that no lunch had been prepared and there was nothing in the family larder but a small sausage. A note taped on the wall announced that his wife had gone to visit her ill mother. Although embarrassed and disappointed, Adolfo took it all in stride, confiding to me that "that's how women are." A man is a fifth wheel in his own house, he noted, adding peevishly that at least he had the consolation of knowing that the "old dragon" would not be bossing him around that day, since she was sick. It is clear that many lower-class men feel marginalized in their own homes.

In addition to her dominance in economic planning (with her mother's active support), the non-elite Andalusian wife usually acts as the unofficial administrator of domestic finances. This is especially true among the rural proletarians in both Fuenmayor and El Castillo, where the husband may surrender his entire day-wage to his wife each night. In return he expects the house to be run properly, and will himself be given a small "allowance" for his expenses at the bar and for his nightly card game. Many laborers refer to their wives in a semi-ironic vein as the *ama* ("boss") or *jefa* ("chief") of the house — words reserved in the wider public context for such authority figures as employers and political leaders. One man in Fuenmayor spoke of his wife seriously as the "generalissima" of household finances (using the feminized form of Generalissimo Franco's[10] title), adding that he did not care what she did with the money he earned so long as he was returned enough to buy refreshments at the neighborhood tavern.

I remember one worker getting up from an exciting card game to run home to wheedle his wife for more money. His fellows remarked that his wife was a "peseta pincher," but they agreed that her supervision of his gambling was probably a good thing, as he tended to bet poorly at cards. Most men present admitted that their own wives held the family purse strings and that this was unavoidable, since they (the men) were rarely at home. They said that a man works (or "sacrifices") to give money to his wife and his family and that a man who withheld his wages from his wife was "mean" and a reprobate: he was depriving his children. Again, male acquiescence here may be seen as morally ambivalent. Men evade onerous responsibilities by giving the wife final authority, but there is a lingering self-doubt about it; as usual, this tension finds expression in self-deprecating humor.

## Domestic Power and Class

This tendency to let the wife and her mother run the family's finances correlates with class status. Among the wealthier peasants, most husbands retain rights over the domestic economy and play a more active part in allocating resources for the family. Among the gentry in Fuenmayor, most husbands take a more active role in finances and may even control the family purse strings through bank accounts and investments that the wife rarely knows about. Or, in some landowning families, a husband may simply provide his wife with a monthly allowance, while she does little more than distribute this to various domestic employees with instructions on purchases.

In the working classes, however, where surplus cash is a rarity and where the domestic economy is often managed on a credit or deficit basis because of the vagaries of agrarian employment, the wife "rules" the household economy and the husband accepts this. Although he may realize that it further diminishes his "power" in the domestic sphere, he is often willing to trade this power for the peace of mind that comes from being shielded form petty fiscal annoyances. Again, working-class male remoteness here is a trade-off in which the man sacrifices control for a modicum of comfort. Conversely, in the propertied classes, comfort is assured through the practice of hiring servants; in addition, or perhaps because of this, the rich tend to live either patrilocally or patrivicinally after marriage: the *suegra* is not "needed."

## Power and Sexuality

Finally, there is the "power" exercised by wives through their ability to withhold sex, which is the same in all classes. Generally it is assumed among men in Andalusia that women are highly sexed, although it is the man who awakens and directs this amorphous source of female sexual energy. Yet there is also a general understanding that in marital relations, it is the woman who "uses" the strategy of withholding sex as a means of controlling or persuading.

Some men naturally are "flojo" sexually (weak or impotent), and their wives may be frustrated by this lamentable failing. But according to informants—both male and female—a husband never withholds sex purposefully in order to manipulate his wife. "He could not do that if he were a man," one man asserted firmly, adding that this is an exclusively feminine weapon that would be humiliating for a man.

Withholding sex is also a weapon that carries more than just psychological weight. I was once talking to a couple of newlyweds, who quite spontaneously asked me and my wife (a medical doctor, as they knew) about the best way to conceive a child. They had heard rumors that the impregnation of the wife could be assured and the sex of the child could be determined by "positions."

Although we could not advise them on this issue, the conversation soon turned to more concrete subjects, such as the importance of having a first child exactly nine months after the wedding. Husband and wife agreed that this is necessary to quell gossip about the man's potency. If a first child is delayed, they added, people assume that the husband has sexual problems and they gossip about his manhood. They also implied that since this is so, some brides are able to "lead the groom about by the nose" by threatening to withhold sex. the man has to placate her so that she quickly becomes pregnant. This is another example of female "power" wielded without respect to "right."

## Conclusions

If power is defined as personal autonomy and the ability to impose one's will regardless of the source of this ability, then one must conclude, along with Rogers (1975) that men have less of this ability than their wives—at least in the lower classes of these Andalusian communities. Although the lower-class men claim that this imbalance is by design and that it "frees" them to concentrate on more important matters, I am inclined to regard this as Rogers seems to do, as farcical face-saving, rather than an inverse "power" to evade work.

Beyond the domestic realm, real power is a scarce commodity denied to most men. Most Andalusian workers have little or no political power; nor do they exercise power in relations with their peers, all of whom start from the same point of equivalency in basically egalitarian relationships. They may have influence with their cronies, but few men can be said to have power, whatever its provenance—except perhaps over their sons, but even this is equivocal (Murphy 1983). Since working-class men have virtually no *alternative* sources of power over their peers in communities like Fuenmayor and El Castillo, one may conclude that they are relatively powerless compared to women, whose domestic power is real and unqualified.

One very important point should be made about relations of dominance and subordination in the context of class-stratified marginal communities like those in rural Andalusia. This is that any approach to the dimension of power that uses only gender as a criterion is probably epistemologically invalid. Where power is concerned, there are men and men, and there are women and women. As Davis has pointed out, what matters is not only sex, but also relative access to resources. One may not speak of a category "men" opposed to another category "women," because this is an oversimplification that, in Herzfeld's phrase, "sacrifices *complementarity* to *opposition*" (1986:215) and conflates theoretically subtle symbols. Europeanist ethnography shows us the pervasiveness of social class and its power to determine, not sex of course, but the principles of group formation. Gender is one additional or parallel dimension of the social organization of production, not an arbitrary symbolic schema imposed independent of structural and historical context (Driessen 1983:131). Almost everywhere we look, "Alpha males"[11] dominate women *because* they dominate men and so one must speak more generally of multidimensional *human* rather than unidimensional gender hierarchies.

# 14

# Contested Order
## Gender and Society in the Southern New Guinea Highlands[12]

*Rena Lederman*

As opposed to the common style of ethnography that lets native male statements and actions stand for the whole of social reality, gender-conscious studies of the past fifteen years have either critically dissected these facts as representations of particular, male interests, or else have sought to describe and account for female experience itself. Either way, such feminist-inspired work helps place the contradictoriness of sociocultural systems center stage. In this paper I treat culture as contested rather than shared, and therefore represent social practice more as an argument than as a conversation.

The Mendi Valley is located in the Southern Highlands Province of Papua New Guinea, a region that largely escaped ethnographic scrutiny until the 1970s. By central Highlands standards, the Mendi people are moderately densely settled on their land, and have an intensive system of agrarian production based on the sweet potato. Sweet potatoes are the human staple food. They are also fodder for pigs, which, along with pearlshells and P. N. G. national currency, are given as gifts at weddings and mortuary ceremonies, and in the establishment of both personal relationships and political alliances. As in many other Highland societies, both individual and group standing are conceptualized as actively produced in gift exchange.

In the Highlands anthropological literature, analysis has focused on the organization and political dynamics of "clans": ideologically

Adapted from *American Ethnologist* 16:2, May 1989, by permission of the American Anthropological Association. Not for sale or further reproduction.

agnatic, exogamous landholding collectivities[13] in the names of which people go to war or sponsor public distributions of wealth (like pig festivals and war-death compensation prestations). In the Mendi valley, as in many other parts of the Highlands, intraclan relations appear "corporate," by which I mean only that the Mendi use clan names to talk about transgenerationally enduring communities of social responsibility, and that as fellow clan members, persons are held to be equivalent (substitutable for one another) and capable of unitary purpose ("one talk" or "one mind"). However, by and large, only men are formally involved in clan affairs.

The Mendi distinguish two kinds of gift-mediated social relations in which men and women are differentially involved. Exclusively male, "corporate" clan (*sem onda*) relationships are distinguished from ego-centered "network" relationships between exchange partners (*twem ol*). *Twem* relationships are ephemeral insofar as they are created by each person over the course of a lifetime and dissolve upon his or her death. In Mendi, all adults—male and female—establish exchange partnerships and transact with their partners for various reasons.

We have for a long time assumed that clans are dominant institutions in the Highlands, and that the exclusion of women (and nonagnatic men) from clan affairs bespeaks a second-class status (that is, nonpublic or nonpolitical). But while the systematic exclusion of some social categories from dominant institutions may be a good cross-cultural criterion of subordination, I argue here that it is not at all clear that clans are dominant—that the two forms of sociality are hierarchically ordered—in Mendi. Nor, then, is it clear that exclusion from them is, in itself, evidence of subordination.

Understanding female exclusion from clan affairs is particularly difficult because of how thoroughly "genderized" social discourse is in the Highlands (Herdt 1981). Gender meanings are a concrete model of the social order. Highlanders do not use gender constructions (categorical distinctions between "male" and "female" qualities) just to refer to relations between men and women. They use such constructs also in thinking, talking and arguing with each other about more elusive matters: about personal agency and ambition, about kinds of social responsibility and continuity of social identity, about productivity and value.

Because genderized terms are used to speak about such a variety of things, they cannot be analyzed as an abstract and formal system of consistent propositions. Divorced from the contexts and politics of their use, Highland gender constructions convey ambiguous information about women's social agency and value, and about their relations with men. Contradictory idioms and conceptions of gender may be applied by the same persons in *distinct* social contexts, and by different people in the *same* context. The meaning of a particular idiom is to be found in its relations with others and its use in practical contexts of social action.

## Women, Men and Networks in Mendi

I begin by describing what is least familiar: Mendi women's participation in exchange networks. Women's activities are not restricted to what we would call a "domestic" domain. Their production and exchange work involves them with people both outside and inside their husband's and their own natal communities. While Mendi women may not be unique among southern Highlanders, their involvements do appear to differ from their counterparts in the northern Highlands, where women engage in exchange predominantly in support of their husbands and brothers and are not recognized by men as "transactors" (M. Strathern 1972). In contrast, Mendi women may participate "in their own names" in exchanges. Both women and men say that women may determine the allocation of sweet potatoes, pigs, and other products of their labor, as well as of objects they have obtained in exchange, and suffer the consequences of their decisions.

In Mendi, each person builds up a network of exchange partners upon whom to depend whenever he or she needs valuables. In contrast to the practice elsewhere in Melanesia, in Mendi people do not inherit partnerships from their parents. The number and type of partners each person accumulates reflects his or her particular level of interest and involvement in transactions and individual strategies of developing exchange relationships. One's *twem* partners may be any kind of relative and may also include nonrelatives—for example, someone met on the road while traveling between communities. People sometimes refer to particular members of their own clans with whom they have personal exchange relationships as *twem ol*. Nevertheless, a person's most important *twem* partners are usually related to him or her by marriage, and marriage is a key context for reproducing *twem* relations.

Affinal relations in Mendi commonly involve people from neighboring, allied clans. Similarly, one's exchange partners are likely to live in localities other than one's own. For example, they may belong to other clans in the tribal alliance with which one's own group affiliates or to groups belonging to other tribal alliances. One may also establish exchange partnerships with (and marry) members of hostile groups. Not only may one's partners come from socially distant clans, but they may come from geographically distant ones as well. Exchange relationships typically extend far beyond a person's local community.

So far I have been describing exchange networks as if gender did not matter. And, in many respects, women's networks are similar to men's. Women's exchange partners are both male and female; they may be relatives or nonrelatives, just as for men. Women's transactions are similar to those of men in the sense that they are not domestic or local. They extend not only to the woman's husband's people (with whom she usually lives) and to male and female residents of her own natal community, but also (for example) to her female agnates' affines, to the kin of women and men married into her husband's clan, and to unrelated people in other communities. A number of my female informants reported that in the period just before and after the Australian administration set up headquarters in the Mendi Valley (1950), women used to travel as far as Kandep (a five-day trek northward) in order to get pigs and salt from their maternal relatives.

While network exchanges are not normatively an exclusive preserve of either men or women, and while men and women transact with one another, men are more active in network exchanges than women are. They have more exchange obligations (gift "debts" and "credits"; *saon* in Mendi) and more exchange partners than women do, and may spend more time at these activities than women.

In part, this reflects the social organization of production. Men are responsible for clearing forest regrowth to make new gardens; but while this work is important and energy-intensive, the need for it is infrequent. Gardens in much of the Mendi Valley are cultivated continuously. The main garden work of Mendi men involves repairing fences and ditches (essential for preventing pigs from damaging gardens as they forage along village paths and in bush areas). While men are also responsible for planting and maintaining special crops (like sugar cane), and may occasionally help their wives in the production of sweet potatoes, their work can be done episodically, and need not be an everyday chore.

In contrast, women are responsible for planting, weeding and harvesting sweet potatoes and greens, a daily cycle of work in a system essentially without harvesting seasons and food storage. Women's garden work provides the staple foods upon which both people and their pigs depend each day. Furthermore, women are expected to do most of the continuous work involved in maintaining the household pig herd (their own pigs, as well as pigs claimed by their husbands, children, and other people). In caring for pigs, women produce one of the most important exchange valuables for both men and women, a fact of critical importance in the comparative understanding of Highlands political economies and their contemporary transformations. Furthermore, unlike men, Mendi women's conventional sense of themselves as social "agents," capable of creating relations and values, is constituted and expressed in their garden work and allocation of garden products.

The quantitative level of involvement of men and women in *twem* exchange differs also because, to a degree, they transact for different reasons. Women establish new exchange partnerships in order to obtain wealth required to maintain existing ones; that is, they treat the interpersonal relationship as an end in itself. They also transact with their partners in order to contribute in their own names to individually sponsored public marriage and mortuary prestations. Men establish *twem* partnerships for these same reasons, but they also engage in network transactions to acquire wealth for display in clan-sponsored ceremonies (for example, warfare death compensation), a concern women do not necessarily share and from which, in any case, they are formally excluded.

Though they may demur, even young, unmarried women are expected to make decisions concerning the allocation of wealth. For example, young girls are given pigs by their relatives, who say that it would be shameful for them to begin their married lives without valuables of their own. Women do not come to their new husbands' houses empty-handed. One man argued privately with his adult son that the latter ought to give his father's-brother's-daughter a pig in return for a bridewealth pig she had promised him during early marriage negotiations with her prospective husband. The man asserted, "It would not be good for her to be in the middle, without any pigs of her own." Mendi brides distribute their own bridewealth, and are held responsible for their decisions by their occasionally disappointed relatives.

Women routinely have exchange partners who are not part of their husbands' or brothers' networks. A woman's exchange obligations vis-a-vis even those partners who are also partners of her husband are not necessarily equivalent to those of her husband; a person may choose to transact separately with a husband and wife. Women have exchange obligations of their own, and do not seek out wealth from their exchange partners merely in response to the requests of their menfolk. Thus, it is not uncommon for men and women to claim that their spouse's transactions are none of their concern (though the degree of husband/wife coordination varies greatly from household to household). Coordination is a widely shared value, but both men and women concede that it is a partnership (sometimes a power struggle) between mutually autonomous persons. Women's autonomy with respect to the exchange interests of their husbands and clansmen is also demonstrated by the fact that network transactions involving female-female links are routine; women are not simply "in between" men — linking or conveying wealth between brothers-in-law — as they are in the northern Highlands (M. Strathern 1972: cf. Feil 1984).

In network exchanges, objectively everyone is "in between." Men not uncommonly receive an item from a woman to give to another woman; women frequently do the same for men, and for other women, as men do for other men. The point is that women are widely expected to be responsible for their own gift-debts.

Mendi women's apparent autonomy — in exchange and as persons — may be unusual in the Highlands. But just as we will see that a Mendi man's "autonomy" with respect to his clansmen — his ability (and not infrequent desire) to withdraw from clan projects and pursue his own schemes — is rooted in his unique set of exchange partnerships, a matrix of intensely *social* obligations, a woman's "autonomy" from her husband also presupposes certain social forms. It is underwritten by the typically strong, though personal, support she receives from her agnatic relatives. Mendi women have very close relationships with individual members of their natal clans, with whom they visit frequently and exchange wealth. Even after they have married, many women continue to work regularly in gardens allocated to them by their fathers and brothers.

While many Mendi women today are quite ready to defend

themselves in disputes with their husbands or husbands' people, and while they not infrequently take the offensive both verbally and physically, their strongest sanction is their ability to leave their husbands either temporarily or permanently. Unlike women in nearby Highland societies (for example, Meggitt 1965), Mendi women are typically welcomed by their brothers or other close clansmen if they return to their natal communities, and may stay indefinitely until a dispute is resolved. While a husband and wife may come to blows, men are constrained by the knowledge that their wives have the power to leave them, and that such a withdrawal of labor and other kinds of cooperation will affect a man's ability to participate in community affairs. Furthermore, a man knows violence is a legitimate basis for divorce; at the least, a woman and her brother can be expected to demand compensation in pigs, pearlshells or money.

Mendi women's autonomy in exchange, and the personal support they receive from their agnates, is evident in many everyday attitudes and situations. Whether in domestic or public settings, they are frequently assertive and vocal in their dealings with one another and with men. They are quick to defend themselves when anyone, male or female, insults them. In local village courts, which most frequently concern disputes between individuals or households (not clans) within or between communities, women play an active role, contributing both testimony and opinion.

## Men and Clans

While women are active and recognized participants in many daily settings in Mendi, they are systematically and conspicuously absent from meetings held to discuss and plan clan-sponsored parades and prestations, and to coordinate preparations by allied clans. Indeed, the exclusion of women is a distinctive feature of clan meetings.

While both men and women have exchange partners with whom they transact for various reasons, only men do so specifically in order to participate in clan ceremonies. Only men are formally involved in clan affairs, determining clan policy and speaking for their clans in discussions with men of other affiliations. Although women may act as an informal audience at meetings held to discuss clan policy, they are explicitly excluded as participants. Such meetings are held either in settings conventionally defined as exclusively male (like men's clubhouses), or in settings that are normally open (like ceremonial grounds where women often congregate) but are defined and organized as exclusively "male" for meeting purposes.

Not only are in-married wives excluded, but also clanswomen: sisters and daughters who, after all, usually move to the communities of their husbands upon marriage. More surprisingly, married agnatic women resident in the community are excluded, even when they are more active in network exchanges and more articulate than their husbands who, though they be in-married men and therefore not formal members of the clan, do take an active part in meetings. This is true despite the respect and strong sense of personal identification and responsibility that Mendi men often express and demonstrate toward their clanswomen.

As such, Mendi society is similar to others in the New Guinea Highlands, which have an anthropological reputation for male dominance. In these societies, men are the predominant actors in ritual and in public political meetings and exchange ceremonies. Highlands men have, for this reason, been more accessible than women to Western outsiders (male and female anthropologists included). But the predominance of male activities in ethnographic descriptions may also be due to our own presuppositions about the relevance and relative value of such distinctions as "public" and "domestic." Our understanding of the symbolism and sociopolitical uses of gender constructions has been based predominantly on statements made by Highland men in the context of discussions about (or performances of) male fertility or initiation cults, and public, clan-sponsored wealth exchanges. Highlands ethnographers have long recognized (but have not always emphasized) that the idioms of agnation or brotherhood that Highlands men use for talking generally about the "maleness" of collective social identities and of transgenerational continuity might in fact articulate an interested perspective: an "ideology" of male dominance over women.[15]

Nevertheless, central Highlands ethnography has foregrounded clans, clan-sponsored ceremonial exchange and the role of leaders ("Big Men") in organizing them. For the most part, we have been left with the impression that clans are the integrative and taken-for-granted framework of social life. From this vantage, the part is taken for the whole: clans are the "social structure" and clan prestations and warfare drive Highlands political economies.

Our attention to collective male action, and lack of attention to the cultural value central Highlanders also accord to exchange partnerships, households, and other kinds of noncollective social relations have had the effect of implying that the latter are simply strategic means to the end of spectacular public prestations made in the names of clans, at which prominent men officiate.

An analytical focus on clanship has also constrained our understanding of male/female relations. For the Mendi case, clan-centered analysis would force us to conclude that "personal" network exchanges, along with "domestic" production, merely facilitate the "public" staging of "political" clan prestations, and have no distinct rationale of their own. Given women's exclusive involvement in network transactions, and their formal absence from clan ceremonies, this interpretation implies not only that women are political nonpersons, but also that even their claims to personal agency—based on control of their own labor and transactions—is a delusion.

In this interpretation, Mendi women's control over the pacing of their garden work and over the allocation of garden crops they have planted, and their assertions about transacting "in their own names," are illusory or superficial despite male concurrence, because men control the timing, planning and import of clan-sponsored wealth distributions. If we treat male collective relations as the overarching context and "end" of all work and all network exchanges, we would have to conclude that, regardless of how indirectly their power is expressed and regardless of their intentions or interpretations, men ultimately control both the function and the meaning of women's creative energies. In the local idiom, women would not even control their own "names"—which they claim to make through the skillful execution of garden work, and through hospitality and gift-giving—if their "personal" reputations were ultimately subsumed or encompassed by "political" clan meanings which only men make.

But if clan-centered structural analyses constrain our understanding of male/female relations, analyses centered on gender constructions and relations contribute to the general reinterpretation of Highlands sociopolitical structure by attending to the signs of a dialectic of cultural perspectives and practices.

## Networks, Groups and the Structuring of Exchange

Clan (*sem onda*) relations are "corporate" in the sense that clan names are used to define collectivities that endure beyond the lifetimes of individuals and that clan affiliation governs access to garden land and bush resources. A man's clan affiliation defines his collective social identity and community of responsibility. All of this helps to create a sense that clan relations are historically "given" facts of cultural structure. But the sociopolitical reality of any particular clan must also be actively demonstrated in exchanges, violent or amicable, aimed at reestablishing or redefining its relationship with other clans.

The specific political significance of such events is mooted at public meetings, during which men seek to establish a persuasive interpretation of events. In order to organize clan prestations, a collectivity of what are represented as "brothers" must agree to coordinate their activities and, in particular, they must hold onto their wealth in preparation for the event. Not only are women formally excluded from clan policy-making, but the "agnatic" biasing of clan genealogies conveys the sense that clan unity and transgenerational continuity are "male."

*Twem* networks are unnamed, ego-centered and unique; each exists only relative to some particular person. The members of one's own network are not necessarily members of one another's networks. Networks are unbounded and inclusive, in the sense that the network of any person articulates with the networks of each of his or her exchange partners, linking that person indirectly with thousands of others, *Twem* networks are as ephemeral as particular persons. At the same time, the specific, cultural sense of personal agency and "autonomy" (a man's with respect to fellow clan members; a woman's with respect to her household) is in large measure actualized through network exchanges of wealth (pigs, pearlshells, and money, the same items exchanged in clan ceremonies). Moreover, these relations are the main way in which a person extends himself or herself beyond the social circle of childhood, a status culturally associated with antisocial consumption.

In contrast to the years-long pacing of a clan's exchanges, the events of active exchange partnerships have a weekly or monthly rhythm. The relationship of clan members involves diffuse, generalized reciprocity,[16] whereas *twem* partners actively request wealth from one another and keep accounts of their gift-debts, often specifying when and how they ought to be repaid. In contrast to the mutual identification and substitutability of clansmen, the *twem* relationship is premised on difference: *Twem* partners have a differential need for wealth, and stand to one another alternately as givers and receivers of gifts. A premium is placed on the rapid circulation of wealth between *twem* partners: one reproduces partnerships and expands one's network by quickly distributing the wealth one has on hand.

It is especially important to understand that the exchange rationales of *twem* partnerships and of clanship are potentially in conflict. Clan and network exchanges demand a different and sometimes mutually incompatible allocation of wealth. That is, while clan ceremonies require the periodic *accumulation* of wealth, the etiquette of exchange partnerships demands the rapid *circulation* of wealth. Exchange partners have what is, in effect, joint or equivalent claims on the wealth any one of them currently holds. When a partner arrives requesting something that one has on hand, one is under some moral pressure to relinquish it. At the same time, men know they ought to coordinate with their fellow clansmen in holding onto wealth in preparation for group-sponsored prestations.

Network and clan obligations are in an important sense necessary to one another, and may be fulfilled simultaneously, as when a man manages to orchestrate his network obligations so that he can call in his "credits" and pay off his "debts" in the very act of participating in a clan event. Moreover, certain exchange conventions may be used to conjoin group and network obligations. For example, the expectation that a man will repay with an incremental value any gifts given to him by his wives' and mother's kin, if they wait for the repayment until his clan festival, encourages those relatives to be patient.

However, without such a premeditated effort of orchestration, the mutual expectations of exchange partners only partially and fortuitously feed into the coordinated projects of a community of clansmen, and may well conflict. In such an event, a man may find himself forced to delay meeting his *twem* partners' requests for wealth and to make heavy demands on his network for gifts or repayments in order to have sufficient wealth available in time for his clan's ceremony. Conversely a man's diverse commitments to his respective *twem* partners may limit his participation in a clan event. Indeed, whether as a deliberate strategy in interclan politics or for want of collective purpose, clan events are often delayed and sometimes cancelled in the name of *twem* responsibilities.

For women this conflict is not the same problem it is for men, since women are excluded from participation in clan affairs and have no voice in discussions about the collective significance of a particular event. In precolonial times of interclan warfare, women suffered the sometimes violent and dislocating effects of men's decisions to make war without the hope of enhancing their personal standing that helped make warfare meaningful to their menfolk. Since warfare has been outlawed, clan decisions made by men have more benign implications for women. Unlike men they need take no initiative in reordering network obligations for these events. However, married sisters may choose to give their brothers valuables to support their participation in clan prestations, and wives expect that they and their kin will receive incremental repayments for any gifts or labor they provide their husbands when his clan sponsors such an event.

Despite the apparent asymmetry in the means available to men and women for shaping the conditions of their own and other's actions, and despite the memory (and possibility) of warfare, these days women do not seem to care very much about their exclusion from clan meetings. While enjoying aspects of the festivities organized in the names of clans, they admit little envy concerning male control over public wealth distributions. On the contrary, they often express indifference or bemusement—and sometimes scorn—about time better spent in other pursuits.

Mendi women explain their husbands' clan prestations as a means of fulfilling obligations to themselves and their own agnates, and men offer this interpretation on occasion as well. After all, prestations sponsored in the names of clans are most often received by members of allied clans, the natal groups of in-married wives. What is more, the wealth accumulated for clan distributions is not held out of networks for long. Major clan events like the Mendi *sai le* (pig kill[17]) are organized as a large number of simultaneous public distributions, first of pearlshells and money and then of pork, by individual clansmen directly to their respective *twem* partners. It is the public discussion beforehand, and the general coordination of personal obligations, that gives these separate prestations their collective effect. Even those prestations formally represented as passing from one clan as a corporate entity to other clans[18] are shared out on the spot to individuals, who are subsequently free to reinvest the wealth in their personal networks in an uncoordinated fashion.

Nor is a network focus exclusive to women. Men agree that *twem* relationships are not simply the sources of wealth to be displayed during clan events. For men no less than for women, *twem* relationships also produce other *twem* relationships. Moreover, clanship may be considered one of the sources of wealth needed to create *twem* partnerships, insofar as clansmen are expected to contribute to one another's marriage prestations, and to establish personal exchange relationships with one another's affines.

Of course, some men rarely attend clan meetings, and do not make any special effort to accumulate wealth in preparation for clan events. While extreme male inactivity is usually derided by both men and women, even well-respected ordinary men do not play a very active role in defining the political contexts and setting the dates for clan prestations. When these are established, the success of collective events becomes a matter of each prospective participant separately reorganizing his own *twem* obligations so that they will coordinate with those of his clansmen. Each man attempts to meet the demands of both his exchange partners and his clansmen simultaneously, preferably with the same valuables. For example, he may attempt to convince particular exchange partners to redefine what were initially simple gift-debts (*saon*) as "initiatory" gifts (*ol topowe*); that is, gifts that solicit group prestations and are repaid with an increment. To the women who have looked after the pigs he plans to kill, he arranges to give "pig rope" gifts (*mok ya ri*). That is, with some effort of reorganization aimed at engaging *twem* (and also female) interests, the two kinds of obligations need not necessarily conflict.

But this is a risky process, and men often face an explicitly politicized choice between two different kinds of relationships with potentially incompatible implications. They cannot hope to coordinate all their network obligations with their group responsibilities and must occasionally decide between allocating wealth to exchange partners or withholding it to participate with their fellow clansmen in a group prestation. This necessity is experienced as a major challenge by most men; it is also what much of the discussion at clan meetings is about. For if clan events are to take place, men *have* to accord them special value some of the time, and give priority to the *twem* obligations that are compatible with their participation.

While women must also make choices, these are not a focus of explicitly public discussion. A woman may choose to give a pig at the request of one or another of her exchange partners outside of any collective project, or she may give the animal to her husband or brother to support his participation in a clan event. The amount and timing of repayment will be different in each case, but she is likely to talk about these alternatives as equivalent, personal relationships. While women who tirelessly support their husband's clan project are praised (especially by men), women with other sorts of exchange involvements are also respected.

Ordinary Mendi men's attitudes are often similar to those of women. They express a preference for uncoordinated network involvements over the coordination of clan events. While they may support particular clan projects, they are more actively concerned with their own *twem* partnerships and with preparations for small-scale, individually sponsored marriage and mortuary prestations. But, unlike women, their preference for network relationships has a negative aspect, since they cannot affect extreme indifference to clan festivals without risking a loss of personal standing. Consequently, they regard with at least mild distress the necessity of synchronizing their exchange network obligations with a clan ceremonial timetable.

However, Big Men do not share with ordinary men this ambivalence of structural commitment. While they are also concerned with developing their network relationships and amplifying their renown by sponsoring small-scale prestations in their own names, Big Men consistently initiate and organize collective events. It is this active association with the collective identity that makes a man "big." The Mendi are quite explicit that one cannot build a regional reputation as a Big Man without organizing and performing well in clan-sponsored events; that is, without playing a creative role in the reproduction or reordering of clan names and interclan relationships.

Prominent among the means by which the advocates of clan projects create a conviction of common male interest is the strategic use of gender constructs in public speech-making during meetings. Emphasizing conventional differences between maleness and femaleness and ranking their respective value, but alluding to sentiments of support and reciprocity about which there is general agreement, a rhetoric of gender idioms deflects attention from and obviates differences between men while effecting a hierarchical ranking of their common clan concerns over their differentiating, network ones. The marked and remarked upon differences of social involvement between men and women in clans and networks are, in these contexts, made to stand for differences among men.

In order to create a consensus for clan action, orators contest the value of *twem* relationships by arguing that to put network obligations first is to be "like women": concerned with personal affairs rather than with the collective interest. Because of their differentiating effect, which works against a unity of purpose ("one talk" or "one voice," as the Mendi say), networks have a "female" value, even though men are in fact more active in them than women. Outside of this rhetorical context, network involvements are not any more simply "female" than they are simply "male"; they are what all adults do. What is more, neither personal network involvements nor women are denigrated.

However, the rhetoric may be interpreted as evidence of women's secondary status by Western observers. The particular ordering of relations emphasized during clan meetings happens to converge with the ordering of personal (domestic, female) concerns as against political (public, male) ones familiar in the West. No wonder it appears definitive. But in Mendi, while the clan view is certainly compelling, it is neither simply "true" nor is it uncontested. The evaluative rhetoric of clan meetings is itself a sign of the problematic character of what it advocates. The successful organization of clan events—that is to say, the persuasive representation of certain actions as collective—is, in fact, a political *achievement*. While one may wish to consider this achievement a hegemonic moment for one version of "male" interests, it is not canonical. Collective "clan" identities and concerns are not taken-for-granted or ritualized inevitabilities in Mendi; they need to be argued for. They do not take precedence over "personal" identities and involvements. The value and priority sometimes accorded to male collectivity is not an objective fact but rather a relative weighting. It cannot be understood without a simultaneous appreciation of what it is an argument *against*. That such an argument is necessary hints at the conventional value of the alternative construction, in which gender difference is not hierarchically organized.

## The Cultural is Political

The cultural values of both personal and collective identities are contested in Mendi. Because these values are constituted in gendered terms, and because women's and men's orderings of them differ, the relative social position and agency of men and women become analytically ambiguous as well. Gender constructions have a bearing on how Highlanders think about men and women; but the male/female distinction also contrasts kinds of men (or women), gives meaning and value to relations among men, and defines kinds of social responsibility and other qualities of *persons* generally, regardless of their sex. In the Highlands, gender constructions have also been among the most potent local media for remaking social value and relationships in dramatically changing times, and for redefining the very contexts (and therefore the meaning) of both men's and women's action.

Along with everything else, both male and female roles and the ways in which gender is used rhetorically is changing throughout the Highlands. These changes are not simply the product of external forces. Highland peoples have also been making a difference, and their actions have been informed by historically constituted interpretations of their circumstances. In Mendi and elsewhere, people argue about exactly how the cultural reworking of new situations ought to be accomplished. In contemporary struggles for cultural control over a changing social world, women are actively engaged in limiting the development of new forms of male power and expanding their own, just as leaders and ordinary men are, each in their own ways, attempting to regain some of the power they lost during a generation of state and mission challenges to local clan autonomy.

The contested order of gender relations is illustrated by an incident that took place very early during our stay in a Mendi village. One day, my husband and I sat in our house talking with a prominent tribal leader, Walipa, about details of the community's history, with the aid of two or three male acquaintances who acted as interpreters. I had begun by asking him about the community's involvement in Pig Festivals, but one thing led to another, and he wound up giving us an account of precolonial warfare practices, with special attention to the particular battles in which he had been involved. While we were listening to an especially vivid description of how he had acquired two scars, Walo (one of Walipa'a wives) and Nande (a woman on whose husband's land our house was built, but whom we did not know very well at the time) came by and called out to us. One of the men in the house opened the door at my request. "Why are you letting them in?" Walipa asked, as the women entered the house. "Women aren't allowed in here!" he asserted, ignoring the sex of the anthropologist. Walo and Nande seated themselves just inside the door, smiling all the while, and Walo asked her husband, "What is it you want to say now, that we cannot hear? Something about sorcery, perhaps?"

Against her husband's view of the matter, Walo suggested that, however it might have appeared, the anthropologist's house was not a "men's house," where a prohibition against women would have been appropriate. Nor were the content and form of our discussion the sort from which women are conventionally excluded. Walo made this point indirectly, but without much subtlety (and not entirely for the anthropologist's benefit), by alluding to sorcery, the only sort of activity that is conventionally secret (though it is equally secret for men and women). She was making fun of Waliba's attempt to apply rules concerning the exclusion of women to what she judged was an inappropriate context. Choosing to ignore the legitimacy of women's exclusion from some gatherings, she asserted that this one was open. By alluding to what is very widely agreed to be a negative kind of "exclusive" activity (sorcery), she attempted to undercut the legitimacy of Walipa's interpretation of the situation: that the activity was exclusive in the positive (that is, male) sense. Both distinctions are culturally recognized, but their application to particular contexts is subject to debate. Walo and Walipa each used the distinction which suited his or her respective meaning, construing the context in contrastive ways.

I agreed with Walo: My house was not a men's house. But not just because I was a woman. As an anthropologist, I had to attend to diverse voices and create a space in which I might hear them. For this and other reasons, I was an outsider and unlike either Walo or Walipa or most other members of their community. However, we are all alike in bearing responsibility for the stories we choose to tell. For, how people represent themselves and how they are represented by others (both within and outside their communities) have serious implications for their worldly behavior by giving it particular meanings and values. From this point of view, a central question in understanding relations of power concerns how notions of difference and value are themselves innovated or transformed and, particularly, how different categories of persons come to create the means by which they may effectively make their case.

# 15

## Breadwinners and Decision-Makers
### Nineteenth-Century Mexican Women Vendors[19]

*Judith E. Marti*

In many historical descriptions of Mexico, particularly those of the nineteenth century, men have been portrayed as the workers, the main family support, and, above all, the decision makers. Women, on the other hand, have been depicted as wives and mothers, the caretakers of children and supervisors of the household. Even when these women worked outside the home, researchers still viewed their position as secondary and submissive, and usually awarded the role of decision-makers to the men.

Ethnohistorical research into the economic lives of women market vendors during the last quarter of the nineteenth century belies the accuracy of these descriptions and shows that these women could and did hold power to make economic decisions, to negotiate with, even to challenge the larger social structures around them.

The view of men as holding the primary position of power outside the home can be partially explained by the nature of the historical documents used as evidence. Men and women sold food products and crafted goods in nineteenth-century Mexican markets, often as a family, a routine still in practice today. But most market fees, licenses, and documents, for that period were held in a man's name, perpetuating the idea that only men had important economic roles. Thus, the part women played in the public markets is often hidden. Unless a woman was a widow, she rarely appeared as a vendor, or among the signatures of vendors acting as a group, for example, petitioning the municipal government. Yet, it is from studying these petitions that we gain a glimpse of the important economic roles of women market vendors. Women emerge as both breadwinners and decision makers. Complaints and petitions give us the voices of the women—of widows and heads of families—shrewd, knowledgeable, and, it appears, effective strategists.

In the nineteenth century, as today, public markets were not only an integral part of daily life, but were crucial to the economy. They were especially important at the turn of the century, which marked the early stages of industrialization for Mexico. As industry grew and concentrated in the cities, it required a large pool of workers. A wave of migration was set into motion as people were drawn to the large urban areas in search of jobs. Guadalajara was one such city which grew rapidly as a center of industry during the turn of the century. By 1900 it was Mexico's second largest city, the only urban center besides Mexico City to reach a population of over 100,000 (Unikel et al. 1976). As immigrants seeking jobs swelled the urban ranks, cities like Guadalajara and Mexico City were faced with the need for a cheap supply of basic goods, food and clothing, for a rapidly increasing, and increasingly poor, population.

Markets and market vendors were extremely important as sources of cheap products in large urban areas. As the population increased, toward the end of the century, so did the number of public markets, and market vendors. Travelers' descriptions and photographs of the period indicate that most market customers were not affluent. The poor depended on market and street vendors for beans, corn, sugar, coffee, ceramic pottery, blankets and used clothes. The wealthier classes also shopped at markets, but were also able to patronize the numerous specialty shops of Guadalajara, where they bought imported goods: sausages from Switzerland, and wines from France and the United States (Gibbon 1893; *El Correo de Jalisco*, various issues, 1895).

A picture of the bustling covered public markets where vendors sold from individual stalls or *puestos* can be gained from the contemporary writings of long time city residents and foreign visitors, from official municipal newsletters, newspapers and photographs. Thomas Brocklehurst, an English traveler to Mexico, left us a vivid sketch of a typical urban public market, which includes descriptions of the women who bought and sold there:

> . . . in the early mornings, indeed, all day, the adjoining streets
> are scarcely passable from the crowds of people pressing to and

from [the market's] attractive portals. It is enclosed by a high wall, and on the right the whole is overshadowed by a still higher wall of some old convent. Against this are a lot of shanties and booths where old cloths and old everythings are exhibited in the greatest abundance. The market is provided with four gates, each gate giving upon a street. Around the walls, inside the enclosure, are shops and projecting piazzas, the remainder of the space being occupied by stalls and booths, which are protected by framework covered with matting, in the shape of gigantic umbrellas. A portion of the market has a zinc roof. The space literally swarms with human beings, from the *dueña*, or housekeeper, of some swell Mexican family, to the Indian woman with the inevitable child strapped across her back in her *rebozo* [long scarf]. Each class of article exposed for sale has its own quarter in the market — meat, fruit, fish, vegetables being in separate places. Venders who are not the possessors of stands spread out their wares on mats, utterly regardless of space; and you will find yourself treading on the stock-in-trade (the owner uttering shrill cries of warning) unless you keep a pretty good look out. Indian women stretched on mats indolently watch their wares, red and green pepper pods, *granadas*, melons, *papaya*, *camote*, *chirimoya*, *chico zapote*, *chiote* (fruit resembling a hedgehog), *jicami*, and fifty other Mexican fruits, whose names I could not note down. . . . Indian maidens with great coops of chickens on their backs, and a dozen live fowl hanging with their heads downwards from their waist-belts, jostle past you, while a donkey places his pointed, unshod foot on your favourite corn. The *dueñas* drive hard bargains in the shrillest possible tones (Brocklehurst 1883: 52-54, author italics).

That women sold goods in the markets is also well documented by photographs of the time. Pictured but silent. What roles did they play? What, if any, input did they have in economic decision making?

The traditional view has relegated Mexican women to the home, and to secondary economic positions outside the home, and portrayed men as breadwinners and decision makers. This view begins to give way when we are introduced to the nineteenth-century women market vendors of Guadalajara: to Sra. Acosta, Sra. Gómez, and Sra. Padilla, three market women, all widows, economically poor, with large families, who sell from *puestos* (small shops or stalls) in two of Guadalajara's most important markets. They are illustrative of the important and dynamic role women played in the market economy.

The Mercado Alcalde is known for its pottery, produced in the nearby village of Tonala. In the market, Sra. Acosta sells *loza* (grazed clay pottery). To sell in the market, she has to pay a daily fee of fifteen centavos, at a time when a factory worker's good wages were under fifty centavos a day (Muriá 1982: 159). Sra. Acosta is barely able to make a living, so she argues. She has a possible, but risky, option: to petition the municipal government for a fee reduction.

Sra. Acosta is faced with a dilemma. To petition the municipal government would require a considerable investment. First, she must pay a scribe to record the claim legibly and in legal language. We know she did not pen her own petition: the calligraphy is well-executed in contrast to her own halting signature. In addition, the *ayuntamiento* (city hall) requires that a ten-centavo fee stamp be affixed to each petition, a fee she can hardly afford.

She weighs the risks and decides to petition the *ayuntamiento* to either exempt her from paying the market fees, or to reduce her quota for one year. Sra. Acosta pays the cost of a scribe but affixes only three centavos in stamps, asking the *ayuntamiento* to consider her petition, "admitting the stamps I am using because I am very poor." The decision pays off. A commissioner is sent to investigate the case and reports that she is, indeed, very poor. He recommends her fee be reduced from fifteen to ten centavos, beginning that very day.[20]

We cannot know what prompted Sra. Acosta to take the risk of losing money on a petition to the city government to lower the fees, but it is probable that her decision, and the knowledge of how to work around the system, came from other cases known to her. The record shows that the majority of market vendor petitions to the *ayuntamiento* requesting reduced fees met with favorable rulings.[21]

Like Sra. Acosta, Sra. Gómez is a widow supporting a large family, who sells in the Mercado Alcalde. She, too, is probably illiterate since her petition is written by her daughter. And like Sra. Acosta, Sra. Gómez asks the *ayuntamiento* for a reduction in market fees. Even though she is not in as desperate a situation, her request is also granted.

In fact, Sra. Gómez sells meats to some of the city's hospitals and orphanages, as the petition mentions. My mother, writes Sra. Gómez's daughter, delivers meat daily to establishments "*de beneficencias.*" The problem is that these establishments generally pay her only part of what they owe. Sra. Gómez's daughter describes her mother as a good citizen, one who has always paid her fees to the municipal government on time, and who has continued to supply the establishments with meat. But this practice, she writes, cannot continue. As it is, she is not making enough money to raise her family. She asks that the municipal government be just and fair by lowering her market fees, "taking into consideration her good works."

The language of Sra. Gómez's petition conjures up an image Guadalajara is striving for—that of a progressive and modern city—an image repeatedly called for in the editorials of the numerous newspapers of the time. One such editorial decries the rowdiness of street fairs, with their cockfights, as "(staining) the image of the second city in Mexico . . . this is not what a civilized city should have" (*El Correo de Jalisco*, 16 July 1895: 1). A civilized city, Sra. Gómez's petition insists, would support important institutions such as orphanages and hospitals. Her wording is aimed at persuading the municipal government that, by lowering her market fees, the city would be taking a step in the direction of progress and modernization.

Again, an inspector is dispatched to the market and reports that Sra. Gómez's stands are some of the best placed in the market and in the best condition. Besides, he continues, "she sells much more than she acknowledges." Nonetheless, perhaps in part because of her role as supplier to city hospitals, her petition is granted.[22]

Our third widow is Sra. Padilla, a vendor in the market *Parián de San Agustín*. If anything, Sra. Padilla is persistent. Twice she petitions the municipal government for reductions in fees, and twice the rulings are made in her favor. Her petition speaks knowledgeably to market regulations, citing volume and page. Moreover, Sra. Padilla is not averse to criticizing the methods by which treasury agents established her fees. Finally, her petition puts forth the rather sophisticated argument that the city would not knowingly sacrifice the individual interest for the public good.

The municipal government has relocated Sra. Padilla to new shops in place of the ones demolished by the city. But the city, says the vendor, is now charging her much more for the new shops than they did for the old ones—even though the new ones are considered to be of equal size and value. This is because, she points out, one of her new stalls is a corner shop. The agent sent to measure her new shops added both the length of the front and side of the shop. According to "page 533 of the volume 14 of the laws of the state," reads her petition, the fee should have been fixed only by the length of the front of the shop. She now has to pay a fee "larger than the shops produce" and asks for a reduction of fees in line with what the shops are worth.

The city complies with her request, prompting Sra. Padilla to petition once again. This time she criticizes the city for giving her a location inferior to the old ones. Not only are her new shops lower in value than the original shops, the petition reads, but her business has suffered with the move. Her second petition uses the rather sophisticated argument that a good government would not knowingly undertake actions for the public good (in the form of taxation — including market fees — collected to repair roads, create parks, construct public buildings, etc.) if these actions were to bring harm to an individual, i.e., put a poor vendor out of business:[23]

> I am begging because I am sure that you know that the public benefit cannot be a motive to harm my own interests, and it will happen if you do not lower my taxes. And knowing of the [problem with the new shops] and the very difficult situation that I am in, I will not be able to pay the tax even if you reduce it as you say you will. So I am asking to have my tax [further] reduced, and let me pay 5 pesos a month even if this is only a portion of the tax required.[24]

This time the city allows Sra. Padilla, rather than an outright reduction in fees, to pay each month only a portion of the market fee, the remainder to be paid to the municipal government at a later, unspecified date.[25]

The stories of these three women challenge the myth of Mexican women as relegated to the home, as occupying secondary positions in the market economy, or as powerless. To have an income, these poor widows had to work outside the home. They chose to run a business in the public markets. There, they found themselves in situations neither of their choice nor of their liking, so they took actions to change them. They were successful, rather than powerless, even when fighting "city hall." They used a variety of strategies to negotiate their positions: Sra. Acosta knew how to work around the bureaucratic system, with its rules and regulations; Sra. Gómez's petition argued cogently by drawing on government rhetoric of progress and modernization; and Sra. Padilla demonstrated knowledge of market rules and regulations, along with a penchant for criticizing government practices and city functionaries.

We encounter these women, and others like them, precisely because they take action and complain. Rather than submissiveness and powerlessness, they display common sense, determination, persistence, knowledge of value, the ability to negotiate, and the willingness to make decisions and take risks. These are the qualities that define these women and allow them to survive. Sra. Acosta, Sra. Gómez and Sra. Padilla may be the exceptions but, in this case, the exceptions belie the rule.

# 16

# Daughters of the Forest

## *Agnes Estioko-Griffin*

I n the textbook-case foraging society, hunting is a man's job. Anthropologists argue that a sexual division of labor makes sense. Women seem less suited physically for such strenuous activity, and in any case, hunting entails many risks that might endanger their children. The woman's role is to bear and raise babies, dig roots, pick berries, and maybe catch the occasional rabbit. Discussing "The Evolution of Hunting," Sherwood L. Washburn and C. S. Lancaster wrote that "when males hunt and females gather, the results are shared and given to the young, and the habitual sharing between a male, a female, and their offspring becomes the basis for the human family" (1968:301).

Taytayan Taginod and other Agta women in the Philippines have not heard this anthropological wisdom and would laugh if they did. Taytayan, now a young grandmother, has long hunted wild "bearded pigs," deer, monkeys, and a variety of smaller forest animals and has spearfished in dangerous rivers.

The Agta live in the Sierra Madre, a heavily forested mountain range that parallels the rugged Pacific coast of northeastern Luzon. The Agta do exploit some ocean resources, but it is the humid rain forest and its streams and rivers that dominate their lives. Traditionally, the forest provided not only food but also bark for clothing, palm fronds and saplings for houses, leaves for bedding, and wood for tools. Today, the Agta obtain metal tools, manufactured cloth, cooking pots, tobacco, and rice in trade for forest products — meat and fish, rattan, orchids, and Manila copal, a tree resin.

With permission from *Natural History*, (May, 1986); Copyright the American Museum of Natural History, (1986).

Extended family groups—clusters of two or three brothers and sisters, the old folks, and the children—are the living and working units of Agta society. All men hunt, except those living where the encroachment of agricultural groups has decimated the forest and game. Where only Agta live, game is plentiful. Wild pig and deer are abundant, although they fluctuate in numbers through various cycles. Plant foods are less readily available. Wild roots are scattered, difficult to dig, and give low returns for the effort expended. Today, Agta dig wild roots only in times of real hardship or when they feel a desire for traditional foods. They grow upland (dry) rice, corn, cassava, and sweet potatoes, but the yield from these crops is low. Given this situation, the Agta say it makes sense for women to be hunters. Women vary in their patterns of living, but many hunt and nearly all join the men in driving game.

Agta women differ from men in hunting tactics. Men love to enter the forest alone, where they stalk with bow and arrow, wait in ambush for hours by fallen fruit, or spot game at night with flashlights tied to their heads. Women are team hunters. They work with other women or with their men. They almost always prefer to drive with dogs and favor killing with long knives instead of bows and arrows (arrows are apt to endanger the dogs). They are seldom the fanatics that men are, but for some women, love of the hunt dominates all their work.

Taytayan is one of the enthusiasts, as my husband, P. Bion Griffin, and I learned as anthropological guests of her family. Taytayan learned to hunt from her husband, Galpong, whose second wife she had become at age sixteen. Taytayan's older sister, Littawan, was Galpong's first wife. Littawan had been unable to conceive; rather than divorce her, Galpong had taken the younger sister as well. Taytayan soon loved hunting with Galpong or Littawan or both. By the time we became acquainted, all three were mature adults and very successful hunters. Taytayan hunts several times a week, choosing, as the more active women hunters often do, to carry the bow and arrow and to nurture a pack of hunting dogs.

I recall the time she ran a deer for two days, until its feet were raw and bloody and exhaustion had slowed it to the point it could be shot. She had given up the hunt the first day, but the next day, she took her dogs, found the deer, and chased it until it collapsed. Other times she and Littawan hunted, Taytayan leaping ahead to shoot and kill, then asking Littawan to carry the carcass home. The kill, she felt, was fun, but lugging a pig home was no joy at all.

Taytayan takes pleasure in the Agta pastime of telling the story of a hunt. The presence of a tape recorder spurs her and others on, and gives the anthropologists (who can seldom keep up during the actual chase) a better insight into the activity. While Taytayan readily tells the stories of both successful and unsuccessful hunts, the following excerpt reveals much of the character and action of a good hunt.

"Littawan and I took off and walked way upstream. . . . 'Say, here are some deer tracks,' I said. We went up the side of Tagemuyo Mountain. No tracks there. We walked up the stream bed and crossed. We saw more deer tracks. The dogs were all over the hillside. We kept on but saw nothing. We crossed the stream again and went farther upstream. Those deer were really hiding. 'Hala, ha, ha, ha,' a monkey cried. 'Huu, huu,' I called to the dogs. Upstream there were more tracks. We continued, and I said, 'There are too many tracks! Where are the dogs?' 'Aah, aah,' I called to the dogs. I grouped the dogs together where the tracks were clustered. The dogs wouldn't stay together, and one, Tighe, was off on his own.

"'Listen! That's a pig!' I said; 'Quick, after it!' Littawan urged the dogs on by calling 'Arah, arah, arah, arah!' 'Hurry up to the next stream!' she yelled. I ran around a pile of fallen rocks and earth and into a swarm of bees. They started stinging me all over my body. My hands became swollen; I was so upset I almost threw away my bow. I ran through the bushes and saw the pig, a large boar. The dogs, Littawan, and I ran after it downstream. I nocked[26] my arrow; Tighe really bit the pig, but it broke loose. I couldn't shoot for fear of hitting the dogs. I finally got an arrow into it but didn't kill it. I then stabbed it several times.

"Littawan arrived and tied the pig for carrying. 'Are we going to butcher it here or carry it home?' she asked. 'Let's butcher it over there,' I said, 'or we'll starve to death.' We roasted the liver and some sweet potatoes I was carrying, and then I said, 'Let's go downriver and spearfish.' On the way, we gathered grass for broom making to sell to the lowlanders. I spearfished but only got three fish.

"When we got home, I hollered, 'Bion, come and take our picture, as we are carrying meat.' I was carrying the grass and my bow and arrows over my shoulder. That would make a good picture."

While Taytayan learned to hunt after she married, most girls learn before they reach puberty. Later they develop into hunters or give it up, as it suits them. In our camp, which contained twenty-five people, girls of age ten and up accompanied fathers, mothers, aunts, and grandmothers on hunts. The girls carried knives or no weapons at all, but ran as game was taken, helped hold and control the dogs, and aided in butchering and carrying home the kills. They learned to recognize the signs of game animals, the fruit and leaves they eat, and how they behave under different conditions. Abey, Taytayan's elderly sister-in-law, recalls learning to hunt as a prepubescent girl:

"My mother and I left for the forest. We took the hunting dogs along. We walked upriver. 'The dogs are chasing a young wild pig!' called Mother. 'Hurry up before they chew it up.' 'I can't walk because of the thorns,' I answered. My mother got angry. 'I am going to leave you behind,' she threatened. I started to cry; I didn't want to be left in the forest. My mother hit me on the head with a stick. She ran off through the undergrowth and I grudgingly followed.

"We reached the place where the dogs had cornered the wild pig. My mother stabbed it with a knife until it died. She also hit the dogs because they kept attempting to drag the pig away. Still angry at me, she told me to carry the pig on my back. I took it down to the river to soak. I wanted to head home since I was already hungry. My mother, however, called the dogs and we proceeded upriver.

"The dogs jumped a deer, chased it, and bit its legs. It got away and ran into the river. Mother ran to it, held one of its legs, and stabbed it. 'Oh!' she screamed, 'It will gore me!' 'Take it into the deeper water!' I called. She grabbed and held the deer's head. It finally collapsed. 'Drag it to where the pig is,' she said. She butchered the deer. I gathered firewood, built a fire, and burned the hair off the pig. After Mother finished the deer, she butchered the pig. I roasted the liver and we both ate.

"Mother sent me to cut vines for making a pack to carry the meat. She gave me three legs to carry and we proceeded downriver. My pack was so heavy I was really staggering."

Now a grandmother, Abey is again the weak one, as she hunts with her older daughter, Iring. On one trip, she and Iring killed a pig; Iring carried her one-year-old son on her back. We photographed the dead pig and recorded Iring's tale:

"'Let's keep on walking, Mother,' I said. She answered, 'Wait there for me, because my thighs hurt from climbing up the mountainside.' I walked along with my baby on my back. I was annoyed at Talengteng [the baby] because he was noisy while I was running. We climbed up the steep trail, I on my hands and knees. . . .

"Mother asked, 'What is that howling?' 'Ho, ho, ho,' howled [the dog] Baklayan. I thought, this old woman has weak hearing. That's just a young pig, judging from the pitch of the howling. I had to go faster because my mother couldn't run fast enough. As soon as the old woman arrived, she clubbed the pig on the head, but it wouldn't die. She clubbed it again, but it still would not die. I cut vines for tying the pig. She finished tying it, and I took the bow and arrows. The pig was still breathing hard tied to Mother's back. We walked and walked, rested, and chewed betel. While we descended the hill, Mother complained, 'That old dog is useless. It would have been better if I had reached the pig and stabbed it.'"

Just how effective are women hunters? My husband and I collected quantitative data and kept daily logs of activities. Of the 296 hunting trips we logged, men made 180, either singly or in groups that included no women. Another 61 trips were male-female team efforts. Trips involving only women numbered 55. Men, then, are more frequent hunters, but women also participate actively.

The greater frequency of hunting by men is reflected in the percentage of carcass weight they bring home. In our sample, men provided 43 percent of the animals by body weight. Hunting by women accounted for 22 percent, while mixed teams got 35 percent. These figures are also the outcome of differences in hunting techniques.

Men use various tactics and often hunt alone. They lie in wait by fallen fruit to ambush the pigs and deer drawn to feed, or they stalk their prey under cover of jungle thickets. The average pig or deer killed by men using these tactics is larger than that brought down by women, although the better women hunters do kill large, adult game. The power of arrows shot from bows with sixty-pound pull also contributes to men's success in killing large animals. Women's bows seldom pull more than forty-five pounds. Of course, only the best hunters, male and female, regularly get the heaviest game.

While women's contribution by carcass weight is smaller, their hunting success rate is high. In the course of the 296 hunts we tabulated, 73 kills were made. The 180 "men only" trips brought in 31 kills, achieving a 17 percent rate of return. In comparison, women totaled 31 percent, and mixed teams of both men and women totaled 41 percent. These figures show that the use of teamwork and dogs yields the highest kill ratios.

Most of the trips by women involved dogs. Dog teams are expensive to maintain, perform poorly in rainy weather, and frequently die from game attacks, illness, or malnutrition. Well-trained, mature, healthy dogs, however, can be of critical importance to the hunt. Two different tactics may be used. In the first, hunters proceed into the forest and station themselves at ambush points where game is likely to pass. Then, one or more hunters with dogs enter the forest, hoping to surprise game and drive it to the ambushers. The second tactic is for a small team, say a husband and wife or two women, to travel with their dogs until an animal is located. Then, as Taytayan recounted, the chase is on, and the hunters expend huge amounts of energy covering rugged terrain. Very often the animal escapes, but good dogs help insure success.

Just as there is overlap, as well as difference, in how men and women hunt in Agta society, so too the division of labor in other areas is a matter of emphasis. Everybody spearfishes, for example. Although women in foraging societies worldwide have usually been excluded from hunting, they have often been fishers in coastal and riverine environments.

Among the Agta, spearfishing is done under water, by swimmers wearing primitive goggles and using a large rubber band to propel a wire projectile. Some fishing is in deep, fast, cold rivers; some in slow and shallow streams. Children start learning to fish when little more than toddlers, eventually turning play into a skill. Boys and girls make forays to streams for safe, shallow-water fishing, their catches becoming picnic snacks. Teen-agers join adults in fishing the larger rivers where large fish abound. Women truly excel in this often daily activity. Nearly all females, from twelve years old to the very old, spearfish.

One of the most important of the Agta's food-getting pursuits, fishing may, in the dry season, provide nearly all their animal protein for days at a time. Even people who are not strong enough for the rigorous fishing occasionally participate in the special fish drives. Women in advanced pregnancy, the elderly, and the lame may drag the rattan lines, tied with fronds, that span the river and chase fish to the swimmers.

Another large part of women's work among the Agta consists of gathering plant foods, shellfish, honey, and the multitude of items needed for medicines and camp maintenance. Even here, however, men are hardly excluded. Everybody collects honey, with women ably climbing the trees to cut down combs, except when young men can be talked into the task. (Women do not like to climb if they are wearing skirts; modest jogging shorts are the favored attire for work in the forest.) Frequently, all the adults and children in a camp take off for an outing along the beaches of rock and coral, where mollusks and crustaceans are to be had. Men limit their beach activities to spear and line fishing, however.

Women and children are the primary gatherers of wild roots and other plant foods. Men seldom join the women in digging up roots, whether cultivated or wild, and although they work at clearing and planting the family's small plot of dry rice, they are less likely to help harvest the crop. Whole families may work together in cutting the caryota palm tree, extracting the starch-laden pith, and packing the food home. More often, however, parties of women and girls do this arduous work, with lots of joking and horseplay throughout the long day.

As we examine all the work done by women, hunting and its supposed limitations on child rearing come into better perspective. Taytayan and her family exemplify efforts to harmonize food getting and general work with the bearing and raising of children.

Taytayan bore four children, two girls and two boys: only the two daughters survived. In this experience she was typical. We found that one-third to one-half of Agta children die before puberty. Tom Headland, a missionary-anthropologist working many miles to our south, found that about half the children die. In his area, the Agta have been more exposed to the destructive effects of newcomers — disease, alcohol, and depletion of game.

Children are a part of nearly all Agta activities. While older children may be left with baby sitters, nursing infants are carried on their mothers' backs not only on occasional hunting trips but also on forest excursions to secure building materials and food. This day in, day out exposure, which sometimes subjects them to wet and cold conditions, certainly contributes to the illnesses that kill many. Mothers shelter their children from bad weather whenever possible, however, and avoid hunting under such condition. So although hunting is rigorous, it does not pose any special danger to infants.

Taytayan's two daughters are now rearing families. The elder has four surviving children, while the younger, married only in 1978, has two. Both women learned to hunt with their mother, but now hunt primarily with their husbands. They neglect bows and arrows, preferring to carry only knives. During pregnancy they hunted less, and not until the babies were about six months old did they begin to carry them on short hunts.

Taytayan continues to go after wild pigs, deer, and monkeys, while also tending her grandchildren, even adopting the eldest. Now her companions include nieces, nephews, and, of course, Littawan. Her daughters find her difficult to keep up with because of her vigor and enthusiasm. Taytayan once expressed her interest in rumored "fertility drugs" to me. I asked how in the world she would hunt if she had another baby. "No problem," she said, "Littawan can carry it while we hunt."

Mothers and females in general are most decidedly the major child tenders in Agta society. Mothers do the greatest share, followed by elder sisters and grandmothers. Fathers are fourth, but still spend a significant amount of time caring for their children. Young fathers of two or three children assist their wives in child care every day. These fathers often carry older children, aged about three to eight, on foraging trips outside of camp, tending the children while mothers spearfish or gather. My husband and I have often joined these family expeditions. One of my husband's favorite activities was to accompany a father or grandfather on some forest task; the anthropologist had no trouble keeping up with the smaller children!

We even know one little girl of about seven, an only child, who was taken by her devoted father on short hunts. Of course, she did not hunt, and she had to be carried for part of the trip. She did, however, begin to take in the whole world of hunting — the sights, sounds, feelings, and spirit of moving through the jungle in hopes of killing prey. As she grows older, she will learn that women and men are not identical in hunting or in any other aspect of their lives. A division of labor by sex does exist in Agta society. But it is flexible, subject to individual needs and preferences. Women adjust hunting and child rearing to each other and to their other subsistence efforts. If they choose, they too can "bring home the bacon."

# PART V

## Gender on Earth and in the Cosmos

## Power as Violence
### Hindu Images of Female Fury
*Ann Grodzins Gold*

## Legendary Heroines
### Ideal Womanhood and Ideology in Iran
*Erika Friedl*

## A Healing Ritual
### The Life and Words of Nisa, a !Kung Woman
*Marjorie Shostak*

## The Woman Who Didn't Become a Shaman
*Margery Wolf*

Not all goddesses are gentle and nurturing. Kali,
the demon-slayer of Hindu mythology, is typically
depicted wearing a garland of human skulls.
*The Bettmann Archive.*

▶

# Suggested Readings

**J. J. Bachofen. 1967.** *Myth, Religion, and Mother Right: Selected Writings of J. J. Bachofen.* **Princeton: Princeton University Press, Bollingen Series LXXXIV.**
As classics go, Bachofen's *Mother Right* is surprisingly readable, especially in this excerpted version translated by Ralph Mannheim. When reading a classic work is this painless, it is a good idea to go to the source, if only to see what all the shouting is about. This edition also includes some of Bachofen's lesser-known writings on other types of myths related to gender, including a commentary on Lesbos, the legendary island from which the term lesbian is derived.

**Jose Ignacio Cabezon, ed. 1992.** *Buddhism, Sexuality, and Gender.* **Albany: State University of New York Press.**
This is a scholarly but readable analysis of various aspects of gender in Buddhist tradition, ranging from the equivocal role of women in early Buddhist belief and practice to the relationship between Buddhism and abortion in contemporary Japan. This wide-ranging survey helps to explain some apparent contradictions in the way Buddhist theology represents women and male homosexuality.

**Maria Gimbutas. 1989.** *The Language of the Goddess.* **San Francisco: Harper and Row.**
This lavishly illustrated book surveys the archaeological evidence for a prehistoric goddess cult in Europe. In the absence of written records, it is difficult to say whether Gimbutas' interpretation of the figures and other designs conforms to the peoples' understanding of what their symbols mean. Nonetheless, this is an impressive work, of interest to anyone seeking to know more about the art and archaeology of Europe.

**Carl Olson, ed. 1985.** *The Book of the Goddess: Past and Present.* **New York: Crossroad.**
The authors in this edited volume explore manifestations of the goddess in such diverse forms as Isis and Hathor of Egypt, the Virgin Mary of Roman Catholicism, Kali the Hindu goddess of destruction, and Amaterasu the Japanese sun goddess and progenitress of the imperial line. These articles can be a revelation for those who presume that goddesses conform to the Western model of women as eternally compliant—and this volume is more readable than most works of this genre!

**Diana Y. Paul. 1985.** *Women in Buddhism: Images of the Feminine in the Mahayana Tradition.* **Berkeley: University of California Press.**
For the dedicated student of religion or of women in culture, this provides an in-depth look at several aspects of women's roles in Buddhism—as goddesses, as nuns, and as mothers, daughters and wives. The author relies heavily on Buddhist scripture and poetry and restricts her analysis primarily to the philosophy expressed in the organization of the book.

**Mark Twain. 1971.** *Eve's Diary.* **In** *The Diaries of Adam and Eve.* **Lawrence, Kansas: Coronado Press.**
Although his feminist credentials were far from impeccable, Mark Twain (aka Samuel Clemens) was an astute observer of human nature. In this irreverent work, he pokes acidic fun at gender relations, God, the universe, and the scientific method, among other things. Adam is portrayed as a well-meaning oaf, Eve seems hardly better, and God appears to represent the Peter Principle, which suggests that individuals inevitably rise beyond their ability to perform.

# Introduction

## *Mari Womack*

Not long ago, I attended a religious celebration honoring a goddess-saint, conducted by a female officiant, at a female-headed ashram where most of the residents were women. Services were held in the evening and candles flickered in the gathering dusk as female voices sang hymns of praise. Flowers banked the altar and their perfume mingled with the scent of the incense that floated in a cloud over the intent worshippers.

The active participation of women in this group was not a political statement; nor was it the product of some New Age religious rebellion. The ashram and the religious celebration were in the Vedanta tradition of Hinduism and the object of reverence was Sarada, the dutiful wife of Ramakrishna, a nineteenth-century mystic and articulator of the Vedanta philosophy of non-dualism. Sarada was no rebel; she rose at four every morning to prepare food for her husband's devotees.

The high visibility of women in the religious service I attended was largely due to happenstance. The ashram leader for the last fifty years was a woman; the female officiant was the highest ranking religious person on the grounds at the time; and women were drawn to the ashram in higher numbers than men.

After the main part of the service was over, I left the chapel and walked out into the moonlit courtyard where I stood gazing up at the stars. Behind me floated the clear, bell-like voices of women singing hymns of praise to Sarada: "Sarada-devi, Sarada-ma,[1] come to me Holy Mother." Their song was echoed by a lilting voice nearer at hand, and in the shadows I saw a young mother crooning to her drowsy child as she cradled and rocked it in her arms—the living manifestation of the mother goddess.

For the first time, I understood the real impact of relegating women to a secondary spiritual role. The loss is not just to the women who are barred from active religious participation, but to the religious community deprived of the singular contribution women can make. The night I attended the celebration for Sarada, the company included several other visitors, drawn by the beauty of the singing and the simplicity of the service. The statement was powerful precisely because no statement was intended.

As an anthropologist schooled in the tolerant stance of cultural relativism, the force of that unintentional affirmation of the feminine took me by surprise. It also forced me to reconsider the interrelatedness of concepts of the human with concepts of the divine, for it is in our relations with the cosmic order that our concepts of humanness are defined and articulated in symbols. Symbols express complex meanings in a condensed form, by reasoning from the known to the unknown and from the simple to the complex.

The mother goddess is an especially potent symbol that links our experience of earthly mothers to cosmic creation and nurturance, which are beyond our mundane experience. Just as Sarada represents this concept for the Vendantist group, the Virgin Mary is the personification of the virtuous mother in Roman Catholic tradition. The Virgin is a human figure that stands for complicated and often contradictory concepts about nurturance and mercy, as well as the oppositions of fertility-virginity and divinity-humanness. Symbols have the power to reconcile oppositions.

Symbols are the language of religion, art, and drama. They shape opinion because they convey ideas in a compelling form that appeals to the emotions. In religion, symbols are expressed in two forms: ritual and myth. Ritual is symbolic behavior, including prayer and formal religious services. Myths are stories that convey information about the nature of human beings and the cosmos, and the interrelationship of these two realms. Symbols may or may not be "true" in the historical sense, but they always convey "truths" about how humans define themselves. Myths are important for gender relations because they define feminine and masculine nature and specify behavior appropriate to each. For example, the Judeo-Christian creation myth suggests that Eve was created to make life more fulfilling for Adam, and that women in general play a secondary role to men. The story of the fall from grace — in which Eve tempts Adam with an apple — attributes human suffering, including the pain of childbirth, to a presumed female susceptibility to evil.

On one level, gods and goddesses personify abstract concepts or forces. The Greek goddess Athena embodies the concept of wisdom;

the Chinese goddess Kuan Yin represents the qualities of mercy and compassion. Social relationships are also defined in the *personae* of celestial beings. The God of Judeo-Christian tradition — omniscient, omnipotent and omnipresent — expresses the characteristics required of male clan heads who led the tribes of Israel on their wanderings through the desert. As adapted to the cosmology of Roman Catholicism, God is a Father-figure; the Virgin Mary is the Holy Mother. As a father, God is somewhat remote, just, and a provider; Mary is an ever-gentle and merciful mother. Celestial figures sometimes act as models for appropriate gender behavior. For example, Catholic girls are instructed to model themselves after Mary's nurturing and self-effacing example.

Scholarly discussions of goddess figures are often based on the assumption that male and female characteristics expressed in the Judeo-Christian model are universal and that goddesses are therefore always gentle and loving. However, this is most assuredly not the case. Nuliajuk, the supreme deity of Netsilik Eskimos, bore a grudge against humans. This stems from the fact that she was once a human herself and was badly treated. When she was a little girl, the people of her village fled their homes on a hastily constructed and over-crowded raft. Because the child Nuliajuk had no family to protect her, she was seized and thrown overboard to make more room. She clung to the edge of the raft, but the people cut her fingers off. Her fingers became seals and Nuliajuk herself sank to the bottom of the sea, where she became mother of the sea beasts and mistress of everything else alive. In order to enjoy successful hunts and stay alive during harsh northern winters, the Netsilik Eskimo had to placate the goddess by observing proper rules of behavior and by ritually soothing her occasional angry outbursts (Balikci 1970). In this case, the goddess is given to fits of anger; she is the provider and the one who enforces the moral order. In these respects, she is more like the Judeo-Christian God than the Virgin Mary.

The Hindu goddess Kali is a personification of rage and destruction. Sometimes called the "Mad Mother," Kali devours human beings, she does not give birth to them. She is a warrior goddess who sprang from the forehead of the goddess Durga (or Candika) during a battle against a host of demons. Kali's first act was to fling herself into the ranks of the demons, scattering their armies by killing some with her weapons and devouring others. She is depicted as having four arms and her four hands hold a bloody sword, a noose, a freshly severed head, and a cup made from half a human skull. Her necklace is made of human or demonic heads; severed human hands dangle from her waistband and two dead infants form her earrings. During a previous period of history, human beings were sacrificially beheaded to satisfy her taste for human blood (Brown 1985). The association of Kali with a mother goddess may seem illogical to those socialized in the Judeo-Christian tradition, but it is consistent with Hindu views of the universe. According to Hindu cosmology, the old order must be destroyed before creation can take place. Thus, Kali is revered because she clears away illusions and deception that stand in the way of authentic understanding. It is the human ego—which clings to individual gratification in defiance of the cosmic order—that is the target of Kali's destructive rage.

Although the personalities and life histories of gods and goddesses shape the attitudes of human beings and play a role in their behavior, it would be misleading to assume that mythology or ideology determines gender relations or human behavior in general, an issue addressed in the first two selections of this part. In "Power as Violence: Hindu Images of Female Fury," Ann Grodzins Gold explores the seeming contradiction between a pantheon of violent goddess such as Kali and the subservient role of actual Hindu women. Gold suggests that such cosmic models subvert social conventions that require Indian women to display restraint and deference before men. She says these images are, in one sense, symbolic acts of rebellion.

Ironically, it is men who are often the most devoted followers of Kali. This may be a case of ritual inversion, in which religious acts reverse everyday reality—not in an attempt to overthrow it, but to demonstrate its validity. Gold notes that, if women have the potential to swell into angry goddesses, men are justified in using whatever means are necessary to restrain them. The two explanations for angry goddesses are by no means mutually exclusive. The same symbol may express different imperatives in different contexts and may have meanings that seem to contradict each other. As Victor Turner (1967) observes in Forest of Symbols, symbols are multivocal—that is, they speak with many voices. It is with this understanding that we may explain the various manifestations of the mother goddess.

Themes introduced in Gold's analysis set the stage for a somewhat different paradox which underlies behavioral models for Shi'a Muslim women. In "Legendary Heroines, Ideal Womanhood and Ideology in Iran," Erika Friedl notes that two women in the life of the prophet Mohammed are almost conceptual opposites. Mohammed's daughter Fateme is the model of self-effacement; his granddaughter Zeynab is a revolutionary heroine who champions her nephew in war. Friedl concludes that both ideals are beyond the reach of most women, who respond to these powerful symbols in ways not anticipated by those who frame them publicly. Because of their different positions in society, Shi'a women interpret the models of Fateme and Zeynab differently than do male Shi'a leaders. By exploring women's private responses to public symbols, both articles help to explain how such concepts relate to the experiences of actual human beings.

Symbols are not static codifications of ideology, but provide dynamic models that stimulate us to reflect on our own place in the social world and in the cosmos. This approach can provide new insight into matriarchy myths, a phenomenon which has stimulated a debate about the origin of gender relations. The issue, framed in anthropology in the nineteenth century and resurrected in the last two decades by feminist theorists, centers on the relationship of myth to social organization. In his monumental work *Das Mutterecht* or *Mother Right* (1861), the nineteenth-century evolutionist J. J. Bachofen speculated that creation myths describing a primitive matriarchy are remnants of a time early in human prehistory when women controlled public political power. The myths, present in many cultures in different parts of the world, postulate an original dominant female goddess and/or a political structure originally controlled by women. The stories typically describe how these strong females were brought under control by men or, alternatively, how they lost their power by using it inappropriately.

Based on events described in these myths, Bachofen suggests that, after an initial stage of promiscuity, women grew tired of the never-ending sexual demands of men, defeated them militarily, and established a matriarchy, or political organization dominated by women. The matriarchy emphasized material existence and the mother principle, reflected in goddess-centered religions stressing fertility. According to Bachofen's model, men ultimately rebelled, overthrew the matriarchy and established a new order based on patriarchy, spirituality and religion formulated according to the "divine" father principle.[2]

Bachofen's theory was later rejected, along with other speculative evolutionary models, on the basis that there is no evidence to support it, since researchers cannot go back in time and observe the behavior of people who lived long before the existence of written records. Studies of contemporary human groups have failed to document any society in which positions of power are reserved for women. However, the myth of the matriarchy has gained new importance in recent years, as feminist scholars have challenged the universality of male authority. On one level, modern scholars are attempting to refute models of biological determinism, which assign women a secondary role in society because of presumed innate differences. On another level, these attempts call on mythology to provide a blueprint for altering the present imbalance of power.

There is one inherent flaw with this line of reasoning: a recurring theme in myths of matriarchy is that women lost control over power because they were unable to handle it. Thus the matriarchy myth is not a blueprint for success, but for failure. Stories of dominant women of the past do not hold out the promise of power for women; instead, they affirm the power of men as appropriate and justify domination of women by asserting that women have earned their secondary role.

However, the debate over the myth of the matriarchy focuses new attention on the importance of symbols in articulating and reflecting upon social values and illustrates the dynamic nature of symbolic statements. Because they express a number of complex and potentially conflicting meanings, symbols are subject to varied interpretations and, moreover, they are continually reinterpreted as their social and cultural context changes. Symbols shape our concept of humanness not because of what they "mean," but because their meaning is continually subject to negotiation. Thus the myth of matriarchy and its expression in feminist theory recapitulates the traditional role of myth: it forces us to reflect upon the interactions of human beings. In its most recent interpretation, the myth of matriarchy gains political importance by providing a symbolic model of power for women, and academic studies of traditional uses of myth become part of the myth-making process by changing our understanding of how these stories might be reinterpreted.

Myths are powerful tools for reflection, but it would be a mistake to assume that understanding the belief system of a religion is equivalent to understanding the religion as a whole. The importance of this simple truth is illustrated by the experience of many Americans who become attracted to the elegance of an Asian religious doctrine, but are horrified when their attempts to practice it become mired in a quagmire of contradictions. Religious practice, or ritual, does not always follow with pristine clarity from religious belief, or myth. And yet it is practice that defines religious experience for adherents. The theological aspect of religion is somewhat rarefied for most "believers" who, when questioned, reveal themselves to be somewhat uncertain of what it is they actually do believe. The finer points of religious mythology is left to the interpretation of religious specialists. Most devotees experience their religion in the form of ritual guided by religious practitioners.

In fact, specialized religious personnel define religious experience for their followers—by interpreting myth and by acting out myth-based rituals. By mediating between human beings and supernatural beings, religious specialists can exert a great deal of power or influence over their followers. This power is especially pronounced in complex societies, such as the United States and Europe, where the stratified organization of the society as a whole is reflected in the institutionalization of religious authority. After Max Weber (1965), anthropologists designate as "priests" those religious figures who have authority to mediate between people and deities by virtue of their *office*. "Priests" are primarily associated with complex, stratified societies.

On the other hand, more egalitarian societies typically are served by "shamans," who must continually reaffirm their religious importance by demonstrating their *ability* to contact and influence the spirit world. In writing about the "prophets" or shamans of the Nuer of the Sudan, E. E. Evans-Pritchard described the different roles of priests and shamans this way: "Whereas in the priest man speaks to God, in the prophet . . . God speaks to man" (quoted in Lessa and Vogt 1965:381). Women are more likely to be accepted as shamans than as priests, since the shaman's power rests on demonstrated ability to contact the spirits and to use them to help others. The experiences of a woman shaman in a generally egalitarian society are described in the third article of this part, "A Healing Ritual: The Life and Words of Nisa, a !Kung Woman," by Marjorie Shostak.

The shaman acts both as a healer and a mediator between human beings and the spirit world, typically gaining power through meeting with a spirit being. The initial contact with a spirit often results from what Western psychologists would call a "psychotic episode," in which the future shaman may experience convulsions, see visions, and/or hear voices. An event of this type is described in the fourth selection of this part, "The Woman Who Didn't Become a Shaman," by Margery Wolf. After the initial and often terrifying contact with a god or spirit, the initiate undergoes a period of training in which she learns to go into a trance (or altered state of consciousness), to control her interactions with the spirits and, eventually, to heal others.

In this article, Wolf demonstrates that the aspiring shaman's ability to contact spirits must be validated by influential elders before she can undergo training. This may make it more difficult for a woman to become a shaman, especially if her social position is viewed as marginal according to criteria other than gender. In the case described by Wolf, the authenticity of the woman's experience was challenged in part because her husband did not occupy a respected role in the community.

The two articles by Shostak and Wolf illustrate similarities in shamanic practice in spite of variations in the shamanic role resulting from differences in the political and economic organization in the two communities. The !Kung of Africa are a foraging society, in which there is no sharp difference in the status of males and females. The basically egalitarian nature of the social organization is reflected in the view that women have the potential to be as spiritually powerful as men. However, even among the !Kung, women are expected to be mothers first and shamans second, and these two roles may come into conflict since the spiritual power n/um is believed harmful to fetuses and young children.

On the other hand, the agricultural Taiwanese village studied by Wolf is organized along patrilineal, patrilocal lines of descent and post-marital residence—a structure traditionally viewed as favoring the status of men over women. Wolf suggests that men are favored in receiving shamanic training and, in the case of Mrs. Chen, the woman who didn't become a shaman, her initial acceptance was reversed when she was rejected by an influential male elder of the community.

Symbolic statements about the universe—expressed in religious belief and practice—profoundly influence our definition of what it means to female and male. But it would be a mistake to view this relationship as deterministic. A symbol that asserts the moral force of the status quo in one context can be a rallying cry for revolution in another. Even the Virgin Mary, that gentle personification of nurturance and self-sacrifice, became a revolutionary symbol of sorts when in 1531 she appeared to a low-status Indian on the Hill of Tepeyac in her guise of the Virgin of Guadalupe and spoke to him in the local language of Nahuatl. By so doing, she affirmed the spiritual validity of native Mexicans. According to some scholars, the Virgin of Guadalupe was the local goddess Tonantzin, Our Lady Mother, dressed in Catholic clothes. The Virgin of Guadalupe became a source of moral authority for insurgents during the Mexican War of Independence. As Eric Wolf describes it:

> The banner of Guadalupe leads the insurgents; and their cause is referred to as "her law." In this ultimate extension of the symbol, the promise of life held out by the supernatural mother has become the promise of an independent Mexico, liberated from the irrational authority of the Spanish father-oppressors and restored to the Chosen Nation whose election had been manifest in the apparition of the Virgin on Tepeyac. The land of the supernatural mother is finally possessed by her rightful heirs. The symbolic circuit is closed. Mother; food, hope, health, life; supernatural salvation and salvation from oppression; Chosen People and national independence — all find expression in a single master symbol (in Lessa and Vogt 1965:153).

Thus, the mother goddess, radiating love and compassion, can inspire the most passionate of revolutionary actions. Perhaps it is not so illogical that Kali, the Hindu goddess who leads an army and devours men, is viewed by her devotees as the divine mother. And perhaps it is not so surprising that a graceful female voice, wafted to me on a twilight breeze, could revolutionize my theoretical position on the role of women in religion — or that the gentle words of surrender in that song, first voiced by the goddess-saint Sarada one hundred years ago, could strike my ear as a clarion call for change:

> Heed not the faults of others;
> Heed rather your own,
> If you would have peace of mind.
> If you would have peace of mind,
> Make the whole world your own.

# 17

# Power as Violence
## Hindu Images of Female Fury

### Ann Grodzins Gold

T
he angry, weapon-wielding female divinities who people India's rich mythology present compelling images. Goddesses like Kali are portrayed with bloody tongues, with weapons in their multiple arms, and garlanded with their victims' skulls. Such larger-than-life figures emerge from and interact with real peoples' minds, hearts and gender politics. The realities of fearsome sword-wielding goddesses somehow interpenetrate the realities of their worshippers. To Western observers, these violent and powerful goddesses have figured largely in constructions of an exotic Asia, along with the neatly complementary stereotype of perfectly passive, submissive wives.

Social scientists often highlight seemingly contradictory aspects of Indian womanhood, as in Susan Wadley's classic essay on "Women in the Hindu Tradition":

> Clearly Indian women present a paradoxical situation for the interpreter of South Asian society. The view of the Hindu Woman as downtrodden represents one behavioral reality; her participation in the highest political and social arenas is another undeniable reality (1977:113).

In this paper, I suggest some ways in which Hindu stories of female fury comment on such broader cultural configurations. I focus on three narratives collected during field work in rural Rajasthan, a state northwest of India's capital New Delhi. These narratives are drawn from a myth, a legend and a tidbit of village

This paper is based on field work in India supported by fellowships from the American Institute of Indian Studies in 1979-1981 and 1987-1988, and the Social Science Research Council in 1980-1981.

gossip. Thus they are set, respectively, in mythic time, in history, and in human memory. A single image links the three narratives: a female arm brandishing a weapon. But the severed or threatened necks vary: her sons', her own, her husband's. Each narrative describes a strong female—divine, transfigured, or mortal. Her actions are in each case molded—with varying results and implications for herself and those around her—by patterns of gender relations given in cosmology and society.

## Cosmology, Gender and Power
### The Cultural Context

All animating power is female in Hindu cosmology. The word for power is śakti and it can be used to refer to energy or strength. It is also a name of the Goddess.[3] Female gender, then, is associated with energy, animation, and creative artistry—not weakness. As Ashis Nandy puts it, "the ultimate authority in the Indian mind has always been feminine," while the Indian male, according to Nandy, identifies with "what he sees as the passive, weak, and masculine principle in the cosmos" (1980:36).

It is therefore in South Asia "natural" or cosmologically appropriate for women to attain and exercise supreme power. A woman prime minister is no surprise; no one worries that she might not be up to the task. In 1979-80, I often heard people in Rajasthan casually refer to Prime Minister Indira Gandhi as "Śakti" and explicitly identify the male assistants serving her interests with the lesser male deities who accompany and serve the Goddess.

But what evidence is there for identity or continuity between mortal women who are not prime ministers and manifestations of an all-pervasive female power? Both psychological studies and research on spirit possession in South Asia reveal links between female lives and mythic images. Based on his work with upper class Western-educated Hindus who have sought psychotherapy, Alan Roland has observed that "Integral to the socially contextual ego-ideal for Hindu Indians is a strong mythic orientation. . . ." (1988:253) He finds that "women, especially, traditionally experience everyday relationships within the framework of myths. . . ." (1988:297) Roland provides an example of a patient who ministers to a sick sister and saves her life by "becoming" the mythic heroine, Savitri, who outsmarted Death himself.

Women do not always identify with life-giving female myth models, as with Roland's patient. Sometimes they express both sexuality and rage through demonic and divine possession. Gananath Obeyesekere reports of Sri Lankan women that many "... who come to be exorcised suffer from severe repressions of both sex and aggression. In rituals there is a myth model that helps to express this problem" (1981:102). Sudhir Kakar writes of a possession case observed in Rajasthan: "Urmilla's expression of rage against her husband and his family is also a rage against her feeling of powerlessness. . . . her identifications are with the powerful figures of the father, the mother-in-law and the Mother Goddess" (1982:79).

Pervasive continuities between women and goddesses are traceable in everyday life. Women's devotional songs typically describe female divinities who like the same things they do (such as jewelry, clothes, fine food and kind attention from loved ones), and who experience the same emotions. Many Hindu women have the names of goddesses (as men do of gods). In Rajasthan, women commonly have "Devi," meaning goddess, as a middle name. Describing a family scene among urban Punjabis in Delhi, Veena Das writes:

> One day Lakshmi, a baby three months of age, was wailing loudly. Her grandfather carried her around in his arms, swinging her and making all kinds of baby sounds. The baby seemed inconsolable. At one stage he said, "Oh Baby, you are Lakshmi. You are the goddess. Then why do you cry?" As it happened, the baby stopped crying, at which time the grandfather turned to me and said, "See, she needed to be reminded who she was." (1989:268)

In the village of Ghatiyali, Rajasthan, where I lived, I was often told that babies of both sexes were like deities to their parents. The way people talked of goddesses mixed familiarity and intimacy with respect for their potency and violent capacity—a capacity not necessarily embodied in weapons. When, on one of my early walks through the village, I met a woman accompanied by a child with a deformed leg, she pointed to it and said to me, shaking her head, *Mataji Mataji*. Naive as I was—and coming from America where issues of child abuse were beginning to surface—I thought the woman was telling me the child's mother had crippled her. As some awkward dialogue soon revealed, she was herself the mother and she was telling me with a mixture of resignation, respect and resentment that this affliction was the work of the goddess. *Mataji*, a respectful term for "mother," is used to refer to the Goddess in all her forms and names.

Even after acknowledging existing links and identifications among goddesses, women, and *śakti* as power, the paradox pointed to by Wadley remains partially unexplained. Why are women subordinated in household hierarchies, kept in seclusion, subjected to discrimination on the job market? Why are sons preferred to daughters, and the health of male children of greater concern than that of females? Why, since the introduction of amniocenteses, has the problem of aborting female babies become a major ethical issue?

Part of the explanation lies on the "other side of the coin." If women have an excess of power, a corresponding excess of sexuality, and the potential to swell into angry goddesses, men have a strong interest in restraining them. Hence the infamous advice from the classical Hindu book of moral law, the *Laws of Manu*, that a woman must be subjected to lifelong control by male kin.[4] Hence the urgency to marry daughters before they attain puberty, the inauspiciousness of widows, and the pervasive male fear of women draining their vital fluids and life force.

But fear of women as agents or possessors of *śakti* doesn't account for other factors in the complex of Indian women's apparent subordination. For example, there are socially and religiously salient reasons for the strong preference for sons that have to do with the nature of patrilineal descent and inheritance, patrilocal marriage and ancestor worship, with village exogamy and dowry, which draws wealth from the woman's lineage and contributes wealth to her husband's lineage. Women are considered unfit to study Sanskrit or offer sacrifices, and are thus unable to perform religious duties essential to the well-being of their natal families. None of these cultural complexes seem based on an understanding of power as female, and uncontrolled female power as dangerous. Rather, a scenario emerges of male biological, political and economic dominance.

Male dominance in Hindu South Asia does not imply sharply differentiated male and female gender identities. As Nandy indicates in his essay on "Woman versus Womanliness," men may be motivated to cultivate womanly traits for positive reasons. Moreover, sources of female power are sometimes located in just that self-restraint and suffering imposed on women by their subordinate roles, but analogous to the self-restraint and suffering embraced by male ascetics to increase spiritual power. Mahatma

Gandhi asserted more than once that women were better than men at self-suffering (his ethical version of effective asceticism) and better, too, at non-violence (*ahimsa*). Gandhi observed: "Woman is the incarnation of ahimsa. Ahimsa means infinite love, which again means infinite capacity for suffering" (cited in Rudolph and Rudolph 1983:61).

Hindu concepts of gender *vis-a-vis* power differ greatly from Western concepts. Some themes underlying gender in India may be usefully summarized as follows:

1. Power is cosmologically associated with female gender.
2. Goddesses are female powers both alien and intimate, not separate and unreachable from the human world, and sometimes incorporated into mortal female identities.
3. Women are socially, politically, economically, and ritually disadvantaged.
4. Suffering is understood to be a source of power, and women are better at it than men.
5. Gender identities are relatively fluid.

These concepts are manipulated, substantiated and articulated through Hindu myths and the following stories of *śakti*.

## Three Narratives of Sword-Wielding Females

***The Creatrix Beheads her Sons.*** Madhu Natisar Nath, an old man in his seventies belonging to a caste of yogi-magician-farmers (Naths) told me this creation myth, as a result of our discussion of his yogis' earrings. Rajasthani Naths are Shaivites, or followers of Śiva, and Madhu said the thick crystal rings in his slit ears were a form of the divine couple, Śiva and Śakti, who are often worshipped as stylized genitals: "The ear is the *yoni* (vagina) and the earring is the *lingam* (phallus), so it is a form (*rūp*) of Śhiv-Śakti." Madhu continued:

> So was the creation of the earth. On the earth were seven oceans. Of its own accord in the water a flame stood up and in it was Niranjan Nirakar [Spotless Shapeless] and a girl, Śakti. And he said to Śakti: "Let's go create the earth." He took the form of a tortoise and got some muck and made the nine continents with it. Then he said, "Śakti, I've made the earth, now you make life."

She said, "I have no mate. How can I do it alone?"

He said, "Do it the best you can because I don't have a body. Do it according to your desire."

Then Śakti was wandering alone, no birds and animals were there, she was all alone. She said, "my left hand is female and my right is a man," so she slapped the right on the left and got three blisters: Brahma, Vishnu, and Śiva[5] emerged from these blisters.

She said to Vishnu: "Be a ruler," and to Brahma, "You study." And Śiva had set up his yogi's campfire [that is, he had begun to practice ascetic meditation], and she thought, "I've had three boys. There is still no one to be my mate. They are my sons. They are my own sons, but I will accept them as my husbands."

She went to Brahma with her hands joined and said, "Marry me."

"Mother, you are my mother, how can I marry you."

She said, "You fucker!" And she cut off his head with her disc and burned him up."

She went to Vishnu and the same thing happened.

She went to Shankar [another name for Śiva], who thought, "she killed my two brothers. If I refuse she'll kill me, too. She's my mother. I'll agree to anything and stay alive."

"Sure, I'll marry you but first calm down. I'll marry you but first give me a promise."

She had three eyes. "Give me the middle one."

So she gave it to Shankar. "Now, let's get married."

"First bring my brothers back to life, and the 33 million goddesses and gods, and fifty-two Bhairujis so they can enjoy the wedding."

So she clapped again and brought Brahma and Vishnu back to life and created the goddesses and gods and Bhairujis.

[Note that the narrator who has called the goddess Śakti up until now, refers to her after her wedding as Parvati, the name of Śiva's consort.]

Parvati had no vagina so Shankar scratched her with his nail and made her a vagina and they collected the blood in a pot and dyed some cloth and Shankar accepted it as ochre [*bhagavá* because it came from Parvati's *bhag*] and from this time the Nath yogis wear this color of cloth.

Parvati kept asking Śiva to make love to her.

> Growing annoyed by her demands, he cut off his penis and threw it up in the air.
>
> Then she spread out her vagina [*bhag*] and sat on the ground and when Śiva's penis fell back down it stuck there and from that time it was worshipped in that way.
>
> So Lord Śiva's *lingam* [phallus] was staked in this *yoni* [vagina].
>
> None of the couples were having children.
>
> So Śiva and Śakti called them all and said, "Worship this lingam and yoni and pour water over it and drink it." Then they had children.

In this myth, a mother is sexually aggressive toward her sons. Thwarted, her sexuality becomes dramatically and effectively murderous, but the resulting deaths are only temporary. Śakti's violence to Brahma and Vishnu persuades Śiva to bargain instead of refusing her offer of marriage, and Śakti is quite willing to bargain. The assaulting, decapitating goddess quite readily relinquishes some power (her masculine power, the third eye) in order to achieve her goal of creation. Cooperation, not murder, is the way to get things done, but it is negotiated only after a violent display.

The erotic mother then becomes transformed into an equally lusty wife. In this myth erotic-violent and nonerotic-procreative females are not separated, as they often are.[6] This Śakti is a mother, the mother of everything; she is also a sexually eager wife, and her serial sexual aggressions—first as mother and then as wife—are the means of creating and perpetuating life. Śiva's self-castration in the second half of the myth seems to balance his brothers' beheadings in the first. Both result from Śakti's sexual aggression, but both are ultimately beneficial.

The myth gives an origin story for two things important to the caste of the teller: the red-orange cloth they wear and the worship of lingam and yoni (neither, of course, unique to Naths). Renouncers' robes are a highly valued symbol of detachment from the world, and from women. Here they are dyed in vaginal blood—perhaps the blood of Parvati's defloration. In ordinary life this blood is very polluting and dangerous. This part of the creation myth could well be viewed as a clear case of male appropriation of female generative power but, alternatively, it might express male and female complementarity. Throughout this story the need for mutuality, for pairing—as expressed in the beginning of the myth—rather than for domination of one sex by the other, seems to resonate. In accepting the color emblematic of their identity as dyed in vaginal blood, yogis thus acknowledge an intimacy with female body substance even as they outwardly reject contact with women.

This myth from a regional oral tradition shows us female violence as readily reversible and having positive results, while female sexuality is fully creative. Although Śakti's excessive sexuality, both as mother and wife, charters both decapitation and castration, the outcome is gender mutuality on several conceptual planes: it takes a pair to accomplish cosmic world-creation; coupled mortals must worship the pair Śiva-Śakti to get children; divine creative coupling is modeled by the teller's earrings, emblems of his yogic identity and microcosms of a paired universe.

**Hadi Rani Beheads Herself.** In the story of Hadi Rani we encounter a very different configuration of female power and human violence. Sexual exuberance is not merely muted, but annihilated. Here the female-wielded weapon is turned on the female self, even as it punishes, defeats and emasculates the male. The emasculation here leads not to union and fecundity but to separation, although in that separation is victory. Unlike Śakti, Hadi Rani has a mother and father, a caste and lineage. Yet transfigured as Śakti, she becomes in the end a singular being.

The tale of Hadi Rani, a popular Rajasthani folk heroine, is located in a turbulent era of Rajasthani history, during the Moghul emperor Aurangzeb's reign (1658-1707), when Rajput princes were either resisting or capitulating to the country's casteless Muslim rulers. Resistance or capitulation was often expressed through the powerful symbolic medium of women. Rajput princes signaled submission by giving a bride to Muslim royalty; they signaled resistance by refusing to do so.

During my stay in Rajasthan I heard Hadi's story from members of both sexes. It was usually told to back up an argument about the ways in which women surpassed men, or to demonstrate the awesome and peculiar valor of Rajput women (women of the "warrior" caste). My summary of Hadi Rani's story is based on an account in a volume of "true romances" about Indian women (Shamsuddin 1967) and the preface to a book of verses in her praise (Mahiyariya 1978).

Hadi's birth and childhood follow a pattern common for women warriors in India. Her father wants a son, but his only progeny is his daughter Hadi. He never treats her like a girl, but gives her instruction in sports and martial skills, calling her "my eldest son." Her father is reluctant to arrange her marriage since, to do so, he must admit she is a daughter. She makes her own choice, however, begging her father to accept the offer of a military chief in the service of the ruler of Udaipur—a kingdom famed for resisting Moghul rule. The husband-to-be is older than Hadi, but she admires his military prowess and valor.

After her wedding ceremony, Hadi goes to her husband's house for consummation of the marriage, as is still the custom. At the same time, a neighboring princess asks for help from the kingdom of Udaipur to keep the Moghul emperor from taking her as a wife by force.

The messenger bearing this news arrives at the door of the couple's bridal chamber and asks Hadi's new husband to come at once with his troops. Her bridegroom attempts to defer his departure for war until morning. Hadi is enraged: "Wear my bangles, and give me your sword and sit secure in the circle of these four walls; and don't ever call yourself a Rajput," she cries.

Hadi's ardor shames her husband into setting off for the battlefield, but he hesitates a second time at the city gates. He sends a messenger to ask his wife for a remembrance to assure him of her *satitva*, her truthfulness or fidelity. By implication, it would also be a pledge for her to become a *sati*—a widow who sacrifices herself on her husband's funeral pyre—should he die in battle.

Hadi is infuriated by this double insult: that her husband should question her honor and also reveal additional reluctance to go to war. "Take this remembrance to my husband," she commands the messenger, seizing a sword and beheading herself in a single stroke, with the words "Victory to the Goddess!" on her lips.

A weeping soldier carries Hadi's head on a platter to her husband, who ties the head around his neck as he might have tied a more conventional token. Stunning the enemy with this gruesome sight, he fights valiantly to his death and to a Rajput victory, while Aurangzeb is "forced to return to Delhi, empty-handed" (Mahiyariya 1978:3).

Nathu Singh Mahiyariya, a male poet of the early twentieth century, honors Hadi's triumph with 131 four-line Rajasthani verses in rhyme. Mahiyariya's poetry plays with heavily gendered images, in which the female becomes "ferocious" without losing her feminine modesty and the male becomes ashamed, like a woman, even in his public deeds of battle:

Hadi is anchored to modesty
Her neck sliced, she still keeps the rules
Her face-veil is sticky with blood
So the wind cannot blow it away.
[From heaven Hadi speaks]
Now that you've opened the enemies' throats
O Husband, come open for me
Hadi's wedding wristbands;
I sit and wait in heaven.

When the mother heard the news about
Hadi giving her head
She cried to her husband, Hada
"How joyful a daughter's birth!"

When Hadi's head reached her husband
The blood-soaked earth turned mud
But Hadi's eyes stayed dry
So her eye makeup didn't smudge.
Cowardly men lowered their heads
Their shame spread throughout the world
Hadi having given her head
Women raised up theirs.

She kept up India's moral courage
She kept her honor before the world,
Hadi did not keep her head, but
She kept her lineage great

These verses present a number of transformations on gender stereotypes: Rajput women should stay inside (keep *purdah*) and, if they must go into public, they should cover their faces and lower their heads. But Hadi emerges from purdah as a bodiless, bloody, but still demurely covered head. This is surely an ironic comment on female coyness as a pose, a masking of superior power. Moreover, Hadi's valor on the battlefield—of which the emblem is her head—inspires all men to take up a pose of shame and gives all women the right to be bold.

Female adornment is an explicitly acknowledged form of restriction, signifying women's submission to men (although women also celebrate their beauty as a form of power). But here the eye makeup with which Hadi was adorned for her wedding night becomes a symbol of her courage, contrasting with male weakness. The male messenger weeps, Hadi's husband's feet are stuck in bloodied mud, but Hadi's eyes are tearless. Her beauty is intact, though totally inaccessible. Further, Hadi only conditionally grants her husband the right to open her wedding wristbands as a prelude to their marital union—after he has opened the enemies' necks.

Sons are desired to carry on a lineage; the birth of a daughter is not joyful. But Hadi, the only daughter, has saved the reputation of both her husband's and her parents' house. She is known, significantly, by her father's name. Her mother is vindicated for giving birth to a daughter, and she wants her husband to know it.

Women are caught up in concerns of home and family while men are capable of selfless acts of valor, but Hadi's husband can't give up his attachment and Hadi can. It is, moreover, his questioning of her capacity for *sati* that propels Hadi to her moral height. Many of Mahiyariya's verses contrast Hadi's single act of selfless valor with her husband's battlefield exploits, which are described as "giving-and-taking." This phrase evokes a concept of war as a kind of commerce, a morally debased activity against which Hadi's act stands out purely as giving-without-taking. It would seem that by cutting off her own head Hadi has thoroughly emasculated her husband, denying him his sexual rights as well as his martial glory. Nothing he does on the battlefield can compare with her single act of courage, as the poet reminds us again and again, framing it as a triumph for the whole race (*jati*) of women. Even as she empowers him to defeat the Muslims, she defeats him with her moral superiority.

Despite all these subversive themes, it is clear that Hadi Rani died to perpetuate a system in which male warfare was the supreme value. Her female energy ultimately served male politics.

***Shobhag Kanvar Threatens Her Husband.*** When I first knew Shobhag Kanvar she was a married woman of about fifty-five, with two grown sons and two married daughters. Her life-course had been much like that of thousands of high-caste women in rural India, patterned by her kinship identities as daughter, wife and mother, mother-in-law and grandmother, and lived in terms of those relationships.

There are, however, ways in which Shobhag Kanvar was not ordinary. Although totally nonliterate, she possessed more knowledge about rituals and knew more worshipful stories and songs than most women in her large, multicaste village, giving her a certain status as a religious expert. As a devotee of the Rajasthani hero-God Dev Narayan—considered to be an incarnation of Vishnu—Shobhag Kanvar was deeply involved in his worship at a shrine just outside her village, and with a mixed-caste group of that deity's devotees.

The central figure among this group was the shrine's charismatic priest, a man of about Shobhag Kanvar's age from a lower caste. Although the terms of their relationship were never fully clear to me, part of it was certainly economic. Shobhag Kanvar assisted women pilgrims at the shrine and, in return, the priest gave her a substantial share of the offerings made there. When I was in the village, the priest and several of his male followers came to Shobhag Kanvar's courtyard every day for tea and often sat for more than an hour, talking freely with her. During festivals, Shobhag Kanvar, along with many other pilgrims, would spend the night at Dev Narayan's shrine, singing songs in his praise. Shobhag Kanvar did not define herself as a rebel, but as a devotee, and her bearing implied an impeccable propriety. However, her behavior, by ordinary standards, was not appropriate for a woman of her caste.

Village gossips told a story about Shobhag Kanvar that explained to their satisfaction how she attained her freedoms, a story notably different from the ones she herself narrated. One day, the gossips said, Shobhag Kanvar's husband had had enough. He forbade her to continue her participation in the group of Dev Narayan's devotees. After a verbal battle, she appeared to accept his authority. However, that night after he was asleep, Shobhag Kanvar took down the family sword from its place on the wall,[7] climbed astride her husband's chest, and poised the weapon over his neck. "Let me continue to worship Dev Narayan as I have been," she demanded. He complied.

The image of a wife astride her husband's chest resonates in village folklore with a bawdy insult song—sung by women about one another, substituting different husbands' names:

> That lewd hussy X's wife lifted a load, yes!
> She climbed on his chest and pissed on his mustache,
> Yes-oh-yes!
> She climbed on his chest and pissed on his mustache,
> Yes-oh-yes!
> Get away, wanton woman, what have you done?
> Yes-oh-yes!

Women seem to be gleefully celebrating a self-image quite different from that of reticent, dutiful wives. Was this song in the minds of scandal-mongers who envisioned Shobhag Kanvar threatening her husband? It might well have been. But the image of a sword-wielding, emasculating female also echoes the creatrix myth and even the story of Hadi Rani, who by beheading herself also emasculates her husband—simultaneously robs her husband of his honor and his wedding night pleasures, as she saves him from his own weakness. In Shobhag Kanvar's life story, resistance to both confinement and devaluation have been perpetual strategies, which may be why village gossips depicted her in that mythic pose.

Like Śakti the creatrix and Hadi the queen, Shobhag Kanvar acted for religiously appropriate ends. She was merely insisting that her husband allow her to continue her devotional activities. The activities to which her husband objected netted her considerable earnings, which she poured into home improvements—enhancing the value of male-owned property, but also making her own life far more comfortable. Certainly, the economic independence Shobhag Kanvar reaped from her work at the shrine added weight and edge to the sword that village gossips liked to imagine her wielding.

## Women, Goddesses and Violence

Despite the verbal and physical deference that South Asian women accord to the husband-god and to the ideology of female subordination, they retain and communicate a sense of gender virtue and virtuosity that can become manifest on both moral and physical planes.

In *Notes on Love in a Tamil Family*, Margaret Trawick reveals an intricate tapestry of subtle interpersonal relationships, observing that "the battle between the male and female modes of existence was not waged exclusively on a mythological level" (1990:70). She narrates a brief episode involving herself and Padmini, one of the main female characters in the family: "Once, when we were picking vegetables in the garden, I came upon a praying mantis. I commented that among these bugs, the wife devours the husband. 'That's just the way it should be,' said Padmini, unsmiling" (1990:71). Many anthropologists who work closely with Indian women have received similar messages.

The female capacity for violence evident in the three narratives presented here is linked to women's positive self-evaluations, as well as to the evident ideological and material disadvantages women suffer in their daily lives. In the myth of a creatrix beheading her sons, female desire becomes murderous, but procreative necessity and vitality reverses any deathly implications. Power subsumes violence; violence is only a strategy of power. The creatrix kills, negotiates and restores.

In the legend of Hadi Rani beheading herself, a bride sacrifices her own gratifications to channel her energy as power to support male valor. As she does so, she demonstrates a moral superiority that makes her better, not only at suffering, but also at war. Rather than terror of uncontrolled female violence, Hadi's legend reflects a subtler and more insidious fear of women's superior self-control. Hadi Rani is able to put her public moral conscience above her private desires when her husband fails to do so.

The story about Shobhag Kanvar threatening to behead her husband engages a bawdy image of acknowledged anti-modesty. But because Shobhag Kanvar's violence was at once in the interests of religious commitment (*dharma*) and profit (*artha*), it also has positive results. Both shrine and household were prospering at the time gossip was circulating, and certainly some jealousy, as well as grudging awe, were at work in spinning the tale.

All three images of female violence unite positive and negative evaluations of female power as creative and destructive. Most rural North Indian women live their lives according to conventions of restraint and deference: they cover their heads, stay in courtyards, and avoid directly addressing their husbands or male in-laws. But these narratives, as manifestations of *śakti*, subvert or deny such conventions. The creatrix does not act shy before her intended husbands; later in the myth she spreads her legs wide to catch Śiva's penis after he has thrown it up in the sky. Hadi Rani's veiled head rides in the public domain of battle. Shobhag Kanvar, envisioned in gossip, straddles her husband's chest. These stories suggest an ironic resistance to the terms of male superiority as they both embody and confound the paradoxes of female mythic power and social subordination.

# 18

# Legendary Heroines
## Ideal Womanhood
## and Ideology in Iran

*Erika Friedl*

he themes of "The True Muslim Woman" and the ideal model of modern Islamic femininity have been played in many variations in the literature on Muslim women. In this paper I will examine the elaboration of two outstanding historical women into Muslim models of femininity in terms of their inner logic, inherent contradictions, and "fit" with the traditional Persian culture as lived and practiced by the majority of people in Iran today.

I will confine myself to Shi'a Iran because their images of women are used as a guide for legislation and are held up as the only acceptable model for attitudes and conduct for women. In addition, major ideological shifts among Shi'a Muslims in Iran over the past twenty-five years have produced more and sharper discontent and discussion regarding women than elsewhere in the Middle East.

Muslim ideals of womanhood have the great advantage over modernist and Marxist[8] ideals espoused by outsiders because they are "home-grown" and they elaborate an ideology which is seen as embedded in an indigenous, traditional and familiar culture. They do not derive from alien, Western-inspired models, but have the authority of holy Islamic writ behind them. In Iran, rejection or criticism of the Islamic model is implicitly taken to mean a criticism of divine will, i.e., a sin as well as a crime.

However, different models not only exist within the Islamic paradigm, but are so variant as to conflict with each other. These differences are based on alternative interpretations of religious texts and the selective manipulation of particular character traits of esteemed female religious figures by ideologues in the media, popular literature, and in the pulpit. In other words, texts and heroines furnish examples for feminine ideals that include a wide range of character traits and behavior.

Depending on politico-socio-ideological goals and life circumstances of the proponents of ideal womanhood, some traits are selected and propagated and others are neglected or played down. For example, one of the most colorful women around the prophet Mohammed was his youngest wife Aisha, by all legendary accounts a spirited, sexy young woman, a model of a loving and well-loved wife. As such, she is acknowledged and promoted as a symbol in Turkey, but not in Iran. In Iran, her youthful good looks and high spirits amount to insolence, and she is linked to alleged treachery against her husband. She is a bad, disloyal, dishonest woman whose name is used as an insult.

In Iran, feminine ideals are embodied in Shi'a Islam's two most famous women, the Prophet Mohammed's daughter Fateme and his granddaughter Zeynab. The very different hagiography and legends associated with the two women furnish clear, if contradictory, exemplary traits for Muslim women to live up to.

Generally, Islamic ideals of gender rest on observed and assumed differences between men and women. According to Muslim theology, men and women are equal before God as souls. As flesh-and-blood beings, they are different and complementary in a divinely ordered authoritarian-hierarchical frame. Women and men can realize themselves optimally and in a morally correct fashion by fulfilling the obligations of their relative positions. This requires that men take responsibility for women and, in turn, must be supported by obedience and cooperation.

The hierarchy and its resulting relationships are justified by assumed innate bodily, intellectual and emotional differences between men and women. The ideal Muslim woman must, above all, endure her innate shortcomings: her physical and moral weakness, which renders her vulnerable; her emotionality, which renders her ineffective; her relative lack of reason, which renders her a poor judge; her sexuality, which renders her potentially dangerous for men and, thus, the community. Acknowledging these inherent traits, she willingly submits to guidance, admonition, protection, seclusion and, if need be, punishment, to keep her on the straight and narrow path of virtue. It leads her to seek and accept proper seclusion, including so-called modest dress, to avoid tempting men and being tempted by them.

The hagiography of Mohammed's daughter Fateme furnishes

many examples of these ideal traits. In one popular story, Fateme is ordered by her father to serve tea to a blind beggar. She does so, but only after having covered herself completely with a veil. Told that this was superfluous because the man was blind, she answered, "I know, but I am not blind and I may be tempted by the sight of this man." Countless stories of unquestioned obedience to her father and her husband are told in a spirit of awe, accompanied by a strong flavor of "This is how women *should* be, BUT. . . ."

On a purely ideological level, such a good woman is spared unpleasant dealings with the harsh outside world in return for her propriety. She is taken care of under the triangular protective roof of father-husband-son, so that she is free for her feminine tasks. She is given specifically and exclusively feminine properties to be proud of: virginity and motherhood.

Seemingly this model is internally consistent: an exact definition of desirable character traits and behavior in a woman is linked to the promise of a fulfilling, sheltered life. As such, it is a frequent theme in sermons. However, Fateme did not enjoy the fruits of her perfection. She is said to have suffered many hardships, from her own child-marriage to the death of her sons and husband. This obvious contradiction in the model of Fateme is not recognized or elaborated. Rather, Fateme's modesty, self-effacement and obedience are held up as ideal feminine behavior, while her incongruent suffering is linked to another realm altogether, that of practical life experience.

Fateme's very human suffering makes her personally accessible to similarly suffering women, who expect her to be compassionate and understanding in a way that Fateme the morally superior woman can never be. Fateme the ideal, and idealized, woman is removed from women's everyday experiences. One might say it is a male image, projected, used and exploited as an instrument of authority. Fateme the suffering mother is appropriated by women, not so much as an ideal of femininity as an emphatic appraiser of their own condition.

Further contradictions emerge when unrealistic assumptions about feminine nature create problems on the level of practical living. To be obedient always, to never say a mean word, to never be inquisitive, impatient, bossy, or exasperated, is to be a saint like Fateme, not an ordinary woman. Fateme was of exalted descent, the daughter of the Prophet. To be like Fateme is to be unlike any other woman, and this is an unattainable goal.

The ideal of a Fateme-femininity marked by docility, acceptance and submission is accepted by women generally as meritorious in a religious sense. However, they realize fully—and freely express the opinion—that the more successful women around them are sharp, assertive, daring, and quick to use their powers—ruthlessly, if need be—to their own advantage and that of their families. Meek and unassuming women are pitied as "dumb, poor, quiet things," and are admired only within the framework of lip-service to abstract "goodness" in a moralistic sense.

The elaboration of the Fateme ideal creates yet another set of contradictions on the theoretical level. Women are declared to be the indispensable maintainers and reproducers of the ideal Muslim society in their functions as guardians of family cohesion and educators of their children, especially in their moral development. In the Islamic Republic, these obligations are explicitly spelled out in the constitution. Proper mothering is proclaimed to be the key to the ideal, God-ordained Muslim society. A woman's husband establishes the material and protective frame within which the wife is to discharge her duty. Women are exhorted to be proud of their important position and to live up to its challenge.

Although rhetorically this image has merits and potential, on the logical and practical level, it creates problems and suspicion: How can an essentially weak, secluded, emotional-irrational, easily betrayed being be the backbone of society? How can she be the keeper and reproducer of her society's most valued morals? How can she be an effective role model for her daughters and socializer of her sons who, by virtue of their sex alone, are her superiors in authority before they even reach puberty? Surely, a society that bases its moral strength on the performance of its morally weakest members is bound to fail. Fateme is said to have accomplished this difficult task, but women say they don't know how she did it. As an example and role model, she fails them.

The Fateme-ideal of modesty and docility is complemented by the image of the tough, wise and courageous woman who stands up to oppression and physically fights for the good cause. Knowledge of the issues of the world and of the larger political picture beyond the confines of family and courtyard leads the list of desirable traits for this feminine ideal. In this case speaking up is a virtue, not a sin; assertiveness is admired, not scorned. This Muslim woman clearly transcends care of her family to include care of larger issues that concern the community of the faithful.

The embodiment of these virtues is Zeynab, Mohammed's granddaughter. Zeynab fought in her father's battles, suffered unspeakable privations along with her brothers, and protected, supported and counseled her only surviving nephew, the successor to leadership of the Shi'a Muslims. Her courage and resourcefulness are recounted in colorful stories of Kerbela, where the decisive battle for the Prophet's successorship was bloodily lost. These legends and descriptions of her role in her nephew's political struggle provide an image of the ideal Muslim woman as an assertive, tough, daring, knowledgeable, brave revolutionary fighter for her religion — the woman guerilla who readily sacrifices herself for the good cause.

During the Iran-Iraq war, Zeynab was invoked by state functionaries whenever Iranian women were exhorted to be brave, to advise their sons to volunteer for the front, and to take arms themselves. Unlike Fateme, Zeynab is not depicted as a *mater dolorosa* or grieving mother, but as an active heroine who exhibits none of the physical and character shortcomings on which the ideology of Muslim male/female relationships are based.

Realistically, women in Iran can identify with many aspects of Zeynab's personality: Zeynab was outspoken, so are they; she resisted oppression, so do they; she gave advice to her male relatives, so do they; she defied force and challenged authority, and so do they, at least occasionally.

Yet this image also contains contradictions: According to Muslim law and theology, at no stage in life is a woman completely a free agent. She can become a freedom fighter or engage in public matters only with the permission of the man responsible for her — her father, husband, or son. This can happen only if she has no other, more pressing obligations to fulfill, such as taking care of her children. On the level of practical living, no respectable woman can leave home, hearth and husband to take up a public cause, much less fight alongside her brothers. The two demands are mutually exclusive. In fact, Zeynab performed her heroics as a loyal defender of her men's causes, on their order, permission or sufferance. She did not perform as a mother at all, but as a sister and aunt. There are very few adult women who stand in this peculiar and unusual kinship position. An unmarried, childless adult woman is an anomaly, not an ideal.

The image of the tough freedom fighter (or the assertive career woman, for that matter) is incompatible with the status of motherhood and caretaker of a home. At best, it can only be realized as a transitory stage in a woman's life, appropriate only for one who is young, unmarried and childless. In addition, it can occur only under certain conditions, which must include proper chaperoning.

The two ideals, personified in Fateme and Zeynab, are realizable only in sequence: first Zeynab, then Fateme.

Even if we concede that these two roles are possible in sequence, there remains another contradiction, a psychological one. The character and personality required and fostered by these two extreme ideals are incompatible: a politically astute, assertive, combat-oriented gunslinger of a young woman must, upon marriage, transform herself into a docile, obedient wife and a caring, housebound mother.

Neither of these images attracts much adherence from Iranian women. For most women, Fateme the Silent Saint is unrealistic, as is Zeynab the Fighter. Women know that, at times, prudence demands subservience to male authority, just as, at other times, women have taken arms in defense of themselves and their families. But for mothers to neglect husband and children for public cause is an unrealistic proposition, just as total effacement is unrealistic in the struggle of everyday life.

Despite these difficulties, Fateme and Zeynab are popular saints in Iran. As sufferers of injustice, their experiences together encompass many situations women find themselves in or can relate to. Out of their sufferings and the strength the two women have shown in bearing them, modern women fashion a bond which allows them to draw on the memory of these legendary heroines as sources of comfort and strength. In virtually every painful or sticky situation, traditional village women and even many sophisticated urban women invoke the name of Fateme or Zeynab as a plea for help or for an expression of sympathy.

My data on the use of Fateme and Zeynab (and of other female saints whose hagiography is less well established and recorded) suggest that saints' personalities and attractive qualities reflect the existential concerns and circumstances of life of their followers, as well as the programs of theological and political authorities who use the saints to manipulate public sentiment. The Iranian case of the construction and use of Fateme and Zeynab furnishes a good example of this simultaneous construction from below and above. Given a wide enough discrepancy between the political agenda of the leaders and the life circumstances of the people, this process can result in the painting of ambiguous or even contradictory images.

# 19

# A Healing Ritual
## The Life and Words of Nisa, a !Kung Woman

## Marjorie Shostak

**N**isa, a woman of about fifty years of age, is a member of one of the last remaining traditional gatherer-hunter societies, a group calling themselves the *Zhun/twasi*, "the real people." The *Zhun/twasi* or !Kung San, as they are known to anthropologists, live in a remote corner of Botswana, on the northern fringe of the Kalahari desert. They have recently started to leave their traditional means of subsistence — gathering and hunting. Gathering and hunting as a way of life has now almost disappeared, but it was the way people lived for nearly 90 percent of the estimated 100 thousand years of human existence.

Women's status in the community is high and their influence considerable. They are often prominent in major family and band decisions, such as where and when to move and whom their children will marry. Many also share core leadership in a band and ownership of water holes and foraging areas. Just how influential they really are and how their status compares with that of men is a complicated question: women may, in fact, be nearly equal to men, but the culture seems to *define* them as less powerful. In other words, their influence may be greater than the !Kung—of either sex—like to admit. This report discusses !Kung attitudes toward illness and the role of women in ritual healing. It includes Nisa's own story of how she came to be a healer and her description of what it is like to heal others.

Reprinted by permission of the publishers from *Nisa: The Life and Words of a !Kung Woman* by Majorie Shostak, Cambridge, MA: Harvard University Press, © 1981 by Marjorie Shostak.

The realm of the spiritual infuses all aspects of !Kung physical and social life, and is seen as a fundamental determinant in the delicate balance between life and death, sickness and health, rain and drought, abundance and scarcity. This realm is dominated by one major god in command of an entourage of lesser gods. Both the greater and lesser deities are modeled on humans, and their characteristics reflect the multitude of possibilities inherent in the human spirit. Sometimes they are kind, humane, and generous; at other times, whimsical, vindictive, or cruel. Their often erratic behavior is thought responsible for the unpredictability of human life and death.

One way the spirits affect humans is by shooting them with invisible arrows carrying disease, death, or misfortune. If the invisible arrows can be warded off, illness will not take hold. If illness has already penetrated, the arrows must be removed to enable the sick person to recover. An ancestral spirit may exercise this power against the living if a person is not being treated well by others. If people argue with her frequently, if her husband shows how little he values her by carrying on blatant affairs, or if people refuse to cooperate or share with her, the spirit may conclude that no one cares whether or not she remains alive and may "take her into the sky."

Interceding with the spirits and drawing out their invisible arrows is the task of !Kung healers, men and women who possess the powerful healing force called *n/um*. *N/um* generally remains dormant in a healer until an effort is made to activate it. Although an occasional healer can accomplish this through solo singing or instrumental playing, the usual way of activating *n/um* is through the medicinal curing ceremony or trance dance. To the sound of undulating melodies sung by women, the healers dance around and around the fire, sometimes for hours. The music, the strenuous dancing, the smoke, the heat of the fire, and the healers' intense concentration cause their *n/um* to heat up. When it comes to a boil, trance is achieved.

At this moment the *n/um* becomes available as a powerful healing force, to serve the entire community. In trance, a healer lays hands on and ritually cures everyone sitting around the fire. His hands flutter lightly beside each person's head or chest or wherever illness is evident; his body trembles; his breathing becomes deep and coarse; and he becomes coated with a thick sweat—also considered to be imbued with power. Whatever "badness" is discovered in the person is drawn into the healer's own body and met by the *n/um* coursing up his spinal column. The healer gives a mounting cry that culminates in a soul-wrenching shriek as the illness is catapulted out of his body and into the air.

While in trance, many healers see various gods and spirits sitting just outside the circle of firelight, enjoying the spectacle of the dance. Sometimes the spirits are recognizable—departed relatives and friends—at other times they are "just people." Whoever these beings are, healers in trance usually blame them for whatever misfortune is being experienced by the community. They are barraged by hurled objects, shouted at, and aggressively warned not to take any of the living back with them to the village of the spirits.

To cure a very serious illness, the most experienced healers may be called upon, for only they have enough knowledge to undertake the dangerous spiritual exploration that may be necessary to effect a cure. When they are in a trance, their souls are said to leave their bodies and to travel to the spirit world to discover the cause of the illness or the problem. An ancestral spirit or a god is usually found responsible and asked to reconsider. If the healer is persuasive and the spirit agrees, the sick person recovers. If the spirit is elusive or unsympathetic, a cure is not achieved. The healer may go to the principal god, but even this does not always work. As one healer put it, "Sometimes, when you speak with God, he says, 'I want this person to die and won't help you to make him better.' At other times, God helps; the next morning, someone who has been lying on the ground, seriously ill, gets up and walks again."

These journeys are considered dangerous because while the healer's soul is absent his body is in "half-death." Akin to loss of consciousness, this state has been observed and verified by medical and scientific investigators. The power of other healers' n/um is all that is thought to protect the healer in this state from actual death. He receives lavish attention and care—his body is vigorously massaged, his skin is rubbed with sweat, and hands are laid on him. Only when consciousness returns—the signal that his soul has been reunited with his body—do the other healers cease their efforts.

The underlying causes of illness that healers discover while in trance seem to reflect an understanding of the role psychological factors may play in disease. The analysis a !Kung healer offered of a young woman's bout with malaria, for example, illustrated his awareness that her father's recent death might have been affecting her health. The healer's soul made a journey to the world of the dead to find out why the woman was sick. He found the spirit of the woman's father sitting on the ground with the spirit of his daughter in his arms. He was holding her tenderly, rocking her and singing to her. The healer asked why his daughter was with him in the world of the dead and not in the land of the living. Her father explained that he had been desolate without her in the spirit world. He had brought her there so he could be with her again. The healer defended the daughter's right—and obligation—to remain alive: "Your daughter has so much work still to do in life—having children, providing for family and relatives, helping with grandchildren." After an impassioned debate, the healer convinced the spirit to give his daughter time to experience what life had still to offer and to grow old: "Then she'll join you." As the father reluctantly agreed, he loosened his grip on the young woman and her spirit returned to her body. A cure was thus effected, and her health restored.

*N/um* reflects the basically egalitarian nature of !Kung life. It is not reserved for a privileged few: nearly half the men and a third of the women have it. There is enough for everyone; it is infinitely divisible; and all can strive for it. Almost anyone who is willing to go through the rigors of apprenticeship can attain it. Not everyone wants to, however. Many apprentices become afraid or lack ambition and drop out. Others—though few in number—try but do not succeed. Although one can often strengthen one's *n/um* by working at it, its limit is said to be determined by God.

The usual way a young man receives *n/um* is from an experienced healer, often a close male relative, during the ceremonial medicine dance. The apprentice follows the healer around—dancing alone or with his arms wrapped tightly around the healer's waist—hour after hour, with only short rests, often from dusk until dawn. Each time the healer's trance state swells with sufficient intensity and power, he rubs the apprentice's body with his sweat, lays on hands, and snaps his fingers repeatedly against the apprentice's waist to shoot spiritual arrows—through which *n/um* is said to be transferred—into him. This process may be repeated several times during the night and may continue for a number of months or years—however long it takes the novice (typically in his late teens or early twenties) to become accomplished.

This apprenticeship involves a profound dependency on the teacher, which seems to help the novice drop his defenses, thereby making possible an altered state of consciousness—or, as the !Kung would view it, a heightened spiritual reality. The beginner often experiences extreme fluctuations in his emotional state as he learns to trance. At one moment, he may grab burning coals, throw himself into the fire, or run out into the bush and the night. He may cry, or rage against the group, or throw coals or hot sand at people, or break things around him. The next moment may find him whining plaintively, like a small child, begging for water or food; given it, he may spit it out on the ground. If the trance becomes too powerful, he may even be overcome and enter half-death, falling violently to the ground.

These actions do not really alarm others around him. Women sitting by the fire prevent him from burning himself and men run after him to bring him back from the bush. The other healers, especially his teacher, are responsible for ensuring that his soul returns to his body after he enters half-death and for helping him to learn to control the trance. Only when trance energy is harnessed can it be used for social good. Younger men, most dramatic and extreme in trance, are therefore usually less powerful as healers than are older men who have mastered the great forces released in trance.

One older man put it this way, "My *n/um* is so strong I can talk to people or even get up and put wood on the fire when I'm in trance." Healers like this one can also usually enter trance easily, almost at will, and depend minimally on external stimulation. For others, however, the weakening of the body that accompanies aging is reflected in a similar weakening of spiritual power.

Toma, another powerful healer, told me how he had received his *n/um*. His father was an experienced and highly respected healer. When Toma, his oldest son, was a teenager, he started to teach him *n/um*. Late one night, not long after his spiritual education had begun, Toma had what he described as a visitation: while he was asleep, God took him from his hut and sat with him because "He wanted to meet me." Frightened, Toma started to cry. His mother woke and found him sitting outside his hut alone in the dark. The next time Toma's father entered a trance, God explained that he wanted to help give the boy *n/um*.

Some time later, again at night, God came to Toma and placed a small tortoise in his hand. In his sleep, Toma buried it under a tree. The next morning he woke with a vague recollection of the encounter. When he went to verify what he remembered, he found the tortoise buried deep in the sand—in the very spot revealed to him in his "dream." He took the tortoise to his father, who cooked it and ate it.

The next night God came again and asked, "Where is the tortoise

I gave you?'' Toma said, "I gave it to my father and he ate it." God was enraged. He said, "I'm going to kill him." The next morning, Toma's father was ill, so ill that it was "as though he were dead." His mother, who had also received *n/um* from his father, entered a trance to pull the sickness out. God came to her and said, "Toma is the only one who can help your husband now. Tell your son to go to his father, to sit beside him, and to hold him. Tell Toma to stay this way until his father's health returns." Toma sat all day with his arms wrapped tightly around his father. They sat and sat and sat. When the sun was near setting, Toma's father opened his eyes. By evening, he was better.

That night God came to Toma again and said, "Does your father have so little sense that he ate something given by God? Tell him, if he ever does that again, I will really kill him." That was the turning point in Toma's relationship with his father — and with God. After that, Toma's *n/um* was greater than his father's. As Toma put it, "My father did the wrong thing."

Despite the serious and dramatic nature of *n/um*, the atmosphere of a ceremonial medicine dance is anything but reverential. It is an important social gathering, a time of general excitement and festivity, a time for people to ensure their safety, to suspend conflicts, and to act out and verify the common bond that unites them. People talk, joke, flirt, and comment on everything that happens. Dances are rarely planned, except in cases of serious illness, and most often occur spontaneously: after the first rains of the season, after a large animal has been killed, or perhaps after children have staged a mock trance dance of their own, tantalizing everyone with their high spirits. Although the healers and apprentices are the central characters, a dance could never be sustained without the active participation of others. Everyone who wants to can join. In the winter months, when people congregate near the permanent springs, dances attract large numbers of participants. Healers report a deepening of their trance states when many men enter trance at the same dance. They believe their *n/um* to be more powerful at such times, as well.

Women, too, are likely to sing and clap more enthusiastically when a chorus of rich voices is available to give the all-enveloping sound they strive for. Men who are not themselves healers impress the gathering with fancy dance steps and elaborate rhythms, sounded out by the dance rattles around their legs, or even with sheer flirtatious appeal. Babies, in slings astride their mothers' hips, variably sleep and wake, as the women improvise melodies with endless variations or, moved by a handsome dancer or just by the spirit of the moment, get up and dance a few turns around the dance circle. As the dance moves deeper into the night, some participants retire to nearby fires, to sleep or to rest. Before dawn, intense trancing is likely to start up again, lasting until sunrise.

!Kung women constitute the chorus at these ceremonial dances. Their singing and clapping are essential to the dance, influencing the strength of *n/um* a healer will be able to summon forth. They also play a fundamental role in protecting those in trance from hurting themselves in and around the fire. Some wives hold or massage their husbands' bodies until the men regain control of their trance states. One or two women, experienced healers themselves, may also lay on hands and cure, side-by-side with male healers. Nevertheless, trance is available primarily to men, and the purpose of a ceremonial medicine dance is to make trance possible. It is men who assume the responsibility for the general well-being of the community.

There is another dance, however, in which women become more actively involved with *n/um* and with the associated spiritual exploration. The women's dance or drum dance seems to be of fairly recent origin in the Dobe area, although it probably came into existence at least one hundred years ago. The presence of a male drummer beating out distinctive rhythms sets the dance apart from the ceremonial medicine dance. So, too, does the semicircle of women standing, instead of sitting, who sing and clap songs of a distinct melody and cadence. The most striking difference is that women are the predominant participants—in singing, in clapping, in dancing, and in entering trance. The drum dance has been occurring with increasing frequency, and is beginning to assume a distinct role in the religious life of the community. Although some men do not bother to attend, others are drawn to it and sit watching.

Nevertheless, the central psychic experience of the two dances seems to be comparable. As the women dance in place, within the half-circle of women singing and clapping, those who possess *n/um* become affected by the beat of the drum, by the heat of their dancing, and by the fire. The intense inward concentration typical of men entering trance is also evident in the women as their *n/um* starts to heat toward boiling. When trance is achieved, however, its physical manifestation is somewhat different: the woman stands in place while a rapid vibration, similar to a shimmy, engulfs her body from head to foot, especially accentuated in the lower torso. Experienced trancers are able to sustain this movement for long periods of time; less experienced ones often become overwhelmed or frightened and sit down to calm themselves. Women who are determined to explore the full force of the trance state often face the same difficulties men do in handling the intensity of feelings released in trance. They may lose control and run off into the bush, or tease themselves and others with fire, or fling themselves violently to the ground.

About one third of !Kung women are capable of entering trance, but only a small number of these learn to lay on hands and cure— without doubt, the most prestigious activity in !Kung spiritual life. The remainder do not channel their *n/um* into helping others, but seem to view the powerful state of trance as an end in itself. Many women express a desire to advance to higher spiritual planes, but most do not attempt it. Some claim this is because women are more afraid of pain than men are. (Intense physical pain is universally seen as closely associated with the !Kung trance.) But the erratic course by which girls and women receive *n/um* and the more limited opportunities available to them to practice their skills are more likely causes.

A girl's first exposure to altered states of consciousness may occur when she is as young as eight years old, when her mother feeds her small quantities of *gwa*, a purportedly psychoactive root. This training tapers off with the approach of motherhood, because *n/um* is thought harmful to fetuses and young children. If the woman's spiritual education, halted in its (as well as her) infancy, does resume, it is likely to be only when she is in her forties, after her last child has grown. By this time, male healers of the same age, having learned their skills when they were still young, physically strong, and more adaptable, have long since become accomplished.

Despite these obstacles, a handful of older !Kung women have always reached high levels of spiritual mastery. When they lay on hands, their *n/um* is considered as powerful and effective as that of men of comparable experience and accomplishment. The current interest in the women's dance is likely to encourage even more women to become actively involved. The few successful women healers are promoting this trend by initiating drum dances in villages they visit, by teaching women to trance, by transferring *n/um*, and by guiding others to lay on hands and cure.

# The Words of Nisa, a !Kung Woman Healer

*N/um*—the power to heal—is a very good thing. This is a medicine very much like your medicine because it is strong. As your medicine helps people, our *n/um* helps people. But to heal with *n/um* means knowing how to trance. Because, it is in trance that the healing power sitting inside the healer's body—the *n/um*—starts to work. Both men and women learn how to cure with it, but not everyone wants to. Trance-medicine really hurts! As you begin to trance, the *n/um* slowly heats inside you and pulls at you. It rises until it grabs your insides and takes your thoughts away. Your mind and your senses leave and you don't think clearly. Things become strange and start to change. You can't listen to people or understand what they say. You look at them and they suddenly become very tiny. You think, "What's happening? Is God doing this?" All that is inside you is the *n/um*; that is all you can feel.

You touch people, laying on hands, curing those you touch. When you finish, other people hold you and blow around your head and your face. Suddenly your senses go "Phah!" and come back to you. You think, "Eh hey, there are people here," and you see again as you usually do.

My father had the power to cure people with trance medicine, with gemsbok-song trance medicine. Certain animals—gemsbok, eland, and giraffe—have trance songs named after them, songs long ago given by God. These songs were given to us to sing and to work with. That work is very important and good work; it is part of our lives.

It is the same with everything—even the animals of the bush. If a hunter is walking in the bush and God wants to, God will tell him, "There's an animal lying dead over there for you to eat." The person is just walking, but soon sees an animal lying dead in the bush. He says, "What killed this? It must have been God wanting to give me a present." Then he skins it and eats it; that's the way he lives.

But if God hadn't wanted, even if the hunter had seen many animals, his arrows would never strike them. Because if God refused to part with an animal, the man's arrows won't be able to kill it. Even if the animal is standing close beside him, his arrows will miss every time. Finally he gives up or the animal runs away. It is only when God's heart says that a person should kill something, be it a gemsbok or a giraffe, that he will have it to eat. He'll say "What a huge giraffe! I, a person, have just killed a small something that is God's.'' Or it may be a big eland that his arrows strike.

That is God's way; that is how God does things and how it is for us as we live. Because God controls everything.

God is the power that made people. He is like a person, with a person's body and covered with beautiful clothes. He has a horse on which he puts people who are just learning to trance and becoming healers. God will have the person in trance ride to where he is, so God can see the new healer and talk to him.

There are two different ways of learning how to trance and of becoming a healer. Some people learn to trance and to heal only to drum-medicine songs. My mother knew how to trance to these, although she never learned to heal. There are other people who know how to trance and to heal to drum-medicine songs as well as to ceremony-dance songs. The n/um is the same in both. If a person is lying down, close to death, and someone beats out drum-medicine songs, a healer will enter a trance and cure the sick person until he is better. Both men and women have n/um, and their power is equal. Just as a man brings a sick person back to health, so does a woman bring a sick person back to health.

My father was a very powerful healer. He could trance to both kinds of songs, and he taught n/um to my older brother [Dau]. He also taught it to my younger brother [Kumsa]. But when my father died, he stole Kumsa's medicine from him. He left Dau with it, but not Kumsa. Today, even if someone is lying down sick, Kumsa doesn't try to cure him. Only Dau does that.

My present husband, Bo, doesn't have n/um. He was afraid. People wanted to teach him but he refused. He said it would hurt too much.

N/um is powerful, but it is also very tricky. Sometimes it helps and sometimes it doesn't, because God doesn't always want a sick person to get better. Sometimes he tells a healer in trance, ''Today I want this sick person. Tomorrow, too. But the next day, if you try to cure her, then I will help you. I will let you have her for a while.'' God watches the sick person, and the healer trances for her. Finally, God says, ''All right, I only made her slightly sick. Now, she can get up.'' When she feels better, she thinks, ''Oh, if this healer hadn't been here, I would have surely died. He's given me my life back again.''

That's n/um — a very helpful thing!

I was a young woman when my mother and her younger sister started to teach me about drum-medicine. There is a root that helps you learn to trance, which they dug for me. My mother put it in my little leather pouch and said, "Now you will start learning this, because you are a young woman already." She had me keep it in my pouch for a few days. Then one day, she took it and pounded it along with some bulbs and some beans and cooked them together. It had a horrible taste and made my mouth feel foul. I threw some of it up. If she hadn't pounded it with the other foods, my stomach would have been much more upset and I would have thrown it all up; then it wouldn't have done anything for me. I drank it a number of times and threw up again and again. Finally I started to tremble. People rubbed my body as I sat there, feeling the effect getting stronger and stronger. My body shook harder and I started to cry. I cried while people touched me and helped me with what was happening to me.

Eventually, I learned how to break out of my self and trance. When the drum-medicine songs sounded, that's when I would start. Others would string beads and copper rings into my hair. As I began to trance, the women would say, "She's started to trance, now, so watch her carefully. Don't let her fall." They would take care of me, touching me and helping. If another woman was also in trance, she laid on hands and helped me. They rubbed oil on my face and I stood there—a lovely young woman, trembling in trance—until I was finished.

I loved when my mother taught me, and after I had learned, I was very happy to know it. Whenever I heard people beating out drum-medicine songs, I felt happy. Sometimes I even dug the root for myself and, if I felt like it, cooked it and drank it. Others would ask for some, but if they hadn't learned how to trance, I'd say, "No, if I gave it to you, you might not handle it well." But once I really knew how to trance, I no longer drank the medicine; I only needed that in the beginning.

When my niece gets older, I'll dig some of the root for her, put it in her kaross[9] for a few days, and then prepare it. She will learn how to drink it and to trance. I will stand beside her and teach her.

Unlike my mother, I know how to cure people to drum-medicine songs. An elderly uncle taught me a few years ago. He struck me with spiritual arrows; that's how everyone starts. Now when the drum starts sounding, "dong . . . dong . . . dong . . . dong," my *n/um* grabs me. That's when I can cure people and make them better.

Lately, though, I haven't wanted to cure anyone, even when they've asked. I've refused because of the pain. I sometimes become afraid of the way it pulls at my insides, over and over, pulling deep within me. The pain scares me. That's why I refuse. Also, sometimes after I cure someone, I get sick for a while. That happened not long ago when I cured my older brother's wife. The next day, I was sick. I thought, "I won't do that again. I cured her and now I'm sick!" Recently, Dau cured her again. I sat and sang the medicine songs for him. He asked me to help, but I said, "No, I was so sick the last time I almost died. Today, my medicine is not strong enough."

I am a master at trancing to drum-medicine songs. I lay hands on people and they usually get better. I know how to trick God from wanting to kill someone and how to have God give the person back to me. But I, myself, have never spoken directly to God nor have I seen or gone to where he lives. I am still very small when it comes to healing and I haven't made these trips. Others have, but young healers like myself haven't. Because I don't heal very often, only once in a while. I am a woman, and women don't do most of the healing. They fear the pain of the medicine inside them because it really hurts! I don't really know why women don't do more of it. Men just fear it less. It's really funny—women don't fear childbirth, but they fear medicine!

# 20

# The Woman Who Didn't Become a Shaman

## Margery Wolf

In the spring of 1960 in a then-remote village on the edge of the Taipei basin in northern Taiwan, a young mother of three lurched out of her home, crossed a village path, and stumbled wildly across a muddy rice paddy. The cries of her children and her own agonized shouts quickly drew an excited crowd out of what had seemed an empty village. Thus began nearly a month of uproar and agitation as this small community resolved the issue of whether one of the residents was being possessed by a god or was suffering from a mental illness. For Mrs. Chen, it was a month of misery and exultation; for the residents of Peihotien, it was a month of gossip, uncertainty, and heightened religious interest; for the anthropologists in the village, it was a month of confusion and fascination.

Mrs. Chen herself had less influence over the outcome of her month of trial than a foreign observer might expect. Even Wang Ming-fu, a religious specialist who lived nearby and who was given credit for making the final decision, was only one factor in a complex equation of cultural, social, ritual, and historical forces. In the pages that follow, I will attempt to reconstruct the events of that spring from field notes, journal entries, and personal recollections and evaluate what happened from the perspective of the anthropologist. I am not concerned here with shamanism per se, but with the social and cultural factors that were brought to bear by various members of the community in deciding whether Mrs. Chen was being approached by a god who wished to use her to communicate with

Adapted from *American Ethnologist* 17:3, August 1990, by permission of the American Anthropological Association. Not for sale or further reproduction.

his devotees, whether an emotional pathology included fantasies of spirit possession, or whether, as a few maintained, her feckless husband hoped to use her as a source of income.

In the hours following Mrs. Chen's precipitous trip into the mud of the rice paddies, an enormous amount of information traveled through the village about her recent behavior, her past, and the attitude of her family and neighbors. The day before, she had taken her six-month-old baby to her sister's house and left her. She had been complaining to her husband that there was a fever in her heart. She had beaten herself on the chest, pleading to be left in peace, and had jumped up and down on the bed so violently that it had broken. Her husband, commonly referred to in the village as Dumb T'ien-lai, had told one of their neighbors that she was probably going crazy "again." Nonetheless, he had done nothing about it until her very public display. Informants who were in the crowd that gathered as neighbors pulled her out of the paddy and took her back to her house reported that she begged to be allowed to go to the river to "meet someone" who was calling her. The nearby river is considered a dangerous place, full of ghosts who have either accidentally drowned or committed suicide. Water ghosts are infamous for trying to pull in the living to take their place in the dark world of unhappy ghosts.

As the long afternoon wore on, I heard other reports. People said that she pleaded with her husband, Chen T'ien-lai, to give her incense so that she could apologize to "the god who crossed the water." When he lit the incense for her, she began to tremble all over, her eyes glazed, and she began to talk in a loud male voice. One of the oldest women in the village, a woman known for her religious knowledge, came to see her and told T'ien-lai that he should call in a *tang-ki* (shaman) to see if she had met a ghost. By then, however, Mrs. Chen's husband had finally taken some action on his own, and the ranting woman was hauled off under some kind of restraint in a pedicab to what was described to me as a "mental hospital" in the nearby market town.

During the three days that Mrs. Chen was out of the village, the Chen family was part of every conversation. Arthur Wolf, our assistant Wu Chieh,[10] and I collected information about the Chens whether we wanted to or not. We discovered that even though the family was extremely poor, Mrs. Chen went regularly to the temple in Tapu and visited other temples within walking distance. Whenever her children were ill she consulted *tang-ki* in Tapu and neighboring areas. At home, she burned incense and made offerings daily to both her husband's ancestors and a variety of spirits and gods. We learned that although she was painfully shy, Mrs. Chen was a fiercely protective mother who had quarreled in recent months with a woman from the Lin household when Mrs. Chen's young son had been slugged by a Lin boy. The Chens had lived in the village for nearly ten years, but by village tradition they were still considered newcomers — it took at least a generation for a new family to be accepted among those whose grandparents and great-grandparents had been in Peihotien. Until then, newcomers were expected to behave like guests, and guests were expected to watch their hosts' faces. It was a Lin village.

When Mrs. Chen returned to the village, pale and drugged, her mother, Mrs. Pai, was called in by Chen T'ien-lai to "help out." Mrs. Pai had none of her daughter's shyness, and the villagers soon learned from her that her daughter had had one previous "episode" of this kind of behavior. When she was a young adolescent the family had come upon hard times and had been forced to give her away "in adoption" to a family in need of a servant. The girl had done fairly well until "something happened" about which the mother was vague in detail but implied that a member of the family had either raped her or attempted to rape her. The girl had run away to her mother, been returned to her adoptive family, and within a few weeks been sent back to her parents because "she was crazy." She stayed with her natal family until her marriage. There had been, according her mother, no recurrence of erratic behavior.

Mrs. Pai also cast new light on what might have precipitated her daughter's current distress. It seems that a couple of weeks earlier a sizable sum of money had been lost from the pocket of her jacket. Mrs. Chen's son said he had seen his father take it before he went out to gamble one night, but Chen T'ien-lai denied it. Mrs. Chen blamed herself for the loss, but at times seemed convinced that it had been stolen by someone from the Lin household. At some point in the days that followed, the money was miraculously found (probably supplied by sympathetic villagers), but the expectation that this would end the problem was disappointed.

Within 48 hours of her return to Peihotien, Mrs. Chen was again drawing crowds. First, she told her mother that she must *bai-bai* (worship) to "the god who crossed the ocean," a god unknown to Mrs. Pai. The old woman I mentioned earlier informed Mrs. Pai that this was probably Shang Ti Kung (a local god) and that it cost only one New Taiwan dollar (a few cents) per day to rent an image. She also urged her to bring in Shang Ti Kung's *tang-ki* to ask what was wanted. All of this was done the next day and, according to a neighbor, the tang-ki said that Mrs. Chen had met a ghost. Later that afternoon the image of another god, Wang Yeh, was brought in, but Mrs. Chen still was not at peace. Then next day, Mrs. Chen, according to her husband, leapt out of bed shouting that the god was in her body and that T'ien-lai must go at once to get the god's image so that she could *bai-bai* to him. They tried to humor her and finally, because she was getting more and more frantic, agreed to purchase the image. However, neither Chen T'ien-lai nor his mother-in-law recognized the god she described. As Chen T'ien-lai was discussing this problem with some neighbors, his mother-in-law came out of her daughter's bedroom and announced that the daughter, using a strange voice, had told her the exact place to purchase the god's image. She sent her son-in-law on his way and, according to my informants, Mrs. Chen calmed down and went to sleep as soon as she heard that he had gone to purchase "the right god."[11]

Once the new god was put on the Chen household altar, however, the activities in the Chen courtyard changed dramatically. Mrs. Chen began to "dance" like a *tang-ki*, speak in a strange language, and make oracle-like statements. For nearly a week, whenever she came out of the house, crowds would gather and she would "perform." We did not attend all of her sessions, but we were told that she revealed knowledge about people's personal lives that "only a god" would have. She behaved and spoke in ways that were most uncharacteristic of the withdrawn, depressed woman to whom the village was accustomed.

One session in which our research assistant was involved is a good example. I quote from our field notes:

> Mrs. Chen suddenly jumped up and pointed at Lin Mei-ling and told her to approach. Lin Mei-ling had been chatting with some other women about some medicine she had put on her eyes, which appeared to be infected. She looked quite scared, and the others had to push her forward toward Mrs. Chen, saying, "Go on, see what she has to say." As soon as Lin Mei-ling reached her, Mrs. Chen touched her eyes and said, "All right. This one will be well." She sounded as if she were reading a formal notice. Mrs. Chen then returned to making *bai-bai* motions with her hands, saying: "Your husband is a good man. He has a kind heart. He took me home one night on his bicycle. Your family will have peace and won't have any troubles." Lin Mei-ling was holding her baby, who began to cry very loudly. Her mother-in-

law came up and tried to take Mrs. Chen's hands off Mei-ling, telling her that the baby was crying because she had to urinate. Mrs. Chen pushed her aside and said in a loud commanding voice, "Never mind." She then began to handle the baby, saying, "You will have peace and you won't have any trouble. It doesn't matter. It doesn't matter." To Mei-ling she said, "In these days everything will be all right for you. Everything will be all right." She made more *bai-bai* motions and then told Mei-ling to go home and not speak with anyone on the way. "Do you understand?" she asked. Mei-ling was still smiling, but she was probably quite frightened, for her face had turned white. She left and Mrs. Chen knelt on the threshold, making more *bai-bai* motions. She called our assistant, Wu Chieh, to come to her.

Wu Chieh was frightened and didn't want to go forward. She asked another woman what to do and was urged to comply. She was told, "Nothing is wrong. The god is in her body, that's all." Several people pushed Wu Chieh, including Mrs. Pai, Mrs. Chen's mother. Mrs. Chen moved her hands over Wu Chieh's body and face and then took her hands and began to "jump" like a *tang-ki*. Some of the people in the crowd laughed and said, "She wants to dance with you, Wu Chieh." Mrs. Chen said, "Older Sister, you come and you are very kind to all of the children. From the top of the village to the bottom, all of the children call you Older Sister. Do you like that? Do you like that?" Wu Chieh was speechless with fear. Mrs. Chen's mother told her to say something, and Wu Chieh blurted out, "Yes." Mrs. Chen hugged her close and put her face against Wu Chieh's. Mrs. Pai said, "She wants to kiss you." Mrs. Chen shouted, "No, no, no!" Her mother quickly said, "No, I am wrong. I am just an old lady who doesn't understand."

Mrs. Chen told the crowd through gestures (reaching in her pocket, smacking her lips, and so forth) that Wu Chieh gives the children candy. "Children, adults, and old people are all the same. You know that, right?" Wu Chieh nodded. Mrs. Chen then began to make wide, sweeping *bai-bai* gestures and pronounced, "People should not be judgmental, saying this person is good and that person is bad." Then she began to jump around the yard, and an older woman hissed at Wu Chieh, "Stupid child, aren't you going to run away now?" Some little boys were giggling and saying, "This crazy lady is dancing and poor Wu Chieh is going to have to wash all of her clothes." (Mrs. Chen was dirty from kneeling and falling in the dusty courtyard.) Mrs. Chen immediately turned on the boys and shouted, "Go away if you don't believe. Go away." She waved them off as if they were curious chickens, and they scattered like chickens. She turned again to Wu Chieh and rubbed her hands, telling her that everything would be peaceful with her.

As she talked, she continued to make *bai-bai* motions and to jump about, and finally she fell over backward on the ground. She lay there for some time, and Wu Chieh said that when Mrs. Chen opened her eyes, only the whites were visible. After a bit, Mrs. Chen got up and told everyone to go away, saying, "If you don't and you meet something bad [by implication, a ghost], don't blame me." People moved off to the edge of the yard, some of them whispering, some of them laughing, but after a bit the crowd slowly began to edge back toward the house. Mrs. Chen told Wu Chieh, "Because they bully me, I am not willing to continue. Do you understand? You must take me out. Do you understand that?" Wu Chieh kept agreeing at the urging of Mrs. Chen's mother, but she wasn't at all sure what was expected of her.

Mrs. Chen told Wu Chieh to go home again and not to talk with anyone she met on the way. "Listen to what I say or it won't go well for me. After you go home, then come back and take me into the house." People urged Wu Chieh to leave then, so she started to walk away, but Mrs. Chen called her back one more time. "I haven't finished talking to you yet," she said. "If you don't listen to me things will go badly for you. Do you understand? Now hurry up and go home and then come back and take me to my room. Will you do that? If you don't, I will come to your house and find you." She repeated these instructions several times and added, "When you come back, if I am still talking to these women, you stand here and don't say anything, do you hear?" This was all said in a loud commanding voice, totally unlike her normal voice, according to Wu Chieh. Mrs. Chen grabbed both of Wu Chieh's hands in one of hers and gestured with the other in the "counting" motions of a *tang-ki* who is "calculating" what goes on in the world. (This is considered an indication of the god's omniscience.)

Wu Chieh finally extricated herself from this session, but returned in a few minutes and led Mrs. Chen, still gesturing and talking oddly, into her bedroom, where she got her to lie down. Wu Chieh then fled, but Mrs. Chen did not forget her. She called for her attendance several times over the next few days. Unlike Mrs. Chen, who had spent ten years in the village and was still an outsider, Wu Chieh in the year she had lived in the village had become everyone's confidante, everyone's friend, even Mrs. Chen's.

Village opinion was divided at best. Before Mrs. Chen was finally taken away "for a rest" by her mother, several village women reported smelling "puffs of fragrant air" in her room, a sure sign that a god was present; several others reported that she had told them things that only a god could know about their family affairs; she had tormented the Lin family, who had treated her so harshly over the quarrel between their children; she had held many sessions not unlike the one described above. Finally, old Wang Ming-fu, who was considered the expert in the region on matters of religion and ritual, came to talk with her. Their conversation, of which we never got a compete report, was not a happy one. He left in a huff.

We began to detect a change in village attitudes shortly after Wang Ming-fu's visit. Dumb T'ien-lai was enjoying the spectacle far too much and talking too openly about how expensive it was for him to have his wife providing free advice to anyone who asked for it. Mrs. Chen spoke too often and too much about herself as Mrs. Chen rather than behaving as a vehicle who was unaware of her pronouncements while "in trance"; her speeches rambled on too long and lost the enigmatic quality that brings authority to the *tang-ki*. And the fact that Wang Ming-fu was unlikely to recommend that she go to a temple where other *tang-ki* got training and experience seemed to end the matter. Within a week, people had begun to refer to her as "poor Mrs. Chen," to regard her displays as a nuisance, and to pressure members of her family "to do something."

## Shamanism in Taiwan

Before I explore in more detail how and why this decision was reached, some background on shamanism, or spirit possession, in China and Taiwan and its role in folk religion is necessary. I will not try to sort out the peculiar amalgam of Buddhism, Taoism, and Confucianism that is involved in folk religion in Taiwan in particular and China in general. Suffice it to say that there are Buddhist temples and monasteries and that their adherents and practitioners are distinguished by dress and diet. There are no Taoist temples, but folk temples devoted to local gods are usually the locus of the activities of Taoist priests and of the lowly spirit mediums.

The average Taiwanese citizen will make use of Buddhist and Taoist practitioners as the need arises, sometimes entertaining both during funeral rituals. Temples nearly always have at least one Buddhist worthy on their altars, and Buddhist temples sometimes have shrines for local gods in side alcoves. To add to the confusion, spirit mediums in rural areas often provide services from their own home in front of their ancestral altar — which is also a shrine to their particular god — or in the home of the family requesting the help of their god. In urban areas some *tang-ki* have shop-front shrines to their gods, and the most successful have cults of followers who may themselves perform in trance.

In his study of folk religion in a Taiwanese village, David K. Jordan describes the function of the *tang-ki* at the village level:

> The *tang-ki* are the prime rural religious arbiters. It is they who diagnose a given case of familial or village disharmony as caused by ghosts; it is they who explore the family tree or village forts for possible ghosts and their motivations; it is they who prescribe the cure. Spirit mediums drive harmful ghosts from the village; spirit mediums perform exorcisms; and spirit mediums represent the august presence of the divine at rites performed in their name. It is likely that in the past it was the spirit mediums who had the final voice in alliances between villages [in local wars] (1972:85).

But, as Jordan goes on to warn:

> The *tang-ki* is not a free man [sic], and his imitation of the gods is not a matter of his own caprice. Not only must he perform in trance (and therefore presumably not be guided by capricious desires but only by unconscious directives), but he is subject to charges of being possessed by ghosts rather than by gods should he become incredible (1972:85).

And if the *tang-ki* is deemed possessed by a ghost, like any other villager, he or she will have his or her soul called back by another practitioner, essentially ending his or her legitimacy as a shaman.

In northern Taiwan, the source of my data and much of the secondary material to which I refer, the village shaman is considered simply a conduit between a god and his or her petitioners. During festivals celebrating the god, the shaman is expected to put on a display of bodily abuse, such as lying on a bed of nails or lacerating the body with swords or a prickball. Although this is often called "mortification" in the literature (Jordan 1972:78), the purpose is not to subjugate the flesh as in early Christian ritual, but to prove that the god does not allow his vehicle to feel pain from these injuries and will protect him or her from permanent damage. The injuries do seem to heal rather quickly, and most observers comment on the absence of any expression of pain. Some shamans draw blood during each session, others only at major public events. In private sessions, they rarely stage such ordeals, but they always trance.

The problems brought to *tang-ki* are varied, ranging from illnesses in humans and animals to economic setbacks to marital disputes to fears of infertility. The following examples indicate the kind of information and acuity required of a practicing *tang-ki*:

> An old lady asked for advice about her husband, who was seriously ill. The shaman said: "He should have been dead by now. Your husband should have been dead yesterday. However, due to 'strengthened fortune and added longevity' [perhaps from earlier treatment?], he has been able to reach the age of 73. His original life was for only 69 years. Even so, it looks to me as if he were supposed to have died yesterday. If he survives the first day of the coming month, he will have great fortune. You can then come to me to further strengthen his fortune, but not before." He gave her a *hu-a* [charm paper].

> A 17-year-old boy asked about a large protuberance under one of his knees. The shaman said: "You have disturbed some ghosts at night." People in the boy's family admitted that he often ran around outside in the evening and said that the swelling had become larger and more painful in recent days. The shaman gave him a *hu-a* and told him to see a doctor.

> An old lady inquired about her lost gold chain. She said she had come several days earlier, but after four days of searching, she had still not found the chain. The shaman said: "Members of your family do not get along with one another and are quarreling. It doesn't matter that you have lost this chain. The quarreling is more important. Take this *hu-a* home and burn it to ashes, mix the ashes in water, and sprinkle it on the roof. You will be in harmony and only then will the chain reappear."

> A middle-aged man asked about his chickens. "I have raised some chickens and they seem to have a lot of sickness lately. I don't know whether they have offended some dirty thing or there is some epidemic." The shaman said: "You did not choose a good date when you built the chicken house. Besides, you have offended the fox ghost. Cleanse the chicken house three times with *hu-a* ashes in water. Offer sacrifices to make the fox ghost go away. Then, everything will be all right."

In order to address the problems brought before her or him, a *tang-ki* must have a quick mind as well as a keen understanding of human motivation. Most *tang-ki* recommend medical help for obvious illness and, where appropriate, are also likely to recommend the assistance of other ritual specialists, such as geomancers and herbalists. They also practice a certain amount of psychotherapy (Kleinman 1980). In the examples given above, the old woman with the seriously ill husband needed resignation coupled with a bit of hope; the boy clearly needed to see a doctor; a dirty chicken house *might* have been causing the man's chickens to get sick; and the old lady who came back because the *tang-ki*'s last bit of advice hadn't helped her recover her gold chain needed distraction—and all families have quarrels.

A successful *tang-ki* must be quick-witted and alert to the needs of his or her clients ("guests" in the literal translation of the term). Other researchers[12] have suggested that *tang-ki*'s successes often rest on their knowledge of the social and economic background of their clients. Kleinman (1980), who interviewed and observed urban *tang-ki* in Taipei, comments extensively on their sensitivity to potential tensions in the Chinese family, even if the particular client/patient does not happen to be known to them.

These "job qualifications" are obviously derived from the observation of professional, experienced shamans. My concern in this article is why Mrs. Chen was eventually considered not to be *tang-ki* material, why she was never allowed to reach this stage. *Tang-ki* come from modest socioeconomic backgrounds; they are preferably illiterate; they must be sincere and honest; they must display clear indications that a god has chosen them to be his vehicle. People fated to become shamans are originally fated to have short, harmless, unimportant lives, but their lives are extended by the gods who possess them in order that their bodies may be put to good use. Many spirit mediums tell of illnesses in which they were brought back from the dead, after which they are troubled by a god who sends them into trances. Nearly all *tang-ki* in Taiwan report that they struggled against possession as long as they could but finally had to give in to the god's will.

*Tang-ki*, incidentally, must not charge money for their services, but it is assumed that reasonable gifts will be made by grateful clients. I suspect that in rural Taiwan, few *tang-ki* receive enough in contributions to support themselves without another source of income. As Jordan reports, in rural Taiwan there are few "divine rascals" because the living is too poor (1972:75).

Anthropologists frequently entertain the theory that spirit possession serves to provide a role for the emotionally disabled, the psychotic, or the epileptic. Kleinman, who studied the *tang-ki* in

Taiwan primarily as healers, dismisses this explanation as impossible because of the complex behavior required of shamans:

> Shamanistic healing clearly demands personal strengths and sensitivities incompatible with major psychopathology, especially chronic psychosis. Thus my findings argue against the view that shamanism provides a socially legitimated role for individuals suffering from schizophrenia or other severe psychiatric or neurological disorders (1980:214).

Kleinman's conclusions and those of others who have studied the Taiwan *tang-ki* are in accord with my own observations. Nonetheless, the behavior of the beginning *tang-ki* and even of experienced *tang-ki* when they are going into trance might well be confused with that of a person who is deranged. And Kleinman himself provides us with a long case study (followed over three years) of a Hakka businessman suffering from acute anxiety and a variety of debilitating physical symptoms, who solved (to his and the shaman's satisfaction) his problems by "accepting the god" of the shrine, trancing, and essentially playing the role of lay shaman in the cult (1980:333-374).

What Western observers might classify as mental illness is not necessarily so classified in Taiwan or China. The Hakka businessman in Taipei was treated for his problems for some time before he was defined as "troubled by the god" who wished to use him as a vehicle. Another of Kleinman's cases, one he classified as "acute, recurrent psychosis," was that of a 34-year-old mother of three who frequently attended *tang-ki* sessions (1980:166-169). When she began to trance regularly at one of the shrines and "asked that shrine's *tang-ki* if she could become a shaman . . . he told her no (an unusual response), because it was "too early" and she was 'not yet ready.'" According to Kleinman, the *tang-ki* did so because "the patient was unable to control her trance behavior and acted inappropriately during her trances" (1980:167). The Hakka businessman seemed to have similar difficulties at the outset, but nonetheless was accepted readily as a lay shaman.

## The Case of Mrs. Chen

Mrs. Chen, our heroine from Peihotien, was eventually deemed "crazy" by her community, or, as Kleinman might more delicately phrase it, to be showing signs of psychopathology. Why? She had as many shamanistic characteristics as others who went on to full *tang-ki* status. Her origins were humble; she was functionally illiterate; she was sincere, devout, and kind-hearted; she had led a harmless and unimportant life; she had a history of psychological breakdown that could be attributed to the god's attempt to make her his vehicle; she had resisted as long as she could; she went into trances and spoke in a voice other than her own. For a fortnight she convinced a fair number of respectable villagers that a god was making his wishes known to them through her. Her lack of finesse in her public performance seemed no more inappropriate than that of other novices described in the literature.[13] Why, then, did she not qualify as a likely apprentice for training?

From the perspective of her village neighbors, the question was not merely whether she was hallucinating the voice of a god or the god was in fact speaking to her. The question included another (for many villagers) more likely alternative: that a malicious ghost rather than a god was tormenting her. When another practitioner diagnosed her illness as a ghost problem this might have ended the matter, but his treatment appeared to have no effect on Mrs. Chen whatsoever, indicating to her would-be followers that his diagnosis was wrong and the god-possession theory was still the best explanation for her behavior. To understand why Mrs. Chen was not accepted as a vehicle for her god, we must look more closely at her position in her community.

A diagnosis of "mental illness" is even less likely to produce a response of care and concern among Chinese villagers than it is among Americans. As long as a family member's oddities can be hidden or explained away, they will be; and whatever they may think privately, the neighbors will go along, for, after all, they, their parents, and their grandparents have lived and worked side by side with this family, sometimes for centuries. Condemning someone with whom your family has that kind of relationship to a status that removes him or her from participation in society as a fully adult human is not done lightly. One might say that the person's genealogical legitimacy in the community is too high.

In the hierarchy of attributes of legitimacy, Mrs. Chen simply did not rank highly enough to protect her from dismissal as a "crazy"; for the same reason, various members of the community who might have recognized her as a potential *tang-ki* decided it was not worth the risk. To begin with, her gender was against her. There are respected female *tang-ki*, but not very many of them. *Tang-ki* are expected to be and do things inappropriate for women, and even though the extraordinary circumstances of a god's demand should make it all right, the sheer incongruity of the expectations of a god's behavior and those of a woman's behavior are enough to create misgivings. *Tang-ki*, even when not in trance and speaking with a god's voice, must be assured and competent individuals. Mrs. Chen's everyday behavior did not inspire this kind of confidence, nor did that of the only known male relative associated with her, Dumb T'ien-lai.

Even had Mrs. Chen been male, I suspect that her legitimacy would still have received closer scrutiny than that of most men in the village. As noted above, the Chens were "outsiders" in a Lin village. They had no relatives in the area whose genealogy would vouch for their respectability. They were better off than the one or two mainlanders who lived nearby and who were considered totally untrustworthy because they had no family anywhere in Taiwan who could be called to account for whatever transgressions their sons might commit. Nonetheless, the Chens by virtue of their newcomer status remained objects of suspicion, people who were considered slightly dangerous because they had no family whose face their misbehavior could ruin. The arrival of Mrs. Chen's mother helped, but the presence of her father and his brothers would have helped even more. And here again, her gender was against her, for women are considered only adjunct members of their husbands' families and temporary members of their natal families. There is no solidity, no confidence in ties through females to families about whom one knows nothing.

At another level of abstraction, Mrs. Chen's failure to be judged a *tang-ki* in the making comes down to her ambiguous status in terms of the Chinese concept of the family. Any *tang-ki* treads dangerously near the edge of respectability in relation to Chinese notions of filiality, and Mrs. Chen's situation tipped her into the area of violation. From the point of view of the Chinese villager, an individual is only part of a more important unit, the family, and the individual's personal inclinations must be subordinated to the needs of the family. Choice of education, occupation, marriage partner, even of medical attention, should be determined by family elders in terms of what is best for the group—and often that group is conceived of as a long line of ancestors stretching into a hazy past and an equally long line of descendants stretching into an unknowable future. The individual is expected to be selfless—even his or her own body is the property of the ancestors. I have seen innumerable village children harshly punished by their parents for playing so carelessly as to fall and injure themselves, thus damaging the body that belongs to the family. Jordan (1972:84) also mentions this ideal in relation to *tang-ki* who regularly slash, cut, and otherwise mutilate their bodies in service to their god. Although divine intervention is supposed to prevent any permanent damage to the ancestors' property, the *tang-ki* nonetheless violates one tenet of filial piety.

More important, *tang-ki* serve another master. They are expected to be totally selfless in that role as well, submitting themselves fully to the god's will in order to enable the god to solve his followers' problems. In fact, the needs of the ancestors and of the possessing god rarely come into conflict, for when out of trance, the *tang-ki* can fulfill all of his or her obligations to parents, grandparents, and so forth. However, in theory, the *tang-ki* has given his or her person to a god to do with as he will. Thus, the *tang-ki* submits to the god that which belongs to the ancestors. This may make the *tang-ki*'s filial piety suspect, but it also highlights the sacrifice the god requires of his vessel. Mrs. Chen's assumed (although demonstrably inaccurate) rootlessness may very well have served to devalue the selflessness of her generosity in submitting to the will of the god.

Had Mrs. Chen been a wife or daughter of a Lin, there might actually have been strong pressures on her to accept the nomination of the god whether she wished to or not. In an intriguing study of shamanism in contemporary China, Ann Anagnost describes the social pressure put on a woman to assume the role of shaman (1987:52-54). During a period of failing health, Zhu Guiying exhibited symptoms that were interpreted as spirit possession. Sought out by fellow villagers as a healer, she at first resisted, but finally submitted to the social expectations of her neighbors. As Anagnost puts it, "To refuse this role would have been tantamount to a denial of social ties and the forms of reciprocity and obligation that bound the community together" (1987:53).

It is conceivable that in another setting, one where she was known in the context of a family, Mrs. Chen might in fact have been encouraged to continue her interactions with the god who approached her in Peihotien. If, for instance, she had moved to Taipei and become involved in some of the cults surrounding well-known urban *tang-ki*, she might have continued to go into trance and might have become a valued member of one of those groups, thereby finding peace and status. In Peihotien she was too low in all of the hierarchies to achieve legitimacy as a full member of her community. As a result, she was not able to overcome her anomaly in either world—that of the village or that of the possessed.

Mrs. Chen failed to become a shaman, by one set of measures, because of the structural context in which she lived; she was an outsider—socially and genealogically. But her failure might be accounted for by another set of reasons, reasons even more intimately associated with her gender. Feminist theorists[14] suggest that the male self is based on a set of oppositional categories (good/bad, right/wrong, nature/culture, and so forth) and that male selves are more rigidly bounded, more conscious of a distinction between the self and the other than are female selves. A female—perhaps because the female infant does not need to transfer her identity from her original caretaker—has a less bounded self. It is not tied into oppositions between self and other, but is constructed instead from connectedness and continuities. A good *tang-ki* must be able to separate his or her behavior as a *tang-ki* from his or her everyday behavior. With a self constructed out of dualisms, a male may find it easier to keep his relations with his deity separate from his conscious mental life. Mrs. Chen clearly could not.

However, there are dangers in applying theoretical concepts developed from observations of white middle-class American parenting styles to the analysis of personalities constructed in a very different culture. One cultural pitfall is that Chinese children usually have a variety of female caretakers during their early childhood and it is unclear how this might affect the formation of adult personality.

In time, Mrs. Chen might have been able to achieve separation of her relationship with her deity from her everyday life—other female *tang-ki* have. But Mrs. Chen had a special problem. Construction of the Chinese female self is highly dependent on the meaning given to the individual by others. Whereas the Chinese male is born into a social and spiritual community that has continuity not only in life but after death, the Chinese female is born into a social community of which she is only a temporary resident, and her spiritual community after death depends upon whom she marries, or, more important, whose ancestors she gives birth to. A Chinese boy's self is defined by this certainty, this continuity. A girl's sense of self develops in an environment of uncertainty—if she isn't sufficiently modest, she won't find a good family; if she isn't obedient, no mother-in-law will want her; if she is willful, she will have trouble with some unknown husband. She reads who she is in the approving or disapproving faces of those around her.

The trauma of Chinese marriage, in which a very young woman is transferred to a distant village where she knows no one, not even her husband, creates for a woman a crisis of identity that is only resolved by the gradual acquisition of a new set of mirrors in which she can identify herself. Mrs. Chen came to Peihotien a stranger, and a stranger she remained. There was no family to smile or frown, no mother-in-law to approve or disapprove of her behavior, and only a husband who was himself a stranger. Without ties to a family that had an accepted place in the village social system, when Mrs. Chen was no longer a novelty, she ceased to have an identity. She was an outsider who was neither dangerous nor useful, and she was more or less ignored. She was in fact nameless, having lost her personal name at marriage (Watson 1986). Unlike other brides, her self was never reconstructed, and her mirrors remained cloudy, except for the self she saw reflected in her children and in the conversations she had with the various gods she visited.

I continue to wonder whether or not Mrs. Chen, on that fateful day when she threw herself into the rice paddy, was not, as some claimed, trying to get to the river. Suicide (often by drowning) is a solution for many (younger) Chinese women who have trouble creating a new self in a strange place. Perhaps when she was pulled out of the muck of the paddy, she made one final attempt to join the social world of the village by way of a god who had more reality for her than the people among whom she lived. Unfortunately, her self was so poorly established that she could not carry it off. The self that spoke with the gods could not be used to construct a self that could survive in a social world constructed by strangers.

# PART VI

# Challenges to the
# Social and
# Cosmic Order

## Debunking Marianismo
Economic Vulnerability and Survival Strategies
among Guatemalan Wives
*Tracy Bachrach Ehlers*

## Poetics and Politics in the Ecuadorean Andes
Women's Narratives of Death and Devil Possession
*Mary M. Crain*

## A Businesswoman among Middlemen
A Case from Siassi
*Alice Pomponio*

## Shades of Blue
Female and Male Perspectives on Policing
*Joan C. Barker*

An officer with the California Highway Patrol
is one of increasing numbers of women
working in jobs traditionally held by men.
*Photo courtesy of the California Highway Patrol.*

►

# Suggested Readings

**Laurel Herbenar Bossen. 1984.** *The Redivision of Labor: Women and Economic Choice in Four Guatemalan Communities.* **SUNY Series in the Anthropology of Work. June Nash, ed. Albany: State University of New York Press.**
Bossen asks: "How does economic development affect women in Latin America?" Using an innovative comparative approach, Bossen examines the impact of economic change on women in four settings: urban shanty, Maya farming village, modern sugar cane plantation, and middle-class neighborhood. Balancing theory with life histories, she shows women's adaptive strategies to changing economic realities.

**Fran Leeper Buss. 1990.** *Dignity: Lower Income Women Tell of Their Lives and Struggles.* **Ann Arbor: The University of Michigan Press.**
These moving personal accounts by ten women from a variety of ethnic backgrounds—white, black, Native American, Japanese—focus on work; economic life; young, single motherhood; and sexual exploitation. They are the stories of poor women who fight to survive the circumstances of their lives. Their stories depict their rage and resignation, their strength and determination. Here is where migrant worker and garment factory worker emerge as union organizers and leaders.

**Sherna Berger Gluck. 1988.** *Rosie the Riveter Revisited: Women, the War and Social Change.* **New York: New American Library.**
During World War II, women replaced men in the building of battleships and airplanes, in welding and riveting, thus occupying what had been exclusively masculine domains. This book, told by former southern Californian women aircraft workers (Anglo, Afro-American, Latina), presents us with ten oral histories chronicling the role of women in nontraditional jobs during World War II. From their stories we gain a better understanding of the processes not only of social change but of personal growth, of how they changed the way they felt about themselves through work. As one woman worker said, "I never realized what I could do." (The book makes a good companion to the film, *Life and Times of Rosie the Riveter.*)

**Rigoberta Menchu. 1985.** *I, Rigoberta Menchu: An Indian Woman in Guatemala.* **Elizabeth Burgos-Debray, ed., Ann Wright, trans. New York: Routledge, Chapman and Hall.**
"My name is Rigoberta Menchu," this story begins. It is told by a Guatemalan peasant Indian woman, famous for her work as a national leader and more recently as the winner of a Nobel Peace Prize. It is a tough, personal story of the horrors of war and of political commitment, all the more poignant for the simple and honest way in which it is told. In the telling Rigoberta Menchu describes her culture's way of life— ceremonies relating to birth, marriage, harvests—and chronicles the fight to preserve the culture through resistance and rebellion. (Rigoberta Menchu's story is also preserved on film.)

**Ilsa M. Glazer Schuster. 1979.** *The New Women of Lusaka.* **Mountain View, California: Mayfield.**
Schuster examines the lives of educated women who are carving out careers in Lusaka, the capital city of the Republic of Zambia. She describes how these women cope with such aspects of their lives as advancement, child care and their relationships with men, who often compare them unfavorably with more traditional women. She notes that these "new women" must also contend with negative portrayals of independent women as "folk devils" in the Zambian media.

# Introduction

## Judith Marti

In any local market of the third world, one can find digital watches displayed next to handwoven cloth; and not a few peasant homes now boast of refrigerators, televisions, radios, and electric blenders, items scarce a few years ago. These items represent the encroachment of the industrial world. What changes has modernization brought to the lives of third-world women? To their status in the home? In the community?

In peasant societies before industrialization, women and men maintained relationships of interdependence, in which both wife and husband exerted control over economic resources. With modernization came an imbalance to that relationship; women lost their autonomy and became dependent on men.

In Guatemala, for instance, industrialization has had an uneven impact. It brought major changes to some communities while all but bypassing others. Laurel Bossen compares the role of women in two communities, T'oj Nam and El Cañaveral. T'oj Nam is a traditional rural community, with a subsistence-based economy where peasants are their own bosses, and each family produces most of its basic needs. Here, men and women are partners, contributing about equally to the household economy: "A man without a wife may have corn without tortillas, cotton without clothing, a house without a hearth" (Bossen 1984:304–305). In contrast, at El Cañaveral, men have to work for cash income in jobs outside the house. Now women no longer contribute equally: "... wives are not needed to haul water, to build fires, nor to weave or sew clothing. Their children are no longer needed as part of the household labor force" (Bossen 1984:306).

Modernization has brought a decline in the status of women. Why? And why have women put up with a new, lower position? The literature on women in Latin America depicts women as unhappy in abusive marriages, writes Tracy Bachrach Ehlers, in

"Debunking Marianismo: Economic Vulnerability and Survival Strategies among Guatemalan Wives," the first article of this part. To explain this situation the *machismo/marianismo* model is commonly used. According to this model, women choose to put up with dismal marriage conditions to gain status. Ehlers summarizes this argument: "women welcome abusive male behavior as the spiritual verification of their true womanhood," since their superior position of near saintliness can only be maintained by comparison to male wickedness. Ehlers disagrees with this model, which she says simply puts the blame on women. Instead, she argues that women's economic value is eroded in the process of changing from isolated subsistence-based economies to modernization. This assigns the male the role as main breadwinner, reducing the woman to a subservient position she must endure because she has no alternative source of income. This explanation suggests that women's status is linked to changes in the developing economy arising from accommodations to the global economy.

Economic and political changes do not necessarily relegate women to subservient positions. There is evidence of women resisting changes that impact negatively on their lives. This opposition has often taken forms that are not easily discernible, resulting in the belief that women are powerless or that it is not in their nature to take action. Silverblatt documents the strategies of resistance women used to combat Spanish rule during the colonial period in Peru (Silverblatt 1980, 1987). In pre-colonial times, women were responsible for ceremonies devoted to female goddesses. Under the Spaniards, women were excluded from religious positions and persecuted as witches for practicing their indigenous religion. "'Now don't you see, the universe has turned inside out; for we are being persecuted,' declared Lucia Suyo Carhua, accused of being a sorceress" (Silverblatt 1980:173).

During the sixteenth century, rural women resisted colonial rule by reasserting indigenous spiritual traditions and refusing to attend Roman Catholic Mass,[1] practices which Spanish officials considered a threat to their authority. These women escaped to the *puna* (high-pastureland), and secretly returned to their ancient customs. Indigenous women not only regained their former power but achieved additional status by taking on the religious duties performed by men in pre-colonial times and by being responsible for preserving their ancient faith. By the seventeenth century an underground religious sect had emerged in which virgins, trained from childhood, played increasingly important roles in maintaining indigenous religions. This female society, called "virgins of the Sun" by Spaniards, became a form of resistance to the changes wrought by European rule.

Today in Andean society, the *puna* is still considered women's territory—"the isolated tableland where they pasture their herds" and practice rites to the mountain spirits or *Wamanis*. "The male members of the *varayoq*, who are obliged to guard the morality of the village, are afraid to go to the *puna*. 'If the women in the puna do not like what we are doing, they will stone us and make us return to our village.' But on the other hand, the *varayoq* add, 'The women in the *puna* are living in the ways our ancestors lived years ago, they are defending our customs, they are defending our culture'" (Silverblatt 1980:180).

In Quimsa, Ecuador, peasant women today practice similar forms of political resistance to the changes brought about by the commercialization of agriculture, as described by Mary M. Crain in the second article of this part, "Poetics and Politics in the Ecuadorean Andes: Women's Narratives of Death and Devil Possession." For several decades, large haciendas in the region have been mechanizing, reducing dependence on peasant laborers. Male peasant protests often take visible forms, such as vandalizing the machinery of large estates, but women have quietly, and effectively, entered the political arena through rumors and gossip, often centered on narratives of devil possession. In one case, a hacienda worker responsible for machinery at a sawmill died suddenly under mysterious circumstances. The man's female relatives whispered that the devil had possessed the machinery and had thus been able to control its operator, driving him to his death. Crain argues that women's narratives send a message to the community as to what will befall the person who benefits from association with commercialized agriculture, and are an example of female power to resist change considered detrimental to their own and their community's existence.

Women can also adapt in innovative ways to economic changes brought by modernization, as evidenced by a New Guinea example recorded by Alice Pomponio in "A Businesswoman among Middlemen: A Case from Siassi," the third article of this part. In this case study, Pomponio notes that a well-born woman was able to succeed where some men in the community had failed, in establishing a business linked to the world market system. As a result she increased her standing in the community and provided jobs for unskilled women that allowed them to contribute cash income to their families.

In American society, women's roles in the workplace have also changed with the economy. During World War II, women entered the work force in large numbers, building warships and manufacturing munitions, replacing husbands, brothers, and sons who were needed as soldiers. But, although their role changed, their image remained the same. Women were portrayed in propaganda films as working housewives rather than as workers. Women were told that cutting patterns out of metal was no harder than cutting a dress pattern out of cloth, a task for which they were well-trained (*Life and Time of Rosie the Riveter*, film).

Since the 1960s, an increasing number of women have entered the labor force to work alongside men. Women are breaking down barriers to what have traditionally been considered male bastions. In her article "Shades of Blue: Female and Male Perspectives on Policing," Joan C. Barker examines the changing role of women police officers. Prior to implementation of affirmative action policies on the Los Angeles Police Department, women officers were assigned to cases considered appropriate to their gender—dealing with rape and incest victims and abused or neglected children. The most dangerous job—responding to domestic disputes—was thought better left to men. In the last decades, the contribution of women to policing has changed both quantitatively and qualitatively. Not only are more women working as "street police," Barker argues, but they typically emphasize a different style of policing than men—relying more on negotiation and persuasion than physical force.

In responding to often dramatic changes in gender relations around the world, women are proving themselves to be neither passive nor uninvolved—though they may at times be powerless to resist pressures that undermine their traditional bases of power and autonomy. As the authors in this part demonstrate, modernization often reduces the importance of domestic-based production, undercutting the economic power of women. In some cases, women are able to increase their stature by developing innovative ideas and techniques, or by applying traditional wisdom to the new context.

# 21

# Debunking Marianismo
## Economic Vulnerability and Survival Strategies Among Guatemalan Wives

*Tracy Bachrach Ehlers*

n highland Guatemala, an old riddle asks, "How is a husband like an avocado?" The answer, "A good one is hard to find," is well known to every woman. My fieldnotes are filled with stories testifying to the truth of this adage. Marcela's common-law husband gambles every night and refuses to marry her because he has another wife — and five children — in the next town. Dona Violeta is called a widow, but everyone knows she was abandoned by her husband after the birth of her third child. Carmen had to send her children to live with her mother since their father left her and her new husband refuses to raise another man's offspring. Dona Magdalena's husband drank up her wages, beat her when she complained about it, then spent the next two weeks with his lover, leaving Magdalena penniless. Rich or poor, in towns and villages across the highlands, rarely a day passes without another woeful tale of offenses, abuses, and bad habits of men.

The research on gender relations in Latin America is replete with descriptions of women tormented by unhappy marriages and with explanations of male behavior in this context.[2] As early as the seventeenth century, Fray Alonso called it *"la mala vida,"* or "the bad life" (Boyer 1989). Where analysis fails us is when we ask why women put up with persistent male abuse and irresponsibility. In trying to explain this pattern, authors have often turned to the *machismo/marianismo* model of gender relations, which suggests

Adapted from: Tracy Bachrach Ehlers, "Debunking Marianismo: Economic Vulnerability and Survival Strategies Among Guatemalan Wives," *Ethnology* 30(January 1991):1-16.

that women welcome abusive male behavior as the spiritual verification of their true womanhood. Men's wickedness, this argument claims, is the necessary precondition for women's superior status as semidivine figures, without whose intercession men would have little chance of obtaining forgiveness for their transgressions (Stevens 1973a).

There are several problems with this model. First, *marianismo* is often considered as a complement to *machismo*, where the passive, long-suffering woman acts in response to male irresponsibility; without *marianismo*, *machismo* could not exist. Second, it alleges that this pattern offers women a positive and private realm and that, relegated to a separate domestic sphere, they are content with their feminine power in the home, and do not wish to change the sexual balance of power. On both counts, *marianismo* blames the victim, suggesting wives accept callousness from men because they benefit from the status of wife/mother. In addition, *marianismo* has evolved into a nearly universal model of the behavior of Latin American women.[3]

Some see *marianismo* as a powerful positive stance,[4] but I maintain that in Guatemala's patriarchal society, the sexual division of labor excludes women from valuable income-producing activities, thus giving them no choice but to accept irresponsible male behavior. Among Mayas and ladinos, the prevailing ideology of male domination in the economy minimizes the contribution women make to family survival and their ability to manage without a resident man. In this system, men are valuable scarce resources who can misbehave with impunity, assured that their wives and mistresses need them for economic reasons. In this paper, I argue that:

1. While female subordination is present, it comes in many different forms and in varying degrees.
2. Women's behavior vis-a-vis men is not merely a response to *machismo*, but is a survival strategy emerging from female economic, social, and sexual dependence in a society where men hold economic, political, and legal power.
3. Gender relations are not a static construction of ideal roles, but evolve and change with the material conditions of women's lives, and over the life span of each woman.

This article focuses on two highland communities where women have distinctly different relations to production. San Pedro

Sacatepequez, San Marcos, is a changing indigenous town (pop. 15,000) in highland Guatemala. San Pedro's rapidly developing economy has created a myriad of income-producing activities for both sexes, reflected in a diversity of male/female relations. In contrast to San Pedro's urbanity, I also examine material from San Antonio Palopó, a traditional Cakchiquel-speaking village on Lake Atitlán. San Antonio (pop. 2600) has a subsistence-based economy, largely dependent upon corn and onion production. In the last dozen years the rapid growth of commercial weaving has resulted in a dramatic change in the sexual division of labor. These contrasting communities have in common a shift in relations of production; i.e., development, albeit on vastly different scales. My discussion focuses on how each town's increasing market integration has changed the sexual division of labor, emphasizing and exacerbating patriarchal relations to the detriment of women.[5]

## The Marianismo Model

Latin American women are aware of the realities of marriage. Safa's (1976) interviews in Puerto Rico revealed that two-thirds of the women regarded marriage as an unhappy situation doomed from the start because of male vices. Similarly, female Mexican textile workers considered marriage to be problem-ridden and thought themselves better off alone (Piho 1975). Still, 92 percent of Latin American women marry (Youseff 1973), and continue to speak fatalistically about the state of marriage. Peasant women in the Dominican Republic also believe marriage to be a matter of luck, that one must suffer whatever comes and make the best of it (Brown 1975).

This fatalistic acceptance of women suffering at the hands of men has been traced to the colonial period, when women were taught to emulate the virtues of the Virgin Mary. The Spanish fostered a nontemporal, spiritual, and therefore secondary, role for women with laws and social codes limiting women's rights and defining women as subservient (Leahy 1986). This tradition relegates the unquestioning, obedient woman to the home, the church and the family.

Stevens (1973a) coined the term *marianismo* to suggest the sacred significance of women's subordinate posture in Latin America, and described the idealized belief that women are semidivine, morally superior, spiritually strong beings who manifest these attributes in personal abnegation, humility and sacrifice. These attributes she believes appropriate, given the tensions surrounding the exaggerated masculinity (*machismo*) of their spouses. Thus women must be patient with frivolous and intemperate husbands. When men are truly sinful, women, who are closer to God, will intervene and, by their prayers, guide men along the difficult road to salvation. Above all, women are submissive and resigned to their status as pure, long-suffering martyrs to the irresponsible but domineering men in their lives.

Women use their subordinate status to their own advantage in "having their *marianismo* cake and eating it too," (Stevens 1973b:98). The myth of Marian martyrdom is perpetuated in order to assure the "security blanket" which covers all women, giving them a strong sense of identity and historical continuity (Stevens 1973b:98). By this way of reasoning, female power emerges from the private, domestic domain where women rule and are as liberated as they wish to be, free from the pressures of the male-oriented business world. Women are satisfied with their domestic domain and will likely work hard to hold onto a system that supports it. However, the price for controlling this powerful resource can be a lifetime of suffering, both in childbearing and in the trials and humiliations of the marriage itself. Nonetheless, as Neuhouser (1989:690) notes, "the positive impact of *marianismo* as a resource for women increases over the life course," as a woman's accumulated pain is transformed into sainthood.

Critics of the *marianismo* concept take issue with the notion that women consciously place themselves within the domestic safety net of *la mala vida*. Bourque and Warren (1981) reject the idea that women enjoy parity with men through their control of the domestic sphere. They argue that where female status is undercut by a hierarchy of men in the larger world, women cannot have power in the home no matter how much they are venerated. Nash (1989) adds that combining public isolation with the spiritual emulation of the Virgin acts to rationalize female powerlessness as it condones male superiority. Moreover, the ideal of the good woman reigning at home rarely corresponds to daily reality (Kinzer 1973; Browner and Lewin 1982). I suggest that as men move away from agricultural dependence, fatherhood becomes an expression of male virility or proof of masculine control over females, and the home becomes the realm of a tyrannical husband, not the idealized domain of women.

Where the *marianismo* model breaks down entirely is among the millions of poor women for whom work is a necessity. They are often underreported and underestimated, especially in subsistence or domestic production. Urban and rural women are rarely idle; their children might not eat if they do not work. Employed as maids, factory workers, in subsistence or export agriculture, as artisans, petty commodity producers, etc., Latin American women work and, when compared to men, occupy the more onerous, insecure, and unrewarding jobs. Female laborers have fewer productive opportunities than men (Deere and Leon de Leal 1981), are severely restricted in what choices they do have (Schminck 1977), and are often forced to accept oppressive conditions and physically taxing work (Piho 1975).

While the sexual division of labor in productive activities is mixed, reproductive responsibilities for Latin American women are relatively uniform. Women perform the bulk of household duties, which proscribes their potential productivity outside the home. Men can find wage labor while many women take up subsistence activities "almost as an extension of domestic work" (Deere and Leon de Leal 1981:360). Even cottage industry, which allows women to direct child labor and is compatible with housework, is usually an extension of labor-intensive domestic skills (Beuchler 1985) and can be a highly exploitative, low-profit endeavor (Ehlers 1982). Moreover, whether a woman works in the informal sector or in the home, she still works two shifts, juggling children, cooking, washing, and cleaning with income-production. Managing these two full-time jobs impinges upon female income potential and diminishes the seriousness with which women are treated in jobs and careers. In short, the *marianismo* model does not fully take into account Latin American male domination.

Male dominance over economic and political institutions limits female access to economic resources. Because it marginalizes women as economic actors, patriarchy does not have to dominate women physically, but can use indirect market control to limit female independence. This may vary by class, ethnicity, or geography, but any examination of gender relations in Latin America shows male dominance in economic control, access to critical roles in society, and in maintaining cultural stereotypes which reinforce male power. Women are therefore economically and socially vulnerable. Modernization and the accompanying elaboration of market relations usually make this situation worse.

Wolf (1966) and Adams (1960) argue that egalitarian relations among indigenous Mayan men and women emerge from a traditional culture that supports a strong, positive husband-father role. Bossen (1984) correctly observes that this argument underestimates the importance of economic roles in determining gender values. In peasant economies where the family productive system functions as a cooperative unit, women's productive and reproductive labor is as valuable as men's work. Loucky's (1988:119) research in two Lake Atitlan towns convinced him that, "so indispensable is this partnership that individual accumulation and highly unequal distribution of goods is rare." Women are confident of their roles and have little reason to be submissive. Both sexes acknowledge the mutuality of their labor contributions within a flexible, supportive social system. This domestic balance would encourage a woman to leave an abusive husband and return to her natal home (Wagley 1949).

All this changes when individualized cash income enters the system, creating a redivision of labor that negatively affects women. The interdependency, cooperation, and equal distribution of labor characteristic of couples in small traditional communities breaks down when men work autonomously outside the home. Male accessibility to private income production establishes female dependency characteristic of nuclear families in a situation of industrialization (Bossen 1984).

The increasing value given to male income from outside employment is problematic for women in the two communities I examine. In each, women's economic status diminishes with the increasing occupational fortunes of their spouses. In one community, new male-dominated industry has begun to make complementary peasant production irrelevant. In the other, modernization has undermined women's independent businesses while it greatly enhanced male external trade opportunities. The evidence suggests that with increased autonomous income, men devalue their wives, who are no longer essential to them. The economic vulnerability of women from these two very different towns compels them to accept male callousness or irresponsibility because they have no alternative sources of economic security. Those middle-class women who are able to manage without a man do so through resources not available to the ordinary Guatemalan wife.

## San Antonio Palopó

San Antonio Palopó is a traditional, Cakchiquel-speaking community on the eastern shore of Lake Atitlán, whose people have depended upon *milpa* agriculture (small-scale corn agriculture) supplemented by small-scale cash crops (namely onions and previously, anise), and seasonal plantation labor. Families live in tiny, one-room houses, few of which have access to running water, and nearly half the households are landless. Harvested maize (corn) lasts about six months, after which cash must be generated to buy food. The precarious quality of life is perhaps best reflected in the poor diet and the high frequency of chronic illness.

Men and women share this impoverished life, but women carry a larger share of the burden. Half marry by age sixteen and 60 percent have their first child by eighteen. Families with six or seven children under twelve years old are common, although 43 percent have lost one or more children to illness associated with malnutrition. Beyond nursing and child care, women bear an arduous and repetitive domestic routine that takes up to nine hours each day, and which diminishes the time for income production.

Although both men and women are poor and socially marginalized, men have more familiarity with and access to the dominant ladino culture. Women are rarely educated (77 percent have no schooling), with only a 15 percent literacy rate, compared with 32 percent for men. Eighty-four percent of men are fluent in Spanish, while women speak Cakchiquel almost exclusively. All indigenous women wear the local costume, compared to three-quarters of men, a figure that will no doubt decrease since men are beginning to insist their sons wear Western dress.

Cultural, economic, and physical isolation handicap Tunecas[6] in many ways. Only a few women regularly travel beyond San Antonio to sell handweavings in the nearby tourist town of Panajachel, and their sales are sporadic at best. In fact, most Tunecas avoid Panajachel, preferring to do their shopping from itinerant traders who charge high prices when they pass through town. Women who choose the forty-minute bus ride to Panajachel to shop are uncomfortable and shy beyond the market, where Cakchiquel is spoken. They usually accomplish their errands quickly and go home on the next bus.

Female social vulnerability is clearest when women interact with outsiders — doctors, teachers, ladino traders — and must defer to men. In part this is because they do not speak Spanish, but also because of cultural prescriptions that deny respectability to those women who openly converse with strangers. Without men present, women can be outspoken about themselves. Tunecas visiting me needed little encouragement to talk about sex and contraception.

They agreed that where children were concerned, women suffered on many counts: they did not like intercourse, they hated pregnancy, feared childbirth, and resented having to care for several small children because it made income production so difficult. Like the women of San Pedro la Laguna interviewed more than fifty years before (Paul 1974), my Tuneca informants characterized men as "curs" who wanted sex all the time, but had little consideration for their wives' needs.

While skewed gender relations have long existed in San Antonio, a clear pattern of male dominance is more evident now than in the past. Until recently, men and women worked together to survive. Men were responsible for agricultural production, women for processing grains, preparing onions for market, and maintaining the home. Both sexes traveled to the coast to pick cotton on large plantations. There was little money to be made beyond this, and the cash generated from migratory labor was quickly absorbed in consumption or fertilizer for corn. In 1978, however, a handful of entrepreneurial men and women worked with the Peace Corps and the Catholic Church to establish a commercial weaving industry in the town. This innovation totally realigned the relations of production, creating a severe discrepancy in the contributions men and women make to the family income.

Today, 60 percent of Tuneco homes have looms. These families generate an average of nearly $50 a month, more than replacing plantation labor as a source of cash income. The average plantation income is approximately $25 a month, and few work for more than one month. Coastal weather is hot and extremely humid, the work is arduous and food and housing are abysmal. Weaving is home-based, often year-round, and clean. One man said he likes to weave because while he works he can listen to his new radio and look at his new watch. Moreover, instead of eating *frijoles* (beans) three times a day, his wife cooks various dishes for him, keeps his clothes clean, and generally provides domestic support services for his productive efforts.

In San Antonio in 1978, no men wove, but nearly all their wives did. Women used their backstrap looms to produce the blouses, shirts, and handcloths for the family and for a small tourist trade. It seemed obvious that women should lead in the introduction of four-harness footlooms since they understood the basic weaving system and could easily adapt to the new technology. In fact, women far outnumbered men at the early co-operative meetings, but later, when it was clear that the new production system was to be ongoing, men signed up in increasing numbers. As an indication of their incipient dominance of commercial weaving, a handful of entrepreneurial male leaders took over as officers of the co-operative, pushing women into peripheral organizational positions.

In a very short time, the sexual division of labor evolved to afford female weavers a small part in the town's new economic profile. Only five percent of commercial weavers are women, despite their prominent role in the establishment of the textile co-operative. Quite simply, with all the other (non-paying) labor they have to do, women do not have the time to weave. Men replace themselves in the fields with day laborers paid from their weaving earnings. The demand for local fieldhands to tend the corn fields has risen with the popularity of weaving and become a secondary occupation replacing plantation labor. In fact, so many men weave there is a scarcity of fieldhands. Women cannot do the same in their domestic work, and this compromises their effectiveness as weavers. While men can start weaving upon rising and work all day, female domestic responsibilities seriously diminish the number of hours available for commercial textile production. Weaving contractors admit they would rather not give work to women because of their longer delivery time compared to men. Despite their traditional skill as weavers, women's labor is now less valuable than their husbands'.

Men have readily taken advantage of the opportunity to weave, as evidenced by the cash purchases of new tape decks, watches, roofs, and cement block houses. Several men have invested their earnings in motorboats, bars, *tiendas* (stores), and other businesses. As soon as they learned how to market belts and table linens, a dozen or so enterprising men began their own weaving organizations as *contratistas* (middlemen), a system paralleling the co-operative, but with one distinction. Rather than putting the standard 20 percent of each order back into the co-operative, the *contratistas* keep it for themselves. Every few months, someone else decides to try being a middleman by drumming up new business. Since looms can produce only so much, new weavers regularly enter the labor pool. Thus, privatization of the weaving business enlarged the small existing bourgeoisie by infusing it with male entrepreneurs. The men of San Antonio Palopó have embraced a new productive activity affording them a better living.

It is too soon to state unequivocally how development has disrupted male-female interactions in San Antonio. However, given the new relations of production accompanying weaving, we might gain some insight by looking to those who have profited most from the individualization of income, the entrepreneurial class. The incidence of *casitas* (parallel marriages) is highest among the town's wealthier men. While few men have the opportunity for more than casual affairs, men with money can take second wives, and they tend to flaunt their behavior. In a flagrant case of polygyny, one of the new *contratistas* built a house for his second wife and their children next to his first wife's house. The families involved have complained to the local authorities about these arrangements, making the affair a public scandal. In another case, one of the town's well-to-do middlemen brought his parallel family to San Antonio's saint's day fiesta, an action so outrageous that his first wife tried to kill him. Both these wives took action to stop their husbands' infidelities, but neither has been successful.

San Antonio women are at a considerable disadvantage in maintaining themselves as partners in the family productive system. Like other rural Maya, they shared their impoverishment with the men in their lives. Currently, a discrepancy in income and control of earnings deprives them of that comfort, however small, and the security of knowing that their husbands need them as much as they need their husbands. It is clear that development has been beneficial to men, creating a large new job category (weaving), and expanding another (day laborer). Although men still require female domestic service, the traditional complementarity of peasant agricultural production has been replaced by individualization of income and concentration of business in the hands of men. At the same time, women's productive contribution has been devalued and marginalized, exacerbating female economic vulnerability and creating worrisome implications for gender relations in the future.

## San Pedro Sacatepequez

San Pedro Sacatepequez is a busy Indian commercial center in San Marcos, located between the high altiplano and the coastal towns and hotland plantations. The town has a heterogeneous, stratified population made even more diverse by the large hinterland comprising seventeen hamlets (*aldeas*), a favorable location for trade. Since World War Two, expansion of commerce, cottage industry, transportation and education has placed San

Pedro and several other large, enterprising Indian towns in stark contrast to the poverty of most highland communities.

The pace of business is such that townsfolk are fully employed, with few families relying entirely upon *milpa* production for food. Evidence of decades of entrepreneurial vigor are found in the town's educated children, handsome new houses, and imported automobiles. Although consumerism is rampant among the growing middle-class, poor townspeople and rural *aldeanos* also have disposable income. Few rural Sampedranos need to work on coastal plantations to feed their families. Those in the four or five nearest *aldeas* are well-integrated into the commercial activity of the town whose middle-class values they now emulate.

The creation of a middle-class (15 percent of the urban population) in a mere forty years is an indication of the potential for material gain in San Pedro. Since the late 1940s, business opportunities have multiplied with better transportation and the demand for more consumer goods, and many commercial families have dramatically expanded their earning power. Nowadays, grandchildren of itinerant textile peddlers have comfortable lives and successful careers as doctors, lawyers, architects, teachers, and engineers. Education has become a valuable and accessible commodity as the desire for learning and diploma-related employment has grown. Oddly enough, the local passion for business often supersedes entering the positions that come with post-graduate training. There are several cases where new professionals postponed establishing a practice to return to their first love, the family store.

The good fortune of the middle-class is built upon the same strategy used by poorer Sampedranos, the family productive system. But middle-class families have been able to educate enough children to generate reliable salaries, thus providing capital for the commercial development of household-based businesses. Poorer families must continue to invest in labor-intensive enterprises and jobs. While the poor, too, are beginning to send their children to school, class differences handicap *aldeanos* as wage earners, making their material progress slower.

Women, more than men, exploit the available labor supply, depending upon the free labor of children working side-by-side with supervising mothers in what I have called the female family business (Ehlers 1982). Female members of the family cooperate in the home, store, or small workshop for the efficient running of both business and household. Domestic functions are undisturbed since daughters care for babies, cook meals, and run errands to free their older siblings and mothers for income production. The family productive system maximizes the potential for under-capitalized, labor-intensive work while socializing girls for the same occupations when they are mature.

Women must engage in several productive activities to survive, and it is the rare woman who has only one strategy for earning money. A teacher is an after-school knitter or shopkeeper or both. A weaver comes to the huge Thursday market to sell the week's *huipil* (a woven blouse or dress), but also stocks up on candies and breads for her little *aldea* store. When their live chicken market closes, three teenage girls help their mother make *piñatas* and paper floral decorations for graves. The woman who sells vegetables returns home at 7:00 P.M. to her knitting machine, and will bake several dozen breads for sale if she has time. The dedication to work is near-constant and Sunday mass provides the only respite most women have from productive activities.

To justify their workaholism, Sampedranas claim they live to work, but the opposite is equally true: they must work in order to live. The pace of commercial development in San Pedro is brisk enough and the new middle-class large enough, that it is an easy mistake to assume that the locals are doing well. They are better off than other highland communities, but in most cases their earnings are grossly insufficient. A growing population, competition, and unstable markets have kept profit margins for female cottage industry or trade only slightly above cost. Labor is never figured into the price of a handmade product since a woman's saleable work is considered part of her normal domestic responsibility. Accordingly, in ten day's time, a woman and her two daughters might produce a *huipil* in which they have invested $50 in thread, but for which they will garner only $60. Their profit of just over one dollar a day is standard.

Weaving and other female family businesses provide women with their own productive enterprises where they control family labor, manage money, and make creative decisions, but profits from female enterprises are so low that few can completely depend upon them to sustain the family. For the family to survive and flourish, men must do their part as well. The standard highland budgetary division of labor assumes men will contribute the household staples of corn and firewood, while their wives provide everything else through domestic manufacture or cash production. Until recently, women were able to fulfil their obligations by producing goods domestically. Today, women are buying more items because the demands of earning a living do not allow for the home manufacture of necessities like bread, soap, candles, or clothes. Budgets from nearby *aldeas* show that families require a cash minimum of $80 each month, far more than a woman can earn by herself.

An alliance with a male pays off for women in another way. Men father children and, most important, daughters. While boys are valuable for potential remittances from salaried jobs, girls are a necessary requirement for their mother's immediate security. In the poorest households, girls help with domestic chores or low-level cottage industry, and mothers benefit from the small income their teenage daughters provide as domestics. Artisan women use their daughters' labor through the female family business and keep up handicraft output. In both situations, women are keenly aware of the crucial productive and reproductive contributions of men.

Middle-class women are in a somewhat different situation, one complicated by the diversity of productive options among the socially mobile. Some middle-class women have jobs as teachers, but most who work are *comerciantes* (business operators). Rarely do they have their own businesses, however. Instead they function as the retail end of a commercial enterprise which their husbands own and manage. Few of these women control the money their stores take in, being little more than front office overseers. Other wives of this class do not work at all, in many cases because their husbands insist they remain at home as a visible sign of male affluence. In either situation, these women control little of their families' resources and are entirely reliant upon their husbands for money. Children in this case legitimate a woman's role as a mother, but require expensive outlays to outfit and educate, rather than being productive assistants. Nonetheless, children of the professional middle-class do contribute to household expenses and are often regarded as fiscal safety nets in the event that their mother is widowed or abandoned.

## Female Vulnerability and Development

Since World War II, men in San Pedro have been able to take advantage of their town's burgeoning commercial enterprises by establishing relatively lucrative commercial networks and artisanal occupations (Smith 1977). Men now control transportation, storefront retail businesses, and professions. Men have more tools for investment than women (among them better education, easier credit and, most important, exclusive control of the external market), and have done remarkably well in taking advantage of the bullish economy. Quite the opposite is true for their wives.

One by-product of modernization has been the undermining of women's traditional occupations in cottage industry and trade. For generations, woman-centered artisan shops satisfied indigenous consumer habits. Now, however, they are unable to compete with the cheaper, commercially manufactured modern products merchandized by local men, and their handiworks are no longer even minimally profitable. Identification with the national culture has also meant that handwoven textiles and handmade household goods are now considered old-fashioned. Without their customary markets, independent female family businesses are dying out. They have been replaced by employment or piece-work jobs which transfer control of production from the woman to a male patron or supervisor. Overall, while most women in San Pedro have work if they want it, the relations of production are changing. Analysis of production data I collected in town and three *aldeas* shows the following:

1. Women's work is segregated into a handful of occupations, while male jobs are spread across a much wider spectrum.
2. Women's occupations were overwhelmingly labor-intensive and based on family production. Men do take advantage of their sons' labor to some extent, but they generally work in more solitary jobs.
3. Nearly half the women surveyed currently worked only in non-paying household duties, compared to a small fraction of men primarily occupied with *milpa* production.
4. Female family business made an average of one dollar a day while solitary male workers made nearly three times as much for about the same hours worked per week.

In sum, women's work is narrowly confined to traditional production systems which are steadily declining as a viable part of the economy. Lacking the skills or capital to begin new businesses, many traditional producers have returned to being housewives, being able to do this because their husbands are making more money. As women's traditional enterprises fade, men's productive opportunities have expanded, particularly in solitary occupations and businesses. Education has afforded them more jobs and access to credit for start-up companies. The result of this transition in the sexual division of labor has been an increase in female economic vulnerability and, correspondingly, a greater dependence upon male wage earners for family survival.

The repercussions of decades of modernization are sizeable, and one clear problem for women is that diminishing economic responsibility translates directly into a loss in female status. Women who no longer manage a household productive system forfeit fiscal independence, supervision of child labor, business decision-making, and personal mobility. Instead they move toward a peripheral productive role in the family, where they are minor contributors to the household budget, dependent upon husbands' earnings, and thus more vulnerable to male domination.

## Mating Patterns

Adult Sampedranas regard marriage and the bearing of children as the only way to fully legitimize their status as women. Emphasis on the domestic role is so pervasive that middle-aged *senoritas* are extremely rare. Women are invariably newly married, married with children, single but with children, abandoned with children, or widowed. Women understand that at some stage in their relationships with men they will become hapless victims of their *mal caracter* (bad character). Even the early stages of married life are seldom enjoyable for women. Sampedranas tend to marry or, more commonly, move in with a man before they know much about sexuality or the reproductive system. In most cases, girls marry when their parents discover they have been seduced and/or impregnated, and few of these *unido* marriages are legally binding. Thus women are mothers before they are out of their teens, often forced into marriages with boys they hardly know or care for. Patrilocal residence extracts them from their natal families and the female family business into which they were socialized. They come under the direction of an often hostile mother-in-law, who may oblige the new wife to work for her for no wages. Young wives begin their marriages lacking power, and remain that way until their daughters are old enough to provide a modicum of economic security.

These mating patterns and the alternatives to *la mala vida* have been disparately affected by developments in San Pedro. Lacking the resources for personal survival, poor unskilled women have little choice but to stay with abusive husbands. Artisans have traditional skills, but their declining market share is quickly rendering them obsolete as independent producers. They are becoming instead a cottage proletariat, dependent upon work orders from their husbands and other men, or they are unemployed. As the productive mobility and individualized incomes of their spouses rises, these women experience more seriously problematic relationships. What they have that unskilled women lack is a family productive system into which they were socialized as children. For the time being, abused artisans can still return to their natal homes and find a certain amount of economic security, however fragile.

Middle-class male infidelity is likely to increase with the advent of an affluent lifestyle and the status that accompanies it. Middle-class women are often powerless to rein in a wayward spouse since their welfare is entirely based upon a male breadwinner. However, middle-class women have more latitude than poor women when they are unmarried. Educated girls have begun to spurn irresponsible suitors, even if the young woman has become pregnant. With schooling, a job, and a family business for support, these young women are not obligated to marry. They can support themselves and their children without men, and can thus afford to be more selective in choosing a husband.

From late childhood, Sampedranas worry about being abandoned, mostly because of the money difficulties involved. They are taught to prepare themselves so that when and if their husbands leave them, they will be able to feed their children. Some women are able to do this better than others, but modernization has made single motherhood more troublesome for many Sampedranas who are forfeiting their traditional businesses and the personal status it provides. Moreover, in today's economy women are making less money and men more, further skewing the relations of production. Sampedranas are more economically vulnerable than ever, with less leverage to control male behavior, and fewer resources to retreat to if abandoned. Survival demands that women passively accept male irresponsibility or suffer the consequences.

## Conclusions

Although *marianismo* has been widely accepted as an ideological explanation for why Latin American women endure abuse, this concept does not address the economic basis for gender relations. Instead, *marianismo* provides a rationale for female subordination and idealizes the harsh reality of women's lives. Women tolerate abusive husbands and continue in bad marriages because they have no alternatives. Most highland Guatemalan women rely upon male economic support and to a lesser extent their children, which men provide. The arrangement between men and women is simple. When men abandon the home, women rarely miss them as much as the money or the corn they supply. Deserted women repeatedly enter into temporary or fragile alliances with married men for the same reasons they originally wed: the money and the children that will result.

The basis for this dependence on men lies in the unprofitable and tangential connection women have to production. In two very different highland Guatemalan communities there exists a trend toward female economic degradation associated with accelerated male integration into entrepreneurial activities, cash income, and the external labor market. While this tendency has just begun in San Antonio, if men continue to monopolize income production, female subordination will eventually come to resemble that of San Pedro, where parallel marriages and abandonment are common.

# 22

# Poetics and Politics in the Ecuadorean Andes

## Women's Narratives of Death and Devil Possession[7]

*Mary M. Crain*

In 1983, in the community of Quimsa, Ecuador, a period of political mobilization involved peasants and local commercial farmers in a struggle over land and employment issues. For some three decades, large farmers had been replacing labor-intensive estate production with capital-intensive mechanized agriculture. The resulting social and economic changes eventually led to political unrest. Although women were active in community-level decision making during this period of peasant political mobilization, it was primarily male peasants who assumed positions of leadership and controlled the public debates.

During this period, a male peasant who worked as a foreman on a neighboring commercial farm died suddenly and mysteriously. Peasant women murmured that his death had been caused by devil possession. Subsequently, other stories emerged about devil possession linking male employees to the capitalist farm economy. This article examines the political implications of these narratives about devil possession, as articulated by peasant women, and their use as an idiom for talking about the women's opposition to material change.

The women's narratives constitute a form of politics, provided we expand our understanding of "the political" to include various modes of resistance occurring in informal domestic domains. Such

Adapted from *American Ethnologist* 18:1, February 1991, by permission of the American Anthropological Association. Not for sale or further reproduction.

domains are often excluded from Western definitions of "the political," which wed it to the formal, public, and visible aspects of social life frequently associated with the hierarchical, institutionalized structures of the state. By assigning all importance to formal political structures, such definitions ignore the more covert dimensions of resistance. This article proceeds by questioning both the hierarchy implicit in the "formal politics" versus "informal politics" distinction and the idea that these entities constitute two closed and separate spheres. This analysis traces the lines of influence connecting private forms of power and resistance to politics exercised in more public arenas. It also explores how the actual practices of individual men and women may at times cross the ostensible boundaries between these two spheres.

## Unsettling Deaths

I was attending my first funeral in Quimsa. A hacienda worker named Lucho Sandoval, with whom I had conversed only three days earlier, had died suddenly at a young age. His was a mysterious death. His body had been found early Saturday morning not too far from my home—at the bottom of a large ravine some thirty meters in depth. The ravine was located on a hillside called Madre de Dios, about half a kilometer from Lucho's home. Lucho had last been seen by two of his *compadres* (male co-parents) in the afternoon around dusk, and they had thought he was heading toward Madre de Dios.

I sat at the wake and watched while several *comadres* (female co-parents) washed his slender body with a damp cloth and dressed it in a long white robe. He was then gently lowered into an open casket. The clothing Lucho had worn on the day of his death was placed inside the casket along with a spoon, a cup, and a bowl, provisions for his sustenance in the afterlife. By early evening, neighbors, friends, and more distant relatives had arrived, bringing food as well as flowers, candles, and wooden images of saints that were placed along both sides of his casket.

A somber atmosphere reigned as peasants huddled together on wooden benches raised only slightly above the earthen floor. Papa Ramon, a lay prayer-reader, began to recite the prayers for the dead and then led the community in singing several Catholic hymns. The singing was interspersed with long wails of lament in Quichua uttered by Lucho's wife, Barbara, and other female relatives, all of whom wept openly. One of Lucho's youngest sons, Carlos, darted in and out through the crowd in order to get closer to his father's casket. While others were busy singing he reached up and gently stroked his father's face.

The prayers and all the solemnity they entailed were broken by the smells of home-cooked foods, roasted guinea pigs and steamed potatoes. Enormous helpings of these dishes were served, and bottles of *aguardiente* (a strong liquor) were freely passed around the room. As the night wore on, many wept, and the drinking was heavy. Those peasants who grew tired and intoxicated spread their ponchos in a haphazard fashion on the earthen floor, and so a mass of men, women, and children drifted into a groggy sleep. At some point after midnight, those who were still awake took part in a gay form of charades. Several individuals rose to the floor and performed pantomimes, pretending to be various animals such as tapirs, horses, roosters, and bulls. Lucho's funeral, in effect, became a space in which to play, to turn away from grief and embrace life.

My life and Lucho's had already become intertwined in several ways. His wife and I had been friends for over a year. He also happened to be the uncle of Susana, my capricious fourteen-year-old kitchen helper and constant companion. I had met Lucho only three days prior to his death. This encounter made the news of his death particularly unsettling to me, as someone who had just entered my social world had suddenly been wrenched from it. Lucho and I had been introduced at a neighborhood store. We had shared a beer while he talked to me about his job as the foreman at the Hacienda La Miranda's sawmill complex. He oversaw a team of nine men who worked felling the pine and eucalyptus trees of the private forest.

Three days after this conversation, Susana had come running to my home to tell me about her uncle's death. She and I had walked together to the deep ravine and watched while several men hauled out Lucho's limp body. Don Tatamuez, the local sheriff, had come from the county seat to confirm the death and examine the body. After half an hour of examination, he turned to the crowd and reported that Lucho might well have slipped into the ravine accidentally, According to Tatamuez, Lucho had apparently suffered a concussion as a result of receiving a sharp blow to the left side of his head. It seemed possible that when Lucho fell, his head had struck against some rocks protruding from one side of the ravine. Following this pronouncement several men, including the sheriff, hoisted Lucho's body onto their shoulders and accompanied his family members back home.

At the wake, I was surrounded by neighbors and friends. Many members of the peasant community had gathered together to mourn Lucho's passing. His death seemed particularly tragic. Lucho was only 36 years old; he was the father of five children, and his wife Barbara was pregnant with another child. In addition, certain aspects of his death made no sense. In the days that followed this unhappy event, there was a great deal of uneasiness whenever his name was mentioned. Most people were puzzled as to the actual cause of his untimely death.

During the wake, I reflected on some of the rumors that had been circulating in the community. How could one account for this mysterious death? Based on the way in which his body had landed in the ravine, one or two individuals agreed with the sheriff's speculation that he might have slipped and fallen from one of the mud footpaths. Many argued that this would have been even more likely had he also been drinking. But, according to the coroner's report issued several days after discovery of the body, there were no indications of intoxication. Others said that someone might have pushed Lucho into the ravine after dark on Friday.

Susana told me her mother believed that Lucho's death might have been the result of sorcery due to *envidia* (envy). When I asked her to explain this, she said that one had to consider Lucho's relatively young age, his high position in the hacienda work hierarchy, and the fact that he had many material possessions. I had visited their home on several occasions and never been particularly struck by a large number of consumer goods, but Susana argued that there were others in Quimsa, particularly co-workers, who were jealous of his apparent success. "Don't you see?" she asked. "His house was painted, he had a refrigerator, an electric blender, and a cassette player, and he also had pigs." According to Susana, the envious person might have pushed Lucho into the ravine or, more likely, have sought the aid of a shaman to cast a spell on him. Susana contended that the envious person bewitching Lucho would have made a *muñeca* de trapos (a doll fashioned of old rags) and brought this, along with a plate of special foods, to a shaman. The *muñeca* represents the person being bewitched and, after a spell has been cast, it is placed in the pathway of the enemy. Bewitched food (typically consisting of eggs, bread, and roasted guinea pig) is marked by a shaman's spell and is always left, anonymously, close to a daily route generally followed by the enemy. In Quimsa, ravines, the pastures of the nearby commercial farm, and the exterior of peasant homes are the three most popular sites for these hexed objects.

Susana and other peasants suggested that additional factors might have heightened Lucho's vulnerability to bewitchment of this sort. Lucho had, after all, evidently been wandering alone at night, near the principal ravine of Madre de Dios. The combination of these three factors—the ravine, solitude, and nighttime—presaged danger. According to local belief, it is dangerous to walk or remain for an extended period of time near certain sites such as ravines, irrigation canals, waterfalls, lakes, high mountain plains, and places where rainbows appear, for such places may be inhabited by evil spirits. Potentially harmful encounters with the spirit world occur most frequently at night and when individuals are alone. Those who are exposed to any combination of these circumstances run the risk of incurring folk diseases such as *mal aire* (evil wind) and *susto* (fright), which can be diagnosed and cured only by *curanderas*, or shamans, and not by practitioners of Western medicine.

Shortly after Lucho's death I visited my friend Rosa. Knowing that she was *de confianza con* his widow Barbara (on closest terms with Barbara), I asked Rosa what she had heard. She looked at me, lowered her voice, and said, "Keep this a secret. Have you ever heard of a pact with the devil? Or the sacrifice of a person for a thing?" I nodded. Rosa said that was what Barbara and some of her closest female relatives were now saying had caused Lucho's death. I asked her to explain and she exclaimed: "Don't you see? Those machines are big, dangerous, and powerful."

At that point we headed off to visit Barbara, whom we found in tears. We stayed for several hours, offering companionship, and we talked about the difficulties of supporting the family without Lucho. At one point, Rosa looked knowingly at Barbara and told her she had mentioned devil possession to me. Barbara then raised her voice in anger, arguing that all their troubles had started with that "damned machine." I asked naively, "What machine?" and she answered, "The sawmill, of course." Barbara believed the sawmill machinery had been momentarily possessed by the spirit of the devil and, using the machine as its medium, the devil had begun to exert a controlling force over Lucho. While Barbara didn't entirely dismiss the sheriff's speculation that her husband might have slipped into the ravine accidentally, she paid little heed to this idea. She felt her husband's death was rooted in a much deeper metaphysical cause that could only be understood by examining the strange sequence of events that had transpired during the last year of his life. Here is Barbara's story:

> At the time that Lucho was made head of the sawmill workgang, he was also assigned a position as caretaker of the hacienda's private forest reserve. In order to keep an eye on the important machinery at the sawmill and to make sure that no one pilfered from the *patrones'* forest, Lucho built this home for our family on hacienda land, close to the sawmill. Lucho had all these responsibilities: he was always agitated, always watching, always keeping his guard, as he was concerned that someone might either steal or damage the sawmill machine or take the really important wood, the recently felled timber from the forest reserve, at night. He also had his duties as the overseer of the workgang, with nine men under his supervision who were occasionally jealous of his position and his demands. And then our house, which Lucho built here, near the forest, was too isolated from others, from our neighbors and our families.

According to Barbara, Lucho had started having crazy dreams a year or so before his death. She would awaken in the middle of the night and hear him talking to someone. He would always say the same thing: "Are you looking for me? Don't bother me." Then he would lie back down and drift back to sleep. The voices would come again later in the night, only this time Lucho would frequently respond: "I'm coming!" At this point he would rise from bed, go outdoors to the sawmill machine, and turn it on and off to hear the sound of the motor running, to assure himself that it was operating satisfactorily. Barbara said there were many nights when her poor husband would start working and then fall asleep out by the machine. Worried, she would go outside and try to bring him back indoors. On several occasions, she and the children had ended up sleeping by the machine alongside Lucho. From time to time neighbors would tell her they had heard the hum of the machine being turned on and off during the night and had wondered what was going on.

Barbara said that Lucho had become obsessed with his work. She whispered that he had been increasingly dominated by the spirit of the devil that had entered the sawmill machinery. Barbara had frequently insisted that they move away from both the machine and the forest, but Lucho had always shrugged her off. Barbara regarded Lucho's nocturnal "conversations," which had continued for over a year, as evidence of a struggle between him and the dark forces.

It had been the *devil* that had finally lured Lucho into the ravine that night and taken his life.

Following this account, I asked Barbara and Rosa who in the community knew about Lucho's strange dreams? Primarily her family, Barbara responded, and Rosa mentioned that she had said something about them to her mother. I then asked if the devil possession version of Lucho's death had been suggested to the local *patrones*, the owners of the Hacienda La Miranda. I had seen the hacienda owners arrive at Barbara's house on that Saturday morning after news of Lucho's death had spread through the community. Rosa looked at me and said, "Oh no! No mention of this was made to them!" And even if the rumor were eventually to reach them, she added, they certainly wouldn't take it seriously. The *patrones* had been told "another version," the version proposed by the sheriff. Though it was clear the two women blamed the commercial farmers for Lucho's death, they were not airing this conviction publicly.

Finally, I asked whether cases of devil possession leading to death had occurred in Quimsa before. They both said yes and began to tell me two stories depicting similar sequences of events. The first of these concerned a 32-year-old man, Ricardo Meno, who had worked as an irrigation canal cleaner for the Hacienda La Miranda. Feeling faint one afternoon, he had lain down at home before going back to work in the pastures of La Cocha (a part of the Hacienda). When he closed his eyes he dreamed that he saw the foreman of La Cocha supervising the construction of two new reservoirs that the owners of the Hacienda La Miranda were having built there: a large bulldozer was scooping up the earth, and the foreman was mounted on a horse of monstrous proportions, with two big black dogs standing watch by his side.[8] Then, just as the reservoirs were filling up with water, the foreman turned into the devil and called out to Ricardo, telling him to come on down to the Cocha area and start working at once. The devil fought to possess him. After this, Ricardo woke from his dream and recounted it to his wife. He rose with the intention of returning to work, but he was weak and his wife put him back in bed. Later that night he died.

The other narrative centered on a death that had occurred shortly after the construction of a new road and bridge leading to the forest reserve of the Hacienda La Miranda. According to Rosa, the *patrones* had decided that a good road had to be built across peasant territory so that big trucks could enter this area to get lumber out of the forest more readily. The master-carpenter of the hacienda,

Jorge Recalde, was responsible for the heavy machinery being used and for the construction team, which included several day laborers. Rosa was cooking the noon meals for these men. She recalled that during the second afternoon one of the workers, Alberto Escola, came to her looking pale and preoccupied. The devil, he said, had just appeared to him in a daydream and told him not to move any more earth or stones. Alberto was frightened and stopped his shoveling. He also asked the other men to quit working and told the master-carpenter to get off the bulldozing machine because something bad was going to happen. Alberto kept saying that the devil insisted that the bridge not be finished. His talk about the devil clearly upset the other men, and everybody looked worried. But the master-carpenter told the others to continue working. When the bridge was finally finished late that afternoon Alberto would not move from the site, and when it grew dark he lay down beside the bridge. Much later that night his wife came and tried to drag him away. After several attempts she was finally able to get him home.

Several months later a tractor driver, Santiago Chaleco (a local peasant), was going along this new road on his way to plow one of the hacienda's wheat fields. After he crossed the bridge, his tractor slipped down the edge of the muddy embankment, killing him instantly. A peasant woman who had been nearby said that the devil had taken control of the driver and his machine. It was because of the devil's possession that Santiago had been unable to jump off the machine and save himself. Rosa and Barbara said that Alberto's devil visitation had portended disaster—it had signaled Santiago's impending death. Both women stated that the bridge and road should never have been completed. They also expressed a great deal of uneasiness about Alberto's future but noted that so far nothing had happened to him.

In each of these narratives, men figured as the devil's victims. Rosa and Barbara remarked that they fully expected further deaths from devil possession. They argued that no one should continue to work at the sawmill, and Barbara announced that she and her children were going to leave the house by the forest.

As the preceding discussion suggests, subaltern explanations are not necessarily all of a piece. Instead, many voices clamor for attention. The multiple versions of Lucho's death reflect the complexity of the local social reality. One version proposes that Lucho's death was an accident, another concludes that it was caused by envy and witchcraft, and yet another posits devil possession. In addition, a variety of factors such as inauspiciousness of place, time of day, and state of being are invoked. To complicate matters even further, many of these explanations are not mutually exclusive. However, each of them was aired in a particular context and was directed to a particular audience. The "envy" version, for example, points to inequalities within the peasant community and emphasizes Lucho's identification with the interests of the landed elite. The heterogeneity of the various versions reflects not only the general factors of gender and class but also the specific personal experiences, attitudes, and idiosyncrasies of the individual storytellers.

In the analysis that follows I will focus on women's stories of devil possession both as explanations of Lucho's death and as a metaphor for the material changes that have transformed everyday life in Quimsa during the past three decades. In this way, we can shed light on the cultural meanings female peasants attribute to wage work. Ideas about the devil, circulated by women, inform Quimseño notions of group identity and construct boundaries between peasant self and dominant other. In the contemporary setting the devil serves as a symbol for foreign technology, Western styles of development, and commercial farming.

## Peasant Cosmology, the Labor Process, and Western Technology

In the traditional cosmology of Quimsa, the devil manifested itself in many different forms. Local peasants held that the spirit of the devil could temporarily enter both animate and inanimate objects, and a person who encountered these objects could become ill or susceptible to the devil's control. For example, several informants explained that the devil could momentarily enter and leave waterfalls and irrigation canals. They also explained that the devil could assume the form of an animal—a bull, a lizard, a black dog— or of a person, known or unknown, such as an abandoned infant crying in the road. Peasants today believe that the devil can penetrate newly introduced Western commodities. Thus, individual deaths that are related in some way to the use of heavy machinery, to construction, or to wage work are described as the devil's handiwork.

For the Quimseño peasantry, large machinery and heavy equipment (tractors, bulldozers, harvesters, sawmills) are symbols of capitalist farming. These peasants had rarely encountered any type of heavy machinery before the 1940s, when equipment was first imported by multi-national firms such as International Harvester and John Deere. Over the next three decades farm operations were progressively mechanized. Since the machines represent a large capital investment, one hacienda owner explained, estate owners usually brought in skilled employees from outside the region to operate them. This pattern has continued into the present. As a result, many local peasants remain somewhat bewildered by such machinery and frequently attribute its inner workings to the devil.

Gender differences are also significant with respect to machinery. While male peasants have in the course of their everyday work gained a nominal familiarity with heavy equipment, female peasants know almost nothing about the technology used on the estates and by development teams. Moreover, heavy machinery is rarely used in peasant forms of production. In contrast to neighboring parishes, where large peasant cooperative farms were formed after the 1960s agrarian reform, in Quimsa the majority of peasants have title to land only in the form of smallholding units. Most of these plots are either too small or on too steep an incline to allow use of heavy machinery. In addition, many peasants lack the money to rent such machinery.

Peasants associate the new machinery with the devil and often regard these products of Western technology as an unnecessary evil. Mechanization has undermined the need for peasants' labor on many large estates and has dealt a deadly blow to their traditional means of livelihood. Second, as peasants lose their employment opportunities, they fear the loss of other perquisites, such as the right to rent pasture space and to draw upon the *patron*'s name and fame as a form of symbolic capital—perquisites which are, in one way or another, tied to local wage work. Finally, changes in the material conditions of life have had profound effects on the structure of household relations, and have forced individual peasants, particularly men, to migrate in search of work.

In the early 1970s, disgruntled workers and unemployed peasant youths invaded the neighboring Hacienda El Cisne, where they reportedly vandalized or stole various items of machinery. Local commercial farmers are quite aware that mechanization has become a volatile political issue, and they fear the possibility of collective action on the part of a peasant labor force displaced by further mechanization. This fear is surely one of the factors informing their recent decision not to introduce imported milking machines, as these would eliminate a number of jobs presently held by peasant milkmaids. (Milking is one of the areas in which the female labor force is concentrated.) To date there is only one commercial farm in the parish, a rather small one, that has installed milking machines.

While both male and female peasants in Quimsa often reject mechanization, at the level of the household it is women who determine which new products of Western technology will be accepted and which rejected. Constituting units of production and consumption, households are the most important economic institutions in Quimseño peasant society, and today it is primarily women who are responsible for managing the household economy and for cultivating each household's subsistence plot.

Many peasant women feel the seductive appeal of new commodities that claim to alleviate domestic drudgery, but they also profess a certain ambivalence about purchased products. For example, while visiting me one day, Rosa spotted a package of instant Maggi soup on my shelf and remarked that such a product was "dangerous." Initially I thought she meant that packaged soups might be harmful to one's health since they contain chemical preservatives. However, I discovered later that she feared these products because she felt she might grow to depend on them. The loss of household autonomy that results from new practices of consumption was particularly apparent during the spring of 1983, when inflationary pressures and hoarding drove the prices of many store-bought goods higher. At this point many peasant women restricted their household expenditures and, where possible, relied on their subsistence production. Such practices constitute an everyday form of resistance, designed to limit the intrusions of the market economy.

## Gender, Politics, and Heretical Discourse

In stories told by female peasants, accusations both of envy and of devil possession link male workers with the capitalist farm economy. Yet these beliefs are not shared across cultural and class boundaries. Instead, most commercial farmers whom I interviewed tended to dismiss them as pure nonsense and peasant superstition. Two large landowners even professed that they had helped banish witchcraft and occult practices from the parish. While large farmers have worked in conjunction with other dominant institutions (such as the Ministry of Health and the Catholic Church) to eradicate native traditions of healing and witchcraft, their actual social practices may conflict with their professed views. Several female peasants told me that they had healed particular landlords when Western medicine had not proven effective.

Given a social climate that generally tries to repress such occult beliefs, Quimseño talk about devil possession forms part of a suppressed, underground discourse.[9] During my fieldwork, I never once heard devil possession discussed in public. Instead, it was discussed informally, in private conversations among women. Communal laundering, embroidering circles, and healing sessions, in particular, drew the women together and served as important channels of communication for the entire community. In such settings women frequently criticized the conditions of wage work on nearby commercial farms.

This exchange of information and opinion is similar to that observed by Harding in northern Spain. Analyzing women's lack of access to institutional power, Harding argues that women's tongues are their most important weapon and that "in gossiping, women are behaving politically because they are tampering with power. . . . Gossip is potentially a challenge to the male hierarchy" (1975:302-303). Talk about the devil in Quimseña women's informal groups was always marked by a change in intonation and prefaced by such comments as "let's keep this between you and me." The decentralized and scattered nature of such groups grants them a veil of secrecy, making it difficult for dominant groups to monitor them.

Although I initially wondered why Barbara and Rosa had decided not to confront Lucho's boss with their version of Lucho's death, I eventually came to see their behavior as a calculated act. It calls to mind James Scott's (1985) remarks on the "onstage" and "offstage" behavior of Malaysian peasants in a highly unequal agrarian class structure. Scott finds that the peasants often defer to members of the elite and take care not to speak disparagingly of their social superiors in public, thus avoiding reprisals. However, when they are in situations of relative privacy and among equals, in an "offstage context," they freely engage in gossip and character assassinations of the rich.

In Quimsa, women chose to represent themselves to "the outside" with a story quite different from the version they circulated in the community. Among themselves they constructed a definition of what constituted "the real" that was in conflict with dominant definitions of the social world, but they protected themselves and kept on good terms with the landed elite by arguing in public that Lucho's death had been an accident. In the Quimseño case, such a strategy of public conformity worked surprisingly well. About a week after the death, Rosa informed me that the *patron* had paid a visit to Barbara and told her that he would try to get life insurance benefits for her family by claiming that Lucho's death had been a work-related "accident."

In studies of resistance movements in Third World societies where state or landlord coercion has worked to stifle overt political expression, Scott (1985) and Comaroff (1985) have noted that the defiance of subaltern groups often takes a disguised or coded form that outsiders may not immediately recognize as a form of protest. The significance of talk about the devil in Quimsa, the coded form of resistance considered in this article, is further compounded by the gender inflections that mark this discourse. Both cultural and historical factors help to explain why it is women who have become the purveyors of this clandestine discourse. As Harding has argued, "The words of women and men follow the lines of their work" (1975:284). In Quimsa, women's topics of conversation are often quite different from men's. While men discuss agricultural matters, political issues, and jobs available outside the community, they rarely speak of family matters. In contrast, women's "work" and therefore their conversation centers on family life and associational ties. And it is generally women who preserve family genealogies and care for the dead. As we saw in Lucho's case, female peasants utter the ritual laments and carefully lay out the bodies of the dead. Given this preoccupation with the family, it seems logical that women would be the tellers of tales of devil possession, tales that keep the memories of their dead relatives alive.

Moreover, women's speech has traditionally been devalued in public settings, where gender hierarchies come into play and where men (male peasants as well as male members of the dominant class) dominate discussion. Barred from full participation in formal politics and often reduced to silence in public settings, women have fashioned a political language that draws on the devil idiom. Although the workplace is the site of struggle, the protest against it is being launched from the domestic sphere.

Discourses of development in Quimsa, articulated by local commercial farmers as well as by state institutions, marginalize women's participation in the modernization process. Promoting the acquisition of imported farm machinery, government loans, and new technical skills, these discourses are primarily addressed to male peasants, who constitute the "proper subjects" of development. Most development agents who visited Quimsa during 1982-84 promoted community work projects that enlisted the labor of young men. Development officials did not—and often still do not—ask women to identify with their programs and step into the modern world in the same manner as men.

In several of the community meetings I attended, members of development teams and certain local men made derogatory remarks about women, suggesting that women came to the meetings only to gossip among themselves, knit, or nurse their babies. Women were present at the meetings, but they voiced their opinions less frequently than men. One limitation on women's public speech is that it has become increasingly important to know oral and written Spanish to communicate with the state agencies that administer the majority of development funds, and men are more likely than women to be able to speak and write Spanish.

But I would also argue that, in certain instances, women's silence or refusal to speak in the presence of outsiders is a positive act of resistance. Peasant women in Quimsa see male peasants as more ready than they to collaborate with "the outside," often without fully considering the implications of such collaboration. The following case illustrates my point. In April 1983 several women accused the acting vice-president of Quimsa, a man named Caesar Pilas, of revealing community secrets and of jeopardizing the political interests of the majority of Quimseños. This man had taped the minutes of a community meeting in which Quimseños discussed the feasibility of taking over the Hacienda La Miranda. This meeting had been held at night, with outsiders and persons of superior social status excluded. The following Saturday, three women found Caesar drunk in a corner of the community football field, his cassette-player blaring out the meeting's heated discussion. These women were horrified to see that the administrator of the hacienda was within hearing range. Later, Caesar was overheard alluding to the meeting in a conversation with one of the hacienda's foremen. Immediately, attacks on his behavior began to circulate in women's gossip networks. He was socially ostracized, accused of being careless and of serving as a spy for the *patron*, and eventually denounced publicly—by women—in community meetings. Caesar was forced to resign from his position as vice-president of the community, largely as a result of politics and power struggles originating in women's domestic domains.

Women's silence in the presence of outsiders does not always imply passivity but may instead be a deliberate strategy. Many times I saw women feign ignorance when questioned by external authorities making brief visits to the community. In several cases I knew that a particular woman was knowledgeable about the topic of inquiry, but heard her respond, "I don't know about these things, *senor*. You will have to ask my husband." Usually the husband was conveniently away at the time.

Women's symbolic power in the community has traditionally resided in their positions as healers and witches,[10] and more recently they have begun directing this power toward the political arena, albeit in a coded form. Although devil possession per se was never openly discussed in the formal political meetings I attended, both men and women used the devii idiom to refer to the local *patron*, the owner of the nearby Hacienda La Miranda. Female peasants often avoided pronouncing the *patron*'s name in public and referred to him simply as a *cuco*, or devil-like figure. Several of the most vocal participants during the political mobilization of 1983 were women who were respected healers, midwives, and witches. In one political meeting, a senior woman and noted curer compared the coming of the large-scale machinery purchased by the commercial farmers to the arrival of the *mata-doctores* (killer doctors) of the Western medical tradition. She emphasized that *her* only doctor was the nettle, a common medicinal plant, which she could use perfectly well by herself or with the aid of another *curandera*. Women who occupy positions as witches and healers have been regarded as "threatening" and as "troublemakers" by development teams and contemporary commercial farmers. Campaigns to wipe out folk practitioners by replacing them with various forms of Western medicine have a lengthy history in the parish. Positioned at the margins of the structures of global capitalism, these women are in a privileged position to launch a critique of the modernization process.

## Gender Relations and Material Change

The traditional tenancy system, which prevailed on the estates through the early 1960s, was based on the labor power of the entire peasant family. Women worked alongside men in agriculture, and they predominated in milking and domestic service. On the large farms today, women are generally excluded from agricultural labor, largely the result of two related trends. First, the shift to commercial dairying has led to a reduction in agricultural jobs. Second, the reduced agricultural sector has been mechanized and estate owners have hired only men in the remaining positions.

Capitalist relations of production ideologically constitute female laborers as "helpmates" and part-time workers who are subordinate to men. Women's labor is accorded less value than men's and so women receive less pay for their work. Moreover, the majority of female laborers do not receive any fringe benefits such as medical insurance or social security pensions. Holding 85 percent of the positions at the Hacienda La Miranda, male workers are more fully integrated into the commercial farm economy than are women. Furthermore, only men occupy those positions of authority, such as overseer, that are particularly important in the reproduction of the hierarchical class structure.

Work defines what a man is, and today it is primarily "wage work" that is a crucial element in the construction of masculine identity. Although Quimseña women seem to work all the time, it is men's work that is socially defined as "real work" and as crucial to family survival. A woman's identity is defined primarily in terms of her relations to others, to kin and community, and her work is perceived to be a derivative of these relations. The greater valorization of the male worker, attested to by his ability to obtain high positions in the work hierarchy and to earn fringe benefits denied to the female worker, promotes a male identification with the commercial farm enterprise that many women lack. Estate owners as well as peasant overseers tend to view female workers with a degree of suspicion and skepticism. The commercial farmers whom I interviewed complained that they had greater problems with their female labor force. I was told that the milkmaids in particular were noted for their lack of work-discipline, tardiness, and tendency to "talk back" on the job.

During the past ten years women's dependence on wage earnings from the local dairy farms has declined while men's has stayed relatively constant. This change is due in part to the commercialization of women's artisanal production. While women have traditionally embroidered clothing and other items for use in the home, they are now producing embroidered goods for sale in extralocal markets as well. Many women combine artisanal production with part-time wage work on commercial farms, but they are often able to earn more cash by selling their embroidered goods than by dairying or domestic work. Indeed, the income they generate from artisanal production sometimes surpasses that of male peasants who work as common day laborers. Artisanal production allows these women a degree of flexibility and control over the pace of their work, and because such production is based in the home, it is compatible with child care and the completion of women's other domestic chores.

As the lowest paid and the first to be reassigned to new positions, many women accord their part-time wage work a low priority. I often heard remarks such as "If I can make twice as much by embroidering a tablecloth, why should I worry about showing up for work at milking time?" Milking demands punctuality, and male overseers are often frustrated when upstart milkmaids fail to appear at the appropriate hour. While the women's stories examined here associated the figure of the devil with commercial farming, on the commercial farms women themselves are often accused of being the devil's accomplices. The overseer of the La Cocha milk station charged peasant milkmaids with bewitching him as well as the livestock of the Hacienda la Miranda. Arriving one morning at the milk station, he found voodoo dolls in the cows' feed troughs and immediately held the milkmaids suspect. Not wanting to touch these items himself, he ordered the women to get rid of them at once. One milkmaid who had been privy to all this told me: "We laughed, and while the overseer was busy inspecting several newborn calves we took the voodoo dolls and cast them into the Calina (a nearby lake)." It is believed that magical spells cast on items thrown into this lake cannot be cancelled, for the lake is reputed to have no bottom and, therefore, no end. Such practices undermine the foreman's ability to maintain order in the workplace, and they have a disruptive effect on dairy production in general. One foreman, furious with the chaos that rumors of bewitchment had created in the workplace, was reported to have said that he would prefer that no women work in dairying.

The new economic possibilities provided by the sale of their artisanal products have afforded women a semiautonomous space within which to criticize commercial dairy production. Women's ability to secure a measure of independence from the work regimen of the commercial farm contrasts sharply with the male peasants' increasing subjugation to wage work. In the narratives presented here, it is women who attempt to pull men away from wage work and to protect them from the dangers it poses. The peasant "imaginary" of daydreams and nightmares, repeatedly evoked in these stories, is haunted by unsettling images of the devil figure who dominates wage work. Women's opposition to the new cultural values, patterns of work-discipline, and standards of consumption consonant with the new mode of production are confirmed by these stories and by the supporting evidence of several examples. In the first story, women's opposition to both the lengthening of the workday and the accelerated rate of wage work is registered in Lucho's constant preoccupation with his work. In this text, Lucho's body and spirit became, in essence, mere appendages of the sawmill machine. In the third narrative, women's objections to new standards of work-discipline and to the form male authority takes in the workplace are evinced when the protagonist, Alberto Escola, stops working at the construction site and encourages fellow laborers to do the same. He refuses to be the labor power that capital requires. Finally, women's everyday acts of resistance, exemplified by their rejection of Maggi's soup and other store-bought products, demonstrate their ability to hold off new patterns of consumption.

Each telling of these stories of devil possession becomes a political act in which women project their concerns about the preservation of life and the destiny of their community while simultaneously negating the dominant meanings assigned to wage work. Another common threat running through these narratives is their opposition to capitalism's radical reshaping of the natural landscape, a reshaping that conflicts with Andean cosmological schemes that assert the unity of persons, spirits, and nature, and seek to maintain a "reciprocal balance" between them.[11] Under capitalist relations of production this balance has been distorted, as nature has become a commodity, pried loose from the norms of reciprocity and increasingly subjected to human domination and rational control. For the tellers of these tales of devil possession, this constant making-over of the landscape — the enclosing and privatizing of forests and pastures, this paving of roads and building of buildings — has been a harbinger of death.

## Conclusions

The devil narratives discussed here reflect a confrontation between the Quimseño peasants' moral economy and an expanding global economy. They should be read as allegories that, in telling stories about the deaths of individual male workers, are in fact foretelling the impending death of an entire way of life. They portray the decentering of the hierarchical peasant world and the installing of a new cultural order in which the logic of commodity production reigns supreme and in which material objects wax large and people small—or, in Rosa's idiom, in which "persons [such as Lucho] are often sacrificed for things."

By focusing on the different "versions" of Lucho's death, I have demonstrated the complexity of local social reality, a reality in which multiple causation is frequently invoked to explain events. Furthermore, by examining the various versions, I have attempted to illuminate the ways in which peasant ideology and politics are constructed and have pointed to conflicting interpretations of the development process. I have argued that aspects of peasant cosmology, as well as class and gender ideologies, are inscribed in these accounts and work to resist the process of commodification. Peasant spirits, such as the devil, and cosmological beliefs about inauspicious places and times of day haunt workers and their respective work sites. Such cosmological impulses disrupt work-discipline and wreak havoc in the workplace. Following Ong (1987), I argue that these spirit attacks can be viewed as an unconscious form of political resistance to the new material conditions of life associated with commercial farming.

This analysis argues for an expanded definition of "the political," a definition that includes both conscious and unconscious forms of resistance generated initially in women's informal domains. It insists that we cannot ignore the gender dimension that shapes the production of this counterdiscourse about the devil. I have drawn attention to the ways in which gender constructs politics—and vice versa—by underscoring the fact of women's marginalization in the realm of official political discourse, and I have demonstrated women's construction of an alternative political language. Focusing on women's statements of resistance in discourse as well as women's everyday acts of resistance to both commercial farming and Western styles of development, this article demonstrates that female peasants in semiprivate contexts confront public issues—namely, the politics of the workplace.

It seems appropriate that it is women, and not men, who are the storytellers and who launch this powerful critique, since women have not been drawn into the world of wage work and the development process to the extent that men have. Women's presence on the land and in the community at a time when large numbers of men have migrated out, moreover, puts female peasants in an ideal position for communicating these concerns about the changes in life wrought by wage work. Thus women, who derive their primary sense of identity from their relations to others and who serve as cultural mediators between the living and the dead, tell stories about the deaths of significant others, deaths that have taken a dramatic toll on life in the community. Dominant groups have tended to represent peasant women themselves as witchlike or as in league with the devil. In the narratives described here, women are turning the discourse of the dominant group back on itself.

Lucho's death disrupted the taken-for-granted nature of everyday life and called into question the routines of wage work. His death called up stories of other deaths, and the ensuing conversations allowed those who had known him to reflect on larger changes taking place in their world. Through these stories and conversations, peasant women were attempting to reshape a society increasingly menaced by forces perceived as being beyond their control. The stories are full of public meanings and they speak of collective troubles facing the community. From amidst the din and hum of mechanized farming, the whirring and buzzing of the sawmill turning, emerges the muffled sound of women's voices disrupting attempts to redefine the meaning of work in their community.

# 23

# A Businesswoman Among Middlemen
## A Case from Siassi

### *Alice Pomponio*

The Siassi Islanders of Papua New Guinea have long been described in the anthropological literature as maritime middlemen who form the central hub of the Vitiaz Strait trade system (Harding 1967). Mandok Island,[12] a raised coral islet off the southern tip of the high volcanic island of Umboi, is one of two islands at the center of this hub. Mandok Islanders have been noted for their canoe manufacture, carving tradition and sailing skills. Although considered locally to be "entrepreneurs," their performance in a market economic system has been uneven, characterized by financial and political disaster.

The Mandok see themselves as mobile maritime middlemen and "kings of the sea," a view at odds with administrative development strategies prevailing since World War II. These have overwhelmingly stressed subsistence farming and cash cropping. For the Mandok, who live on a ten-acre coral islet with no source of fresh water, increased land productivity would require relocation to Umboi Island, where they garden a supplemental plot of about three hundred acres. They have had several false starts and attempts at relocation, but in the end they staunchly refuse to move.

While most government administrators have defined "rural development" in terms of agricultural intensification and cash cropping, individual Mandok have defined "development" to mean "personal access to cash." This definition has affected their appraisal of and participation in various development projects through time. In their view, even educating children became a "development project" because educated children got jobs in town and sent money home to their village relatives (Pomponio 1993). Most business enterprises initiated on Mandok Island from the 1960s until about 1977 were communal village projects. In the late 1970s a village schism pushed individuals and family "lines" to start independent businesses. With the minimal and episodic exception of copra[13] sheds, most Mandok business ventures, village-centered or independent, have either been trade stores or have keyed into Mandok's self-perceptions regarding mobility, maritime orientation, or middleman trade. Until the late 1980s, most businesses failed. This analysis examines a notable exception to this pattern. Before describing the case, however, I shall discuss the broader social and cultural context in which it developed.

## A "Woman of Knowledge"

Mandok social and political systems revolve around age, generation and sex. The kinship system is nominally patrilineal, though matrilateral ties are also very important and can be invoked when necessary or desirable. Leadership positions on Mandok favor firstborn males born to a loose hierarchically organized system of patrilineal groups called *runai*. Firstborn people have higher status than latterborns, regardless of sex. But leadership positions require more than heredity: leaders must also display *ngar* or "wisdom." A knowledgeable man who is respected is called a "man of knowledge." A woman who demonstrates these qualities is likewise called a "woman of knowledge." At a relatively young age, in her early forties, Agnes Keke was already considered to be a "woman of knowledge." She has some hereditary advantage, which I discuss below, but more importantly *she used it* in innovative and extra-ordinary ways to become a businesswoman among middlemen and a respected "woman of knowledge" in her own right.

Agnes Keke was born on January 15, 1948. Although she was not a firstborn, she was the only daughter of a "big man" and *runai* elder. Through *his* adoption her father was feted as a firstborn and kept that status; some of this extended to her as his daughter. At the age of ten Keke started school on Mandok Island. In 1960, the school was moved to Por Island (adjacent to Mandok) and was expanded to teach children through the fourth grade. Keke was a student during the expansionist era of education (mid to late 1960s) in Papua New Guinea,[14] and also part of a "first generation" of school children from Mandok Island. She was therefore encouraged by her parents, the Catholic Mission, and by nationwide economic and political circumstances, to continue her education. She attended boarding school at the Catholic Mission station in east New Britain through the ninth grade.

In 1967-68 she attended teacher's college in east New Britain and, after graduating, returned to Mandok Island and taught in its community school for two years. In 1971 she was appointed a senior teacher in a Catholic primary school in Lae. The following year she became the school's headmistress.

In 1973 Keke attended a six-month headmaster's course in Port Moresby, capital of Papua New Guinea. This qualified her for a post as an associate lecturer and Dean of Women at Madang Teacher's College. In 1974 she completed a one-year course at the Canberra College of Advanced Education in Australia. After this she lectured at Holy Trinity Teacher's College in Mt. Hagen from 1975 to 1977.

Keke married a Dutch expatriate in 1975, and they had four children. She had also adopted a daughter before she was married, for a total of five. In 1978 she transferred to Port Moresby Teacher's College, where she taught until June 1981, when she accompanied her husband for a three-year posting in Japan. Upon her return in 1984 she decided to devote herself to being a full-time housewife.

This occupation did not last long, however. In late 1986 Keke answered a newspaper ad and started a business on Mandok to collect, process, and sell sea cucumbers (also called *beche de mer* or *trepang*). She called her business "*Panu* (Village) Enterprises." This business was notable for several reasons, not the least of which was that it represented a series of "firsts" in Mandok commercial enterprise. First among "firsts" was that the business was conceived, owned, and operated by a woman. The second "first" was that most of the labor was female. In 1986-87, 208 Mandok were employed by this project: females numbered 148 (70 percent) and males numbered sixty (30 percent). Males (especially teenagers) did some diving, and they collected and cut firewood. Youths and young men supervised the overnight smoking phase and bagged the dried sea cucumbers. Women did the rest: most of the diving and all of the cooking, cleaning, burying, and sun drying.

The third "first" was that the owner had a clear road to a market: she dealt directly with buyers first in Taiwan and later in Hong Kong as well. Fourth, she supplied herself with starting capital by taking out a personal bank loan. As of July 1990, though not yet showing a profit, she had good credit at the bank, was still in business, and was very hopeful about the future.

Another remarkable characteristic of this business was that it did not earn money off the Mandok; the Mandok earned money by working for the business. Well-versed in Siassi history, Keke knew that trepang had long been a popular commodity for external markets, and she learned from the experience of her business predecessors. Workers were paid for their labor rather than the product. In this way she controlled its quality.

In 1986, almost everyone was excited about this business, particularly the women. Some of the elders were dubious at first and complained that the business was born of personal greed, not communal beneficence, but their wives and daughters usually overruled them. Even if the elders could not quell their anxieties, Keke, as a daughter of a "big man," could not be dismissed lightly. She also had earned respect in her own right. The work force tripled within months. Within a short time, most of the original dissenting elders had changed their thinking, and several actively encouraged their wives and daughters to work for Panu Enterprises.

## Harvesting Sea Cucumbers

Sea cucumbers just lie on the reef. To harvest many species, all one has to do is bend over and pick them up. Other species require deeper diving,[15] but Mandok women are accustomed to diving for sea clams (Pomponio 1992). Although it is time-consuming and tiring to dive all day, the process is not hazardous, except perhaps for the presence of stonefish and other dangerous reef creatures. But these are commonplace dangers of daily life in the Vitiaz Strait. Collecting sea cucumbers requires no training, no talent, and no special equipment. Other stages require more tedious work, but none require special skill: anyone can do it. In general, younger women and teenagers do most of the diving and heavier, more physical work. Older women do the more tedious village jobs: watching the boiling trepang and scraping the cooked ones.

Different stages of the process take longer than others and workers are paid accordingly. Collecting and other full-day jobs earn workers about US $1.10, while boiling and other half-day processes earn them about US $.55. Prior to the establishment of Panu Enterprises, only skilled women earned cash through the tedious and time-consuming craft specialties of making trochus shell and beaded arm bracelets, and weaving betel nut baskets and grass skirts. These brought a price of about US $1.10-4.40 for several weeks' work. Although some species of sea cucumber require deep diving, and some stages of processing trepang are time-consuming and tedious, women are still earning money more quickly and in larger quantities than they would by producing traditional crafts. The newness of the project, and its promise of still more money, made it very popular with Mandok women in 1987. The success of Panu Enterprises seemed assured, as virtually nothing was consumed locally, and participants were all motivated by the same incentive: personal access to cash.

The initial loan for the business was for US $2200, with which Keke paid for processing equipment, for operating a motorized dugout canoe,[16] and for gasoline, personal travel, and wages. The initial contract was for a monthly shipment of sea cucumbers, but from 1987 to 1989 Keke averaged two shipments per year, partly because of her desire to limit the amount of time she spent away from her family. Each shipment consisted of about 1.5 tons of mixed species, valued at about US $8800. Keke expected this figure to more than double for 1990, owing to a rise in market prices in general and the addition of a market in Hong Kong, which was considerably better than the one in Taiwan.

As the business developed, workers became more efficient, and Keke borrowed more money to improve her equipment. In 1989 she bought an outboard motor and an eighteen-foot boat for collection; in 1990 she built a new drier made of more permanent materials than the bush materials she had used previously. These changes, combined with increased worker efficiency at the various jobs, allowed her to decrease the actual numbers in her labor force (and, consequently, her labor costs) by half, though the ratio of females to males remained the same.

## Investments in People

Elsewhere I have described Mandok's social system as a network of long-range investments in people (Pomponio 1992). These investments work on a principle of delayed reciprocal exchange (Sahlins 1972). That is, if I go fishing today, I give you some. If you harvest sweet potatoes tomorrow, you give me some. There is not a precise reckoning, as participants expect the exchange of food to continue *ad infinitum*. I refer to this kind of debt as "gift debt."[17] "Gift debt" is an interest-free exchange of objects that keeps the parties in a state of "mutual reciprocal dependence." The motivation of any individual transactor is to maximize net outgoings

(Gregory 1980:636). The Mandok describe this as "giving freely." This type of system supports a subsistence existence by distributing unequal resources more equitably. Overseas trade partnerships, while cast in an idiom of kinship, keep a somewhat closer reckoning of who has given what to whom, over how much time, and under what circumstances. Both these systems, however, are flexible; both presume value equivalence in the objects traded and mutual interdependence of the traders. They also assume equitable access to resources.

The etiquette of Mandok kinship obliges kin to give generously to one another. If someone has something he or she does not wish to give away, the request will be answered with the lie, "Sorry, I have no more," rather than by rebuke or refusal. Children are drilled in this sense of sharing from early childhood. When they become adults and marry, the same value system is reinforced. Young brides, for example, are admonished never to cook in a small pot, for a hungry kinsperson passing by would feel rejected.

I call this the "Marimari Rule." Marimari is a Tok Pisin (a New Guinea form of pidgin English) term that means "mercy," "pity," or "sympathy." Missionaries introduced the term, as might be surmised from its meaning. In Mutu this idea was expressed idiomatically in the phrase, lolo isamini, translated as "one's insides are dirty/ruined for him/her," and meaning "one is sorry for him/her." The Mandok adopted the shorter Tok Pisin term into their language.

Marimari breaks down with purchased goods, unless there was a previously agreed-upon equivalence, but such equivalence is not usually stated. Individual Mandok do not have equal access to kerosene, gasoline, or trade store goods because, within Mandok, individual access to cash varies greatly. This was also partly why the larger village investments failed. In a capitalist system, debts incurred are of the sort Gregory calls "commodity debt," which stands in opposition to "gift debt." "Commodity debt" accrues interest and keeps the participants in a state of "mutual reciprocal independence." The motivation of an individual transactor is to maximize net incomings and to accrue capital (Gregory 1980:636). When a village business society or an independent business owner takes out a bank loan, they incur "commodity debt." When a relative asks for food, money, or material items, he or she is incurring "gift debt."

Many Mandok personal businesses failed partially as a result of unfamiliarity with standard business practice. Much of this failure, however, has also entailed a confusion of "gift debt" with "commodity debt." Mandok people did not distinguish business assets from personal hoards: they were therefore subject to the *Marimari Rule* of the kinship system. This placed any business owner in a dilemma: those who were most likely to support the business (e.g., kin) were also the most likely to undermine it. They did this by exacerbating the owner's "commodity debt" while incurring their own "gift debt." They bought things on credit or "borrowed" things according to their kinship rights, and never repaid them under the commercial obligations of "commodity debt." Personally owned trade stores went bankrupt because relatives "ate the profits." What good son or daughter could stand by and make an older relative and his or her family go hungry for want of a bag of rice and a can of fish?

Keke's trepang business is an important exception to a more general pattern of defeat experienced by other independent businesses on Mandok. Her project has a certain immunity to the *Marimari Rule* for several reasons. First, there is nothing to beg, borrow, or steal. Eating dry-roasted sea cucumbers struck me, with my Western palate, as somewhat like chewing on the sole of a rubber thong that has been marinated in sea water. Most Mandok shared my appraisal. Older men and women told me that in the past sea cucumbers were a "famine food." They also recounted with great bellows of laughter how their parents and grandparents sold them (literally and figuratively) to the Umboi Island bush people as a "specialty food" in order to get a better exchange value against Umboi vegetable staples.

Second, rather than work against the kinship system, Keke used it to her financial benefit. Anyone who wanted to work could, and would be paid. The project soon had enough labor to support three complete and distinct work crews, each from a different part of the village and each, therefore, organized around extended family groups. The crews rotated, so that each group went in turn for different stages of production. Thus, individual women could organize their family's activities around a larger group's schedule and work according to their own abilities and time constraints (e.g., sharing babysitting, food gathering for their own families, etc.). From the business perspective, this ensured a constant work force, smooth interaction, and happier workers.

Third, as a former school teacher, Keke had some valuable practical skills. She knew how to plan ahead and organize people into work groups. She took attendance in a roll book and kept accurate records of each worker's wages in addition to her own costs. She understands basic concepts of supply, demand, overhead, and profit margin.

Finally, she parried the elders' reservations about her community spirit by formally recycling some wealth back into the village. In 1990 she supplied ten houses with sheet metal for roofing—at a personal cost of about US $4950—and was hoping to get a loan and supply ten more. This is partly why, after almost three years in business, she has yet to show a profit. From the perspective of evaluating "development projects," however, her workers feel the project is a success because it brings cash into the village. She seems content, as the following excerpt from a letter shows:

> Because of all the expenses...I have continuously large overdrafts. Though I would love to make a small profit, I am satisfied that because of my efforts, especially the women in the village have, for the first time, an opportunity to earn some cash. This enables them to be partially independent. I have calculated that those families which work for me can earn more than K200 [about US $220] per year. As you know until last year this was the only way to make some money [on Mandok]. Only recently have the people from Siassi started selling fish to the Siassi Development Corporation in Lablab through its agent on Mandok.

Note that this project utilizes extant skills, social ties, and culturally appropriate strategies for large undertakings. It also is culturally consistent with Mandok self-perceptions as "sea people." These are major factors in its success. Note too that, rather than break the rules or step outside her gender role, Keke managed to utilize both to her advantage. Her ability to integrate her advanced education and international experiences and still "know herself" is extraordinary. In this sense she is truly a good businesswoman and "woman of knowledge."

Although there still are obstacles to overcome, Keke's business shows independent action, long-range planning, and the tenacity necessary to sustain long-term development projects. In 1989 she was selected by the Papua New Guinea government to attend a course in Kiribati (formerly the Gilbert Islands, near Western Samoa) on fish processing for women entrepreneurs in the South Pacific. She was also nominated to participate in a workshop on export marketing for women executives in Vanuatu (formerly New

Hebrides) sponsored by the United Nations in October 1990. Her business history, her biography, and her continued successes have been an inspiration to Mandok women and a boon to the local economy.

# 24

# Shades of Blue
## Female and Male Perspectives on Policing

### *Joan C. Barker*

**P**olicing has long been perceived as a male occupation. Yet, in the last few decades, women have been taking their place among the "fellowship" of law enforcement officers. In a self-defined male domain this represents quite an adjustment. For a subculture with a richly documented and well-earned reputation for clannishness, *machismo*, and solidarity, the adjustment is cataclysmic.

Female and male officers define the job and their roles differently, producing tension between the groups and providing fertile grounds for mutual misunderstanding. This is expressed in differing views on such issues as the use of physical coercion, the concept of danger, the importance of "command presence," the need for "back-up" of fellow officers, and even the course of the police career.

The importance of these concepts for policing became evident during my long-term study of street officers working for the Los Angeles Police Department. Policing is especially problematic in this city of extraordinary diversity. Not only must officers contend with often intense inter-group and neighborhood rivalries, but they must also cope with communication barriers in an area where an estimated eighty to ninety languages are spoken. The L.A.P.D. is the nation's smallest urban police force in terms of the ratio of police to population, and the Department patrols a large geographic area. My fifteen-year study began in 1976, at a time when the Department began implementing affirmative action programs that emphasize hiring and promoting women and minorities. Officers distinguish "traditional" police—those hired before affirmative action programs were implemented—from "new police," those who were hired under affirmative action guidelines.

Views of officers reported in this paper reflect differences by generation and gender. The relevant categories are: traditional male police, traditional female police, new male police and new female police. As will become evident, generation is a more important predictor of attitudes toward policing than gender, though there are some important female-male differences as well. There is also significant individual variation related to differences in economic and educational background and personality attributes of the officers. This paper focuses on the interrelationship of gender and generation.

Before implementation of affirmative action policies, women served as police officers in the L.A.P.D., but their numbers were few and they were generally restricted to cases involving home and hearth: abused and neglected children, truancy, and interviewing female victims of physical abuse, rape and incest. Female officers were not assigned to patrol duty, regarded by most traditional officers as "real police work," nor were they assigned to domestic disputes, since these were viewed as being too dangerous.[18] One consequence of these policies is that it was difficult for female officers to get the kinds of varied experiences that led to promotions.

In the early days of affirmative action implementation, when women were first being assigned to street patrol, concerns of white male officers focused on logistics: sexual attraction, self-esteem and physical danger. Logistical concerns included such problems as separate locker rooms, showers, and bathroom facilities for female officers. As women have become integrated into the police force, problems of logistics are less acute, but sexual attraction, self-esteem, and physical danger continue to plague relations between female and male officers.

Concern over sexuality centers on the fact that officers on street patrol spend long hours in close association with their partners and in isolation from others. Some male officers note their wives and girlfriends are fearful that the intense relationship based on interdependency that can develop between "fellow" officers might threaten their personal relationships. In fact, there have been incidents involving "fraternization"[19] and there have been marriages between "fellow" officers. Clearly, the sentiments and experiences that bind police officers into a "fraternity" can also form the basis for the marriage bond.

Male officers suffer an assault on their self-esteem through their perception that standards of physical fitness and job training have been eroded as a result of affirmative action. They also see "easy promotions" for women as devaluing the work of people who, in their view, had to wait much longer and work harder for the same recognition. White males view affirmative action as a barrier to promotion for them. This problem is exacerbated by the fact that female officers tend to have more formal education than male officers. Thus, females often are better at organizational skills, such as report writing, that bring them to the attention of "supervision" and may result in what males perceive as preferential treatment in assignment to indoor jobs and promotions.

Perception of danger, however, is perhaps the most serious issue dividing male and female officers. Male officers think females increase the danger on the job in many ways, but especially because they lack "command presence," which is defined as looking so formidable "perpetrators" will not challenge their authority. "Command presence" involves physical size, the uniform (replete with visible weapons), and attitude. As an attitude, "command presence" is taught in the training academy and practiced on the streets. It is believed that "command presence" increases efficiency and reduces danger for all concerned. As one officer put it, " ... all you needed on the street was the brains God gave you, your gun and command presence. If it came right down to it, you could do without the brains and the gun, but God help you if you didn't have command presence."

To be taken seriously by male officers, female officers must convey "command presence." Since females are typically smaller than males, it is difficult for them to intimidate "perpetrators" by size alone. Therefore, they express "command presence" primarily through attitude, but this can lead to other problems perceived as increasing the danger of the job. Some female officers, in attempting to project "command presence," are viewed by male officers as being excessively aggressive. Just as over-zealous male officers are said to exhibit the "John Wayne" syndrome, overly aggressive female officers are called "Jane Waynes." Both are considered to be dangerous work partners. The difference is that male officers are assumed to be able to "back" themselves. Female officers, on the other hand, are perceived as lacking the physical ability to "back" themselves and thus are viewed as being more likely to draw their partners into a confrontation.

Male officers view their female partners as lacking the physical ability to provide adequate "backup" in the event of an altercation, and some men charge that they have received injuries as the result of their female partners' lack of physical ability or inclination to come to their aid. This has become part of the folklore of male officers. One man describes his horrified reaction to a training film, in which a policeman is stabbed repeatedly while his female partner is unable to come to his aid. The story reflects the ambivalence of the officer in identifying the cause for the lack of back-up by the injured officer's partner:

> It was unbelievable. Unnerving. . . . It was worse than the worst horror movie. This suspect was on the back of a police officer stabbing him with an ice pick. And the officer had to reach around, put his arm across his body and try to shoot the suspect while the suspect was still stabbing him. . . . And it goes on and on, stabbing and shooting and each time the guy gets shot he's telling the officer about the shot. Unbelievable — and the female partner, was either killed or didn't jump in, or — I don't know — She was killed, but the officer lived. He lived, he was on the tape and you could see in his description how heavy it was.

Female officers also describe themselves as being reluctant to become involved in physical altercations because they acknowledge themselves to be at a physical disadvantage. However, this does not mean they do not get into fights. In fact, every police officer finds that the job sometimes requires such action, and every female officer interviewed stated that she had been in many such encounters. One new female officer commented:

> It's survival really. I mean you don't really think about whether you're a female or male, or whether this guy's bigger than you are. When you're actually out on the street trying to fight, and you're fighting for your survival, whatever goes, goes in order to come out alive as far as you and your partner is concerned. The priority is coming out alive, coming out of the situation unscathed, and you just do whatever you have to do. You don't have time to think about whether you're afraid or whether you're going to get hurt. . . . My perspective is that I have a lot more to lose than my partner. . . . If a guy gets cut from ear to ear, . . . they're a hero, and it's basically just a battle wound. For a woman . . . you know, it's different, . . . so I have a lot more to lose. If a suspect wants to blow me or my partner away out on the street, with my partner they're just going to blow him away. . . . [With] me, with the women, they want to disfigure you, do sexual things. . . . I figure I've got a lot more to lose.

After the first wave of women had settled into their jobs, their male partners often stated that they tend to avoid situations they view as "too dangerous" to deal with while working with a female officer. A recurring theme in the complaints of traditional male police is that working with new female officers gets in the way of doing the job as they were taught to do it. According to one male, it is now necessary to bypass verbal persuasion in favor of physical force using a baton because "new police" are physically too small to take risks:

> The new training with all the A.A. [affirmative action] police emphasizes baton because so many of the new police are female—smaller muscle mass and generally short, or shorter—and small males, guys that would never have made it on the job before. It's not safe. They're too easily overpowered.

On the other hand, female officers assert that male officers have placed them in situations to "test" their willingness to be "stand up" officers. A "stand up" officer is one who does not shirk his/her duty, takes responsibility for his/her actions and has an aggressive or assertive attitude.

Male and female describe the job of policing in similar ways, but with different emphases. Both see it as requiring many different talents and abilities—a job which involves public relations and social work as well as "fighting crime"—but they tend to stress their own perceived strengths. For example, males emphasize enforcing the rules, the physical danger, and the need for physical power for safety and to enforce compliance. Females stress the sociological aspects and the need for understanding and negotiation. Male officers complain that they feel fettered in doing "real police work" when they have female partners. Female officers think the males are too aggressive in their approach to policing and, therefore, tend to exacerbate potentially violent situations. Females see nothing wrong with "sweet talking" or verbally empathizing with suspects, whereas males see this as inappropriate behavior that is demeaning to the uniform. One female officer observes:

> I know it frosts my male partners sometimes, but hey, if it works. . . . Sometimes some gang-banger is all attitude and right on the edge. If I can get him cuffed and in the car with "hey homeboy," or "honey," or his name if I know it, "I know you aren't going to give me any trouble today," and turn on the sweetness and the smiles. . . . I mean, I know how it can go, but if sugar works, why not?

Another female officer links the utility of maintaining an empathic demeanor with the necessity of distancing herself from some grimmer aspects of the job:

> . . .it's kind of like role-playing . . . it just depends on what the role is. There are times when you go into a situation and you have to portray a caring role, but you don't really care. In order to do your job you portray a caring role. . . . Some people will say, how can you respect someone that just raped a three-year-old kid? But then you kind of have to portray that in order to keep from losing it, and to do what you're supposed to do and not get overly involved.

It is difficult to tell how much of this difference in approach is related to differences in female and male socialization and how much to biology — including greater physical size and strength, as well as higher testosterone levels, for males — but it is clear that biology forms the basis for what some male officers view as preferential treatment for their female colleagues. When female officers become pregnant, they are relieved of street patrol and given desk jobs, where they remain for the duration of their pregnancy and, often, for prolonged periods following delivery. Women may also be given "inside" assignments for other "female problems," such as painful menses and the aftermath of miscarriages. Filling "inside" slots with female officers means the positions are unavailable for their traditional use as assignments for officers who have been injured during street patrol.

Male officers express resentment because, they say, female officers receive the same pay but do not do the same work, and their physical complaints are not subject to the same levels of scrutiny as that given to physical complaints of males. Male officers value conformity to an ethic which includes "working hurt" without complaint. When they do seek "light duty" and find that women with undisclosed "female complaints" have filled the available positions, they often question the value of female officers on the job.

Differences between male and female officers extend to background and motivation for joining the force, as well as to attitudes about the job itself. Whether male or female, "traditional" police were mostly white and came from "police families." That is, they had fathers, brothers or uncles who were also in the Department. This is particularly true for traditional female officers.[20] In addition, males were likely to have had military experience, a significant factor since the Department is structurally very similar to the military model. Officers hired after implementation of affirmative action, or "new police," are much more varied, both in terms of ethnicity and background.

Motivation for becoming a police officer differs for males and females. Males are much more reluctant to discuss their reasons for joining the Department but, when urged to do so, describe motivations related to idealism, status, or money—in that order. One officer joined the force on the suggestion of a much-admired buddy from the war in Vietnam:

> ... my friend, he had been a "dust off" pilot in Nam, a great guy, one of the greatest . . . Those guys, the pilots, especially the "dust off" guys would go in, no armament. You were allowed a pistol, but nothing serious, no cover. And they'd go in and pick up the wounded. [He] saved . . . thousands of guys that wouldn't have made it, had no chance at all . . . Anyway, he, my friend, is a copper in Newton and he told me about the job. He said he thought . . . I would make a good cop. I truly respected him and figured if he was. . . . Well, being a cop might be a way to do something. . . . It sounds stupid, but I thought I could do something for the good . . . to help people, to save people. I don't know, but to help make it better where I live. . . . Grown up Eagle Scout stuff.

Another officer was drawn to policing by a combination of idealism and frustration over the direction his career was taking. After returning from a stint with the Army in Vietnam, he worked at a number of jobs—in a factory, in construction, and as a truck driver:

> ... I felt like I was wasting my life. Not that I expected to do something, really. . . . I mean I wasn't going to save the world or anything, but it seemed like I could do something better. . . .[The L.A.P.D.] was advertising, and it paid good money. They paid a hundred dollars more than I was working for, and I decided to take the test. And I passed. I figured it was a job I could go home and be proud to tell my parents about. It made me feel pretty good at the time.

Women are more likely to join the L.A.P.D. looking for excitement, or because they "thought it would be fun." They cite the excitement, novelty of the career choice, economic motivations, and idealism—in that order. According to one, "First off, it was the excitement that appealed to me. I didn't just want to be another nine to five-er . . . and I have to admit I love it when people ask what I do because then I get to tell them and watch their reaction."

This officer's eagerness to discuss her job also sets her apart from male police, who typically conceal their occupation from what they consider the intrusive questions of outsiders. Female officers are also much more likely to buy sweat shirts and tee shirts with the Department logo and wear them "in public" — to the market and while running errands. In contrast, traditional male officers often carry two wallets while off-duty so their police identification can be kept totally private when conducting everyday errands.

In spite of publicly identifying themselves with the L.A.P.D., women officers typically do not express the "gung ho" attitude expected of males. One new female officer notes that policing was her second choice:

> I always wanted to either be a fireman or a police officer growing up, and I think I leaned more toward being a fireman until I kind of realized it's real physical. Not that I'm not in good shape, and I like to work out but, you know, I kind of just got turned off by all that, and I decided to be a police officer instead.

Another new female police officer stated that she thought the job would never get dull and, if it did, she would leave it. She added that she hoped to find a husband before she left the job. Her observation that it is the best job she ever had in terms of meeting eligible, economically stable males is echoed by a number of new female officers. Such attitudes are viewed with disdain by traditional officers of both sexes. Traditional female officers appear more reluctant than their male counterparts to acknowledge the accomplishments and value of the new female police. Over lunch at a restaurant, a black traditional female assessed the new officers:

> The females are just here to find husbands. I wouldn't want to work with them. They're not here to do police work. . . . The other day [a male officer] was working with [a female officer], and he was struggling with this suspect. His partner didn't come to his aid. . . . She just stood there. She didn't do anything. Finally, some citizen helped [him]. . . . When it was all over she just called it in. No discussion. [He] was so mad. So I ask you, you see these waitresses and folks around here. If someone came in here and started pounding on one of them, don't you think they would come to the aid of their co-worker? And they're just waitresses. They're not cops. I swear, I won't work with any of them.

Male officers emphasize solidarity with other officers as a driving force in their lives. They socialize with fellow officers, share the same hobbies and, often, live close to each other. Female officers express an interest in maintaining a balance and separation between the demands of the job and other aspects of their lives, including relationships with their spouses and children. Women, more than men, are concerned about the danger of "burn out," of not being able to leave the job behind them at the end of their shifts. They worry that demands of policing will interfere with their ability to be sensitive, caring people. Females sometimes express the feeling that male officers are too consumed with "the job" and that it might be better for them to relax more. One woman, who switched to policing after working with psychiatric emergency intervention teams, put it this way:

> . . . I know these people who just LIVE for the Department, twenty-four hours a day. And I guess it's really good to be loyal to that extent, but I don't think that it's healthy. And I know from having been in my own therapy, and my own psych advice I used to give is, "You need to have a balanced life." You need your off time to go off and travel and vacation and have fun, see your friends, and do all that other stuff.

Male officers more emphatically separate their off-duty lives from their on-duty persona. They leave their non-working persona in the locker room, where they switch from "soft clothes" or "street clothes" to their uniforms. They are aware of psychologically "suiting up" in the same way that they dress for survival on the street. They don their bullet-proof vests and put on "backup" weapons (usually two-inch revolvers), in addition to the regulation firearm, mace, handcuffs and restraints (braided nylon cords). Long before they sit in roll call or hit the streets, the officers have prepared for the kind of dangerous shift they know is a possibility.

Female officers make something of the same transition, but not to the extent the males do. They wear the same gear, but are less likely to carry a "backup" weapon, which is not required by the Department. Women say the "backup" weapon is too uncomfortable, too bulky, and too heavy. Unlike male officers, they do not consider it an essential part of their equipment.

On this issue alone, male officers feel that female officers do not understand the reality of the job and, therefore, are dangerous to work with. Male officers see policing as being much more dangerous than female officers perceive it to be. In fact, males are more likely than females to become injured. This may be partly because males tend to define the job in more physical terms. Some male officers have been injured while they acted to protect their female partners. Often this physical intervention is "preemptive"—they act decisively and physically to maintain control and effect an arrest. The males act sooner than they would if they were working with a male partner and felt they could count on a backup. Instead, they count on the element of surprise. They do this, they say, to protect their more vulnerable partner.

The female officers tend to see their male partners as being overly aggressive, and females define the danger level as being lower than do male officers. In some ways, the attitude of female officers is more like that of seasoned officers in the past. Experienced officers did not feel themselves to be especially vulnerable on street patrol, and were less likely to be injured than officers new to the job.

Males tend to see policing as a career, but new female officers usually do not plan to stay on "the job" much more than six or seven years. New male officers typically do not plan to spend their entire careers in the L.A.P.D., but express a desire to "lateral," transfer to another department where they may have a better chance for promotion. New female officers, on the other hand, expect to leave policing altogether. While 90 percent of traditional female officers intend to retire from the Department, 75 percent of the new female officers interviewed do not plan to stay until retirement. These figures may represent a bias based on self-selection, however, since many traditional officers are nearing retirement age. The less dedicated officers may well have left the Department earlier in their careers.

New female officers typically reassess their commitment to policing when they become mothers. None of the new female officers with children anticipate staying with the Department until retirement, and this is partly because they have reevaluated the dangers of police work in light of motherhood. They typically express concern about not being physically and emotionally "there" for their children. One female officer stated that she used to enjoy the excitement of the job, but has since reconsidered:

> [A]s you get older and have children, or just start being more aware of things, it's not that important any more to risk your life. . . . You do it because that's how you're trained to act, . . . [to] automatically do certain things when you're put in that situation, but you try not to get yourself in that situation as much, I think.

Motherhood propels female officers away from the job for other reasons as well. Female officers often express the need to spend nurturing time with their children:

> I want to leave and be home with my babies now. My whole attitude has really changed. I see myself as coming inside and being off the streets. . . . I'd prefer not to have to work and be a police officer. I never thought I'd say that—but I didn't think I'd have two more babies, either.

Male officers usually feel an even greater commitment to the job when they become fathers, and this is related to the cultural definition of the male parental role as provider. Many traditional and new male officers cite financial obligations of child rearing as a primary reason for working overtime and staying until and beyond retirement.

In spite of placing greater emphasis on their off-duty lives than males, female officers do not appear to be dissatisfied with their chosen careers. One woman notes:

> [Policing] is everything I thought it would be as far as helping people and having a good career. And I feel satisfied and I go home feeling good most of the time, knowing that I do something that makes me feel good, that I like. All my family and friends are proud of me. People kind of look up to you when you're a police officer. . . . There's not really one part I don't enjoy, but you have days when you don't enjoy, where you see something you don't want to see, or something you don't want to hear, or something happens to you. . . . .[Then] I think, "Oh, why do I do this?"

Morale is increasingly a problem for all Los Angeles police officers. The former psychiatric worker quoted above, who is respected by other officers for her "street smarts," expressed some ambivalence about policing:

> I'm back to enjoying what I do and I can stay for a while but, you know, ten years, something else happens, it wouldn't be such a big deal to get into something else, get into business. I never try to get locked into something, like this will be the job forever. . . . I have gone through cycles, especially these last six months, of this job . . ., you can have it. I'm moving to Maui to sell puka shells on the beach, and . . . before my last vacation, I felt like, "just leave me alone."

Male and female officers make complementary contributions to the difficult job of policing. Establishing an effective "police" presence in a city that is ethnically, economically and linguistically diverse calls on a variety of verbal skills and experience in interpreting such cues as body language. With the influx of female officers, different perspectives have been forced on the Department. As one new female officer put it:

> Women bring a balance . . . balance in the sense that, women don't get caught up in the ego trip like the men do. When you have female suspects, sometimes as a female I'll run up against more hostility—it would take my partner to calm down the situation. . . . [But] some of your hard-core criminals will still say "Yes, Ma'am," and then curse out your partner and want to take them to the deck, but they will do what you say because you are a woman. Try to figure it.

Both male and female officers appear to be moving toward a more varied approach to policing. In some instances, this represents a synthesis; in others, the result is a balance of complementary approaches.

During 1991 and 1992, the L.A.P.D. became engulfed in a crisis that tested the confidence and commitment of all officers, traditional and new, female and male. The Department was shaken by accusations of brutality against four officers involved in beating Rodney King, a black man stopped for traffic violation after a high-speed chase. Pressure intensified in the spring of 1992, when the Department was accused of slow response to riots and looting, which broke out after a jury returned "not guilty" verdicts in the trial of the four officers. The incident focused harsh light on the dilemmas of policing and forced individual officers to new awareness of their limitations. Males weren't able to plunge in and solve the problem through a display of physical strength. On the other hand, females weren't able to negotiate a successful solution, either.

# Endnotes

## Preface

[1] These figures are drawn from the United Nations' world population estimates for the period 1985-1990 (1991:27).

[2] For a discussion of sex ratio differences, see Sieff (1990:25-48).

## Part I

[1] Lyrics by Alan Jay Lerner.

[2] The two discussed their experiences at a gender roles class taught by anthropologist Gale Loof at California State University, Northridge.

[3] Some feminist scholars suggest the ordering of concepts into opposing categories is a male attribute, growing out of the socialization process in which "maleness" is socially constructed and is defined as being in opposition to "femaleness." See Chodorow (1974); Gilligan (1982, 1988); Hartsock (1983); and Martin (1988).

[4] Forager societies meet their subsistence needs by hunting, gathering and fishing, rather than through food production, which includes herding and agriculture.

[5] This model of the division of labor in foraging societies is challenged by an article in Part IV of this volume, "Daughters of the Forest," which describes hunting activities of women in the Philippines.

[6] On the other hand, psychoanalyst Bruno Bettelheim (1954) suggests that a dominant theme of male puberty rites is to address what might be described as "womb envy." He observes that subincision may be a ritual attempt to construct a vagina and that homosexuality rites further emphasize the initiate's symbolic female role.

[7] Creek field research (1980-81) was supported by the National Science Foundation, the Wenner-Gren Foundation for Anthropological Research, the American Philosophical Society, and the Whatcom Museum of History and Art.

[8] Ankipaya translates as "my enemy." *Ankipáya i:tálwa* are those outside a clan group united by marriage. *I:tálwa* united by marriage are *anhússi* ("my friend").

[9] My fieldwork among the Bena Bena took place from January 1, 1961, to May 15, 1962, at which time I held a predoctoral fellowship and

supplemental research grant from the National Institute of Mental Health, U. S. Public Health Service, and October 1970 to September 1971, at which time I had a Fulbright research fellowship and supplemental support from the New Guinea Research Unit of the Australian National University.

10 The author is referring to sister exchange, a form of marriage exchange discussed in Alice Schlegel's article "Status, Property and the Value on Virginity," in Part III of this volume.

11 Bena Bena, like many other groups, are polygynous, meaning that men may marry more than one wife (See Part III of this volume).

12 Pu'a planned to make the donation for a pig feast, a ceremonial occasion through which New Guinea men gain status and prestige.

13 See C. Lévi-Strauss: *Les Structures elementaires de la parente*. My thanks are due to C. Lévi-Strauss for his kindness in furnishing me with the proofs of his work. . . .

## Part II

1 Quoted in Charles Rollo, *Psychiatry in American Life*, 1963.

2 At the time Margaret Mead went to Samoa she was married to her first husband Luther Cressman, a theological student. He did not accompany her to the field. (EDITOR'S NOTE)

3 "Zande" is the singular and adjectival form of "Azande."

4 My field work (1983-1985) was partly supported by a grant from the Department of Anthropology, University of California, Los Angeles, and a University of California Chancellor's Patent Fund Grant.

5 The word "àbàrémù" literally means "clothed males," and earlier referred to slavers, explorers and colonialists. Its meaning now includes "government men."

6 The chief at the time of my arrival was the son of the chief presiding during Evans-Pritchard's time.

7 For confidentiality, I have provided pseudonyms for all Azande I mention in this article. The form combines a Christian and Zande name linked by a hyphen.

8 Seligman and Seligman utilized Evans-Pritchard's notes for their chapter on the Azande. They did not show Evans-Pritchard the final text, however, so his responsibility for it is limited (Evans-Pritchard 1971b:130).

9 Another reason why Evans-Pritchard may have missed ritual activities is that some of them occur in the hours before dawn during a very long party/feast/dance.

10 The Protestant church opposed commemorative feasts because they include the drinking of alcoholic beverages. The Government of Equatoria opposed the practice of giving away all a widow's possessions and forcing her to abandon her old homestead.

## Part III

[1] Data on adolescence come from Schlegel and Barry (1991), a cross-cultural study of the behavior and treatment of adolescents in preindustrial societies.

[2] This part summarizes material originally presented in Schlegel and Eloul (1987, 1988).

[3] The dower consisted of a portion of or interest in the real estate of a deceased husband given by law to his widow during her life.

[4] A *puja* is a religious ceremony in honor of a particular god or saint. In the passage cited, the goddess Bhagavati is the object of worship.

[5] The rate of "illegitimate" births is approximately 70 percent (Powell 1986:83).

[6] I conducted historical and legal research at the University of the West Indies, Barbados, followed by field work in Antigua and Barbuda from January 1985 to March 1986, and again for three months in 1987.

[7] This paper is based on research funded by the National Institute of Mental Health and the National Institute on Aging.

[8] In anthropological analyses of kinship, "ego" is the individual from whose point of reference kinship is figured.


## Part IV

[1] Lamphere follows Talcott Parsons' (1963a; 1963b) model of persuasion and influence.

[2] Research for this study was made possible by grants from the National Institute of Mental Health, the National Science Foundation, the Wenner-Gren Foundation, the National Endowment for the Humanities, the Council for the International Exchange of Scholars, and the H. F. Guggenheim Foundation.

[3] See, for example, Giovannini (1985); Uhl (1985); Dubisch (1986). I also follow Dubisch (1986:16); and Salamone and Stanton (1986:97) in use of the term "domestic power."

[4] Names of both towns are pseudonyms.

[5] A latifundium is a landed estate on which workers in a state of partial servitude practice labor-intensive agriculture.

[6] Agnates are kin related through the male line.

[7] From a poem by Marcelin Lora.

[8] From a poem by Juanillo "El Gato."

[9] From a poem by Juanillo "El Gato."

[10] Generalissimo Franco ran Spain with an iron hand from 1936 until his death in 1975.

[11] "Alpha male" is a term developed in studies of nonhuman primates. It refers to the dominant male of a local primate group.

12 The field work on which this paper is based was conducted during 1977-79 supported by the National Institutes of Mental Health and National Science Foundation, and in 1983 with grants from the American Philosophical Society and Princeton University.

13 Clans are kin groups that trace descent from a common ancestor. Agnatic groups are those linked by kin ties through males; exogamous refers to the fact that members must marry someone from outside the clan. Endogamous groups are in-marrying.

14 See, for example, Ortner (1974:69).

15 See, for example Langness (1974); A. Strathern (1969); Lederman (1986).

16 Generalized reciprocity is a form of economic exchange in which there is no immediate expectation of a return in kind.

17 The pig kill is the last event in a decade-long series making up the *mok ink* or Pig Festival.

18 For example, components of warfare compensations or the parades leading up to the pig kill.

19 Research was funded by a U.C.L.A. Anthropology Department Research Grant and a U.C.L.A. Mexus Research Award.

20 From the records of the *Archivo Historico Municipal de Guadalajara*; exp. 12, 1893.

21 Ibid., exp. 12, 1893.

22 *Archivo Historico Municipal de Guadalajara*; exp. 11, 1893.

23 *Archivo Historico Municipal de Guadalajara*, exp. 14, 1893.

24 Ibid.

25 Ibid.

26 To "nock" an arrow is to fit it against the bowstring preparatory to shooting.

**Part V**

1 The suffix 'devi' is a reverential title for a goddess; "ma" acknowledges the motherly role of Sarada.

2 I am indebted to Webster (1975) for her succinct formulation of Bachofen's model.

3 Animate, diversified nature, *prakriti*, is also female and is opposed to an originally inanimate, undifferentiated substance or selfness or man: *purusa*. Illusion, *maya*, the power that spins the universe along in delight and ignorance is female. *Maya*, like *śakti*, is a name of the goddess. In its positive aspect it is entrancing art; negatively it is a deathly snare.

4 A woman should obey her father until married, her husband until widowed, and her son until death.

5 Brahma, Vishnu and Śiva are three great male Hindu deities. Commonly, Brahma is known as the creator, Vishnu as the preserver, and Śiva as the destroyer. Note that here the existence and power of the goddess precedes all three.

[6] The madonna-whore dichotomy familiar in the West is an example of a somewhat different expression of the conceptual dichotomy between the procreative and erotic aspects of femininity.

[7] Rajput families keep swords dating from a glorious and lamented past when Rajput men fought heroically in the service of local overlords. The weapon is emblematic of an era when male power had deeper foundations among the Rajputs than it does today.

[8] Marxist theorists approach the position of women in society as related to class struggle; others view the position of Iranian women in terms of Western middle-class images of emancipation.

[9] A kaross is a leather covering made from the hide of a large antelope. Worn almost exclusively by women, the kaross is draped along the back and two ends are tied at the shoulder. A rope holds it close over the abdomen. The pouch formed in the upper back is used for carrying ostrich eggshell water containers, gathered foods and older children.

[10] Wu Chieh is a pseudonym.

[11] We never did get a name for this god, who needed a special paint job (with half his face black and half white) but still looked and acted very much like Shang Ti Kung to some of the people in the village who knew about such things.

[12] See, for example, Elliot (1955:92); Gould-Martin (1978:59); Kleinman (1980:217); Potter (1974:210, 214).

[13] Jordan describes the initiation of another village woman: "Throngs of village people looked on as she flailed her back, shouting, sputtering, drooling, and muttering. When it was over, she was, willy-nilly, a *tang-ki*" (1972:167).

[14] Nancy Chodorow's (1974) contribution to this issue is discussed in the introduction to part I of this volume. See also Gilligan (1982, 1988); Hartsock (1983); and Martin (1988). [EDITORS' NOTE]

## Part VI

[1] Roman Catholics use the term "Mass" for their weekly church service.

[2] See, for example, Basham (1976); Lewis (1959, 1961); Peñalosa (1968); Hewes (1954).

[3] Some writers exclude traditional indigenous families who maintain their "cultural purity" (Stevens 1973b).

[4] See, for example, Paul (1974); Neuhouser (1989); Stevens (1973c); Jacquette (1976).

[5] Research in San Antonio began in 1988. In the summer of 1989, I administered a comprehensive sociodemographic survey of 80 Tuneco families form which the current analysis emerges. The study of San Pedro Sacatepequez began with a year's dissertation research (1976-1977) and research visits continued in the 1980s.

6 Female residents of San Antonio are called Tunecas; males are called Tunecos.

7 Funding for the fieldwork on which this study is based was provided by the Doherty Foundation at Princeton University and by the Institute of Latin American Studies at the University of Texas at Austin.

8 Black dogs are emblematic of hacienda farming. They are the ominous gatekeepers without whom a traditional hacienda would not be complete. Peasants fear them because of their ferocity and size.

9 See, for example, Favret-Saada 1980; Price 1983; Taussig 1987.

10 According to Silverblatt (1980) women occupied important political and religious roles during the pre-Columbian period, but were excluded from formal positions of power under Spanish rule. Spanish colonial officials strengthened ties between men and appointed native political chiefs, but accused women of being witches and of making pacts with the devil. This realigned gender relations and led to the perception that men were allies with the intruders, while women were "true representatives of Andean society" (Silverblatt 1980:176).

11 See, for example Bastien (1978); Nash (1979).

12 I conducted fieldwork in Papua New Guinea focusing on Mandok Island for over two years: eighteen months from 1979-81, and eight months from October 1986 to May 1987. The research on which this paper is based was funded by The Wenner-Gren Foundation for Anthropological Research and by a St. Lawrence University Faculty Research Grant. Parts of this chapter have been excerpted from Pomponio 1992.

13 Copra is dried coconut meat from which coconut oil is made.

14 See Pomponio and Lancy (1987); Pomponio (1993).

15 The commercial species of sea cucumber can be found as deep as thirty to fifty meters but, as of this writing, divers were not going deeper than about six meters.

16 Keke's father, a World War II veteran, used his compensation money to buy an outboard motor and had a motorized dugout canoe built in the village. Keke still had to fuel it and pay for a "captain" to run it, as this would have been inappropriate for a woman to do.

17 This is based on Gregory's (1980) formulation which is, however, much more complex and on the whole less applicable than my interpretation here.

18 Police view domestic disputes and regular traffic stops as the two most dangerous types of activity.

19 The term "fraternization" is an interesting one when applied in this context, because it is used to describe behavior that is "loverly" rather than "brotherly."

20 Ninety percent of traditional female officers in this study came from police families, as opposed to 15 percent of new female officers.

# References Cited

Adams, R. N. 1960. "An Inquiry in the Nature of the Family," in G. Dole and R. Carneiro, eds., *Essays in the Science of Culture: In Honor of Leslie A. White.* New York: Thomas Y. Crowell.

Anagnost, Ann S. 1987. "Politics and Magic in Contemporary China." *Modern China,* 13:40–61.

Anantha Krishna Iyer, I. K. 1912. *The Cochin Tribes and Castes.* Madras: Higginbotham.

*Archivo Historico Municipal de Guadalajara.* 1893. exps. 11, 12, 14.

Balikci, Asen. 1970 (reissued 1989). *The Netsilik Eskimo.* Prospect Heights, IL: Waveland Press.

Bardwick, Judith M. 1974. "The Sex Hormones, the Central Nervous System and Affect Variability in Humans," in Violet Franks and Vsanti Burtle, eds., *Women in Therapy: New Psychotherapies for a Changing Society.* New York: Brunner/Mazel.

Barfield, Ashton. 1976. "Biological Influences on Sex Differences in Behavior," in Michael Teitelbaum, ed., *Sex Differences: Social and Biological Perspectives.* Garden City, NY: Anchor Books.

Basham, R. 1976. "Machismo," *Frontiers,* 1:126–143.

Bastien, Joseph W. 1978 (reissued 1985). *Mountain of the Condor: Metaphor and Ritual in an Andean Ayllu.* (American Ethnological Society Monograph No. 64.) Prospect Heights, IL: Waveland Press.

Bem, Sandra. 1983. "Gender Schema Theory and Its Implications for Child Development." *Signs,* 8:598–616.

Berleant-Schiller, R. 1977. "Production and Division of Labor in a West Indian Peasant Community." *American Ethnologist,* 4:253–272.

Bettelheim, Bruno. 1954. *Symbolic Wounds: Puberty Rites and the Envious Male.* Glencoe, IL: Free Press.

Beuchler, J. M. 1985. "Women in Petty Commodity Production in La Paz, Bolivia," in J. Nash and H. Safa, eds., *Women and Change in Latin America.* South Hadley, MA: Bergin and Garvey.

Bohannan, P. 1971. *Divorce and After.* New York: Anchor Books.

Bossen, Laurel. 1984. *The Redivision of Labor: Women and Economic Change in Four Guatemalan Communities.* SUNY Series in the Anthropology of Work, June Nash, ed. Albany: State University of New York Press.

Bourque, S. C., and K. B. Warren. 1981. *Women of the Andes: Patriarchy and Social Change in Two Peruvian Towns.* Ann Arbor: University of Michigan Press.

Boyer, R. 1989. "Women, 'La Mala Vida' and the Politics of Marriage," in A. Lavrin, ed., *Sexuality and Marriage in Colonial Latin America.* Lincoln: University of Nebraska Press.

Brandes, Stanley H. 1980. *Metaphors of Masculinity.* Philadelphia: University of Pennsylvania Press.

Brocklehurst, Thomas Unett. 1883. *Mexico To-Day: A Country with a Great Future, and a Glance at the Prehistoric Remains and Antiquities of the Montezumas.* London: John Murray.

Brøgger, Jan. 1990. *Pre-Bureaucratic Europeans.* Oslo: Norwegian University Press.

Broude, Gwen J. and Sarah J. Greene. 1980. "Cross-Cultural Codes on Twenty Sexual Attitudes and Practices," in Herbert Barry III and Alice Schlegel, eds., *Cross-Cultural Samples and Codes.* Pittsburgh: University of Pittsburgh Press.

Brown, C. MacKenzie. 1985. "Kali, the Mad Mother," in Carl Olson, ed., *The Book of the Goddess Past and Present.* New York: Crossroad.

Brown, Judith K. 1970. "A Note on the Division of Labor by Sex." *American Anthropologist,* 72:1073–1078.

Brown, S. E. 1975. "Love Unites Them and Hunger Separates Them: Poor Women in the Dominican Republic," in Rayna R. Reiter, ed., *Toward an Anthropology of Women.* New York: Monthly Review Press.

Browner, C. and E. Lewin. 1982. "Female Altruism Reconsidered: The Virgin Mary as Economic Woman." *American Ethnologist,* 9:61–75.

Carrasco, Pedro. 1963. "The Locality Referent in Residence Terms." *American Anthropologist,* 65:133–134.

Casselberry, Samuel F. and Nancy Valavanes. 1976. "Matrilocal Greek Peasants and Reconsideration of Residence Terminology." *American Ethnologist,* 3:215–226.

Chamove, A., H. Harlow and G. D. Mitchell. 1967. "Sex Differences in the Infant-Directed Behavior of Preadolescent Rhesus Monkeys." *Child Development,* 38:329–335.

Chiao, Chien. 1971. "Female Chastity in Chinese Culture." *Bulletin of the Institute of Ethnology (Hong Kong),* 31:205–212.

Chodorow, Nancy. 1974. "Family Structure and Feminine Personality," in Michelle Zimbalist Rosaldo and Louise Lamphere, eds., *Woman, Culture and Society.* Stanford: Stanford University Press.

Comaroff, Jean. 1985. *Body of Power, Spirit of Resistance: The Culture and History of a South African People.* Chicago: University of Chicago Press.

Cook, H. B. Kimberley. 1991. "Female Aggression and Social Control in Margariteño Society." Paper presented at the American Anthropological Association annual meeting.

*El Correo de Jalisco* (newspaper). 1895. various issues. Public Library of the State of Jalisco.

Craig, D. 1979. "Immortality Through Kinship: The Vertical Transmission of Substance and Symbolic Estate." *American Anthropologist*, 81:94–96.

Das, Veena. 1989. "Voices of Children." *Daedalus*, (Fall):263–294.

Davis, John. 1973. *Land and Family in Pisticci*. London: Athlone Press.

Deere, C. D., and M. Leon de Leal. 1981. "Peasant Production, Proletarianization, and the Sexual Division of Labor in the Andes." *Signs*, 7:338–360.

Devereux, George. 1976. *A Study of Abortion in Primitive Societies*, revised edition. New York: International Universities Press.

DeVore, Irven. 1963. "Mother-Infant Relations in Free Ranging Baboons," in H. L. Rheingold, ed., *Maternal Behavior in Mammals*. New York: Wiley.

Doering, C. H., H. Kraemer, H. Brodie, and D. Hamburg. 1975. "A Cycle of Plasma Testosterone in the Human Male." *Journal of Clinical Endocrinology*, 40:492–500.

Douglas, Mary. 1966. *Purity and Danger*. London: Routledge and Kegan Paul.

Draper, Patricia. 1975. "!Kung Women: Contrasts in Sexual Egalitarianism in Foraging and Sedentary Contexts," in Rayna R. Reiter, ed., *Toward an Anthropology of Women*. New York: Monthly Review Press.

Driessen, Henk. 1983. "Male Sociability and Rituals of Masculinity in Rural Andalusia." *Anthropological Quarterly*, 56:125–133.

Dubisch, Jill, ed. 1986. *Gender and Power in Rural Greece*. Princeton: Princeton University Press.

Dyer, K. F. 1985. "Making Up the Difference: Some Explanations for Recent Improvements in Women's Athletic Performances." *Search*, 16:264–269.

_____. 1986. "The Trend of the Male-Female Differential in Various Speed Sports 1936–1984." *Journal of Biosocial Science*, 18:169–177.

Edwards, D. A. 1969. "Early Androgen Stimulation and Aggressive Behavior in Male and Female Mice." *Physiology and Behavior*, 4:333–338.

Ehlers, T. B. 1982. "The Decline of Female Family Business: A Guatemalan Case Study." *Women and Politics*, 7:7–21.

_____. 1990. *Silent Looms: Women and Production in a Guatemalan Town*. Westview Special Studies on Latin America and the Caribbean. Boulder: Westview Press.

Ehrhardt, Anke A. 1973. "Maternalism in Fetal Hormonal and Related Syndromes," in Joseph Zubin and John Money, eds., *Contemporary Sexual Behavior: Critical Issues in the 1970s*. Baltimore: Johns Hopkins University Press.

Ehrhardt, Anke A. 1985. "Gender Differences: A Biosocial Perspective," in Theo B. Sonderegger, ed., *Nebraska Symposium on Motivation, 1984: Psychology and Gender*. Lincoln: University of Nebraska Press.

Ehrhardt, Anke A., and Susan W. Baker. 1974. "Fetal Androgens, Human Central Nervous System, Differentiation, and Behavior Sex Differences," in R. C. Friedman, ed., *Sex Differences in Behavior*. New York: Wiley.

Elliott, Alan J. A. 1955. *Chinese Spirit Medium Cults in Singapore*. London School of Economics and Political Science Monographs on Social Anthropology, No. 14. London: University of London.

Englander-Golden, Paula, Frank J. Sonleitner, Mary R. Whitmore, and Gail J. M. Corbley. 1986. "Social and Menstrual Cycles: Methodological and Substantive Findings," in Virginia L. Olesen and Nancy Fugate Woods, eds., *Culture, Society and Menstruation*. Washington, DC: Hemisphere.

Ericksen, Karen Paige. 1984. "Menstrual Symptoms and Menstrual Beliefs: National and Cross-National Patterns," in Benson E. Ginsburg and Bonnie Frank Carter, eds., *Premenstrual Syndrome: Ethical and Legal Implications in a Biomedical Perspective*. New York: Plenum.

Evans-Pritchard, Edward Evan. 1928. "The Dance." Africa, 1:446–461. (Reprinted in *The Position of Women in Primitive Societies*. 1965. London: Faber and Faber, Ltd.)

———. 1937. *Witchcraft, Oracles, and Magic among the Azande*. Oxford: Clarendon Press.

———. 1940. *The Nuer: A Description of the Modes of Livelihood and Political Institutions of a Nilotic People*. Oxford: Clarendon Press.

———. 1971a. *The Azande: History and Political Institutions*. Oxford: Clarendon Press.

———. 1971b. "Sources, with Particular Reference to the Southern Sudan." *Cahiers d'etudes africaines*, 11:129–179.

———. 1973. "Some Reminiscences and Reflections on Fieldwork." *Journal of the Anthropological Society of Oxford*, 4:1–12. (Reprinted as Appendix IV in *Witchcraft, Oracles, and Magic among the Azande*. 1976. Oxford: Clarendon Press).

———. 1974. *Man and Woman among the Azande*. London: Faber and Faber.

Fabes, Richard A. and Erik E. Filsinger. 1988. "Odor Communication and Parent-Child Interaction," in Erik E. Filsinger, ed., *Biosocial Perspectives on the Family*. Newbury Park, CA: Sage.

Fang, Ying. 1990. *The Pattern of Marriage Transactions in China*. M. A. Thesis. Department of Anthropology, University of Arizona.

Farrell, H. B. 1954. "Dearth of Children among the Azande: A Preliminary Report." *Sudan Notes and Records*, 35:7–21.

Fausto-Sterling, Anne. 1985. *Myths of Gender: Biological Theories About Women and Men*. New York: Basic Books.

Favret-Saada, Jeanne. 1980. *Deadly Words: Witchcraft in the Bocage.* Cambridge: Cambridge University Press.

Fedigan, Linda Marie. 1982. *Primate Paradigms: Sex Roles and Social Bonds.* Montreal: Eden Press.

Feil, D. 1984. *Ways of Exchange.* St. Lucia: University of Queensland Press.

Fletcher, Alice, and Francis LaFlesche. 1911. "The Omaha Tribe." *Annual Reports of the Bureau of American Ethnology,* 17:17–672.

Friedl, Ernestine. 1978. "Society and Sex Roles." *Human Nature.* (Reprinted in Phillip Whitten and David E. K. Hunter, eds. *Anthropology: Contemporary Perspectives, sixth edition,* 1990. Glenview, IL: Scott, Foresman/Little, Brown Higher Education.)

Gacs, Ute, Aisha Khan, Jerrie McIntyre and Ruth Weinberg, eds. 1989. *Women Anthropologists: Selected Biographies.* Urbana: University of Illinois Press.

Garfinkel, H. 1956. "Conditions of Successful Degradation Ceremonies." *The American Journal of Sociology,* 61:420–424.

Gaspar, D. B. 1985. *Bondmen and Rebels: A Study of Master-Slave Relations in Antigua.* Baltimore: Johns Hopkins.

Gero (Father Filberto Giorgetti). 1968. *Death Among the Azande of the Sudan (Beliefs, Rites and Cult).* W. H. Paxman, trans. Bologna: Editrice Nigrizia.

Gibbon, Eduardo A. 1893. *Guadalajara, la Florencia mexicana.* Guadalajara, Jal.: Imprenta del Diario de Jalisco.

Gilligan, Carol. 1982. *In a Different Voice: Psychological Theory and Women's Development.* Cambridge: Harvard University Press.

———. 1988. "Adolescent Development Reconsidered," in C. Gilligan, J. V. Ward, and J. M. Taylor, eds., *Mapping the Moral Domain.* Cambridge: Harvard University Press.

Gilmore, David D. 1990. "Men and Women in Southern Spain: 'Domestic Power' Revisited." *American Anthropologist,* 92:953–970.

Giovannini, Maureen J. 1985. "The Dialectics of Women's Factory Work in a Sicilian Town." *Anthropology,* 9:45–64.

Godelier, M. 1986. *The Making of Great Men.* New York: Cambridge University Press.

Goldstein, Melvyn C. 1987. "When Brothers Take a Wife." *Natural History.* (Reprinted as "Polyandry: When Brothers Take a Wife," in James P. Spradley and David W. McCurdy, eds., *Conformity and Conflict: Readings in Cultural Anthropology.* 1990. Glenview, IL: Scott, Foresman/Little, Brown Higher Education.)

Goody, Jack. 1973. "Bridewealth and Dowry in Africa and Eurasia," in Jack Goody and S. J. Tambiah, eds., *Bridewealth and Dowry.* Cambridge Papers in Social Anthropology No. 7. Cambridge: Cambridge University Press

———. 1976. *Production and Reproduction.* Cambridge: Cambridge University Press.

Gough, E. Kathleen. 1955. "Female Initiation Rites on the Malabar Coast." *Journal of the Royal Anthropological Institute*, 85:45–80.

_____. 1959. "The Nayars and the Definition of Marriage." *Journal of the Royal Anthropological Institute*, 89:23–34.

Gould-Martin, Katherine. 1978. "*Ong-la-Kong*: The Plague God as Modern Physician," in Arthur Kleinman, Peter Kunstadter, E. Russell Alexander, and James L. Gate, eds., *Culture and Healing in Asian Societies: Anthropological, Psychiatric and Public Health Studies*. Boston: G. K. Hall & Co.

Gregory, C. A. 1980. "Gifts to Men and Gifts to God: Gift Exchange and Capital Accumulation in Contemporary Papua." *Man*, 15:626–652.

Gregory, James R. 1984. "The Myth of the Male Ethnographer and the Woman's World." *American Anthropologist*, 86:316–327.

Harding, Susan. 1975. "Women and Words in a Spanish Village," in Rayna Reiter, ed., *Toward an Anthropology of Women*. New York: Monthly Review Press.

Harding, T. G. 1967. *Voyagers of the Vitiaz Strait: A Study of a New Guinea Trade System*. Seattle: University of Washington.

Hartsock, Nancy. 1983. *Money, Sex, and Power: Toward a Feminist Historical Materialism*. Boston: Northeastern University Press.

Hays, T. E. 1987. "Initiation as Experience," in L. L. Langness and T. E. Hays, eds., *Anthropology in the High Valleys*. Novato, CA: Chandler and Sharp.

Henry, P. 1985. *Peripheral Capitalism and Underdevelopment in Antigua*. New Brunswick: Transaction Books.

Herdt, G. H. 1981. *Guardians of the Flutes*. New York: McGraw-Hill.

Herskovits, Melville J. 1971[1937]. *Life in a Haitian Valley*. Garden City, NY: Doubleday.

Herzfeld, Michael. 1986. "Within and Without: The Category of 'Female' in the Ethnography of Modern Greece," in Jill Dubisch, ed., *Gender and Power in Rural Greece*. Princeton: Princeton University Press.

Hewes, G. W. 1954. "Mexicans in Search of the 'Mexican': Notes on Mexican National Character." *American Journal of Economics and Sociology*, 13:209–305.

Hibbard, Judith H. and Clyde R. Pope. 1983. "Gender Roles, Illness Orientation and Use of Medical Services." *Social Science and Medicine*, 17:129–137.

_____. 1986. "Another Look at Sex Differences in the Use of Medical Care: Illness Orientation and the Types of Morbidities for Which Services Are Used." *Women and Health*, 11:21–36.

Hoyenga, Katherine Blick, and Kermit T. Hoyenga. 1979. *The Question of Sex Differences: Psychological, Cultural, and Biological Issues*. Boston: Little, Brown.

Jacquette, J. 1973. "Literary Archetypes and Female Role Alternatives: The Woman and the Novel in Latin America," in A. Pescatello, ed.,

*Female and Male in Latin America*, Pittsburgh: University of Pittsburgh Press.

———. 1976. "Female Political Participation in Latin America," in L. B. Iglitzin and R. Ross, eds., *Women in the World, A Comparative Study*. Santa Barbara: ABC-Clio.

Jay, P. 1963. "Mother-Infant Relations in Langurs," in H. L. Rheingold, ed., *Maternal Behavior in Mammals*. New York: Wiley.

Johnson, C. 1983. "A Cultural Analysis of the Grandmother," *Research in Aging*, 5:547–567.

———. 1985. "Grandparenting Options in Divorcing Families: An Anthropological Perspective," in V. Bengston and J. Robertson, eds., *Grandparenthood*. Beverly Hills, CA: Sage.

———. 1988. "Active and Latent Functions of Grandparenting During the Divorce Process." *The Gerontologist*, 28:185–191.

Johnson, C. and B. Barer. 1987. "Marital Instability and Changing Kinship Networks of Grandparents." *The Gerontologist*, 27:330–335.

Johnson, C., C. Schmnidt, and L. Klee. 1988. "Conceptions of Parentage and Kinship Among Children of Divorce." *American Anthropologist*, 90:24–32.

Jordan, David K. 1972. *Gods, Ghosts, and Ancestors: The Folk Religion of a Taiwanese Village*. Berkeley: University of California Press.

Kakar, Sudhir. 1982. *Shamans, Mystics and Doctors*. New York: Alfred A. Knopf.

Kanippayyur Sankaran Nambutirippad. 1963. *Ente Smaranakal*. Kunnamkulam, Kerala: Pancangan Press.

Keesing, Roger M. 1985. "Kwaio Women Speak: The Micropolitics of Autobiography in a Solomon Island Society." *American Anthropologist*, 87:27–39.

Kinzer, N. S. 1973. "Women Professionals in Buenos Aires," in A. Pescatello, ed., *Female and Male in Latin America*. Pittsburgh: University of Pittsburgh Press.

Kleinman, Arthur. 1980. *Patients and Healers in the Context of Culture: An Exploration of the Borderland between Anthropology, Medicine, and Psychiatry*. Berkeley: University of California Press.

Kopytoff, Igor. 1987. "The Internal African Frontier: The Making of African Political Culture," in Igor Kopytoff, ed., *The African Frontier: The Reproduction of Traditional African Societies*. Bloomington: Indiana University Press.

Lagae, C-R. 1926. *Les Azande ou Niam-Niam: L'Organisation Zande Croyances Religieuses et Magiques Coutumes Familiales*. Brussels: Vromant.

Lamphere, Louise. 1974. "Strategies, Cooperation, and Conflict among Women in Domestic Groups," in Michelle Zimbalist Rosaldo and Louise Lamphere, eds., *Women, Culture and Society*. Stanford: Stanford University Press.

Langness, L. 1974. "Ritual, Power and Male Dominance in the New Guinea Highlands." *Ethos*, 2:189–212.

LaRossa, Ralph, and Maureen Mulligan LaRossa. 1989. "Baby Care: Fathers vs. Mothers," in Barbara J. Risman and Pepper Schwartz, eds., *Gender in Intimate Relations: A Microstructural Approach*. Belmont, CA: Wadsworth.

Leahy, M. E. 1986. *Development Strategies and the Status of Women. A Comparative Study of the United States, Mexico, the Soviet Union, and Cuba*. Boulder: Westview.

Lederman, Rena. 1986. *What Gifts Engender*. New York: Cambridge University Press.

_____. 1989. "Contested Order: Gender and Society in the Southern New Guinea Highlands." *American Ethnologist*, 16:230–247.

Lee, Richard B. 1965. *Subsistence Ecology of !Kung Bushmen*. Ph.D. dissertation, University of California, Berkeley.

Lessa, William A. and Evon Z. Vogt, eds. 1965. *Reader in Comparative Religion: An Anthropological Approach*. New York: Harper & Row.

Lévi-Strauss, Claude. 1963. *Structural Anthropology*. Claire Jacobson and Brooke Grundfest Schoenpf, trans. New York: Basic Books.

Lewis, O. 1959. *Five Families*. New York: Basic Books.

_____. 1961. *Children of Sánchez*. New York: Random House.

Loucky, J. 1988. *Children's Work and Family Survival in Highland Guatemala*. Ph.D. dissertation, University of California, Los Angeles.

Lutz, Catherine. 1990. "The Erasure of Women's Writing in Sociocultural Anthropology." *American Ethnologist*, 17:611–627.

Maccoby, Eleanor E. and Carol Nagy Jacklin. 1974. *The Psychology of Sex Differences*. Stanford: Stanford University Press.

Mackie, Marlene. 1977. "On Congenial Truths: A Perspective on Women's Studies." *Canadian Review of Sociology and Anthropology*. 14:117–128.

Mahiyariya, Nathu Singh. 1978. *Hadi Satak*. Jaipur: Sohanlal Jain, Jaipur Printers.

Malinowski, Bronislaw. 1932. *The Sexual Life of Savages in Northwestern Melanesia*. London: Routledge and Kegan Paul.

Martin, Emily. 1988. "Gender and Ideological Differences in Representations of Life and Death," in James L. Watson and Evelyn S. Rawski, eds., *Death Ritual in Late Imperial and Modern China*. Berkeley: University of California Press

Marvin, Garry. 1984. "The Cockfight in Andalusia, Spain: Images of the Truly Male." Anthropological Quarterly, 57:60–70.

Mathew, K. S. 1979. *Society in Medieval Malabar*. Kottayam, Kerala, India: Jaffe Books.

Mazur, Allan. 1985. "A Biosocial Model of Status in Face-to-Face Primate Groups." *Social Forces*, 64:377–402.

Mead, Margaret. 1972. *Blackberry Winter: My Earlier Years*. New York: William Morrow.

Meggitt, M. 1965. *The Lineage System of the Mae-Enga of New Guinea.* New York: Barnes and Noble.

Meigs, A. S. 1984. *Food, Sex, and Pollution.* New Brunswick, NJ: Rutgers University Press.

Money, John and Anke A. Ehrhardt. 1972. *Man and Woman: Boy and Girl.* Baltimore: Johns Hopkins University Press.

Money, John, and Patricia Tucker. 1975. *Sexual Signatures: On Being a Man or a Woman.* Boston: Little, Brown.

Moyer, Kenneth E. 1976. *The Psychobiology of Aggression.* New York: Harper & Row.

———. 1987. *Violence and Aggression: A Physiological Perspective.* New York: Paragon.

Muriá, José Maria. 1982. *Historia de Jalisco: Desde la consolidación del Porfiriato hasta mediados del siglo XX,* vol. 4. Guadalajara, Jalisco, Mexico: Gobierno del Estado de Jalisco, Secretaria General de Gobierno, Unidad Editorial.

Murphy, Michael. 1983. "Emotional Confrontations between Sevillano Fathers and Sons: Cultural Foundations and Social Consequences." *American Ethnologist,* 10:650–664.

Nandy, Ashis. 1980. *At the Edge of Psychology: Essays in Politics and Culture.* Delhi: Oxford University Press.

Nash, June. 1979. *We Eat the Mines and the Mines Eat Us: Dependency and Exploitation in Bolivian Tin Mines.* New York: Columbia University Press.

———. 1989. "Gender Studies in Latin American," in Sandra Morgen, ed., *Gender and Anthropology: Critical Reviews for Research and Teaching.* Washington, DC: American Anthropological Association.

Neuhouser, K. 1989. "Sources of Women's Power and Status among the Urban Poor in Contemporary Brazil." *Signs,* 14:685–702.

Newman, R. 1986. "Symbolic Dialects and Generation of Women: Variations in the Meaning of Post-Divorce Downward Mobility." *American Anthropologist.* 13:230–252.

Obeyesekere, Gananath. 1981. *Medusa's Hair: An Essay on Personal Symbols and Religious Experience.* Chicago: University of Chicago Press.

O'Kelly, C. G. and L. S. Carney. 1986. *Women and Men in Society.* Belmont, CA: Wadsworth.

Ong, Aihwa. 1987. *Spirits of Resistance and Capitalist Discipline: Factory Women in Malaysia.* Albany: State University of New York Press.

Ortner, Sherry B. 1974. "Is Female to Male as Nature is to Culture?" in Michelle Zimbalist Rosaldo and Louise Lamphere, eds., *Women, Culture and Society.* Stanford, CA: Stanford University Press.

Otten, Charlotte M. 1985. "Genetic Effects on Male and Female Development and on the Sex Ratio," in Roberta L. Hall, et al, eds., *Male-Female Differences: A Bio-Cultural Perspective.* New York: Praeger.

Panikkar, T. K. Gopal. 1900. *Malabar and Its Folk*. Madras India: G. A. Natesan.

Parsons, Talcott. 1963a. "On the Concept of Power." *Proceedings of the American Philosophical Society*, 107:232–262.

_____. 1963b. "On the Concept of Influence." *Public Opinion Quarterly*, 27:37–62.

Paul, L. 1974. "The Mastery of Work and the Mystery of Sex in a Guatemalan Village," in Michelle Zimbalist Rosaldo and Louise Lamphere, eds., *Women, Culture and Society*. Stanford: Stanford University Press.

Peñalosa, F. 1968. "Mexican Family Roles." *Journal of Marriage and the Family*, 30:681–689.

Piho, V. 1975. "Life and Labor of the Women Textile Worker in Mexico City," in Ruby Rohrlicht-Leavitt, ed., *Women Cross-Culturally: Change and Challenge*. The Hague: Mouton.

Pina-Cabral, João de. 1986. *Sons of Adam, Daughters of Eve: The Peasant Worldview of the Alto Minho*. Oxford: Clarendon Press.

Pomponio, A. 1992. *Seagulls Don't Fly into the Bush: Cultural Identity and Development in Melanesia*. Belmont, CA: Wadsworth.

_____. 1993. "Education IS Development on a Ten-Acre Island," in V. Lockwood, T. Harding, and B. Wallace, eds., *Contemporary Pacific Societies*. Honolulu: University of Hawaii Press.

Pomponio, A. and D. Lancy. 1986. "A Pen or a Bushknife? School, Work, and 'Personal Investment' in Papua New Guinea." *Anthropology and Education Quarterly*, 17:40–61.

Potter, Jack M. 1974. "Cantonese Shamanism," in A. P. Wolf, ed., *Religion and Ritual in Chinese Society*. Stanford, CA: Stanford University Press.

Powdermaker, Hortense. 1966. *Stranger and Friend: The Way of an Anthropologist*. New York: W. W. Norton.

Powell, D. 1986. "Caribbean Women and their Response to Familial Experiences." *Social and Economic Studies*, 35:83–130.

Press, Irwin. 1979. *The City as Context: Urbanism and Behavioral Constraints in Seville*. Urbana: University of Illinois Press.

Price, Richard. 1983. *First-Time: The Historical Vision of an Afro-American People*. Baltimore: Johns Hopkins University Press.

Puthenkalam, Fr. J. 1977. "Marriage and Family in Kerala." *Journal of Comparative Family Studies Monograph*. Calgary: Department of Sociology, University of Calgary.

Radcliffe-Brown, A. 1950. "Introduction," in A. Radcliffe-Brown and D. Forde, eds., *African Systems of Kinship and Marriage*. London: Oxford University Press.

_____. 1952. *Structure and Function in Primitive Society*. New York: Free Press.

Ramey, Estelle. 1976. "Men's Cycles (They Have Them, Too, You Know)," in Alexandra G. Kaplan and Joan P. Bean, eds., *Beyond Sex-Role*

Stereotypes: Reading Toward a Psychology of Androgyny. Boston: Little, Brown.

Rapp, R.. 1982. "Family and Class in Contemporary America: Notes Toward an Understanding of Ideology," in B. Thorne, ed., *Rethinking the Family: Some Feminist Questions.* New York: Longman.

Read, Kenneth E. 1965. *The High Valley.* New York: Charles Scribner's Sons.

———. 1982. "Male-Female Relationships among the Gahuku-Gama: 1950 and 1981," in F. J. P. Poole and G. H. Herdt, eds., *Sexual Antagonism, Gender, and Social Change in Papua New Guinea,* special issue of *Social Analysis,* No. 12:66–78.

Reid, Anthony. 1988. *The Lands Below the Winds. Southeast Asia in the Age of Commerce 1450–1680.* Vol. 1. New Haven, CT: Yale University Press.

*Report of the Malabar Marriage Commission with Observations Thereon by the Madras Government and the Government of India.* 1894. Madras, India: Price Current Press.

Robbins, S. 1982. *Auyana: Those Who Held onto Home.* Seattle: University of Washington Press.

Rogers, Susan C. 1975. "Female Forms of Power and the Myth of Male Dominance: A Model of Female/Male Interaction in Peasant Society." *American Ethnologist,* 2:727–756.

Roland, Alan. 1988. *In Search of Self in India and Japan.* Princeton, NJ: Princeton University Press.

Rudolph, Susanne H., and Lloyd I. Rudolph. 1983. *Gandhi: The Traditional Roots of Charisma.* Chicago: University of Chicago Press.

Sacks, Karen. 1979. *Sisters and Wives: The Past and Future of Sexual Equality.* Westport, CT: Greenwood.

Safa, H. I. 1976. "Class Consciousness among Working Class Women in Latin America: A Case Study in Puerto Rico," in J. Nash and H. Safa, eds., *Sex and Class in Latin America.* New York: Praeger.

Sahlins, M. 1972. *Stone Age Economics.* Chicago: Aldine.

Salamone, S. D., and J. B. Stanton. 1986. "Introducing the Nikokyra: Ideality and Reality in Social Process," in Jill Dubisch, ed., *Gender and Power in Rural Greece.* Princeton: Princeton University Press.

Salisbury, R. F. 1962. *From Stone to Steel.* Melbourne: Melbourne University Press.

Sanday, Peggy R. 1974. "Female Status in the Public Domain," in Michelle Zimbalist Rosaldo and Louise Lamphere, eds., *Women, Culture and Society.* Stanford, CA: Stanford University Press.

Schlegel, Alice and Herbert Barry III. 1986. "The Cultural Consequences of Female Contribution to Subsistence." *American Anthropologist,* 88:142–150.

———. 1991. *Adolescence: An Anthropological Inquiry.* New York: Free Press.

Schlegel, Alice, and Rohn Eloul. 1987. "Marriage Transactions: A Cross-Cultural Code." *Behavioral Science Research*, 21:118–140.

_____. 1988. "Marriage Transactions: Labor, Property, and Status." *American Anthropologist*, 90:291–309.

Schminck, M. 1977. "Dependent Development and the Division of Labor by Sex: Venezuela. Women and Class Struggle." *Latin American Perspectives*, 4:153–179.

Schneider, D. 1965. "American Kin Terminology and Terms for Kinsmen: A Critique of Goodenough's Componential Analysis." *American Anthropologist*, 67:288–308.

_____. 1968. *American Kinship: A Cultural Account*. Englewood Cliffs, NJ: Prentice-Hall.

_____. 1980. "Twelve Years Later: An Afterword," in *American Kinship: A Cultural Account*. Chicago: University of Chicago Press.

Schneider, Jane. 1971. "Of Vigilance and Virgins: Honor, Shame, and Access to Resources in Mediterranean Societies." *Ethnology*, 10:1–24.

Scott, James. 1985. *Weapons of the Weak: Everyday Forms of Peasant Resistance*. New Haven, CT: Yale University Press.

Seligman, C. G., and Brenda Z. Seligman. 1932. "The Azande," in *Pagan Tribes of the Nilotic Sudan*. London: George Routledge and Sons.

Shamsuddin. 1967. *The Loves of Begum Sumroo and Other True Romances*. Delhi: Orient Paperbacks.

Shore, Bradd. 1981. "Sexuality and Gender in Samoa: Conceptions and Missed Conceptions," in Sherry B. Ortner and Harriet Whitehead, eds., *Sexual Meanings*. Cambridge: Cambridge University Press.

Sieff, Daniela F. 1990. "Explaining Biased Sex Ratios in Human Populations: A Critique of Recent Studies," *Current Anthropology*, 31:25–48.

Siemens, Stephen David. 1990. *Azande Rituals of Birth and Death: Ethnography and Formal Analogy*. Ph.D. dissertation. Department of Anthropology, University of California, Los Angeles. Ann Arbor, Michigan: University Microfilms.

Silverblatt, Irene. 1980. "'The Universe has turned inside out. . . There is no justice for us here': Andean Women under Spanish Rule," in M. Etienne and E. Leacock, eds., *Women and Colonization: Anthropological Perspectives*. South Hadley, MA: Bergin and Garvey.

_____. 1987. *Moon, Sun, and Witches: Gender Ideologies and Class in Inca and Colonial Peru*. Princeton, NJ: Princeton University Press.

Slocum, Sally. 1975. "Woman the Gatherer: Male Bias in Anthropology," in Rayna R. Reiter, ed., *Toward an Anthropology of Women*, New York: Monthly Review Press.

Smith, W. R. 1977. *The Fiesta System and Economic Change*. New York: Columbia University Press.

Sorenson, E. R. 1976. *The Edge of the Forest*. Washington, DC: Smithsonian Institution Press.

Spiro, M. E. 1982. *Oedipus in the Trobriands.* Chicago: University of Chicago Press.

Stevens, E. P. 1973a. "Machismo and Marianismo." *Society,* 10:57–63.

_____. 1973b. "Marianismo: The Other Face of 'Machismo' in Latin America," in A Pescatello, ed., *Female and Male in Latin America.* Pittsburgh: University of Pittsburgh Press.

_____. 1973c. "The Prospects for a Women's Liberation Movement in Latin America." *Journal of Marriage and the Family,* 35:313–321.

Stillion, Judith M. 1985. *Death and the Sexes: An Examination of Differential Longevity, Attitudes, Behaviors, and Coping Skills.* Washington, DC: Hemisphere.

Stoller, R. J. 1985, *Presentations of Gender.* New Haven, CT: Yale University Press.

Stoller, R. J. and G. H. Herdt. 1985. "Theories of Origins of Male Homosexuality." *Archives of General Psychiatry,* 42:399–404.

Stone, Lawrence. 1977. *The Family, Sex and Marriage in England 1500–1800.* New York: Harper & Row.

Strathern, A. J. 1969. "Descent and Alliance in the New Guinea Highlands." *Proceedings of the Royal Anthropological Institute for 1968,* 37–52.

Strathern, M. 1972. *Women in Between.* New York: Seminar Press.

Tanner, Nancy. 1974. "Matrifocality in Indonesia and Africa and Among Black Americans," in Michelle Zimbalist Rosaldo and Louise Lamphere, eds., *Women, Culture and Society.* Stanford: Stanford University Press.

Taussig, Michael. 1987. *Shamanism, Colonialism and the Wild Man: A Study in Terror and Healing.* Chicago: University of Chicago Press.

Thurston, Edgar. 1909. *Castes and Tribes of Southern India.* Madras, India: Government Press.

Tieger, T. 1980. "On the Biological Basis of Sex Differences in Aggression." *Child Development,* 51:943–963.

Tierney, Helen, ed. 1991. *Women's Studies Encyclopedia,* Vol. 1: *Views from the Sciences.* New York: Peter Bedrick Books.

Tiger, Lionel. 1970. *Men in Groups.* New York: Vintage Books.

Travis, Cheryl Brown. 1988. *Women and Health Psychology: Biomedical Issues.* Hillsdale, NJ: Erlbaum.

Trawick, Margaret. 1990. *Notes on Love in a Tamil Family,* Berkeley: University of California Press.

Troll, L. 1971. "The Family of Later Life: A Decade Review," in C. Broderick, ed., *Decade Review of Family Research and Action.* Minneapolis: National Council of Family Relations.

Trumbach, Randolph. 1978. *The Rise of the Egalitarian Family.* New York: Academic Press.

Turner, Victor. 1967. *The Forest of Symbols.* Ithaca, NY: Cornell University Press.

Uhl, Sarah C. 1985. "Special Friends; The Organization of Intersex Friendship in Escalona (Andalusia) Spain." *Anthropology*, 9:129–152.

Ullrich, Helen E. 1977. "Caste Differences between Brahmin and Non-Brahmin Women in a South Indian Village," in Alice Schlegel, ed., *Sexual Stratification: A Cross-Cultural View*. New York: Columbia University Press.

Unikel, Luis, et al. 1976. *El desarrollo urbano de México: Diagnóstico e implicaciones futures*. Mexico City: *Centro de Estudios Económicos y Demográficos, El Colegio de México*.

United Nations. 1991. *World Population Prospects 1990*. Population Studies No. 120. New York: United Nations.

Verbrugge, Lois M. 1976. "Sex Differentials in Morbidity and Mortality in the United States." *Social Biology*, 23:275–296.

_____. 1989. "Recent, Present, and Future Health of American Adults." *Annual Review of Public Health*, 10:333–361.

Verdon, Michel. 1988. "Virgins and Widows: European Kinship and Early Christianity." *Man*, n.s.23:488–404.

Wadley, Susan S. 1977. "Women and the Hindu Tradition," in Doranne Jacobson and Susan S. Wadley, eds., *Women in India: Two Perspectives*. Columbia, MO: South Asia Books.

Wagley, Charles. 1949. *The Social and Religious Life of a Guatemalan Village*. Menosha, WI: American Anthropological Association.

Washburn, Sherwood L. and Lancaster, C. S. 1968. "The Evolution of Hunting," in Richard B. Lee and Irven DeVore, eds., *Man the Hunter*. Chicago: Aldine.

Watson, J. B. 1983. *Tairora Culture: Contingency and Pragmatism*. Seattle: University of Washington Press.

Watson, Rubie S. 1986. "The Named and the Nameless: Gender and Person in Chinese Society." *American Ethnologist*, 13:619–631.

Weber, Max. 1947. *The Theory of Social and Economic Organization*. A. M. Henderson and Talcott Parsons, trans. New York: Oxford University Press.

_____. 1965. *The Sociology of Religion*. E. Fischoff trans., T. Parsons, ed. London: Methuen.

Webster, Paula. 1975. "Matriarchy: A Vision of Power," in Rayna R. Reiter, ed., *Toward an Anthropology of Women*. New York: Monthly Review Press.

Weiner, Annette B. 1976. *Women of Value, Men of Renown*. Austin: University of Texas Press.

_____. 1988. *The Trobrianders of Papua New Guinea*. New York: Holt, Rinehart and Winston.

Whiting, Beatrice Blyth and Carolyn Pope Edwards. 1988. *Children of Different Worlds: The Formation of Social Behavior*. Cambridge: Harvard University Press.

Whiting, Beatrice B. and John W. M. Whiting. 1975. *Children of Six Cultures: A Psychocultural Analysis.* Cambridge: Harvard University Press.

Whiting, J. W. M., R. Kluckhohn, and A. Anthony. 1958. "The Function of Male Initiation Ceremonies at Puberty," in E. E. Maccoby, T. M. Newcomb, and E. L. Hartley, eds., *Readings in Social Psychology.* New York: Henry Holt.

Wolf, E. 1965. "The Virgin of Guadalupe: A Mexican National Symbol," in William A. Lessa and Evon Z. Vogt, eds., *Reader in Comparative Religion: An Anthropological Approach.* New York: Harper & Row. (Originally published in the *Journal of American Folklore*, 1958)

———. 1966. *Peasants.* Englewood Cliffs, NJ: Prentice-Hall.

Wolf, Margery. 1972. *Women and the Family in Rural Taiwan.* Stanford: Stanford University Press.

Womack, Mari. 1982. *Sports Magic: Symbolic Manipulation Among Professional Athletes.* Ph.D. dissertation, University of California, Los Angeles.

The World Bank. 1985. *Antigua and Barbuda Economic Report.* Washington, DC.

Yanigasako, S. 1977. "Women-Centered Kinship Networks in Urban Bilateral Kinship." *American Ethnologist,* 4:207–226.

Youseff, N. H. 1973. "Cultural Ideals, Feminine Behavior and Family Control." *Comparative Studies in Society and History,* 15:326–347.

Zihlman, Adrienne. 1989. "Woman the Gatherer: The Role of Women in Early Hominid Evolution," in Sandra Morgen, ed., *Gender and Anthropology: Critical Review for Research and Teaching.* Washington, DC: American Anthropological Association.